THE ASTROLOGY OF THE FOUR HORSEMEN

How You Can Heal Yourself and Planet Earth

ELIZABETH CLARE PROPHET

SUMMIT UNIVERSITY PRESS®

I dedicate this book to
my Lord and Saviour Jesus Christ—
the same yesterday
and today
and forever

THE ASTROLOGY OF THE FOUR HORSEMEN
How You Can Heal Yourself and Planet Earth
Elizabeth Clare Prophet

Copyright © 1991 Summit University Press
All rights reserved.

Library of Congress Catalog Card Number: 90-070840
International Standard Book Number: 0-922729-06-9

This book is set in 11 point Electra with 1.5 points lead.
Printed in the United States of America
First Printing: 1991

SUMMIT UNIVERSITY 🦢 PRESS®

Contents

PART III
THE ASTROLOGICAL CHARTS
OF THE U.S. AND THE USSR:
A Profile of the Superpowers

PART IV
THE MARS-SATURN-URANUS-NEPTUNE
CONJUNCTION:
*The Four Horsemen in Capricorn Influence
Economic Affairs*

PART VI
CANADA'S ASTROLOGY:
Discover Your True Identity!

PART VII
HOW TO HEAL YOURSELF
AND PLANET EARTH:
*The Violet Flame, Key to Self-Knowledge
and World Transmutation*

The Handwriting on the Wall

Then Daniel spoke up in the presence of the king. Keep your gifts for yourself, he said, and give your rewards to others. I will read the writing to the king without them, and tell him what it means.

O king, the Most High God gave Nebuchadnezzar your father sovereignty, greatness, glory, majesty.

He made him so great that men of all peoples, nations and languages shook with dread before him: he killed whom he pleased, spared whom he pleased, promoted whom he pleased, degraded whom he pleased.

But because his heart grew swollen with pride, and his spirit stiff with arrogance, he was deposed from his sovereign throne and stripped of his glory.

He was driven from the society of men, his heart grew completely animal; he lived with the wild asses; he fed on grass like the oxen; his body was drenched by the dew of heaven, until he had learned that the Most High rules over the empire of men and appoints whom he pleases to rule it.

But you, Belshazzar, who are his son, you have not humbled your heart, in spite of knowing all this.

You have defied the Lord of heaven, you have had the vessels from his Temple brought to you, and you, your noblemen, your wives and your singing women have drunk your wine out of them.

You have praised gods of gold and silver, of bronze and iron, of wood and stone, which cannot either see, hear or understand; but you have given no glory to the God who holds your breath and all your fortunes in his hands.

That is why he has sent the hand which, by itself, has written these words.

The writing reads: Mene, Mene, Tekel and Parsin.

The meaning of the words is this: Mene: God *has* measured *your sovereignty and put an end to it;*

Tekel: *you have been* weighed *in the balance and found wanting;*

Parsin: *your kingdom has been* divided *and given to the Medes and the* Persians.

At Belshazzar's order Daniel was dressed in purple, a chain of gold was put round his neck and he was proclaimed third in rank in the kingdom.

That same night, the Chaldaean king Belshazzar was murdered, and Darius the Mede received the kingdom, at the age of sixty-two.

Daniel 5:17–31 Jerusalem Bible

Foreword

The Four Horsemen of the Apocalypse is an image burned deep into the subconscious of everyone who has grown up in the Western world over the past two millennia. In the Book of Revelation, the Four Horsemen are symbolic of the "end time"— the time at the end of an age, when a 2,000-year-old world order collapses.

It's an image that haunts no one more than Elizabeth Clare Prophet, who has seen it in her dreams and visions more and more frequently over the last several years—and especially since February 1988, when four planets aligned in the sign Capricorn. Now, as the twentieth century draws to a close and we stand at the threshold of a new millennium, she explains her visions and their relevance to world events in *The Astrology of the Four Horsemen: How to Heal Yourself and Planet Earth.*

Like so much of mystical and prophetic tradition, the idea of world ages is astrological in origin. The scriptures of Judeo-Christian tradition rely heavily on the symbolism of astrology: the 12 tribes correspond to the 12 signs, and the references in the

Book of Revelation to the eagle, man, calf and lion are thinly veiled allusions to the signs Scorpio, Aquarius, Taurus and Leo respectively.

Mrs. Prophet's new book revives this ancient symbolism and puts it on the cutting edge of tomorrow, in the hope of giving us warning in time that we may mitigate what she sees in the astrological portents for the remaining years of this century: "an ascending series of karmic challenges, including the possibilities of war, revolution, depression and major earth changes."

Nearly 800 years ago, the scientist and philosopher Roger Bacon noticed astrological configurations which seemed to indicate that war was imminent in Europe. His warnings went unheeded, and a period of conflict ensued. "Oh, how great an advantage might have been secured," he later reflected, "if the characteristics of the heavens in those times had been discerned beforehand by scientists, and understood by prelates and princes, and transferred to a zeal for peace."

Mrs. Prophet sees similar portents in the heavens, and clearly explains them for us in her latest book.

Will prophecy fall on deaf ears again?

The prophetic tradition is one of warning and exhortation rather than mere prediction. Prophets tell us what will happen if we do not change our ways and prepare ourselves—what will befall us if nothing is done to prevent it, in other words.

The possibilities for the future described in

The Astrology of the Four Horsemen are apocalyptic indeed: plague and famine, worldwide depression, even a possible nuclear attack on the United States by the Soviet Union. As little as 10 years ago, all of these things might have seemed incomprehensible. Now, given the AIDS epidemic and the shaky state of the world economy, some of them are already on our doorstep—fulfilling the warnings Mrs. Prophet has issued throughout the 1980s right up to the present day.

Most recently, Iraq's invasion of Kuwait, which precipitated a worldwide crisis that has not yet been resolved as I write this, took place within days of the August 6, 1990 lunar eclipse—a celestial alignment described by Mrs. Prophet as having the potential of "igniting a war anywhere on earth." Given Iraq's chemical and possibly even nuclear arsenal, who knows how close we may already be to Armageddon?

What's the schedule for the rest of this century and what can we do to prepare ourselves and possibly even ward off the unthinkable?

The answers lie in *The Astrology of the Four Horsemen: How to Heal Yourself and Planet Earth.* It's a powerful, gripping book. In quieter times, it would have read like fantasy or science fiction. Today it reads like tomorrow's headlines.

RICHARD NOLLE

It's Greek to Me
A Note to the Reader

Astrologers secretly guide the fortunes of Hollywood stars, politicians, businessmen, investors, brokerage houses and Middle Eastern sheiks.

Sheik Ahmed Zaki Yamani, for many years the oil minister of Saudi Arabia, is an avid astrologer. Ronald Reagan benefited from the advice of astrologers for decades. Joan Quigley, his most recent astrologer, says with only slight exaggeration that she was the Teflon in Reagan's "Teflon presidency."

Americans are surrounded by astrology. Yet when they first encounter it, they often shrug and say, "It's Greek to me!"

And with good reason. Suddenly the non-astrologer is confronted with a series of hieroglyphs like ☉ ♒ ☾ ♏ ♄ ♑. He hears incomprehensible phrases like "the Moon in Leo is square to my Neptune in Scorpio in the fourth house. *That's* why I didn't get out of bed this morning."

Or he is informed that because Mercury is moving *backwards* it is a bad time to sign a contract. Or that a certain aspect between Venus in Taurus and Uranus in Capricorn makes this an ideal week-end for a heavy romance.

But astrology is not Greek. Or kooky. Or hard to understand. Even if you know absolutely nothing about astrology, you can understand this book. But it will help if you have a little painless background information.

Let's start with something almost all of us have experienced—too many times perhaps. You are in a social situation. Someone asks, "What sign are you?"

"I'm an Aries," you reply. Or you might name one of the other signs of the zodiac. The signs, in order, are: Aries, Taurus, Gemini, Cancer, Leo, Virgo, Libra, Scorpio, Sagittarius, Capricorn, Aquarius and Pisces. (If you are mischievous, you might say, "I'm a stop sign," and the other party will get the hint.)

But knowing your Sun sign is just a starting point. The basic unit of astrological analysis is a horoscope, or astrological chart. A horoscope is simply a diagram, or map, of the heavens show-ing the relative position of the Sun, Moon and planets in relation to an event at a specific time and place on earth, usually the birth of a person. But a horoscope can also be drawn for the birth of a nation, corporation, school, space program, sports team—in fact, for anything that has a point of origin.

There are many branches of astrology. The two used in this book are natal astrology and mundane astrology. Natal astrology is the study of the influences of the Sun, Moon and planets on the life and character of a person.

Mundane astrology (literally, "the astrology of the world") is the study of the influences of celestial bodies on nations, world leaders and national and international economic trends. The practitioner of mundane astrology evaluates the potential for war and peace, political stability and chaos, economic prosperity and recession.

The astrological chart is a circle that represents the zodiac, an imaginary belt in the heavens divided into 12 equal segments of 30 degrees each. These are the signs of the zodiac.

The signs have distinct influences. For example, Aries tends to be assertive, Taurus practical, Gemini versatile, Cancer sensitive, Leo dignified, Virgo analytical, Libra cooperative, Scorpio incisive, Sagittarius broad-minded, Capricorn ambitious, Aquarius independent, and Pisces understanding.

The chart is also divided into 12 segments known as houses. The houses, which are distinct from the signs, rule certain areas or departments of life. While the signs always span 30 degrees of the zodiac, the houses vary in size.

The signs, reflecting the earth's rotation on its axis, are constantly moving. Every four minutes a new degree of the zodiac rises on the eastern horizon. The degree of the zodiac on the eastern horizon when a chart is cast is known as the Ascendant, and the sign of the zodiac on the eastern horizon is known as the rising sign.

The sign on the Ascendant at dawn is the same as the sign the Sun is passing through. If, for example, the Sun is in Sagittarius (approximately November 22 to December 20), the sign of Sagittarius will be on the horizon at sunrise. About two hours later, Capricorn will be rising, two hours after that Aquarius will be rising, and so on throughout the day.

The sign on the Ascendant, which is also the first-house cusp, determines which of the signs will fall on each of the house cusps. If the chart has Sagittarius on the Ascendant, then the sign of Capricorn (with few exceptions) will fall on the second-house cusp, Aquarius on the third-house cusp, and so on in order through Scorpio on the twelfth-house cusp. Likewise, if the chart has Aries ascending, then Taurus will be on the second-house cusp, Gemini on the third, and so on.

The date of birth tells the position of the planets in the signs of the zodiac. The time of birth determines in which houses those planets fall.

The diagram on the next page gives a thumbnail sketch of natal astrological information. It shows the zodiac starting with Aries and the approximate dates the Sun is in each sign. It also shows the 12 houses, what they govern (for example, the first house rules self, personality, appearance and temperament) and the planet that rules the house. Finally, it shows the symbol for each planet and the basic influences of each planet.

The planets, signs and houses are the building blocks of astrology. How do they interact? Astrologer

Traditional Astrological Information

Outer Ring: Astrological Signs
Inner Ring: Houses

CAPRICORN
the Goat
"I Use"
Dec. 21 - Jan. 20

SAGITTARIUS
the Archer
"I See"
Nov. 22 - Dec. 20

AQUARIUS
the Water Bearer
"I Know"
Jan. 21 -
Feb. 18

SCORPIO
the Scorpion
"I Desire"
Oct. 23 -
Nov. 21

PISCES
the Fish
"I Believe"
Feb. 19 -
March 20

LIBRA
the Scales
"I Balance"
Sept. 23 -
Oct. 22

ARIES
the Ram
"I Am"
March 21 -
April 20

VIRGO
the Virgin
"I Analyze"
Aug. 23 -
Sept. 22

TAURUS
the Bull
"I Have"
April 21 -
May 20

LEO
the Lion
"I Will"
July 22 -
Aug. 22

GEMINI
the Twins
"I Think"
May 21 - June 20

CANCER
the Crab
"I Feel"
June 21 - July 21

Father, career, status, reputation — Ruler: SATURN — 10th

Long trips, higher mind, higher education, philosophy, religion — Ruler: JUPITER — 9th

Joint finances, taxes, inheritance, death and regeneration — Ruler: MARS — 8th

Friends, hopes, wishes, community affairs — Ruler: URANUS — 11th

Hidden friends and enemies, work behind the scenes, institutions — Ruler: NEPTUNE — 12th

"Others," business and marriage partners, legal affairs, open enemies — Ruler: VENUS — 7th

Self, personality, appearance, temperament — Ruler: MARS — 1st

Health, work, service — Ruler: MERCURY — 6th

Money, possessions, values, sense of self-worth — Ruler: VENUS — 2nd

Romantic affairs, creative affairs, children, social life — Ruler: SUN — 5th

Communications, short trips, brothers and sisters — Ruler: MERCURY — 3rd

Home, mother, environment — Ruler: MOON — 4th

The Planets

☉ THE SUN — individuality, will power, vitality, leadership, creativity, authority, masculine principle, father.

☽ THE MOON — emotions, habit, memory, subconscious, nurturing impulse, feminine principle, mother.

☿ MERCURY — concrete mental faculties, thought, speech, communication, perception, intelligence, reasoning ability, mobility, adaptability.

♀ VENUS — harmony, love, pleasure, beauty, art, social affairs and graces, financial matters.

♂ MARS — action based on desire, construction and destruction, assertiveness, aggression, executive authority.

♃ JUPITER — abstract and creative faculties, expansiveness, higher mind, wisdom, optimism, benevolence, generosity, hypocrisy.

♄ SATURN — concentration, crystallization, organization, caution, pessimism, responsibility, perseverance, stability, discipline, limitation, tradition, obstacles.

♅ URANUS — impulse for freedom and individuality, originality, ingenuity, intuition, independence, inventiveness, eccentricity, disruption.

♆ NEPTUNE — inspiration, illumination, refinement, mystical tendencies, idealism, compassion, escapism, illusion, confusion, delusion.

♇ PLUTO — regeneration, transformation, renewal, destruction, manipulation, denial, coercion, annihilation.

⊕ PART OF FORTUNE — A fortunate place in the chart where, by sign and house, the native has resources to draw upon.

☊ MOON'S NODES: North Node — talents to be
☋ developed. South Node — talents already developed.

Howard Sasportas explains how the signs, planets and houses interact. He writes:

> Like verbs, [planets] depict a certain action which is going on—for example, Mars *asserts*, Venus *harmonizes*, Jupiter *expands*, Saturn *restricts*, etc. . . . The drive of a planet is expressed through the sign in which the planet is placed. Mars can assert in an Arien way or Taurean way; Venus can harmonize in a Geminian or Cancerian fashion, and so on. *Houses*, however, show the specific areas of everyday life or fields of experience in which all this is occurring. Mars in Taurus will assert itself in a slow and steady manner, but its placement by house determines the exact area of life in which this slow and steady action can most obviously be observed—whether it is in the person's career that he or she acts that way, or in his or her relationships, or at school, etc. Put very simply, the planets show *what* is happening, the signs *how* it is happening, and the houses *where* it is happening.*

Combining the influences of the planets, signs and houses requires some experience. But the horoscopes in this book (with 48 easy-to-follow charts) have been interpreted for you. All you have to do is follow the text. In most cases, the interpretations

The Twelve Houses: An Introduction to the Houses in Astrological Interpretation (Wellingborough, Northamptonshire, England: Aquarian Press, 1985), p. 19.

note which planet, house or sign produces the influence in question.

The astrological charts used in natal and mundane astrology are the same; only the interpretation varies. Mundane astrology uses the same principles of interpretation as natal astrology but applies them to nations.

For example, in natal astrology the Sun represents the individual. In mundane astrology the Sun represents the head of state. In natal astrology the second house rules a person's money, possessions and finances. In mundane astrology the second house rules a nation's economy, treasury and Gross National Product. In the glossary at the end of this book, there are detailed lists of what each house and planet rules in natal and mundane astrology.

Astrology has its own symbols, vocabulary and syntax. But it's easier to learn than Greek. And Greek, come to think of it, may not be all that hard to learn. Generations of Greek children have done it without a second thought.

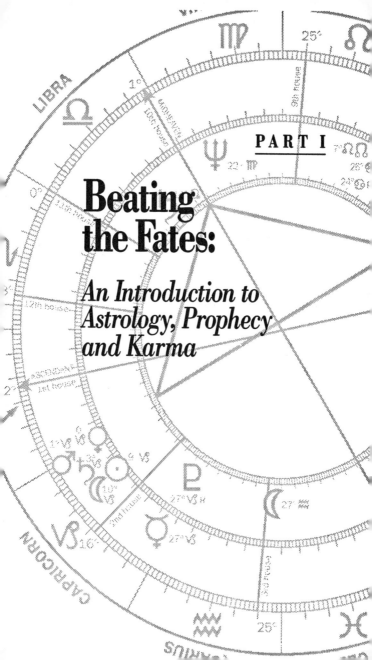

PART I

Beating the Fates:

An Introduction to Astrology, Prophecy and Karma

CHAPTER 1

Astrology and Karma

When most people think of astrology, they think of the sun-sign writeups that appear in newspapers and magazines.

Here's a syndicated horoscope for July 26, 1990, for Geminis—anyone born between May 21 and June 20:

"You might be humming, 'I'm in love, I'm in love!' Emphasis on style, romance, fresh start. You'll exude sensuality. Relationship that seemed 'impossible' is due to flourish. Leo could play major role."

Of course, the Gemini reading the column could be an 80-year-old spinster or a happily married man who isn't interested in a new relationship.

Or what about Scorpio? "Focus on home, special arrangements, 'visual delights.' Member of opposite sex presents gift, expects something in return. Secret passageway could be part of scenario. Another Scorpio plays role."

What happens if the Scorpio doesn't get a gift from a member of the opposite sex? Does it prove that astrology is bunk? Hardly.

Astrology columns must tell how the daily position of the sun, moon and planets affects everyone born in a particular sign; thus they make no pretense of being complete or accurate for all their readers. Since there are 12 signs of the zodiac, the reading for each sign would theoretically apply to one-twelfth of the people in the world.

An astrologer can only perform a thorough and accurate reading for you based on your individual birth chart. Your birth chart applies only to you and anyone else who may have been born at the exact time and place you were. Which brings us to a commonly asked question:

What about the case of two babies born in the same hospital at the same time? One could be born to a wealthy family and one to a poor family. They would have identical birth charts but would likely lead vastly different lives. The skeptic would ask: In the face of situations like these, how can astrology be valid?

Astrology tells you your potential. How you fulfill that potential depends on the circumstances of your birth and family, environmental and hereditary factors, and whether you choose to overcome your negative karma and capitalize on your positive karma.

A lot of people think that astrologers believe that our lives are controlled by "the stars," as illustrated in the *Calvin and Hobbes* cartoon on p. 5. A few astrologers believe in predestination, but the majority do not. Most believe in free will and the ability of the individual to determine his destiny using astrology as a road map.

The fault is not in ourselves but in our stars?

("The fault, dear Brutus, is not in our stars, But in ourselves, that we are underlings." Shakespeare, *Julius Caesar*, Act I, Sc. ii.)

Karma Is the Key

Astrology's purpose can be found through the study of karma. The first thing I should make clear is that neither astrology nor karma determines your future actions.

"Karma does not constitute determinism," we read in *The Encyclopedia of Eastern Philosophy and Religion.* "The deeds do indeed determine the *manner* of rebirth but not the *actions* of the reborn individual—karma provides the situation, not the response to the situation."[1]

Astrology tells you what karma you will face day by day in this life; you decide what to do about it. Karma predestines you, but your exercise of free will allows you to break the shackles of your karma—within parameters.

What is karma? Karma is the causes we have set in motion and the effects we will reap from those causes. Many people think it means fate, something inevitable, and so it does. But karma is more than fate and more than the inevitable.

Karma comes from the Sanskrit word for "deed." The Hindu definition is:

1. a mental or physical action; 2. the consequence of a mental or physical action; 3. the sum of all consequences of the actions of an individual in this or some previous life; 4. the chain of cause and effect in the world of morality.

Each individual's karma is created by that

person's *samskaras* [impressions, tendencies, and possibilities present in consciousness that have arisen through one's actions and thoughts, including those of earlier births. The sum total of *samskaras* form the person's character].

This potential directs one's behavior and steers the motives for all present and future thoughts and deeds. Thus every karma is the seed for further karma. Its fruits are reaped in the form of joy or sorrow according to the type of thought or action accomplished.

Although every human being creates his own limitations through his past thoughts and actions, once having formed these tendencies he has the option of continuing to follow them or resisting them.[2]

In the Buddhist sense, karma is defined as "the universal law of cause and effect." André Bareau writes in *Die Religionen Indiens:*

The deed (karma) produces a fruit under certain circumstances; when it is ripe then it falls upon the one responsible. . . . Since the time of ripening generally exceeds a lifespan, the effect of actions is necessarily one or more rebirths, which together constitute the cycle of existence.[3]

Astrology is the great chronicler of our karmic self. It measures the cycles of our karmic returns and tells us a twice-told tale of a karma sown and a karma reaped day by day.

Astrology engages us as the storyteller. It gives us material to work with, karmic material drawn from our many performances on the stage of life. And we decide how the plot will unfold and how the players—the sun, moon, stars and planets—will interact with us in the moving scenes of life.

God gives us the opportunity to enter the drama entirely according to free will. How we react to this chemistry of our karma will determine our present and future.

Yes, we can make our lives sublime (or ridiculous) and leave behind us footprints, positive or negative, for the next round in these changing sands of time.

Karma in the Bible

The law of karma is set forth throughout the Bible. The apostle Paul makes clear what our Lord taught him and what he learned from life:

> Every man shall bear his own burden . . . .

> Be not deceived; God is not mocked: for whatsoever a man soweth, that shall he also reap.

> For he that soweth to his flesh shall of the flesh reap corruption; but he that soweth to the Spirit shall of the Spirit reap life everlasting.

> And let us not be weary in well doing: for in due season we shall reap, if we faint not.

> As we have therefore opportunity, let us do good unto all men.[*]

*All Bible verses in this book are from the King James Version unless otherwise indicated.

Since it is often not possible to reap all of our harvests in one lifetime, the law of karma is fulfilled through the corollary law of reincarnation. Reincarnation is God's mercy that allows us to reap the harvest of our past sowings here on earth instead of consigning us prematurely to "heaven" or "hell," when we are ready for neither and we still have things to do on earth.

Take, for example, the case of Avianca Flight 052, which went down while trying to land at Kennedy International Airport in January 1990, killing 73 and injuring 85. After controllers and bad weather had delayed its landing, the jet ran out of fuel and crashed into a hillside in Cove Neck, New York.

The first officer's poor communication was one of the primary reasons for the crash. From what I can tell from the official transcript of the cockpit voice recorder,[5] the first officer, whose job it was to communicate with air-traffic controllers, told the control tower that the plane was low on fuel but never used the word *emergency*.

The pilot said to his first officer, "Tell him we are having an emergency," referring to their fuel status. Instead of repeating those exact words, the first officer told the controller, "We are running out of fuel."

Fourteen seconds later, the pilot said, "Tell him we are having an emergency. Did you tell him?" The first officer replied, "Yes, sir. I already told him." Half a minute later, when the pilot said, "Tell him we don't have fuel," the first officer told

the control tower, "We are running out of fuel."
Again, he did not use the exact words given him.
The words "running out of fuel" do not carry the
same urgency that the words "don't have fuel" do.
The pilot then asked, "Did you already tell him that
we don't have fuel?" And the first officer replied,
"I already told him."

For his failure to say, "This is an emergency! We
are out of fuel!" and for his failure to obey the order to
do so while telling the pilot that he had, the first officer
was at least partially, if not totally, karmically accountable for the deaths and injuries of everyone on board.

Having died in the crash himself, how would he
be able to pay his debt to the people he had harmed
by his negligence? Would God send him to hell?

I don't believe so. I believe he would allow him
to reembody that he might make amends for his
mistake. I believe God would, according to the
necessity of the law of cause and effect, put the first
officer in a position whereby he might serve those
who had suffered. And I believe God would return
to embodiment those whose opportunity to fulfill
their destiny in this life may have been impaired or
cut short.

Reincarnation gives us the opportunity to learn
the lessons that our returning karma, good and bad,
teaches us with its exacting discipline. Then free
will allows us to choose to capitalize on our harvest
of talents and good works and to pay the debt for, or
"balance," our misuses of God's light, energy and
consciousness.

Karma can bring boon and blessing to those who have sown well according to the golden rule: "Do unto others as you would have them do unto you." But to those who have sown the bad seed of selfishness and self-love (as we all have in one lifetime or another) karma is a taskmaster—exacting every jot and tittle of the law till all be fulfilled.[6]

Yet, even when karma as the great initiator comes knocking at our door, we may still choose not to make things right and go on violating the rights of others as we freely use and abuse God's energy.

But we cannot get away with it forever. The cosmic law of compensation will not allow it. For God, inasmuch as he embodies his law of karma, will not be forever mocked: Either we cast ourselves upon the Rock of Christ and allow our negative momentums to be broken, else, as it is written, the Rock of Christ as the avenger of our karma will grind us to powder.[7]

In my discussions with Christians, I have found that they deny the law of karma based on certain passages in the Epistles that emphasize salvation by faith and grace. They say that good works, though an important part of Christian life, are no guarantee of salvation. And they say that because Christ died for our sins, we are not required to pay the price for them.

I believe that we are saved through the grace of our Lord and Saviour Jesus Christ. But I also believe that the real meaning of "saved" is that Jesus' grace allows us the time and space through reincarnation to atone for our misdeeds and mistakes.

We are "bought with a price,"[8] as Paul said. And Christ, as the great burden-bearer of our karma, has paid the ransom. But inherent in Christ's grace is our obligation to enter the path of atonement unto the resurrection and eternal life.

When we come of age spiritually and are ready as joint-heirs with Jesus Christ[9] to receive our inheritance of the Light he bore, then the Father-Mother God requires us, as Paul said, to bear our own burden of karma and transmute it through service to life and by the alchemical fires of Love—specifically the "violet flame," which we invoke from the Holy Spirit.

The law of cause and effect and of free will is affirmed by Jesus over and over again in his parables to his own and in his warnings to the seed of the wicked. Our Lord speaks often of the day of judgment, which is the day of reckoning of every man's karmic accounts as recorded in his own book of life. In Matthew 12:35–37 he lectures to the scribes and Pharisees on the law of cause and effect:

> A good man out of the good treasure of the heart bringeth forth good things [i.e., positive karma]: and an evil man out of the evil treasure bringeth forth evil things [i.e., negative karma].
>
> But I say unto you, That every idle word that men shall speak, they shall give account thereof in the day of judgment.
>
> For by thy words thou shalt be justified, and by thy words thou shalt be condemned.

Jesus says that a man will be justified for his righteous and truthful words and condemned for his unrighteous and untruthful words. The Lord's grace will save him only if he is obedient to the law of Love—"that ye love one another as I have loved you."[10]

This law of Love is embodied in the first and great commandment that Jesus taught us:

> Thou shalt love the Lord thy God with all thy heart, and with all thy soul, and with all thy mind.

And it is embodied in the second that is like unto it:

> Thou shalt love thy neighbour as thyself.

Jesus said that "on these two commandments hang all the law and the prophets."[11] Truly, love is the fulfilling of the law of karma; and our obedience to Love's calling is our greatest assurance that we will not continue to make negative karma, whose harvest we will surely reap.

In Matthew 25 Jesus illustrates that the final judgment is based on the karma of an active (positive) or an inactive (negative) Christianity. Here works of love (i.e., charity) are *the* key to salvation. The Lord promises to those who minister unto him even in the person of "one of the least of these my brethren"[12] that they shall inherit the kingdom, whereas to those who do not minister unto him for the very love of Christ in all people, he says:

> Depart from me, ye cursed, into everlasting fire, prepared for the devil and his angels:
>
> For I was an hungered, and ye gave me no meat: I was thirsty, and ye gave me no drink:
>
> I was a stranger, and ye took me not in: naked, and ye clothed me not: sick, and in prison, and ye visited me not . . . .
>
> Verily I say unto you, Inasmuch as ye did it not to one of the least of these, ye did it not to me.
>
> And these shall go away into everlasting punishment: but the righteous into life eternal.[13]

The apostle Paul, in his exhortations to the stubborn Romans, confirms Jesus' teaching on the wages of karma:

> [God] will repay each one as his works deserve. For those who sought renown and honor and immortality by always doing good there will be eternal life; for the unsubmissive who refused to take truth for their guide and took depravity instead, there will be anger and fury. Pain and suffering will come to every human being who employs himself in evil . . .; renown, honor and peace will come to everyone who does good . . . . God has no favorites.[14] (Jerusalem Bible)

Truly, the Great Lawgiver, who teaches us through our experiments with free will, conscience and the law of cause and effect, is no respecter of persons,[15] and that is why his law of karma is irrevocable.

In his Sermon on the Mount, Jesus states the mathematical precision of the law of karma: "With what judgment ye judge, ye shall be judged: and with what measure ye mete, it shall be measured to you again."[16] In fact, the entire sermon (read Matthew 5–7) is Jesus' doctrine on the rewards of righteous and unrighteous conduct. It is his teaching on the consequences of thoughts, feelings, words and deeds. It is the greatest lesson on karma, as the law of personal accountability for one's acts, you will find anywhere.

Paul teaches Christ's doctrine of the rewards for labor when he writes to the church at Corinth:

> Every man shall receive his own reward according to his own labour. . . .
>
> Every man's work shall be made manifest: for the day shall declare it, because it shall be revealed by fire; and the fire shall try every man's work of what sort it is.
>
> If any man's work abide which he hath built thereupon, he shall receive a reward.
>
> If any man's work shall be burned, he shall suffer loss: but he himself shall be saved; yet so as by fire.[17]

Now, the author of Hebrews says, "Without faith it is impossible to please God;"[18] and Paul writes to the saints at Ephesus, "By grace are ye saved through faith; and that not of yourselves: it is the gift of God: not of works, lest any man should boast."[19]

Here it is evident that good works alone do not satisfy the whole law of salvation. Yet without them we have no proof of our discipleship in Christ, called as we are by our Lord to be "doers of the Word and not hearers only."[20]

The apostle John wrote in Revelation 20:12, "The dead were judged out of those things which were written in the books, according to their works." The books referred to here are each man's own book of life in which are inscribed the recordings of his works—his positive and negative karma. Revelation 20:13 repeats the statement that the dead were judged "every man according to their works," i.e., their karma.

Nowhere in Revelation do we read that these violators of Christ's love are saved by a last-minute, death-bed confession of Jesus Christ as their Lord and Saviour. Rather, as James reminds us, "faith without works is dead."[21]

Moreover, Revelation does not say that the dead are judged or vindicated by faith alone, or by grace alone, or, for that matter, by works alone; for all three are indispensable to eternal life.

Revelation 21:7, 8 and 22:12–14 establish with a ring of finality Jesus' teaching on karma. Dictating through John the Revelator, Jesus defines two paths— the path of the overcomers and their reward, and the path of the violators of God's laws and their end in the "second death," which is the merciful cancelling out of the soul potential that has denied the incarnation of God within her temple:

> He that overcometh shall inherit all things; and I will be his God, and he shall be my son.
>
> But the fearful, and unbelieving, and the abominable, and murderers, and whore-mongers, and sorcerers, and idolaters, and all liars, shall have their part in the lake which burneth with fire and brimstone: which is the second death . . . .
>
> And, behold, I come quickly; and my reward is with me, to give every man according as his work shall be.
>
> I am Alpha and Omega, the beginning and the end, the first and the last.
>
> Blessed are they that do his command-ments, that they may have right to the tree of life, and may enter in through the gates into the city.

For anyone to deny that the law of karma is in the New Testament, he would have to deny the full weight of all the verses I have cited. He would also have to deny the law and the prophets of the Old Testament, because Jesus, who is the author and finisher of our faith,[22] said he came not to destroy but to fulfill the law and the prophets.[23] The evi-dence is conclusive that the law of karma is inescap-able in the Judeo-Christian tradition.

And absent the gift of prophecy, clairvoyance,

an active sixth sense, a source of accurate psychic prediction or a prophet next door, astrology is our chart that enables us to navigate the minefield of karma. This is that karma which descends with "sudden destruction,"[24] yet can be foreknown.

Yes, astrology provides us with mathematical formulas predicting the weights and measures, and most especially the timetable, of our karmic returns in all our todays and tomorrows till the end of karmic time and space.

The Moving Finger of Free Will

Astrology *is* the prophecy of our karma. Your birth chart tells you exactly what positive karma, in the form of talents, attainments and blessings, and what negative karma, in the form of challenges and obstacles, you are bringing with you from your past lives.

In one sense of the word, your birth chart is not a predestination; in another sense it is. It is a record of what you have written, for better or for worse, on your book of life. When Omar Khayyám wrote the following verse, he wrote of the indelible recording of our karma by the Moving Finger of free will, as I would interpret it:

The Moving Finger writes; and, having writ,
Moves on: nor all your Piety nor Wit
Shall lure it back to cancel half a Line,
Nor all your Tears wash out a Word of it.[25]

But you must not look at your astrological chart with the sense that it is signed, sealed and delivered and that there is nothing you can do about it. There is everything you can do about it! Because the handwriting on the wall is *your* handwriting! And what Omar Khayyám didn't know is that because it is yours *you can erase it,* by the grace of God.

Consider the principle of the mist and the crystal. The mist is the unformed, the uncongealed. It is the energy of returning karma not yet clothed with physical form. Before it crystallizes, the mist can be read and known as a record of nonresolution whose time for resolution has not yet run out. When it does run out we say the mist has become the crystal—the sands have fallen in the hourglass.

Therefore, time and space grant us the option to balance karma before that karma falls due—to pay off the mortgage, so to speak, before "the bill collector" takes our farm, our business or our house. And that's precisely what being in embodiment on planet earth is all about!

We have a window of opportunity to undo the unrighteous deeds we have done and to do righteous deeds in their place—and to implore the merciful intercession of the Almighty—before the karma becomes an indelible record on our book of life and we are judged for our words and our works.

CHAPTER 2

Does God Condemn Astrology?

Some Christians believe that the Bible condemns astrology. In *Dark Secrets of the New Age*, which alleges that New Age leaders have a plan to establish a one-world religion and a global government, Texe Marrs writes, "The Old Testament is replete with warnings against these anti-God practices, which included necromancy (communication with familiar spirits), witchcraft, sexual perversions, astrology, psychic forecasting, divination, the worship of idols, and the upholding of men as deities."[1]

Hal Lindsey writes in *The Late Great Planet Earth*, "Whenever a person gets sold out by things like astrology, it will be like the Israelis. Israel was judged and virtually destroyed and taken to Babylon in 606 B.C. because the people became devoted to idolatry, especially astrology."[2]

The prevailing negative view of astrology in some church circles makes it necessary for me to take the time to demonstrate that astrology was not condemned in the Bible. A closer reading of the passages cited by Lindsey and others will show that their conclusions are based on outdated translations and faulty logic. Furthermore, their assumption that God condemns astrology belies the abundant traditions which say that astrology was an integral part of Hebrew life.

The Biblical passages that they say "prove" that astrology is forbidden can be divided into two groups: those that have been thought to mention astrology but don't and those that mention astrology but don't denounce it.

The King James Version of Leviticus and Deuteronomy condemns "observing times." Through the centuries "observing times" was thought to mean astrology. Leviticus 19:26 reads:

Ye shall not eat any thing with the blood: neither shall ye use enchantment, nor observe times.

Enchantment means the act or practice of employing magic or sorcery. *To enchant* is to exert magical influence upon, to bewitch or to lay under a spell. Magic seeks to control events; astrology seeks to discern them.

Observe times does not appear in modern translations, which are considered to be more accurate and literal than the King James Version. The Jerusalem Bible translates *observe times* as *practice divination* and the Revised Standard Version translates it as *practice augury*.

Webster's Third New International Dictionary defines *divination* as "the art or practice that seeks to foresee or foretell future events or discover hidden knowledge usually by means of augury or by making use of a psychical condition of the diviner in which supernatural powers are assumed to cooperate (as in the case of a spiritualistic medium or a crystal gazer)." *Augury* is defined as "divination by the interpretation of omens or portents."

The practice of astrology does not require psychic or supernatural skills. While it is not considered to be a science, it is a time-honored discipline based on the observation of natural phenomena.

The second reference to observing times in the King James Version is found in Deuteronomy 18:10–12:

> There shall not be found among you any one that maketh his son or his daughter to pass through the fire, or that useth divination, or an observer of times, or an enchanter, or a witch, or a charmer, or a consulter with familiar spirits, or a wizard, or a necromancer.
>
> For all that do these things are an abomination unto the LORD: and because of these abominations the LORD thy God doth drive them out from before thee.

In modern translations *observer of times* is rendered as *soothsayer*, which means "a person who predicts or pretends to predict the future." Soothsaying is associated more with psychic readings than with astrology.

Are the condemnations of divination in Leviticus and Deuteronomy meant to include astrology? Although astrology is sometimes loosely included among the forms of divination, it is significantly different.

A. Leo Oppenheim, a renowned Assyriologist, says in his classic textbook *Ancient Mesopotamia: Portrait of a Dead Civilization* that the primary form of divination used in ancient Mesopotamia was the prediction of the future through the examination of animal entrails. Diviners also observed the behavior of birds, the movement of oil poured into a bowl of water, and the shape of smoke rising from a censor. They often attempted to obtain yes or no answers from the gods through these methods.

If the writers of the Bible wanted to condemn astrology, wouldn't they have done it more specifically than by naming the general term *divination?* In his book *The Astrological Secrets of the Hebrew Sages*, Rabbi Joel C. Dobin observes, "Hebrew is a very specific language, and the Bible is quite forthright in saying what it means."[3]

Dobin goes on to discuss the methods of divination that are prohibited in Deuteronomy 18:9–14:

> This entire section enumerates quite specifically nine different types of divination, among which Astrology is conspicuous by its absence. If indeed, the Bible meant to include Astrology among the forbidden

processes, there are good Hebrew words for
the Bible to use. That the Bible in its spec-
ificity includes all other types of divination
but does not include Astrology among
those that are forbidden should be ample
evidence that Astrology is accepted as a valid
discipline.[4]

Another supposed condemnation of astrology
is taken from the Book of Daniel. Daniel the
prophet interpreted a dream for the Babylonian king
Nebuchadnezzar. He did so after all of the king's
other advisers had failed. In the King James Version,
Daniel 2:2, the king's advisers included the "magi-
cians, and the astrologers, and the sorcerers, and the
Chaldeans."[5] *Astrologers* is translated in some modern versions as *enchanters*.

Even if the writer of the passage meant to
include astrologers among the king's advisers, it
doesn't mean he was condemning astrology. Astrology and the interpretation of dreams are separate
disciplines. The astrologers' failure to interpret
the king's dream casts doubt neither on their ability
to read the skies nor on the acceptability of the
practice.

The next example comes from a passage in
II Kings that lists the sins for which God allowed the
children of Israel to be carried into Assyrian captivity. During the reign of Ahaz, the Israelites "caused
their sons and their daughters to pass through the
fire, and used divination and enchantments."[6]

Again, *divination* and *enchantment* do not mean astrology.

More than 100 years after the Israelites had been carried into captivity, Josiah, king of Judah, instituted a series of reforms designed to save his people from a similar fate. Some argue that this included wiping out astrology.

Josiah ordered the destruction of the vessels made for Baal that were in the Temple at Jerusalem. He also "put down the idolatrous priests, whom the kings of Judah had ordained to burn incense in the high places in the cities of Judah, and in the places round about Jerusalem; them also that burned incense unto Baal, to the sun, and to the moon, and to the planets, and to all the host of heaven."[7]

Worship of celestial bodies was an integral part of pagan worship. But astrology is the study of celestial bodies, not the worship of them or the gods they were named after. "Burned incense unto" in this passage means "sacrificed to." The cult of sacrifice to the sun, moon and planets was part of Sumerian and Assyrian religion, which identified the celestial bodies with gods.

Isaiah 47:10–15 is crucial to the argument that astrology was frowned upon by the Hebrew prophets. Isaiah is pronouncing the LORD's judgment upon Babylon:

> You [Babylon] were bold in your wickedness and said, "There is no one to see me."

That wisdom and knowledge of yours led you astray. You said to yourself, "I, and none besides me."

A calamity shall fall on you which you will not be able to charm away. A disaster shall overtake you which you will not be able to avert. Unforeseen ruin will suddenly descend on you.

Keep to your spells, then, and all your sorceries, for which you have worn yourself out since your youth. Do you think they will help you? Do you think they will make anyone nervous?

You have spent weary hours with your many advisers. Let them come forward now and save you, these who analyze the heavens, who study the stars and announce month by month what will happen to you next.

Oh, they will be like wisps of straw and the fire will burn them. They will not save their lives from the power of the flame. No embers these, for baking, no fireside to sit by.

This is what your wizards will be for you, those men for whom you have worn yourself out since your youth. They will all go off, each his own way, powerless to save you. (Jerusalem Bible)

If you look at the passage in context, you will see that Isaiah is not condemning the Babylonians for their practice of astrology but for their failure to show mercy to the children of Israel in captivity. This is revealed earlier in the chapter when God says:

> I was angry with my people, I had profaned my heritage. I had surrendered it into your hands, but you showed them no mercy. On the aged you laid your crushing yoke. You said, "For ever I shall be sovereign lady."[8] (Jerusalem Bible)

Isaiah is not, by any stretch of the imagination, implying that the Babylonians are doomed because they practice astrology. He is saying that now no one—not even the astrologers—will be able to save the Babylonians from the LORD's judgment. This shows that although astrologers, stargazers, prognosticators and prophets alike may warn people of impending karma, they cannot turn it back when the mist has already become the crystal.

The most persuasive evidence that God does not condemn the practice of astrology is found in the New Testament. In Matthew 2 we read, "Behold, there came wise men from the east to Jerusalem, saying, Where is he that is born King of the Jews? for we have seen his star in the east, and are come to worship him."[9]

They visited Herod, inquiring about the child, and "when they had heard the king, they departed; and, lo, the star, which they saw in the east, went before them, till it came and stood over where the young child was."[10]

Wise men is the King James rendering of the

Greek *Magoi*, or *Magi*. Who were the Magi? They were most likely astrologers. The Living Bible translates *Magi* as *astrologers*: "At about that time some astrologers from eastern lands arrived in Jerusalem."

The Expositor's Bible Commentary says: "The 'Magi' are not easily identified with precision.... The term loosely covered a wide variety of men interested in dreams, astrology, magic, books thought to contain mysterious references to the future, and the like. Some Magi honestly inquired after truth; many were rogues and charlatans....Apparently these men came to Bethlehem spurred on by astrological calculations."[11]

This description of Magi is consistent with the idea that astrology is a tool that can be used properly by serious seekers after truth and abused by "rogues and charlatans."

The Book of Matthew may contain specific astrological terminology. The New English Bible translates "We have seen his star in the east" as "We observed the rising of his star." And it translates "the star, which they saw in the east, went before them" as "the star which they had seen at its rising went ahead of them."

Do these phrases refer to a star the Magi had seen on the Ascendant, or rising sign, of a chart they had drawn for Jesus Christ? Bible scholar Sherman E. Johnson writes, "The words 'in the east' might be translated 'at its heliacal rising,' i.e. its first appearance in the east at the time of sunrise."[12]

Johannes Kepler, a German astronomer (1571–1630), surmised that the "star" might have been a conjunction of the planets Jupiter and Saturn that occurred in Pisces in May, October and November of the year 7 B.C. He also speculated that the star was a supernova.[13]

Astrology in the Book of Revelation

We find astrological symbolism in the Book of Revelation. For example, Revelation 4:6–8 describes four winged beasts surrounding the throne of God: the first was "like a lion," the second "like a calf," the third "had a face as a man," and the fourth beast "was like a flying eagle."

Astrologers have noted that these four beasts correspond with four of the signs of the zodiac—the lion with Leo, the calf with Taurus, the man with Aquarius and the eagle with Scorpio.[14]

Martin Rist, a professor of New Testament literature and interpretation, says the four beasts were astrological symbols of Babylonian origin, "for the Babylonians had four winged genii or guardians in the form of an ox, a lion, a man and an eagle." Rather than seeing this correspondence as John the Revelator's acknowledgment of astrology, Rist chooses to assume that John "was probably unaware of the Babylonian origin."[15]

Rist does, however, say that the "crown of 12 stars" on the head of the woman clothed with the sun represents the 12 constellations of the zodiac, symbolizing "her power over the destinies of mankind."[16]

The 12 stones at the foundations of "that great city, the holy Jerusalem"[17] correspond with the 12 stones on the breastplate of the high priest of ancient Israel. "According to the ancient Jewish writers Philo and Josephus," notes Rist, "these 12 stones on the high priest's breastplate are to be equated with the 12 signs of the zodiac."[18]

It seems simplistic to argue that John was unaware of the astrological symbolism in Revelation, the most symbolic of the books of the Bible. It is much more likely that he used it for a purpose. As Rist suggests, he may well have been trying to show God's power over mankind's destiny.

It is my view that God is the governor of all astrology and that he uses the heavenly placements to tell us of his true and righteous judgments. Job deals with the age-old dilemma of man's contending with God and his unbending law of karma. He stands in awe of his power and asks, "How can man be in the right against God? Who, then, can successfully defy him?"[19] and then contemplates the Omnipotent One midst the constellations:

> He is wise in heart, and mighty in strength . . .
> Which shaketh the earth out of her place, and the pillars thereof tremble.
> Which commandeth the sun, and it riseth not; and sealeth up the stars.
> Which alone spreadeth out the heavens, and treadeth upon the waves of the sea.
> Which maketh Arcturus, Orion, and Pleiades, and the chambers of the south.

> Which doeth great things past finding
> out; yea, and wonders without number.
> Lo, he goeth by me, and I see him not:
> he passeth on also, but I perceive him not.
> Behold, he taketh away, who can hinder
> him? who will say unto him, What doest
> thou?[20]

Job's lesson is well taken when it comes to facing the power of God as he communicates his omnipotence both to us and over us through the astrology of the constellations. Job's original questions can be answered only in man's acceptance of the justice of the law of karma signaled in the prophecy of the stars. Truly the answer is found in man's pursuit of the giving and getting of mercy, i.e., the process of atonement, to mitigate the powerful judgments of the Almighty.

Thus, it behooves us not to strive against the LORD but to study astrology as God's instrument of power, that we may learn, as Job did, to deal with the justice and the wisdom of "acts of God" in our lives meted out through his law of karma or through the initiations of Light and Darkness. In my opinion, this is the reason why the ancient Hebrews studied the stars.

Astrology in Judaism

There is ample evidence of astrology in Jewish writings such as the Talmud, the Midrash and the Kabbalah.

The Talmud, compiled between the sixth century B.C. and the sixth century A.D., is the paramount source of Jewish law. Rabbi Dobin cites the following passage from the Talmud:

> Rabbi Zutra ben Tuviah said in Rab's name: "He who is able to calculate the cycles and the planetary courses but does not, one may hold no conversation with him!"
>
> Rabbi Shimon ben Pazzi said: "He who knows how to calculate the cycles and the planetary courses but does not, of him the Scripture saith: 'but they regard not the work of the Lord, neither have they considered the operation of His Hands!' (Isaiah 5:12)"
>
> Rabbi Samuel ben Nachmani said: "How do we know it is one's duty to calculate the cycles and the planetary courses? Because it is written: 'for this is your wisdom and understanding in the sight of the peoples.' (Deuteronomy 4:6) What wisdom and understanding is 'in the sight of the peoples'? It is the science of the cycles and the planets!"[21]

Rabbi Dobin explains the passage:

> The rubric "one may hold no conversation with him" is a euphemism for excommunication! Thus the astrologer-rabbi who knows how to cast horoscopes but refuses to do so is subject to the highest punishment the community can inflict.

Rabbi Shimon's statement indicates that the one who refuses to cast horoscopes is at the same time refusing to bear witness to the greatness and the glory of God!

Finally, Rabbi Samuel's statement indicates that, if one does not know how to cast a horoscope, one must go out and learn the science, for this science links one to God! . . .

The rabbis of the Talmud indicate that the method most easily available to us to link ourselves to God's daily communication is astrology![22]

Most people think the Jewish greeting *Mazzal Tov* means "Congratulations." Its literal translation is "May you have fortunate constellations." This is hardly a coincidence. As Rabbi Dobin notes, "Expressions such as these do not become part of a language (there is no other way of saying 'good luck' in Hebrew) unless backing them up are centuries of use during which the basis for the expression was believed in and acted on."[23]

Astrology is also found in the Jewish wedding song *"Siman Tov Umazzal Tov Y'hey Lanu v'al kol Am'cha Yisrael!"* According to Rabbi Dobin, it is generally translated as "May we, and all Thy people Israel, have good luck!" It literally means "May we, and all Thy people Israel, enjoy good planetary aspects in fortunate constellations!"[24]

The first-century Jewish historian Josephus makes a number of references to astrology. He claims that the children of Seth, who was the third son of Adam and Eve, "were the inventors of that peculiar sort of wisdom which is concerned with the heavenly bodies, and their order."[25]

Josephus also says that the children of Noah lived long lives "on account of their virtue and the good use they made of it in astronomical and geometrical discoveries."[26] While there is no way to verify the historical accuracy of Josephus' reports, they serve to demonstrate that the first-century Jewish community was tolerant of astrology.

Roger Bacon Gets to the Heart of Astrology

Roger Bacon (c.1214–1294), one of the greatest minds of the thirteenth century, was a Franciscan friar and a vigorous proponent of astrology. In his day, the words *mathematician* and *astronomer* were interchangeable with *astrologer*. Although astrology flourished in the Middle Ages inside and outside the Church (several popes had court astrologers), it had earlier been condemned by the Church Fathers.

In his *Opus Majus* Bacon argues that the Church Fathers did not denounce astrology as a whole but rather the fatalism of some practitioners. According to Bacon, the problem exists in "lying or fraudulent mathematicians, full of superstition," who "imagine that necessity is placed upon those things in which there is choice, and particularly in matters which proceed from free will."[27] In other words, those who claim that astrology is predestination are misusing it.

He says that on the other hand "true mathematicians and astronomers or astrologers, who are philosophers, do not assert a necessity and an infallible judgment in matters contingent on the future."[28]

Astrology is like any other branch of knowledge. It can be used for good or for ill, properly or improperly, by skilled and unskilled practitioners alike.

Bacon writes that "philosophers do not maintain that there is an inevitable happening of events in all cases due to celestial influences, nor is their judgment infallible in particular instances, but in accordance with the possibility of this science."[29]

According to Bacon, Avicenna, a tenth-century Arab philosopher, shows that "the astrologer is not able to give certain assurance in all cases nor should he, owing to the instability of generated and corruptible matter, which does not in all cases obey the celestial force."[30] Free will and individual circumstances must be taken into account.

Bacon demonstrates that the great philosophers believed in the supremacy of the Creator over the creation. Expounding on their thoughts, he writes:

> They know that the divine rule can change all things according to its will, and for this reason they add always at the end of their decisions the qualification, "Thus shall it happen if God wills it." But they themselves know and testify that the rational soul is able to change greatly and impede the effects of the stars, as in the case of infirmities and

pestilences of cold and heat, and famine, and in many other matters.[31]

For Bacon, the purpose of studying astrology is to avoid its negative portents: "When men see beforehand these evils, they are able to prepare remedies."[32]

Bacon believed that it was possible to avoid wars through the study of astrology. He said that if leaders of the Church had read the astrological warnings, such as the comet of 1264, which preceded the battles that broke out all over Europe, they might have averted the wars of their times.

In his *Opus Majus* he writes: "Oh, how great an advantage might have been secured to the Church of God, if the characteristics of the heavens in those times had been discerned beforehand by scientists, and understood by prelates and princes, and transferred to a zeal for peace. For so great a slaughter of Christians would not have occurred."[33]

All who, like Roger Bacon, have the alchemist's heart know the truth of this statement: As long as the mist is still the mist and not the crystal, no future is inevitable. Nevertheless, in the final decade of this century we the people of planet earth will write and sign our destiny with the future—not in the mist, but in the crystal. And this time, having writ, "nor all your Piety nor Wit shall lure it back to cancel half a Line, nor all your Tears wash out a Word of it."

And we may weep and reap an opportunity lost.

Yet the message of this book is that God is not

ruled by astrology. Through the grace of Jesus Christ, a true entering in to the Word and Work of the Lord, and the violet flame of the Holy Spirit all *can* balance their negative karma in due season.

Or, under fortuitous constellations, we may preemptively pluck the karmic fruit from our tree of life—ere it ripen and fall upon our heads—and cast it into the fire. By the right hand or the left, God willing, we can beat the Fates!

CHAPTER 3

What Is Prophecy?

When I appeared on "Larry King Live!" on April 27, 1990, I found that Larry shared the misconception many Americans have about prophecy—that once a prediction is given the outcome cannot be changed.

LARRY KING: I guess what confounds people is, what's the difference whether we believe or don't believe if your prophecy is ordained? What's the difference?

ELIZABETH CLARE PROPHET: Well, I don't believe in predestination and I don't really engage in psychic prediction. But I think that the prophets come to warn us that if we don't do certain things and come close to God, obey his laws and prepare, certain calamities may come upon us.

LK: But that then always gives you the answer to say, "Well, we did good, so the prophets were wrong." In other words, the prophets can't be wrong. I could prophesy the end of the world next Saturday unless we're good, and then all I've got to do next Saturday is say we were good.

ECP: Well, I didn't make the rules, Larry. That's exactly what Isaiah and Jeremiah did. And when the people received an awakening to their God and became close to him, these calamities did not fall. Because we do move by free will . . . .

I don't think prophecy is final until it happens, ever, because of free will . . . .

LK: If there is free will, all prophecy is bunk. Isn't that true? It has to be bunk. If I can change my mind tomorrow, you can't tell me what I'm going to do tomorrow.

ECP: The scriptures aren't bunk, Jesus' prophecies aren't bunk and Revelation isn't bunk.

LK: Ah, then there's no free will.

ECP: But it still depends on free will.

LK: Then, wait a minute. If you prophesy that the Soviets are going to drop a bomb Saturday and they do drop a bomb, that wasn't free will. It was going to happen.

ECP: Nothing is predestined. You and I are deciding to talk tonight. We didn't have to decide that. We could have changed our minds at the last minute.

LK: Elizabeth, I'm a little lost. If nothing is predestined, how can you prophesy anything?

ECP: Because there is karma. And the law of karma decrees: As we sow, so we reap.

LK: But I can change my sow.

ECP: That's right.

LK: If I change my sow, your karma's wrong and your prophecy's wrong.

The folly of fatalism...

ECP: There is always hope. But karma brings the circumstance of its return. And if people don't change, then it's pretty clear that the karma they have sown is what they're going to reap.

A study of prophecy in the Old Testament bears out what I was saying to Larry.

Jonah's Prophecy Fails

Prophecy concerning future events is *always* delivered as a warning of the impending return of karma so that the people can invoke divine intercession and save themselves before it is too late. One of the best Old Testament examples of this is the story of the prophet Jonah. The message of the Book of Jonah is unmistakable: Repentance can turn back God's prophecies of judgment.

Most scholars believe that the book was written between 400 B.C. and 200 B.C. Its author used the figure of Jonah, a historical eighth-century B.C. prophet, in a parable designed to expose the Jews' intolerant attitude toward their Gentile neighbors.

The narrative opens with God's commission to Jonah: "Up! Go to Nineveh, the great city, and inform them that their wickedness has become known to me."[1]* Instead of going to Nineveh, which was the capital of the Assyrian empire, the prophet fled in the opposite direction and boarded a ship sailing for Tarshish.

Why did Jonah resist the LORD's call? At one point in the drama, Jonah confesses to the LORD:

---

*Quotes from the Book of Jonah in this chapter are from the Jerusalem Bible.

"That was why I went and fled to Tarshish: I knew that you were a God of tenderness and compassion, slow to anger, rich in graciousness, relenting from evil."[2]

Jonah feared that if the people of Nineveh were warned of God's wrath, they might repent of their evil ways. And that if they repented of their evil ways, God might not punish them. The heathen Assyrians had been the cruel enemies of the Jews. Simply put, Jonah did not *want* God to save them.

Jonah's attempted escape to Tarshish was futile. A violent storm threatened the ship and its passengers; when the sailors cast lots to see who on board was responsible for bringing the wrath of the gods upon them, the lot fell on the disobedient prophet.

Realizing that he was to blame, Jonah admitted to the sailors that he was trying to escape from God. He instructed them to throw him overboard in order to calm the sea. They did so reluctantly and the waves subsided. Jonah was swallowed by "a great fish" and remained in its belly for three days and three nights until the fish vomited him onto dry land.

Once again the LORD commanded his prophet to preach to the people of Nineveh. This time Jonah obeyed. He cried out to the people, "Only forty days more and Nineveh is going to be destroyed."[3]

Upon hearing Jonah's warning, the people "believed in God."[4] Everyone, "from the greatest to the least,"[5] fasted, put on sackcloth (which signified their state of mourning) and prayed that God would change his mind. The king of Nineveh "took off his robe, put on sackcloth and sat down in ashes."[6] He issued a decree: "Let everyone renounce his evil behavior and the wicked things he has done."[7]

The people's penance had the desired effect. "God saw their efforts to renounce their evil behavior. And God relented: he did not inflict on them the disaster which he had threatened."[8]

Jonah was indignant that the Ninevites had changed their ways and that God had had mercy on them. He begged God to take away his life, for, he said, "I might as well be dead as go on living."[9] Jonah was angry because he was prejudiced against the Ninevites and he was piqued because his prophecy had not come true.

After building himself a shelter on the east side of the city, he sat and waited to see what would happen. God then caused a gourd, or castor-oil plant, to grow up to shade Jonah as a comfort to him. This made the prophet happy.

The next day God sent a worm to attack the plant and it withered. As the sun beat down on Jonah's head and a scorching east wind blew, he again begged for death and told God he had a right to be angry with him for destroying the plant.

The Book of Jonah ends abruptly as God unmasks Jonah's self-pity and bigotry: "You are only upset about a castor-oil plant which cost you no labor, which you did not make grow, which sprouted in a night and has perished in a night. And am I not to feel sorry for Nineveh, the great city, in which there are more than a hundred and twenty thousand people who cannot tell their right hand from their left, to say nothing of all the animals?"[10]

The lesson is that God shows abundant mercy in the face of repentance. Forty days of fasting would hardly have been enough for the people of a city to balance the karma that had occasioned God's warning. But they showed good faith. Although they did not know "their right hand from their left," although they were heathens and had no morality, they still recognized the voice of God through Jonah and they obeyed.

The Book of Jonah carries such a strong message of the power of repentance that it is read publicly in its entirety on the Jewish holiday of Yom Kippur (the Day of Atonement). The book also defines the role of a prophet in precise terms. Since God's prophecies can be revoked, a prophet must not only speak God's decrees but exhort the people in order to initiate a deep and enduring change of heart.

Scholar R. Alan Cole summarizes the message of prophecy that comes across throughout the Bible:

> God's summons to judgment is, in the Bible, not normally a pronouncement of irrevocable doom, but an opportunity for repentance. All the temporal judgments of God are thus also manifestations of His grace, designed to lead us to a change of heart. Israel is always called to 'return', to 'turn back' to God because, as His people

initially, she enjoyed a relationship which she has now lost. That is why, in the New Testament, the parable of the prodigal son (Lk. 15:11–32) had such point to a Jewish audience.[11]

Defining Prophets and Prophecy

So we see that prophecy is not crystal-ball gazing or psychic prediction. The word *prophet* has a much broader meaning than the popular sense of *fortune-teller.*

Prophet derives from the Greek *prophētēs,* literally "to speak for." *The Oxford English Dictionary* gives the following as the first definition of *prophet*:

> One who speaks for God or for any deity, as the inspired revealer or interpreter of his will; one who [has] or (more loosely) who claims to have this function; an inspired or quasi-inspired teacher. In popular use, generally connoting the special function of revealing or predicting the future. The Greek [*prophētēs*] was originally the spokesman or interpreter of a divinity, e.g. of Zeus, Dionysus, Apollo, or the deliverer or interpreter of an oracle.

This definition applies to the Old Testament prophets. They did not confine themselves to predictions but delivered whatever message the LORD had for the people.

Only in the last sense given in *The Oxford English Dictionary* is *prophet* defined as "one who predicts or foretells what is going to happen; a prognosticator, a predictor. (Without reference to divine inspiration.)"

Oxford defines *prophecy* as "divinely inspired utterance or discourse; specifically in Christian theology, utterance flowing from the revelation and impulse of the Holy Spirit." *Prophecy* is also "the interpretation and expounding of Scripture or of divine mysteries: a function of the prophet in the apostolic churches; applied in the 16th and 17th centuries, and sometimes later, to exposition of the scriptures, esp. in conferences for that purpose, and to preaching."

The apostle Paul elaborates on the purpose of prophecy in the Christian church in his letter to the Corinthians: "He that prophesieth speaketh unto men to edification, and exhortation, and comfort."[12] The Jerusalem Bible translates these words as *improvement, encouragement* and *consolation.*

Edify is defined as "to build up, establish, organize (a system, institution, or law, a moral quality, etc.), to establish or strengthen (a person). In religious use: To build up (the church, the soul) in faith and holiness; to benefit spiritually; to strengthen, support. To inform, instruct; to improve, in a moral sense."[13] Therefore prophecy is a teaching that enables us to build, to establish and to organize our lives and our churches.

Edify has also been defined as "to enlighten, elevate, uplift."[14] When instruction comes forth from God it always improves us in our moral and religious knowledge, hence in the application of the law of God.

The second purpose of *prophecy* is exhortation. *To exhort* is "to admonish earnestly; to urge by stimulating words to conduct regarded as laudable."[15] It also means "to incite by argument or advice; urge strongly: advise, warn" and "to preach" in the sense of urging "acceptance or abandonment of an idea or course of action."[16] To exhort, therefore, is to impel or compel people to right action by the Holy Spirit as one states the truth and the law.

Paul tells us that the third purpose of prophecy is to bring comfort. "Comfort ye, comfort ye my people, saith your God" were the words of Isaiah as he delivered the message:

> Prepare ye the way of the LORD, make straight in the desert a highway for our God.
>
> Every valley shall be exalted, and every mountain and hill shall be made low: and the crooked shall be made straight, and the rough places plain:
>
> And the glory of the LORD shall be revealed, and all flesh shall see it together: for the mouth of the LORD hath spoken it.[17]

The prophet's comfort is the promise of the coming of John the Baptist preparing the way of the LORD, who would appear to us in his Son Jesus Christ. Truly our Lord took upon himself our sins. He has borne our karma, too hard for us to bear alone, that we might step by step, life after life offer

ourselves in redemptive service and be saved by
his grace.

The message of karma and reincarnation is a
great comfort. When you can see that it is the causes
you have set in motion, whether in this or a past
life, that have produced the predicament you are in,
you can liberate yourself from your negative momentums and go forward with a positive attitude to
tackle your problems. And by the intercessory grace
of Jesus Christ and your faithfulness in enduring
temptation you can be assured of your soul's victory
and the crown of life—if you finish the course of
your karma and fulfill your life's mission.

Prophecy, then, is edification: the Holy Spirit
teaching us, bringing us to a higher level of understanding, and enlightening us to God-centeredness
within. It is exhortation: God admonishing us and
compelling us to right action. It is comfort: the
assurance of salvation through faith, grace and good
works. And lastly prophecy is a warning: the prediction of what personal and planetary karma will bring
to our doorstep if we do not heed the prophet's call
to action.

Prophecy is delivered to God's messengers by
those Higher Intelligences—Ascended Masters,
Archangels and Cosmic Beings—who guide the
planetary spheres and their evolutions. They read
our karma as the handwriting in the skies and the
recordings of *akasha** and they tell the messengers

**akasha* [Sanskrit]: primary substance, the subtlest, ethereal essence which fills the
whole of space; "etheric" energy vibrating at a certain frequency so as to absorb, or
record, all of the impressions of life. The recordings in akasha, called akashic
records, can be read by adepts or those whose soul (psychic) faculties are developed.

what will come upon us and our generation if we do not obey the laws of God.

Prophecy predicts returning karma. But prophecy can be altered, mitigated or entirely turned back at any time before that 'mist' becomes the 'crystal'—before the energy of karma is precipitated in the physical plane as a sudden destruction that cometh upon us.[18]

You may think that this is impossible, but Jesus said, and I believe it: "With men it is impossible, but not with God: for with God all things are possible."[19] With God we can turn back the unformed before it crystallizes into the formed.

Just so, with God we can turn back returning karma before it hits us as tornado, flood or fire. By invoking the violet fire of the Holy Spirit and directing it through our chakras (spiritual energy centers in the body) into vortices of misqualified energy lodged in the mind, memory, emotions, soul and body, as well as in planet earth, we can transmute that returning karma, whether it be personal or planetary, before it manifests.

And so as you read the prophecies in this book, I ask you to always bear this in mind: these prophecies do not have to happen! Wherever I deliver Saint Germain's prophecy, this is the message: God has given you the power to change yourself and your world. Use it!

Sources of Prophecy

This book is a prophecy of karma. Although the prophecy written in the skies as astrology is my primary means of illustrating what God has shown me in my vision of the Four Horsemen, in my other writings I draw upon additional sources of prophecy that corroborate my reading of the causes behind today's returning karma:

1. The Old and New Testaments, especially the prophets and the message of Jesus on the Great Tribulation in Matthew 24 and 25, Mark 13 and Luke 21, and the Book of Revelation.

2. Mother Mary's prophecies to the children at Fátima in 1917 and to the teenagers in Medjugorje, Yugoslavia, from 1981 to the present. They contain an update on the prophecies of scripture and what the Blessed Virgin has projected as karmic retribution for our time—unless good people do better.

3. The writings of Nostradamus, the sixteenth-century French seer about whom I have spoken and written since 1986. Saint Germain has given me the correct interpretations of key quatrains that apply to the twentieth century and the superpowers. He has told me that to a certain extent the prophet has been misread by well-meaning commentators who have inserted their world view into their interpretations, thus casting a shadow of erroneous calculations on current events.

I have published Saint Germain's interpretation of Nostradamus in my book *Saint Germain On Prophecy*. It is an eye-opener and well worth reading.

4. The dictations of the Ascended Masters, which come to us directly through the agency of the Holy Spirit. I will explain Ascended Master

dictations in the next chapter. The prophecies of the Ascended Masters, like Old Testament prophecies, are not final. They can always be mitigated or turned back if the people change their ways and pray for divine intercession.

More than anything else, we need divine intercession to make it through this century! Our generation is ill-equipped to meet the challenges of personal and planetary karma that are foretold by these prophecies. Events and conditions in our time have gone too far.

How can we, as the one or the many, deal with the monumental problems we face today—such as drugs, which have impaired the minds of several generations?

Or toxic and radioactive waste spoiling the earth, the air, the water and animal life?

Or the plagues of our time, signaled by cancer and the AIDS epidemic?

Or child abuse inside or outside the womb?

Or manipulation of people and money at every hand?

Or the loss of human dignity through one euphoric escape after another—until people would rather succumb to nuclear death than summon the will to live?

We must realize that we stand on the pinnacle of an age. And which way the age shall go, whether it shall be known as the golden age of Aquarius or the dark age of Aquarius, depends on the decisions we the people of planet earth make in the coming days.

CHAPTER 4

A Messenger and a Prophet

My calling is to be a prophet of God. *Prophet* means one who speaks for God, hence a messenger.

Coincidentally (although I don't believe in coincidences), my name matches my calling. Prophet is the surname of my late husband and teacher, Mark L. Prophet. It was the family name that had been carried through generations from France to Ireland to Canada to Chippewa Falls, Wisconsin.

Mark was a prophet and a messenger, called by God through the Ascended Master El Morya to found The Summit Lighthouse in Washington, D.C., in 1958. He was and is the most amazing person I've ever met—the most humble, the most holy, the most human.

We were together for 12 years, were married, had four children, wrote many books, lectured around the world and built our movement. And then he passed on in 1973, his soul now one with God, yet ever with me.

In 1964 I received the "mantle" of Messenger, including gifts of the Holy Spirit. And throughout my ministry, by God's grace, I have built upon the foundation of prophetic teachings already laid by my husband.

As a Messenger of God, I see myself as the servant of God's Light within you. And the servant is not greater than his lord.[1] My Lord is the Christ of Jesus and the Christ of you, who are one and the same. For as John the Beloved wrote, that Christ was and is "the true Light, which lighteth *every* man that cometh into the world."[2] Therefore I come as a servant of that Light—your Light, my Light, your Christ, my Christ.

The Path of Personal Christhood

By way of introducing to you the Ascended Masters and their prophecies, I would like to tell you my beliefs concerning the path of personal Christhood.

I believe all sons and daughters of God have a divine spark, which is their potential to become, or realize, the Christ within and ascend to God as Jesus did. This concept is at the heart of the major religions, East and West. And it was part of Jesus' original teachings to his disciples, many of which were either obscured by Church Fathers or destroyed.

There is no record in the scriptures of Jesus saying that he is the only Son of God, having exclusive right to Divine Sonship. What our Lord did say is that the Son of man must be lifted up, as we read in chapter 3 of the Book of John:

As Moses lifted up the serpent in the wilderness, even so must the Son of man be lifted up: that whosoever believeth in him should not perish, but have eternal life.[3]

And then the Saviour revealed God's greatest gift to us—the gift of himself through his Son:

For God so loved the world, that he gave his only begotten Son, that whosoever believeth in him should not perish, but have everlasting life.
For God sent not his Son into the world to condemn the world, but that the world through him might be saved.[4]

I believe that the "only begotten Son" whom God gave to the world is the Divine Mediator, indeed the Universal Christ, whose Body is individualized ("broken") for each one of us in the person of our "Holy Christ Self." This is the Son of man, whom we must "lift up" into predominance in our lives. We must give him the seat of authority in our minds and hearts.

This is the Light, symbolized in the brazen serpent, that Moses raised up before the children of Israel.[5] It is the Light of the I AM THAT I AM that truly is the Light of all men.

I believe Jesus is telling us that if we are to have eternal life, we must believe in this Universal Christ, whose incarnation he fully and perfectly was and is. I believe that the Universal Christ is personally

manifest not only in the Christ, Jesus, but also in
the Christ of every son and daughter whom God has
made. And I believe that we must follow in Jesus'
footsteps as his disciples to realize the fullness of this
Christ in our lives, for only thereby can we work his
works on earth.

My faith in the love of the Father-Mother God
for us all is rooted not only in John 3:14–17 but also
in I John 3:1, which reads:

> Behold, what manner of love the Father
> hath bestowed upon us, that we should be
> called the children of God.

To this Paul added:

> The Spirit itself beareth witness with our
> spirit, that we are the children of God: And if
> children, then heirs; heirs of God, and joint-
> heirs with Christ; if so be that we suffer with
> him, that we may be also glorified together.[6]

Because our Father made us joint-heirs with
Jesus of the Christhood he bore, we are the inheri-
tors of his promises to us:

> Verily, verily, I say unto you, He that
> believeth on me, the works that I do shall he
> do also; and greater works than these shall he
> do; because I go unto my Father.
>
> And whatsoever ye shall ask in my name,
> that will I do, that the Father may be glorified
> in the Son.

> If ye shall ask any thing in my name,
> I will do it.
> If ye love me, keep my commandments. [7]

The word *Christ* comes from the Greek *Christos*, meaning "anointed." Hence, the 'Christed one' is one who is anointed with the Light of the LORD, the "I AM" Presence. This is the I AM THAT I AM (the YOD HE VAU HE) witnessed by Moses, [8] whose Presence God individualized for each of his sons and daughters. (See the Chart of Your Divine Self, Part VII.)

The early Christian Gnostics, whose writings were suppressed by orthodoxy, taught the same principles. The Gnostic Gospel of Philip describes the follower of Jesus who walks fully in his footsteps as "no longer a Christian but a Christ." [9] In the Gnostic Gospel of Thomas, Jesus says, "I am not your Master . . . . He who will drink from my mouth will become as I am: I myself shall become he." [10]

What I believe Jesus is saying here is "The 'I' that is the Christ in me is the same 'I' that is the Christ in you. Thus when you shall have become (one with) the same Christ that I AM (for there is but one Christ) then I shall become you and you shall become me—*as I AM*."

Buddhist texts also speak of a divine nature that each soul can externalize. They describe it as "the Buddha-essence" that is "in all beings at all times." [11] In the West, this concept of the potential incarnation of the Light of God, of the Inner Buddha and the Inner Christ, in every child of God has been effectively removed from church, synagogue, mosque and temple.

The culmination of the path of Christhood is the ascension, a spiritual acceleration of consciousness that takes place at the natural conclusion of one's final lifetime on earth. Through the ascension, the soul merges with Christ her Lord and returns to the Father-Mother God, free from the round of karma and rebirth.

The Great White Brotherhood

The Ascended Masters are our elder brothers and sisters on the path of personal Christhood. Having balanced their karma and accomplished their unique mission, they have graduated from earth's schoolroom and ascended to God.

They are a part of the Great White Brotherhood, spoken of in Revelation 7 as the great multitude of saints "clothed with white robes" who stand before the throne of God. [12] (The term "white" refers not to race but to the aura of white light that surrounds these immortals.) The Brotherhood works with earnest seekers and public servants of every race, religion and walk of life to assist humanity in their forward evolution.

Among these saints are Gautama Buddha, Maitreya, Jesus Christ, Saint Michael the Archangel, Zarathustra, Moses, Melchizedek, Mother Mary, Saint Francis, Saint Germain, El Morya, and unnumbered and unnamed loving hearts, servants of

humanity who have ascended to the I AM THAT
I AM and are a part of the living God forevermore.

Dictations from the Ascended Masters

I received my training from the Ascended Master El Morya under the tutelage of Mark Prophet
and I was anointed Messenger for the Ascended
Masters by Saint Germain. My commission is to
deliver God's prophecy and the Ascended Masters'
teaching for the age of Pisces as well as the everlasting gospel[13] for the new age of Aquarius.

I receive this prophecy through the power
of the Holy Spirit in the manner of the ancient
prophets and apostles. When the transmission is
about to take place, I enter a meditative state and
attune with the LORD God or his representative.
The LORD's presence or that of an Ascended Master, a Cosmic Being or an Archangel comes upon
me and the words and the light flow in a power and
a personality not my own.

This congruency of my soul with the living
Word of God I call a dictation, for the words are
being dictated to me even as I am speaking them
in the vibration of the divine speaker. It is truly a
divine happening of which I am but the instrument.
It is a gift of the Holy Spirit and not something I can
make happen.

The only way to describe this experience is to
say, in the words of the prophet: "The Spirit of the
Lord GOD is upon me, because the I AM THAT
I AM hath anointed me to preach . . ."[14] Jesus spoke

of the role of prophet, or messenger, when he said, "He that believeth on me, believeth not on me, but on him that sent me. And he that seeth me seeth him that sent me."[15]

I don't call myself a channeler because as far as I'm concerned channeling is just another word for spiritualism. Seeking advice from departed spirits has been going on since the witch of Endor conjured up Samuel the prophet for King Saul—and a long time before. While Samuel was a high soul, you can never be sure what you're going to get with channeling.

A discarnate entity is a disembodied being who has not ascended to God; hence he is not karma-free nor is he free from the wheel of rebirth. Since such a soul has not passed through the ritual of the ascension and become fully God-identified, he is as subject to error as anyone in embodiment. Still possessed of elements of a human ego as well as momentums of negativity, he may transmit these intentionally or not.

Discarnate entities may be benign but they are not omniscient. They may impart truth but they can be opinionated, proud and self-seeking. They are known to use people to achieve their ends and to take people's light.

Discarnate entities consume vital soul energies, draining the channeler as well as those present of the spiritual essence necessary to true progress on the path. Some well-known channelers admit they are exhausted after their channeling sessions, and many people report feeling depleted after attending a "seance."

By contrast, the energy released by the God-free ascended beings who speak from the highest octaves of Light, one with the universal Mind, is stupendous. It is exhilarating. It charges and recharges the body, mind and spirit of each person in the congregation, clears the chakras and draws the soul nigh to her own inner God Reality.

Dictations are not self-fulfilling psychic predictions, nor are they centered on building up the personalities or the egos of those present. They are the Word of God delivered by fully integrated immortal beings who are counted among the hosts of the Lord.

These beings come to initiate us in the ancient mysteries of Christ and Buddha and the everlasting gospel for the new age of Aquarius. And they come to exhort us so that we will rise to the great God flame within ourselves and defeat the momentums of returning karma that are coming upon the age.

The Ascended Masters present a path and a teaching whereby every individual on earth can find his way back to God. The books that Mark Prophet and I have written and the weekly *Pearls of Wisdom* that we have sent to the Ascended Masters' students throughout the world since 1958 are intended to give people the opportunity to know the Truth that shall make them free.

My purpose in life is to help all people to become acquainted with their own God Reality— the I AM Presence who overshadows them—that they may walk the Homeward path with Jesus, our

Lord and Saviour, and the Ascended Masters.

I do not claim to be a Master nor do I claim to be perfect in my human self. I am but the instrument of the Ascended Masters. My mission is to take true seekers, in the tradition of the Masters of the Far East (which Jesus exemplified), to the level of consciousness where they can meet their Teachers face to face.

An Introduction to Saint Germain and El Morya

I would like to introduce to you the Ascended Masters Saint Germain and El Morya, who play an important role in this book.

Both of these Masters spent many, many lifetimes upon earth, as all of us have. Among Saint Germain's most notable embodiments were the prophet Samuel (c.1050 B.C.); Saint Joseph, protector of Jesus (first century); Roger Bacon, philosopher, persecuted scientist and Franciscan monk (c.1214–1294); and Francis Bacon, statesman, essayist and father of inductive reasoning and the scientific method (1561–1626).

After his ascension in 1684, Saint Germain devoted himself to the advancement of government and science. He is the Aquarian-Age Master, ready to assist us with innovation in every field.

Some of El Morya's embodiments were the Hebrew patriarch Abraham (c.2100 B.C.); Melchior, one of the three Magi (first century); Saint Thomas Becket, chancellor of England, archbishop of Canterbury and adviser to Henry II (1118–1170); Saint

Thomas More, statesman, lord chancellor and adviser to Henry VIII (1478–1535); and Akbar, Mogul emperor (1542–1605). El Morya attained the ascension in 1898.

These five lifetimes give you a sense of the Ascended Master El Morya and his concerns today. From inner planes he works with the leaders of governments and nations and instructs in wise management of the affairs of state.

I have written in greater detail about the past lives, mission and message of El Morya and Saint Germain in *Lords of the Seven Rays, Saint Germain On Alchemy* and *Saint Germain On Prophecy*.

As Ascended Masters, El Morya and Saint Germain have become one with God, transcending all of their former selves, just as you, too, will do when you shall have fulfilled the special mission God gave you for this and previous lives.

Therefore the Ascended Masters are no longer the people they were when living upon earth, just as you are not your former selves, though you bear the momentums of your achievements from past lives and use these talents daily. An Ascended Master can access all the positive good he has externalized throughout his incarnations on this and other worlds—multiplied by the Power, Wisdom and Love of his Holy Christ Self, I AM Presence and Causal Body.

I often must correct the impression people have that I am receiving messages from, for example, the departed spirit of Roger Bacon. Not so.

I deliver the words and the power of the ever-present Ascended Master Saint Germain, who is neither a "departed spirit" nor a "dead man" but an immortal being of Light who is equal to and greater than the sum of his past lives. To stand in his presence as I do, or to be in the audience when he delivers God's prophecy, is to know that he is wholly God-identified, the fullness of his Mighty I AM Presence made manifest.

Every Ascended Master is unique in the cosmic sense of the word, having a unique Causal Body by which he or she may bless, heal, instruct and endow lesser-evolved lifestreams such as ourselves. Even so, when you shall have accomplished your reason for being to the glory of God and balanced your karma, you will have much to offer life as a result of all the constructive good that you have brought forth on earth.

Saint Germain and El Morya have instructed me in the uses of astrology as a means to chart both personal and planetary karma. Saint Germain has shown me what the future holds but he has sealed my lips so that I may not speak of all that I have seen. He has not, however, forbidden me to talk about the prophecy of astrology, which I call the handwriting in the skies.

Astrology is a means of anticipating the future as a series of probabilities that are still subject to change by free will. It behooves us to study the stars and read what the heavens are telling for the United States, for the Soviet Union, for our planet and for each one of us. For the handwriting in the skies is unmistakably clear. And not long are the days for any one of us before we will give an accounting before God's emissaries for our words and works that make up the sum total of this life.

May we sow and reap brightly in the Lord our GOD, that we may be worthy of the approbation: "Well done, thou good and faithful servant: thou hast been faithful over a few things, I will make thee ruler over many things. Enter thou into the joy of thy Lord."[16]

CHAPTER 5

What You Can Do about Your Karma

Now that you understand that your personal astrology is the prophecy of your returning karma, what can you do about it?

When you can read the handwriting in the skies and then calculate the geometry of your karma outlined in your astrology, you can make incisive calls to the Seven Archangels and other great beings of Light to enter your world on the precise lines and degrees of both positive and negative aspects in your astrological chart.

For, you see, your astrological chart is an extension of yourself. Like the rings of Saturn, your chart is with you wherever you go.

And so you can call to your Mighty I AM Presence and Holy Christ Self and to Saint Germain to direct the violet flame into all positive and negative portents of your astrology for the maximum resolution of your karma and the balancing of relationships. And once you get on top of your own world with the violet singing flame, as it is called, you can be God's instrument to mitigate or entirely transmute world karma.

Personal and national charts, when accurately read, are a means of predicting and interpreting coming events. In addition, they give us the information we need to formulate a specific prayer to the Ascended Masters and angelic hosts, asking them to stand between us and a calamity foreseen.

Remember, the Magi predicted the date and place of Jesus' birth in Bethlehem by their knowledge of astronomy and astrology. And by that prediction they, instead of Herod, who would have killed the child, arrived at the scene to bless the "King of the Jews." (Herod had told the wise men to "bring him word" when they found the young child, but God warned them in a dream not to return to Herod; and "they departed into their own country another way."[1])

Your astrology is a record of your creations of the past. Because you have a Mighty I AM Presence, a Holy Christ Self, a divine spark and free will, you are a co-creator with God. This means you can create, and once you have created you can decide to preserve your creation because it is worthy of God and man or you can decide to destroy it because it is not worthy. These three options are ours under the offices of the Trinity as defined in Hinduism: Creator (Father), Preserver (Son), and Destroyer, or Transmuter (Holy Spirit).

The Hindus tell us that there are three ways to "loosen the bonds imposed by the law of karma." As *The Encyclopedia of Eastern Philosophy and Religion* explains it, they are (1) "surrender to God,"

(2) "the creation of good karma" and (3) "the dissolution of bad karma."[2]

The best way to dissolve bad karma is through the science of the spoken Word. I have seen people deter or diminish the impact of impending karma by using the science of the spoken Word to direct the mighty light rays of God and the fullness of the Cosmic Christ consciousness into the negative astrological configurations which signaled that karma, thereby transmuting it before it could manifest in their lives. I have seen them dissolve their diseases and lengthen their allotted lifespan by good works, obedience to cosmic law, prayer and fasting, and forgiving and loving all life free.

I have seen that when people determine to walk a path of discipleship under Jesus Christ, Mother Mary, Saint Germain and all of the Ascended Masters, they gain a self-mastery that enables them to ride the wave of their karma instead of being inundated by it—to ride the bull of their human creation instead of being trampled by it.

I have seen and therefore I believe that in all things, with God and through his Christ, we can emerge the living conqueror—whether in this life or the next, whether on earth or in heaven. We can be the victors as long as we become one with the Light from the heart of the beloved Mighty I AM Presence, the Pure Person of the living God who is with us—the Light that descends even in this moment into the place prepared, our waiting heart-chalice here below.

In the face of *any* negative predictions—whether they be psychic readings or astrological portents or quatrains of Nostradamus or the prophecies of Fátima and Medjugorje—we the people of earth turning to our God can make them fail before the mist of the Fates becomes the crystal (i.e., the crystallization) of karma.

Unless we invoke this violet flame under the law of forgiveness to erase the cause, effect, record and memory of our past violations of the Great Law, sooner or later we will be compelled to balance our personal and planetary karma (a) by serving the individuals or institutions we have injured or dealt unjustly with or (b) by bearing that karma in our bodies as diseases, disorders, debilitation, aberration, accident or death.

What we have to come to grips with is that once the mist becomes the crystal, it is impossible, short of direct divine intervention, to turn it back.

I am delivering the warning to tell the world the worst and the best that can happen in the decade of the 1990s and beyond. And I tell it as I see it in the heavenly signs of astrology, in the earthly signs of the Four Horsemen and in the handwriting on the wall of karma, karma everywhere telling us to hurry up and do something about the mess we've made of this blessed earth and our earth bodies before it is too late.

A lot of people see the karma and hear what it's telling us but they don't know what to do about it. When Moses said, "Our God is a consuming fire,"[3] he was telling us what we could do for our time and for all time: When we have misused God's fire to create unjustly, we must use God's fire to "uncreate," or "transmute," our unjust creations. And this is our work even as it is the work of the Holy Spirit working in us and through us.

The sacred fire of the Lord's Spirit, when invoked by his sons and daughters on earth, will pass through and "uncreate" any and all untoward creations, as well as thoughts and feelings, words and deeds.

The karma of the planet has been held in abeyance for thousands of years by the Light, i.e., the God consciousness, of the saints and Christed ones of all ages. But the end of the age of Pisces marks the day of personal and planetary reckoning. Unless we foresee the due dates of karma as prophesied by the Ascended Masters and direct God's gift of the violet flame into the mist of the negative karma of planet earth, that karma will descend with the Chaos and old Night of ancient cataclysm recorded only in the memory of the race.

Therefore I recommend the following:

1. Read this book and underline the Ascended Masters' warnings and prophecies and the astrological predictions.

2. Study the teachings on the violet flame given in Part VII of this book and use the violet flame daily for the mitigation or the complete transmutation of all negative prophecies and astrological predictions. And expect God's miracle and his victory in your life!

3. Use my violet flame audiotape, *Save the World with Violet Flame! by Saint Germain,* and compose your own prayers to God, imploring divine intercession and violet flame transmutation for the karmic conditions outlined in this book and for the problems affecting you, your loved ones, and planet earth.

A million or 10 million people invoking the violet flame could, according to God's mercy, turn back the karma earth's evolutions have created before it seals our fate. It will take centuries or millennia to undo that karma if it descends physically on planet earth.

That is why we have to transmute this karma now—while there is yet time. No one can "endure permanently half-slave and half-free,"[4] as we do while under the cudgel of our karma and the threat of its swift and sudden descent.

We can decide to make our lives count for one purpose, the victory of the age. And we together, one-times-one-times-one in the Divine One, *can* beat the Fates. Yes, we can in God's name transmute past-present-future by the violet flame and move on to fulfill the cycles of the fiery destiny of our calling in God!

This is the day when we must make our decision to live in Reality, to choose to be and to enter the mainstream of life as God intended us to live it. If we do not make that choice today, if we just let ourselves bob along on the waves of human emotion in and out with the tides of the moon and the astral sea, we will witness at some level of our psyches the disturbances in the earth body that Saint Germain showed me in his vision of the future.

If I didn't *believe* with all my heart and soul that God has placed within us the will to change, the power to change, the wisdom to know when change is possible and when it is not, and the love of change when it is ordained, then I would not be writing this book.

If I didn't *know* with all of my mind and spirit that God has placed in us his divine spark whereby his all-consuming fire is kindled for alchemical change in the microcosm and the macrocosm of our worlds, then there would be no point in placing before you the prophecies of Saint Germain.

Because I know there is time and space to turn the tide of karma, I *must* deliver this the Lord's message. For not only has he empowered me with his mantle, he has impelled me with his fiery Spirit.

Today, then, is our day of decision. This is not an altar call. It is a call from the heart of God to your soul to *remember*.

Let the divine memory unfold as you remember your beginnings in the Great Central Sun with your beloved twin flame. Remember the foreknowledge you had that one day you would be at this crossroads in time and space on a planet in distress called Earth, and that you would be told *how you could make all the difference*.

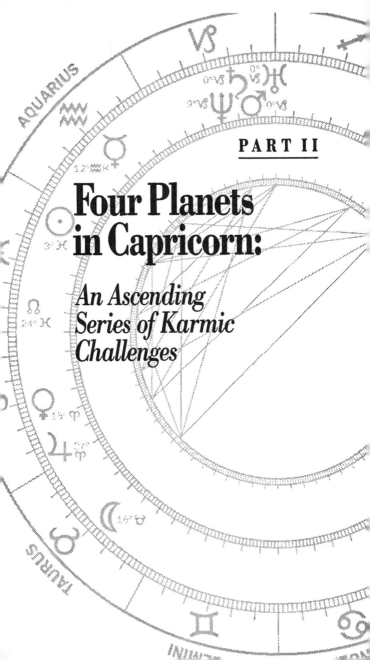

PART II

Four Planets in Capricorn:

*An Ascending
Series of Karmic
Challenges*

CHAPTER 6

An Eventful Two Years

On February 13, 1988, I told a San Francisco audience: "The astrological configurations of the next 12 years show that we will face an ascending series of karmic challenges, including the possibilities of war, revolution, depression and major earth changes."

I talked about a number of configurations, most importantly the conjunction of Mars, Saturn, Uranus and Neptune in Capricorn on February 22 and 23, 1988. This configuration, which has occurred only twice in the last 2,200 years, could have monumental consequences. I said:

> This conjunction of Mars, Saturn, Uranus and Neptune in Capricorn marks the formal starting point of a period of upheaval and change on the planet. The era of financial expansion related to oil and international finance will come to a halt and . . . national economies will contract.
>
> This is a time when nations will become conservative and reactionary, there will be

massive debt liquidation, the real price of commodities will fall, a crash in the real-estate market is likely, a pessimistic mood will sweep the earth, the potential for war is extremely high and the U.S. government will be in danger of being destroyed or reformed beyond recognition.

In short, this Capricorn conjunction and other astrological phenomena I will soon discuss show that the period between late February 1988 and the year 2000 will be a time of karmic summing up. Not one of us is exempt from that karmic summing up . . . .

During this period we are likely to see the reform, disruption or dissolution of economic and political systems, revolution, major cataclysm and war.

Let me now review with you some of the prophecies that have already come to pass.

"The era of financial expansion related to oil and international finance will come to a halt and . . . national economies will contract."

The era of financial expansion related to oil and international finance *has* come to a halt and national economies *have* contracted.

According to one financial analyst, Robert Kwasny, this is "a time of contraction throughout most of the world."[1] The economies of the United

States, Japan, Britain, the Soviet Union, South Africa and most Latin American countries are contracting.

Reactionism around the Globe

"*Nations will become conservative and reactionary.*"

In this context, *conservative* means "tending to preserve established traditions or institutions and to resist or oppose any changes in these." *Reactionary* means "characterized by or advocating reaction, especially in politics." *Reaction* means "a movement back to a former or less advanced condition; extreme conservatism."[2]

We have seen the forces of conservatism and reactionism prevail in many nations throughout the world since February 13, 1988.

On February 26, 1988, Panamanian dictator Manuel Noriega, in a reactionary move, ousted the democratically elected president Eric Arturo Delvalle. Noriega, as you know, was removed from power by the U.S. military on December 20, 1989.

On June 4, 1989, the Communist leaders of the People's Republic of China crushed the budding student democracy movement in a bloody massacre in Tiananmen Square.

Romanian dictator Nicolae Ceausescu stood as Eastern Europe's most visible defender of reactionary Communism until he was toppled by a revolution on December 22, 1989.

In Cuba, Fidel Castro has rejected *perestroika*

and is one of the few vocal apologists for socialism in the age of *glasnost.*

And even the Soviet Union, despite *glasnost*, has been conservative and reactionary. Mikhail Gorbachev is popular in the West. Most Westerners think he's trying to institute irreversible change and establish Western-style democracy in the Soviet Union. Yet many citizens of Russia and other Soviet republics see Gorbachev as the conservative who is trying to preserve the power of the *nomenklatura*— the top Soviet leaders—and the Communist party.

But, you may say, the Soviet people are gaining new individual freedoms every day. The Berlin Wall has been opened. East and West Germany will be allowed to unite peacefully. Well, take a look at these incidents:

On April 9, 1989, Soviet troops broke up a nationalist demonstration in Soviet Georgia using clubs and poison gas against their own citizens. Twenty people were killed.

Moscow is standing in the way of independence in Lithuania, Estonia and Latvia.

On June 20, 1990, the Soviet republic of Uzbekistan proclaimed itself sovereign. As Reuters reported, the Uzbek Parliament "declared the supremacy of Uzbek laws in the republic and placed domestic and foreign policy under the authority of the local government."³ Uzbekistan, however, did not secede from the Soviet Union. Apparently the Uzbeks did not think they could go that far without provoking a hostile reaction from Moscow. Their actions leave no doubt about what they'd like to do.

On July 16, 1990, the Ukraine, the Soviet Union's second largest republic, also declared itself sovereign. Like the Uzbeks, the Ukrainians stopped short of secession, but they claimed for themselves virtually all the rights of a sovereign nation. As Adrian Karatnycky, co-author of *The Hidden Nations: The People Challenge the Soviet Union*, pointed out in *The Wall Street Journal*, the Ukraine Supreme Soviet asserted "the republic's right to create its own currency, raise its own army, collect tariffs and erect enforceable borders."[4]

It is certain that the non-Russian republics would leave the Soviet Union immediately if they thought they could get away with it.

If the views of the Lithuanians, Estonians, Latvians, Uzbeks and Ukrainians about the military and the government of the Soviet Union are correct, then the Soviet Union is conservative and reactionary. Gorbachev the visionary, who launched *perestroika*, has become Gorbachev the reactionary, who denies independence to Soviet republics and opposes popular reforms.

The Economy Heads Downhill

"There will be massive debt liquidation."

To liquidate means "1. to settle by agreement or legal process the amount of (indebtedness, damages, etc.) 2. to settle the accounts of (a bankrupt business firm that is closing, etc.) by apportioning assets and debts 3. to pay or settle (a debt)."[5]

There has been so much debt liquidation since February 1988 that it is hard to report it briefly. On June 15, 1989, the House of Representatives approved the largest government bailout in history, $157 billion, in order to salvage the savings and loan industry.

Even then it was clear that the S&L bailout would cost a lot more than $157 billion. On May 21, 1990, *Newsweek* reported, "The General Accounting Office has said the total bill, counting interest, may total as much as $500 billion."[6] *Newsweek* called the S&L debacle the worst scandal in the history of the United States.

And it may be just the beginning. The nation's commercial banks are in trouble, too. As banking experts Robert E. Litan, R. Dan Brumbaugh and Andrew S. Carron write, "It is possible that losses in the banking industry could eclipse those of the thrift [savings and loan] industry."[7]

Debt liquidation is in full swing in other sectors of the economy. On January 15, 1990, Allied Stores Corp. and Federated Department Stores Inc., two U.S. retailing giants owned by Robert Campeau, filed for protection from creditors under Chapter 11 of the U.S. Bankruptcy Code. According to *Business Week*, the Campeau debacle was "the largest retailing bankruptcy in history."[8] Within a month it was followed by the bankruptcy of what had once been Wall Street's most profitable firm, Drexel Burnham Lambert.

On February 14, 1990, a headline in *The Wall Street Journal* announced: "Wall Street Era Ends as Drexel Burnham Decides to Liquidate." The *Journal* reported, "Drexel Burnham Lambert's remarkable journey from Wall Street mediocrity to junk-bond powerhouse to admitted felon ended last night when the securities firm's parent announced plans to file for bankruptcy."[9]

Even the great real-estate developer Donald Trump couldn't survive this financial crisis. Trump's $3.3 billion debt greatly exceeds his assets. On June 26, 1990, Trump and his bankers reached a last-minute deal that enabled him to avoid personal bankruptcy. But the agreement amounts to an out-of-court bankruptcy. Robert Kwasny writes, "Whatever the specifics of Trump's ultimate negotiations, he will, over time, be forced to liquidate some, if not all, of his empire."[10]

Between June 12 and June 22, 1990, former multibillionaires Nelson Hunt and William Hunt auctioned off more than $20 million worth of ancient gold and silver coins and art objects to pay creditors and back taxes.

The big boys aren't the only ones having problems. Americans are filing for bankruptcy in record numbers. According to *Newsweek*, "The number of nonbusiness bankruptcy filings rose to 580,459 for the year ended June 30, 1989."[11] And the pace of debt liquidation is likely to accelerate in the United States as we move into the next recession.

"The real price of commodities will fall."

The price of commodities turned down across the board in 1989. On August 2, 1990, the Commodities Research Bureau Futures Index (a commodities price index) was 234, down from 275 in June of 1988.

"A crash in the real-estate market is likely."

The real-estate market crashed in parts of New England, New York and New Jersey in late 1988 and early 1989, and real-estate prices, with a few exceptions, are down throughout the rest of the nation.[12]

Falling real-estate prices were integral to the Trump catastrophe. However, *U.S. News & World Report* explained on July 2, 1990, that "the problem is hardly limited to Donald Trump and his lenders. It signals the potential acceleration of a banking crisis brewing for two years that now threatens to break out on a national scale."[13]

The real-estate crisis can only grow worse as Resolution Trust Corporation, created to sell the assets of failed S&Ls, places billions of dollars of real estate on the market. Prices will drop as the number of properties for sale exceeds the demand.

"A pessimistic mood will sweep the earth."

The collapsing real-estate market is leaving many homeowners in a black mood. On April 13, 1990, *The New York Times* reported that "the financial drain and insecurity have created a climate of hopelessness for many homeowners" and that many feel "a sense of impending doom."[14]

Things aren't going well in the world economy either. Financial pessimism has even cropped up in the one place you would least expect it— Japan. *Time* magazine of April 2, 1990, described the situation:

> Suddenly Japan is caught in a powerful downdraft of pessimism. A vexing combination of tightening financial conditions, trade tension with the U.S. and political weakness at the top has sent Tokyo's financial markets into a funk. The slide is threatening to choke the country's economic growth and sap the ebullient confidence that has filled Japanese investors and businessmen in recent years. "The pendulum has once again swung in Japan," says Richard Koo, a senior economist at the Nomura Research Institute. "It's now over to the doom-and-gloom side, when objectively speaking, Japanese companies remain the strongest in the world."[15]

As we go to press, financial pessimism abounds in the wake of Iraq's August 2, 1990 invasion of Kuwait. The United States is in the midst of the biggest troop deployment since the Vietnam War. U.S. soldiers have been dispatched to Saudi Arabia, and Iraq has massed troops from its million-man army near the border of Saudi Arabia and Kuwait.

World leaders and U.S. military men are pessimistic about the outcome of this situation. They doubt it will be peaceful.

Challenges of this nature can be foreseen. In February 1990 I predicted that Saudi Arabia was one of several nations that would face life-and-death challenges between 1988 and 1992.[16]

The Stock Market Separates from the Economy

Speaking about the stock market in my February 13, 1988 lecture, I said:

> The decline since August 25, 1987, is only the first leg of the market's descent. The second leg will be related to the February 23, 1988 Capricorn conjunction and the eclipse of the Sun. The eclipse occurred on September 22, 1987. . . .
>
> Once the market starts down on the second leg, the big drop in the market is likely to come around November 13, 1989, when Saturn makes an exact conjunction to Neptune at 10° Capricorn and both make an exact opposition to Jupiter at 10° Cancer. . . .
>
> This opposition will affect much more than the stock market. It will be a critical factor in triggering major debt liquidation and could lead to the dissolution of much of the Western banking system.

Some journalists interpreted this to mean that I had predicted a stock-market crash for November

13, 1989. However, I only said that the drop was "likely" to come "around" November 13. And it did. The biggest stock-market drop (190 points) since the 508-point crash on October 19, 1987, happened on October 13, 1989.

Perhaps I should have said "economy" instead of "market" in this analysis. When most people think of the "stock market" they think of the Dow Jones industrial average (or Dow). The Dow is popularly considered to be the bellwether of the economy: if the Dow is up, the economy is supposed to be strong and growing; if the Dow is down, the economy is supposed to be weak and headed for a recession.

In general, this relationship holds true. But in 1989 and the first half of 1990, the Dow was an inaccurate indicator of the health of the economy. Until Iraq's invasion of Kuwait on August 2, 1990, the Dow and the economy were moving in opposite directions. The Dow was at an all-time high—nearly breaking 3000—and the economy was either in, or on the verge of, a recession.

Why did this happen?

The Dow is only one measure of the stock market. It is based on the performance of the stocks of 30 large companies. Most of these are industrial companies, but this select club also includes consumer-product companies like Coca-Cola, McDonald's, Philip Morris and Procter & Gamble.

The Dow has been high because of the strong performance of a relatively small number of stocks, particularly the stocks of consumer companies. Coca-Cola, for example, reported increased earnings for the second quarter of 1990, and its stock promptly rose an additional 5 percent. "Coca-Cola's gains have helped move the Dow Jones Industrial Average up to just seven points away from 3000 as of yesterday's close,"[17] Craig Torres reported in *The Wall Street Journal* on July 20, 1990.

But we have to remember that consumer product stocks are characteristically the last to fall as the economy moves into a recession. As Robert Kwasny puts it, "You don't need to borrow money to eat at McDonald's or see a movie."[18]

However, the Dow stocks that rely on the sale of capital goods (real estate, machinery, cars, furniture, etc.) are weak. "A recession begins," Kwasny says, "with a slowdown in the capital goods sector."[19] In 1990 the demand—and hence the stock prices—for capital goods has been down. Through July 1990, IBM, for example, was doing well for a stock in the capital goods sector, but it was about 60 percent lower than it had been before the 1987 crash.[20]

There are other stock averages that show that the Dow Jones industrial average is not a good indicator of the state of the economy.

For instance, the Dow Jones company publishes an average for utilities and transportation stocks in addition to its industrial average. While the Dow industrials have been high, the Dow utilities and Dow transportation issues have been down.

The utilities average is seen as a good indicator of the direction of the economy.

The Dow Jones industrial average rose 5.52 percent between December 31, 1989, and July 31, 1990. But in the same period the Dow Jones utilities average dropped 10.65 percent and the Dow Jones transportation average dropped 7.16 percent.[21]

Broad-based stock indexes give a clearer picture of the health of the economy than the narrowly based Dow industrials. The Russell 2000, an index of 2000 stocks, is down. The Value Line Composite Price Index, another measure of the value of a broad group of stocks, is also down.

All in all, most measures of the stock market other than the Dow Jones industrial average have been declining. And the select group of stocks that pushed up the Dow are by no means invulnerable. Douglas R. Sease and Craig Torres noted in *The Wall Street Journal* on July 24, 1990, "If nothing else, the Dow's dive yesterday—it was down more than 105 points early in the day—illustrates what can happen in a stock market dangerously dependent on a handful of supposed winners."[22]

With Iraq's invasion of Kuwait, the Dow went into a tailspin. The drop can be partially attributed to the spectre of prolonged higher oil prices. But the real reason the Dow dropped is that there were underlying weaknesses in the economy that became more obvious in the post-invasion climate. There was simply nothing to support the Dow soap bubble at levels approaching 3000.

Political Turmoil on a Grand Scale

"We are likely to see the reform, disruption or dissolution of economic and political systems [and] revolution."

In 1988, who could have predicted how that prophecy would be fulfilled?

There has been a remarkable amount of political and economic turmoil in the last two years. These are the highlights:

On August 17, 1989, Solidarity gained enough support to lead a governing coalition in Poland.

On October 18, 1989, Hungary adopted constitutional changes to form a democratic government.

On November 9, 1989, East Germany opened the Berlin Wall and granted East Germans free travel to the West.

On November 24, 1989, the entire ruling Politburo of Czechoslovakia resigned and by December 29 former dissident Václav Havel was elected president.

On December 15, 1989, a bloody revolution began in Romania. President Nicolae Ceausescu was overthrown on December 22 and executed on December 25.

On December 20, 1989, the United States military ousted Panamanian dictator Manuel Noriega from power and on January 3, 1990, brought him to Miami to face drug charges.

On February 11, 1990, South Africa released Nelson Mandela, a leader of the African National Congress, from prison.

On March 11, 1990, Lithuania declared its independence from the Soviet Union. Shortly thereafter, its sister republics, Latvia and Estonia, declared their transition to independence. Around the same time, the Soviet Union was racked by political and military upheaval, especially in Armenia and Azerbaijan.

On July 1, 1990, East and West Germany officially merged their economies after eight months of dismantling portions of the Berlin Wall and eliminating border checkpoints. Combined elections are scheduled for December 2, 1990, and reunification is expected to be complete sometime in December.

The upheaval in Eastern Europe is related to a number of astrological configurations that I will discuss in future chapters.

War or Mortal Challenges Other Than War

On February 13, 1988, I talked about the transit of Pluto in close conjunction to the Soviet Union's natal Sun at 14° Scorpio and in opposition to the U.S. natal Sun at 10° Taurus. I said:

"Pluto transits of this sort are associated with the outbreak of wars and with mortal challenges other than war. As a result, even if the nations do not go to war, they will face severe challenges. These could include financial problems, nuclear power accidents, power struggles, civil unrest, terrorism and a challenge to both governments' grip on power."

We have seen that the United States has experienced serious financial problems. Thus far these have not presented a mortal challenge to the current administration or to our form of government. But we have not yet felt the full weight of our economic burdens.

Civil unrest and political upheaval have, however, constituted a mortal challenge for the Soviet Union. Were it not for the use of military force and the threat of greater military force, their government would probably have fragmented by now and the top Soviet leaders been deposed.

Intelligence analyst Stephen Cole writes:

> British television reports said that the Soviet Union was poised on the brink of civil war last 25 February, when the Red Army forced a showdown with Gorbachev. There was a huge pro-democracy demonstration in Moscow, while the Army deployed 6,000 troops. No violence resulted, but the Army reportedly forced some policy changes on Gorbachev. The Red Army reportedly believes that the country has become ungovernable due to economic disruptions caused by recent reforms. The British reports could not be confirmed, and Soviet spokesmen denied that the incident ever occurred.[23]

We don't know if this showdown really took place but, given the political climate and the astrological influences of the time, the report is plausible.

Some observers are concerned that the Soviet Union will become violent in the wake of the changes in Eastern Europe. On April 25, 1990, former national security advisor Zbigniew Brzezinski appeared on "Nightline" and said, "My prognosis for the Soviet Union is a pessimistic one."

He said that the Soviet Union has only three possible futures:

1. A belated attempt to reimpose a Soviet Empire, possibly with a veneer of Communist internationalism.

2. Fragmentation. The Soviet Union would simply dissolve and cease to exist as the republics secede.

3. A Romanian-type anti-Communist revolution resulting in the overthrow of the government.

Brzezinski sees a violent outcome in all three cases. And in all three cases, the question is: Who will control the Soviet military and especially their nuclear arsenal?

French president François Mitterand recently warned that if Gorbachev's reforms fail, "the rise of nationalism threatening the implosion of the Soviet Union will set off a cycle of confrontation and violence which will have grave international repercussions."[24]

Update on Canada

Following is a brief update on my April 16, 1988 lecture on Canada's astrology given in Toronto and published as Part VI of this book.

In that lecture I said that if Canada did not express the highest aspects of her natal chart by November 13, 1989 (when transiting Jupiter in Cancer conjoined Canada's Sun and Uranus and opposed transiting Saturn and Neptune in Capricorn), "there could be a social, economic and political cataclysm of considerable duration. At the very least, the government in power could be threatened. More likely, the Canadian form of government could be drastically and unpredictably altered for the worse."

On June 23, 1990, the Meech Lake accord expired without receiving the necessary ratification from the ten provincial governments. This agreement was an effort to head off a move for independence by Quebec. It would have granted certain powers to Quebec that would increase her influence over her own internal affairs. Most importantly, it would have given the Province of Quebec status as a "distinct society" within Canada. Having lost this opportunity for "distinct society" status, Quebec might now opt for independence and therefore cause the breakup of Canada.

In just two years, we have seen the partial or complete fulfillment of many of the predictions I made for the period between 1988 and 2000.

The events that are yet hanging in the balance, as heaven waits to see if the people of earth will take up the challenge to alter or mitigate them, are an economic depression in the United States, a war between the superpowers, and major cataclysm.

CHAPTER 7

The Astrology of World Karma

This chapter is an excerpt from an address I gave on February 13, 1988, at the Sheraton-Palace Hotel in San Francisco. It has been edited for print.

Today we are about to enter an era that is unprecedented in this century and perhaps in all of recorded history—both in its opportunity for spiritual and scientific progress and in its potential for destruction.

All destruction is self-destruction. This we must remember. Nothing can destroy us from without unless we are first self-destroyed from within. Abraham Lincoln said, "If destruction be our lot, we must ourselves be its author and finisher. As a nation of freemen, we must live through all time, or die by suicide."[1]

Make no mistake about it, we do have the power to destroy ourselves from within. For we have been co-creators with Life for aeons. But as I have said, what man has done, man can undo. Therefore we must learn to exercise the power of the spoken Word to deliver ourselves from our self-destructive creations of the past.

Ours is to decide what of our human creation is constructive, leading to world and individual acceleration, hence Good. This we must preserve. Ours is also to decide what of our human creation is destructive, leading to world and individual deceleration, hence Evil. This we must not preserve.

In order to "destroy" our miscreations, or "transmute" them, as the Ascended Masters say, we must first call upon the law of forgiveness for having miscreated, i.e., for having misused God's Power, Wisdom and Love given to us to create after the heavenly patterns. Then we must invoke the violet flame to transmute our miscreations, even as we must go about replacing them with renewed soul creations patterned after the divine.

We are gathered on the shores of the Motherland* this evening to consider these truths and to apply them directly to the portents of coming events. We as a planetary evolution have sown the wind of our collective misqualified energies and we are about to reap the whirlwind.[2]

Our karma for these miscreations, held in abeyance for centuries, is returning to our doorstep daily at a stepped-up rate because we are living at the end of the age of Pisces on a world in transition. But if we decide to apply the alchemy of the violet flame by calling it forth from the Holy Spirit and

---

*The California coast was part of the "Motherland," a term used to refer to Lemuria, or Mu, the lost continent that once existed in the Pacific Ocean. According to the findings of archaeologist James Churchward, Lemuria was made up of three land masses stretching more than 5,000 miles from east to west and was destroyed by earth changes approximately 12,000 years ago.

directing it into the karma of a planet and a people, we just might set the earth on a course of victory!

Therefore this evening we shall read the destiny of our untransmuted karma written in the skies, that on the morrow we may write the destiny of our *transmuted* karma and seal it in the sacred fire of God.

The astrological configurations of the next 12 years tell us that we will face an ascending series of karmic challenges, including the possibilities of of war, revolution, economic upheaval and major earth changes.

The primary indicator of these events is a conjunction of Mars, Saturn, Uranus and Neptune in Capricorn that is about to take place. This is a momentous event. Saturn, Uranus and Neptune have conjoined only twice in the last 2,200 years. Their conjunctions inaugurate cycles of major political, economic, social, cultural and geophysical changes on Earth. When Mars joins the configuration, the effects of the other three planets are likely to be more intensely expressed.

Saturn and Uranus Enter Capricorn

Today, at exactly 3:53 p.m.,* Saturn entered the sign of Capricorn. It will remain there until February 6, 1991, except between June 9 and November 12, 1988, when it will retrograde into Sagittarius. Uranus will also enter Capricorn on February 14, 1988, at 4:31 p.m. It will remain there until January 11, 1996, with a brief period of retrogradation into Sagittarius

*All times in this chapter are given in pacific standard time unless otherwise noted.

between May 26 and December 2, 1988.[3]

Saturn, Uranus, Neptune and Pluto are the four slow-moving outer planets. When these planets shift from sign to sign, they indicate important changes in society. The type of change depends on the character of the sign.

As an earth sign ruled by the planet Saturn, Capricorn governs political, governmental, economic and social power in their positive and negative manifestations. Capricorn tends to limit or bring to an end unrealistic behavior.

Saturn, the ruler of Capricorn, is not a "bad" or "unlucky" planet, even though it is traditionally known as a "malefic" and is often associated with unfortunate circumstances. Saturn is a teacher and a tester. Its influence, particularly when in Capricorn, is supportive when a person or group has acted wisely, practically and responsibly. It is then associated with wealth, honors, freedom of action, respect, justly gained or administered power, good government and an orderly society.

But when a person or group has acted unwisely, Saturn forces them to suffer the consequences of their actions. Thus Saturn is also associated with hard times, difficult challenges, recessions and depressions, delays, misfortune, debt, loss of honor or respect, periods of little or no opportunity, limitation or loss of freedom as a result of increased governmental authority, and dictatorships and repressive regimes. Under its influence people are often pessimistic, gloomy, depressed and despondent. They become victims of their own sense of limitation.

Saturn's movement into Capricorn could do much to depress the world economy and place severe stress on the government of the United States and a number of other nations.

Enter Neptune

On February 22, 1988, Neptune will be at 9°33' Capricorn, forming a wide-orbed conjunction with Saturn and Uranus. When Neptune transits (travels) through earth signs—that is, Virgo, Capricorn or Taurus—it tends to trigger downturns in the economy. This is partly because the illusions and illusory behavior associated with Neptune become grounded in the earth signs.

Two preliminary but significant events tell us what we may expect from the rest of Neptune's transit of Capricorn, which concludes January 28, 1998—the fall of oil prices and the decline of the dollar. Neptune rules a number of commodities, most notably oil.

After Neptune's transit from Sagittarius into Capricorn in 1984,* oil prices fell. This is because Sagittarius is a fire sign that tends to be optimistic and expansive, while Capricorn is an earth sign that tends to be pessimistic and deflationary.

The drop in prices surprised many experts who believed that oil prices could only continue

*Neptune entered Capricorn in two phases. It first entered Capricorn on January 18, 1984, but retrograded back into Sagittarius on June 22, 1984, and stayed there until November 21, 1984, when it entered Capricorn the second time. It will remain in Capricorn until January 28, 1998.

to rise. They were victims of their own illusory thinking about oil, which was stimulated by Neptune in Sagittarius. Shortly after Neptune entered Capricorn the dollar also began to decline.

[Note: Oil prices rose sharply following Iraq's invasion of Kuwait on August 2, 1990. The price rise resulted from the sudden loss of 4 million barrels of oil per day that had been produced by Iraq and Kuwait and the fear of greater losses from war. But this is no guarantee that prices will remain high. Saudi Arabia, the United Arab Emirates and oil producers not located in the Middle East, such as Venezuela, have the capacity to replace most of the 4 million barrels per day that were formerly supplied by Iraq and Kuwait. And there are readily available substitutes for oil, such as natural gas. In addition, world demand for oil may drop because the international economy is entering a recession. Thus, if the nations of the free world play it right and the seven sisters do not artificially manipulate the price of oil, it is reasonable to expect that the real price of oil, adjusted for inflation, will be lowered by market forces.]

Although Neptune's entry into Capricorn in 1984 began to depress the dollar and oil prices, the world economy did not begin to rapidly implode because Uranus was still in Sagittarius. Saturn entered Sagittarius on November 16, 1985, giving the international financial system another shot of optimism.

Huge quantities of debt, however, made possible in large part by the Federal Reserve Board's double digit expansion of the U.S. money supply, burdened both the U.S. economy and the international financial system. But the markets ignored the debt overhang and economies continued to expand.

Confidence in the health of the economy began to wane in the fall of 1987, as Saturn and Uranus neared the end of their transit in Sagittarius. Other astrological factors (which I will explain later) entered the picture, exposing the weaknesses of the U.S. and world financial systems and triggering the great stock-market crash of October 19.

Mars, the Trigger Horse

Mars is the fourth horseman of the famous four that ride neck and neck in Capricorn.[4] On February 22, 1988, Mars will enter Capricorn and make an exact conjunction with Uranus at 0°18' Capricorn and a wide-orbed conjunction with Neptune at 9°33' Capricorn.* On February 23, it will make an exact conjunction with Saturn at 0°45' Capricorn. This, then, is the four-planet conjunction in Capricorn (fig. 1).

These four riders—Mars, Saturn, Uranus and Neptune—as harbingers[†] of our karma and our karmic destiny, have contradictory influences that make it difficult for us as individuals to deal with them, and even more difficult for entire nations of peoples to deal with them.

---

*Although conjunctions and other aspects are generally most powerful when exact, they do not need to be exact to be operative. The arc of space, expressed in degrees, in which an aspect is operative is called the orb of influence, or "orb." There is a good deal of controversy over how many degrees astrologers should allow for an orb. A number of astrologers agree that a major aspect is effective up to 8° from the point at which it is exact, and in mundane charts perhaps as much as 10°.

†*harbinger:* a person or thing that comes before to announce or give an indication ot what follows; often applies to something that arrives as the omen or symbol of something to follow.

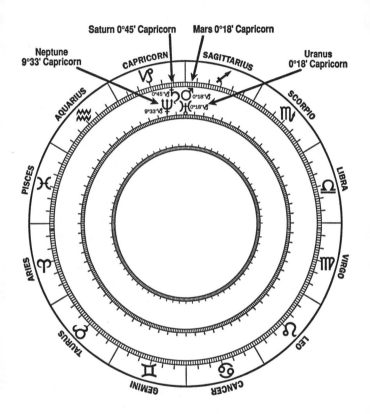

FIGURE 1 On February 22 and 23, 1988, Mars, Saturn, Uranus and Neptune formed a conjunction that marked the beginning of a period of upheaval and change on the planet. Mars was transiting between 0°18′ and 0°45′ Capricorn, Saturn was at 0°45′ Capricorn, Uranus was at 0°18′ Capricorn and Neptune was at 9°33′ Capricorn. Saturn-Uranus-Neptune conjunctions are extremely rare. The last one occurred in 1307 and was the primary astrological impulse for the Black Death, or bubonic plague, which devastated Europe and Asia in the fourteenth century.

Saturn rules institutions, the state, lands, legal systems, tradition and authority. It tends to limit freedom. It gives you freedom only by your own self-discipline and the path of your soul's initiation under the Great White Brotherhood.

Remember, Saturn is our tester. You might see it as the instrument of Lord Maitreya, who is known as the Great Initiator, testing you; or you might see it as Antichrist, depending upon your perspective. It doesn't really matter, because Saturn will get you coming or going. Under its influence you will be tested by forces of Light and forces of Darkness *and* by your own returning karma, positive and negative.

You earn your freedom under Saturn by self-mastery and you hold on to it by self-mastery. Without that discipline, you don't make it either way with Saturn.

Uranus, on the other hand, governs progress, revolution, economic and political change, scientific and social innovation, aspects of warfare, civil unrest, strikes, the breakdown of authority and the wise (or unwise) use of nuclear energy. It gives the impulse for freedom.

Neptune rules enlightenment, spiritual inspiration and intuition, drugs, subversion, disillusionment, treachery and scandal. It gives the impulse for illumination.

Mars, although it is part of the conjunction for only a matter of days, gives the entire configuration a warlike character and acts as a trigger to release or activate its energies.

The Four Planetary Horsemen in Capricorn
Mark a Period of Upheaval and Change

This conjunction of Mars, Saturn, Uranus and Neptune in Capricorn marks the formal starting point of a period of upheaval and change on the planet.

The era of financial expansion related to oil and international finance will come to a halt and, with the exception of one last brief expansionary period when Saturn and Uranus will retrograde into Sagittarius between May and December of 1988, national economies will contract.

This is a time when nations will become conservative and reactionary, there will be massive debt liquidation, the real price of commodities will fall, a crash in the real-estate market is likely, a pessimistic mood will sweep the earth, the potential for war is extremely high and the U.S. government will be in danger of being destroyed or reformed beyond recognition.

In short, this Capricorn conjunction and other astrological phenomena I will soon discuss show that the period between late February 1988 and the year 2000 will be a time of karmic summing up. Not one of us is exempt from that karmic summing up. For the Four and Twenty Elders[5] have said, "The time has come for the people of earth to balance their personal as well as their planetary accounts."

During this period we are likely to see the reform, disruption or dissolution of economic and political systems, revolution, major cataclysm and war. Moreover, if the psyche of the nation does not collectively integrate with the Inner Self, we will see a national schizophrenia, a schism so wide as to be irreparable absent total conversion of the soul by the Holy Spirit to the Universal Christ.

CHAPTER 8

The Portents of
Saturn-Uranus Conjunctions

In 1988, Saturn and Uranus formed an exact conjunction in Sagittarius and a nearly exact conjunction in Capricorn.* These were powerful
conjunctions in their own right, even without considering the larger impact of the Mars-Saturn-
Uranus-Neptune conjunction.

Saturn-Uranus conjunctions, which occur
about every 45 years, have coincided with momentous events throughout history. Astrologer Richard
Nolle compiled an excellent summary of the conjunctions of Saturn and Uranus from 600 B.C. to the
present. He found that they have marked important
turning points in three areas: (1) economic change,
especially periods of inflation or deflation, (2) global
or regional military conflict, primarily along East-
West lines, (3) religious persecution and changes
in the status of religious institutions.[1]

---

*Since planets periodically go retrograde, exact conjunctions often occur in sets of
three within a few degrees of each other. For clarity, these "sets" are often referred
to as a single conjunction. When I discuss the exact Saturn-Uranus conjunction
of 1988, I am referring to three conjunctions: (1) February 12, 1988, at 29°55′
Sagittarius, (2) June 26, 1988, at 28°47′ Sagittarius, (3) October 18, 1988, at
27°49′ Sagittarius. Nearly exact conjunctions do not necessarily occur in sets of
three. The nearly exact Saturn-Uranus conjunctions of 1988 occurred on February 14 at 0°5′ and 0°0′ Capricorn and on December 2 at 2°10′ and 0°0′ Capricorn.

The Saturn-Uranus conjunction of 598 B.C. at 14° Aquarius, for example, coincided with the first stage of the Babylonian captivity—the Babylonian invasion of Judah, capture of Jerusalem and exile of the king and key officials.

The Saturn-Uranus conjunction of 326 B.C. at 2° Taurus coincided with the military zenith of the Greco-Macedonian empire, represented by Alexander the Great's invasion of India. But that victory marked the end and not the beginning of further greatness. In fact, as Nolle points out, it was "the last gasp for ancient Greece: within four years the classic period in Greece was at an end."[2]

The next Saturn-Uranus conjunction, which occurred in Sagittarius, took place in 281 B.C. and coincided with the collapse of the Greek economy.[3]

Saturn-Uranus conjunctions have long been associated with wars. The pattern holds in modern times. The Saturn-Uranus conjunction of 1897 in Scorpio coincided with the Spanish-American War (1898), the Boer War in South Africa (1899–1902), and the Boxer Uprising in China (1898–1900). The Saturn-Uranus conjunction of 1942 in Taurus coincided with World War II (1939–45).

Not all Saturn-Uranus conjunctions have the same influence or strength. Much depends on the sign in which they occur. We can get an idea of what to expect from a Saturn-Uranus conjunction in Sagittarius by reviewing what took place during past conjunctions in this sign.

There have been four Saturn-Uranus conjunctions in Sagittarius since 600 B.C. The first, as noted, marked the collapse of the Greek economy. The second took place between A.D. 309 and 311 and coincided with a period of bitter persecution of Christians by Diocletian and the joint Roman emperors Constantius and Galerius. This finally ended with Galerius' edict of toleration that legalized the practice of Christianity within the Roman Empire. The third Saturn-Uranus conjunction in Sagittarius occurred between 1397 and 1399, close to the beginning of the Renaissance.

The fourth Saturn-Uranus conjunction in Sagittarius took place in 1988. Based on past history, this conjunction could be expected to coincide with any of the following: war, economic collapse, religious persecution and/or toleration, and the renewal of culture and learning.

The exact Saturn-Uranus conjunction in Sagittarius has a good deal of power. But the nearly exact Saturn-Uranus conjunction in Capricorn is even more powerful. This is because the influences of Saturn and Uranus conjoined in the abstract sign of Sagittarius are carried over and more easily and powerfully expressed in the concrete sign of Capricorn.

Saturn is naturally powerful in its sign of rulership, Capricorn, where it can easily express its characteristics, including the capacity to crystallize or precipitate planetary energies (both good and bad karma) in the Capricornian environment. Moreover, the influences signified by the exact Saturn-Uranus conjunction in Sagittarius—war, economic collapse, et cetera—tend to be more concrete and physically expressed as these planets move into Capricorn.

The energies of the Saturn-Uranus conjunction can be easily transferred from Sagittarius to Capricorn because the three exact conjunctions in Sagittarius (referred to as a single conjunction) took place within three degrees of the Capricorn cusp, giving the aspect a Capricorn character to start with. In fact, the first of the series took place at 29°55′ Sagittarius, just five minutes from the Capricorn cusp. In other words, the Sagittarius conjunction is really more of a Sagittarius-Capricorn conjunction and already carries part of the Capricorn vibration.

Saturn and Uranus Conjoin the Galactic Center

There is another element to consider. The three exact Saturn-Uranus conjunctions of 1988, which took place between 27° and 29° Sagittarius, conjoined a point in space known as the Galactic Center at 26° Sagittarius.

Simply speaking, the Galactic Center is the center of gravity of our galaxy. Just as the Earth orbits our Sun every 365 days, so our Sun orbits the Galactic Center about every 250 million earth years.

Astronomers are not certain what the Galactic Center really is. Some think it may be a black hole. One thing is certain: the Galactic Center emits astronomical quantities of energy.

The astrological influence of the Galactic Center is not completely understood. Although astrologers are in the early stages of researching its importance, some influences have already been observed.[4] Theodor Landscheidt, for example, accurately predicted a period of economic recession and uncertainty in 1982 based on a conjunction of Neptune with the Galactic Center.[5]

In gauging the influence of the Saturn-Uranus conjunction with the Galactic Center, we can look at the one previous Saturn-Uranus conjunction with the Galactic Center since 600 B.C. This Saturn-Uranus conjunction took place over a two-year period between A.D. 400 and 402 and was exact at 16°21' Capricorn on February 1, 401. The position of the Galactic Center, which precesses backwards at the rate of about 1° every 72 years, was then about 18° Capricorn.

What did this rare conjunction coincide with? The demise of the mightiest political and social entity the world had known to that time—the Roman Empire. Upon the death of Theodosius I in 395, the Roman Empire permanently split into eastern and western divisions. The Eastern Empire was called the Byzantine Empire. Alaric, leader of the Visigoths, invaded the Western Empire in 401 (just as Saturn and Uranus were making their conjunction in alignment with the Galactic Center) and sacked Rome in 410.

Will history repeat itself today? This correlation of astrological and historical events should at least give us pause and compel us to consider whether we will allow the potential influence of the configurations we have been discussing to cause cataclysmic changes in our time—changes on the same scale as the fall of the Roman Empire.

George Santayana said, "Those who cannot remember the past are condemned to repeat it."[6] Knowing what we know about the past, we can hypothesize by the geometric coordinates of the heavens that there is the possibility of a major international conflict in the next few years.

If we are to deal successfully with this and other upcoming challenges, we must learn from our astrological history: the configurations of the planets, the events that coincided with them, and the consequences of the choices made by players on the historical stage.

Our decade mandates that we also learn from the karmic portents of that astrology, which were evident in the social, economic and political signs of the times and circumscribed the choices of those involved.

Will we forever ignore the warnings of our sages and our prophets or of the little child who in holy innocence would lead us when we choose to ignore the prompting of the Inner Self?

Paraphrasing Santayana I would say, "Those who cannot remember their astrological past, signifying their karmic past, are indeed self-condemned to repeat it."

CHAPTER 9

The Portents of Saturn-Uranus-Neptune Conjunctions

Saturn-Uranus-Neptune conjunctions are extremely rare. The last time these three planets were conjoined was in 1307. The last time before that was in 234 B.C. In other words, Saturn-Uranus-Neptune conjunctions come around about every 700 to 1500 years.

The impact of these conjunctions cannot be overstated. Saturn-Uranus conjunctions alone can trigger wars and are related to the onset of depressions. Saturn-Neptune conjunctions alone can trigger earth-shaking events. Between 1988 and 1993, we will see multiple conjunctions of these three planets: Saturn and Uranus, Saturn and Neptune, and Uranus and Neptune.* But as I said in chapter 7, in February 1988 all three planets were grouped together.

While the short-term effects of multiple-planet alignments may appear within a few years, the

*The Saturn-Uranus conjunctions occurred on February 12, 1988, at 29°55′ Sagittarius; on June 26, 1988, at 28°47′ Sagittarius; and on October 18, 1988, at 27°49′ Sagittarius. The Saturn-Neptune conjunctions occurred on March 3, 1989, at 11°55′ Capricorn; on June 23, 1989, at 11°15′ Capricorn; and on November 13, 1989, at 10°22′ Capricorn. The Uranus-Neptune conjunctions will occur on February 2, 1993, at 19°34′ Capricorn; on August 19, 1993, at 18°49′ Capricorn; and on October 24, 1993, at 18°33′ Capricorn.

long-term effects may take decades or centuries to become apparent. Later astrological events, such as an eclipse or a major conjunction aspecting the original conjunction, may bring into manifestation the potential long-term influences of the original conjunction.

The Calamitous Fourteenth Century

The Saturn-Uranus-Neptune conjunction of 1307 inaugurated a century of woe. It was characterized by unenlightened leadership, exorbitant taxation, the breakdown of social institutions, immorality, religious ferment and persecution (including the slaughter of Jews), destruction of farms and villages by bands of marauding mercenaries, peasant uprisings and anarchy.

What is known as the Little Ice Age, a period of extreme cold, began about 1307 and lasted until about 1700. Famine devastated Europe in 1315–16 as a shorter growing season and incessant rains caused crops to fail. People were reduced to eating dead bodies, reportedly even their own children. Corruption in the Church reached new levels as Pope Clement V removed the papacy from Rome to Avignon, France, in 1309. The Hundred Years War between France and England broke out in 1337 and the expansion of the Ottoman Empire into Europe began in 1345.

The worst tragedy of the century was the Black Death (bubonic plague), which from 1347 to 1351 wiped out as much as half the population of England

and at least one-third of the population of Europe. It recurred throughout the century in both Europe and Asia. The conjunction of Saturn, Uranus and Neptune was the primary astrological impulse for the plague.

Later astrological events brought into manifestation the influences of the Saturn-Uranus-Neptune conjunction. The Medical Faculty of Paris ascribed the plague to a conjunction of Mars, Jupiter and Saturn in Aquarius on March 20, 1345. Astrologer Dylan Warren-Davis says that that conjunction certainly showed the potential for an epidemic.[1] But it could not have been the sole or even the primary astrological cause of the Black Death, which was the worst disaster in history. It simply wasn't powerful enough.

The Mars-Jupiter-Saturn conjunction of 1345 formed a square to and activated the Saturn-Uranus-Neptune conjunction of 1307. The Medical Faculty of Paris could not have known about the earlier Saturn-Uranus-Neptune conjunction, of course, since Uranus and Neptune had not yet been discovered.

There may have been other astrological factors related to the virulent spread of the Black Death that the Medical Faculty of Paris was unaware of. Astrologer Diana Rosenberg points out that the Jupiter-Saturn conjunction of 1345 occurred at the time of the "Great Mutation,"[2] i.e., the point in the cycle of conjunctions between Jupiter and Saturn when they move from a series of conjunctions in astrological signs of one element (fire, air, water or earth) to a series of conjunctions in signs of another element. The ancients paid careful attention to the "Great Mutation" in their mundane predictions and considered it to be particularly powerful.

The fourteenth century was a remarkable but tragic period, a time of troubles with historical and astrological parallels to our own. In *A Distant Mirror: The Calamitous 14th Century,* Barbara W. Tuchman suggests that we have much to learn about the present by studying the events of the fourteenth century. In effect, we can put our time in perspective by viewing it in the "distant mirror" of the fourteenth century.

Tuchman writes in her foreword:

> The genesis of this book was a desire to find out what were the effects on society of the most lethal disaster of recorded history— that is to say, of the Black Death of 1348–50, which killed an estimated one third of the population living between India and Iceland. Given the possibilities of our own time, the reason for my interest is obvious. The answer proved elusive because the fourteenth century suffered so many "strange and great perils and adversities" (in the words of a contemporary) that its disorders cannot be traced to any one cause; they were the hoofprints of more than the four horsemen of St. John's vision, which had now become seven—plague, war, taxes,

brigandage, bad government, insurrection, and schism in the Church....

Although my initial question has escaped an answer, the interest of the period itself—a violent, tormented, bewildered, suffering and disintegrating age, a time, as many thought, of Satan triumphant—was compelling and, as it seemed to me, consoling in a period of similar disarray. If our last decade or two of collapsing assumptions has been a period of unusual discomfort, it is reassuring to know that the human species has lived through worse before. [3]

Now, for the first time since the fourteenth century, we face the challenge of a Saturn-Uranus-Neptune conjunction. As we embark on a perilous journey into the future, let us remember that the fourteenth century was more than a time of misery. The disastrous events that took place ultimately changed economic, political and sociological patterns.

As astrologer Richard Nolle points out, the Saturn-Uranus-Neptune conjunction caused a revolution in military technology that brought the feudal period to a close, hastened the rise of the monarchies and catalyzed the power struggles that resulted in the exile of the papacy to France. [4] The widespread mortality caused by the Black Death started an economic revolution by consolidating wealth in fewer hands.

By acting in time and space we can anticipate events just as momentous in our time and, as Roger Bacon prophesied, we can forestall the tellings and foretellings of the Four Horsemen that ride across the celestial window before our gaze.

AIDS and Astrology

The Black Death, or bubonic plague, is a bacterial disease that has been largely under control since the development of antibiotics such as tetracycline. In our time the condition that thus far best meets the criteria of a plague is the acquired immunodeficiency syndrome, or AIDS.

According to the currently accepted theory, AIDS is caused by a virus that attacks an important part of the immune system—the white blood cells known variously as T-4 leukocytes, T-helper cells, or simply T-cells, which are essential for the neutralization of viruses and certain foreign bacteria. With a decline in the number of T-cells, the body is not able to fight off otherwise controllable infections. Thus, the AIDS patient gets one or more opportunistic infections that would normally be suppressed by his immune system. These infections, rather than the AIDS virus itself, ultimately kill the AIDS victim.

Like the Saturn-Uranus-Neptune conjunction in Scorpio of 1307, the Saturn-Uranus-Neptune conjunction in Capricorn of 1988 is related to the rise of diseases of the immune system and epidemics. Both the planet Saturn and the sign it rules, Capricorn, have partial rulership of the immune system. Negative Saturn-Capricorn energies can have a depressing effect; hence they may be associated with a depressed immune response.

Uranus rules new conditions, circumstances or technologies as well as diseases of the blood and circulatory system—all characteristics of AIDS, particularly if one looks at AIDS as a blood-borne disease. Neptune can have a degenerative effect on the immune system and is also associated with hard-to-define problems and elusive causes, both of which are unquestionably related to AIDS.

The combined effects of Saturn, Uranus and Neptune conjoined in Capricorn suggest that a modern plague would be characterized by a degenerative condition related to a weakened or debilitated immune system with hard-to-define, novel causes. AIDS is precisely that, a previously unknown degenerative condition in which a depressed immune system leaves the body vulnerable to opportunistic infections.

There are several other astrological influences related to AIDS and other kinds of epidemics that act synergistically with the influences of the Saturn-Uranus-Neptune conjunction in Capricorn. For instance, Pluto in Scorpio is related to plagues. Pluto has been transiting in Scorpio since November 5, 1983, and will remain there until January 17, 1995.

The areas of life that Pluto and Scorpio rule are especially related to AIDS. Scorpio rules or is related to sex, sexuality, medicine, the healing arts, the drug industry, joint financial affairs and matters of life and death. Pluto rules or is associated with decay, death and regeneration, investigation, power and its misuses, secret and underhanded dealings, destruction, the threat of annihilation and annihilation itself. In combination with Neptune in Capricorn, Pluto in Scorpio indicates the strong possibility of deception or intrigue with long-term consequences.[5]

During the Capricorn megaconjunction of January 11, 1994 (see chapter 18), Saturn in Aquarius will square Pluto in Scorpio. Among other things, this could precipitate widespread plagues and famines, the plagues being an expansion of the existing AIDS epidemic, something new, or both.

On January 28, 1998, Neptune will enter Aquarius. As astrologer John Townley says, "Neptune in Aquarius. . . is quite consistently associated with the great plagues, extending all the way back into Roman times."[6] Again, it is not clear whether this might relate to an expansion of the AIDS epidemic, something new, or both.

CHAPTER 10

The Spirit of the Prophets
Then and Now

I said in chapters 6 and 7 that we are entering a period of karmic summing up. In the decade of the 1990s we are likely to see the reform, disruption or dissolution of economic and political systems, revolution, major cataclysm and war.

As you ponder these prophecies, remember that prophecy is sent by God so that those who have ears to hear *will hear* and *will act* in time. They must act to save their souls through supplications to God and they must act to mitigate that prophecy, or turn it back entirely, through prayers to the Holy Spirit for the conversion of mankind to the Lord.

As we have already seen in the Book of Jonah, when the prophets of Israel and Judah warned the people of the judgments of the LORD (the I AM THAT I AM), they would say, "If you do not repent of your indulgences, your going after pleasure and selfish pursuits and the murdering of your firstborn, if you do not take care of the poor, the LORD will deliver these calamities upon you."

In the words of the prophet Ezekiel:

> I will judge you, O house of Israel, every one according to his ways, saith the Lord GOD. Repent, and turn yourselves from all your transgressions; so iniquity shall not be your ruin.
>
> Cast away from you all your transgressions, whereby ye have transgressed; and make you a new heart and a new spirit: for why will ye die, O house of Israel?
>
> For I have no pleasure in the death of him that dieth, saith the Lord GOD: wherefore turn yourselves, and live ye.[1]

The prophet Isaiah delivered this message of the LORD to the people of Judah:

> Wash you, make you clean; put away the evil of your doings from before mine eyes; cease to do evil;
>
> Learn to do well; seek judgment, relieve the oppressed, judge the fatherless, plead for the widow.
>
> Come now, and let us reason together, saith the LORD: though your sins be as scarlet, they shall be as white as snow; though they be red like crimson, they shall be as wool.
>
> If ye be willing and obedient, ye shall eat the good of the land:
>
> But if ye refuse and rebel, ye shall be devoured with the sword: for the mouth of the LORD hath spoken it.[2]

Karma and Prophecy

The LORD explained to the inhabitants of Jerusalem through the prophet Jeremiah that the outcome of his prophecies was dependent on their response:

On occasion, I decree for some nation, for some kingdom, that I will tear up, knock down, destroy; but if this nation, against which I have pronounced sentence, abandons its wickedness, I then change my mind about the evil which I had intended to inflict on it.

On another occasion, I decree for some nation, for some kingdom, that I will build up and plant; but if that nation does what displeases me, refusing to listen to my voice, I then change my mind about the good which I had intended to confer on it.

So now, say this to the men of Judah and the citizens of Jerusalem, "The LORD[3] says this: Listen, I have been preparing a disaster for you, I have been working out a plan against you. So now, each one of you, turn back from your evil ways, amend your conduct and actions."[4] (Jerusalem Bible)

When we read in the Bible that God, having given the people ample warning and opportunity to turn from their errant ways, pronounces his judgment, it means that the time has come for the return of mankind's karma for their disobedience to God. Judgment means the descent of karma after a period of mercy during which the people have not repented of their deeds.

As we study the prophecy of God and how God chastises a holy people, we find that he often allows their karma to descend upon them through pagan nations. Even those who do not worship the LORD become the LORD's instrument for the judgment of his people.

In the case of Israel and Judah, God delivered their karma by allowing them to be invaded by the powerful nations of Assyria and Babylonia. Jeremiah said, "Thus saith the LORD, . . . I will give all Judah into the hand of the king of Babylon, and he shall carry them captive into Babylon, and shall slay them with the sword."[5]

History records that when the children of the Light disregard the commandments and disobey their Father-Mother God, then karma becomes their Teacher and they become vulnerable to "the rulers of the darkness of this world."[6]

Karma brings back to our doorstep exactly what we send out, both good and bad. Negative karma is our unredeemed energy coming for redemption. It is the untransmuted coming for transmutation. It is the unresolved coming for resolution.

Karma teaches us our violations of the laws of physics and metaphysics, of chemistry and spiritual alchemy, and of the balance of forces yang and yin.[7] Any state of mind or being that compromises the equilibrium of the Masculine and Feminine polarity of God within us, any out-of-alignment state begets its own negative karma that sooner or later will require its own resolution. By a like token, all the good we send out returns to us multiplied by the Greater Good and we receive abundant blessings in kind.

The law of karma is God's law. It is inexorable. Therefore we say, "Even so, LORD God Almighty, true and righteous are thy judgments."[8]

I would like to tell you that I deliver the prophecies of Saint Germain as I receive them, looking neither to the Right nor to the Left. I am neither conservative nor liberal, nor do I position myself in the middle of the road.

Some people ask me why I don't confine myself to spiritual topics, why I speak on political issues. Well, I am a prophet and I come in the tradition of the prophets of Israel and Judah, who spoke out in the midst of political and social upheaval as well as spiritual crisis. They rebuked kings, counsellors, priests, family, friends and enemies alike. And they told the people exactly what they had to do to get on the right side of God and his laws.

Popularity was not their concern. Like Jesus, they made themselves of no reputation and took on the form of a servant.[9] But their reputation has followed them to the present. And the voices of these servants of God and of the people still resound in the Holy City.

O Israel, O Judah revisited in this wilderness land, will you not hear, will you not hear!

The Unpopular Prophet

I love the ancient prophets. As a child I turned to them for consolation and wisdom. They stood apart as gurus fierce and uncompromising in their courage. I was in awe of them. They were my heroes.

Today I walk in their shadow, as I would walk in the shadow of the Almighty, a student of their words and their works. God's spokesmen they were as they stood before the mighty men of old, the false prophets and the betrayers of the people—and still stood—until their calling was through.

Jeremiah is one of my favorite prophets. My heart goes out to him, for his message was enormously unpopular. He prophesied death and destruction in a time when people wanted to hear about peace, not war. And he went unheeded for 40 years.

Jeremiah preached in Judah, the Southern Kingdom of the Hebrews, starting in about 627 B.C. In the tenth century B.C., the 12 tribes had split into two kingdoms: Israel in the north and Judah in the south, with two capitals, Samaria and Jerusalem. Israel had fallen to the Assyrians under Sargon II in 721 B.C. and most of her inhabitants had been deported.

Jeremiah's career began during a time of upheaval in the Near East. The once-powerful Assyrian Empire was crumbling and the Babylonian Empire was beginning to rise. Judah was a vassal state of Assyria. When Assyria fell in 612 B.C., Judah gained independence—but only until 609 B.C., when she became an Egyptian vassal.

Jeremiah said that the people of Israel had been taken into exile because of their faithlessness and worship of idols. He preached God's imminent judgment upon Judah for her sinfulness. He warned that if the people did not turn wholeheartedly to their God in time, they would meet the same fate as Israel at the hands of an "evil from the North."[10]

What were the sins of Judah? Idolatry, apostasy (renunciation of one's faith), corruption and moral degeneracy.

The Hebrews had adopted pagan religious practices while Judah was under Assyrian control. They had erected altars to a host of foreign gods, whom they worshiped alongside the LORD. And the fertility cult's sacred prostitution was practiced in the Temple at Jerusalem.

Western civilization is guilty of the sins of Israel and Judah. To this day the children of God haven't stopped going after idols or misqualifying the sacred fire of God's altar.

Who do we worship? We worship the stars, the celebrities, the rich and the powerful, few having any morality, any principles or any God in them. Our idolatry even extends to ourselves, our materialism and our pleasure cult. We worship sex. We have made a god of it. And if we expect to avert the karmic consequences of our actions, we must tear down these idols that we have placed before our God!

The prophet also challenged social injustice: immorality, official corruption, stealing, murder and lying, as well as the oppression of strangers, orphans and widows. Some of the people even partook of the pagan practice of human sacrifice, making "their sons and daughters pass through fire in honor of Molech."[11] (Jerusalem Bible)

Child Sacrifice in the Twentieth Century

Child sacrifice—otherwise known as abortion. Each year in America 30 percent of all women who become pregnant abort their children. Family planning using scientific methods of birth control is one thing, and it's a good thing. But the practice of abortion as a means of birth control is fraught with the most severe karma and the most severe judgment of Almighty God.

What is abortion? It is not only the abortion of a body, it is the abortion of the divine plan of a soul whose body temple is being nurtured in the womb. It is the abortion of an individual calling; for God chooses the special moment in history for each soul to return to earth to take part in the Divine Plan of the decades and the centuries.

I believe abortion to be first-degree murder of God. God as a living potential, Christ as a living potential, is in that child from the moment of conception.

When a father and a mother sacrifice their child to the god of lust, they are killing a part of themselves. Moreover, they are aborting the reason for being of the mother, whose mission it is to walk in the footsteps of the Mother of God, and they are aborting the divine calling of the human father unto the heavenly Father to sire His own on earth.

Abortion is the greatest crime that has ever been committed by a people against their God. The child in the womb, and the soul who is already a part of that body, has consciousness, has awareness of its mother and father, and looks forward to being born and fulfilling its mission in life.

Because I believe in reincarnation and in the continuity of being, because I know that we retain our faculties of cognition and recognition from one lifetime to the next, I am agonizingly aware of what a baby goes through during an abortion. Yes, the "child-man" in the womb is a mature soul, having complex thoughts and deep feelings. Only the body is undeveloped.

The baby's body, the greatest miracle of God's gift of Love to man and woman, is a brand-new house that the soul will enter sometime after conception or as late as at birth. The soul, attached to this fragile form, pleading entrance to life at the portals of birth, is defenseless and at the mercy of its parents and society.

The abortion of a lifestream in the womb is the greatest child abuse on earth. And it is suffered in silent crucifixion. O America, as I live, I know that the child you abort suffers the most horrible death — just as you and I would if we were mugged in Central Park, knifed and cut up in pieces. But because the child's scream is a silent scream, we can silence the voice of our conscience who yet pronounces the sixth commandment, "Thou shalt not kill."

How much more, then, do we silence the Holy Spirit itself that "beareth witness with our spirit, that we [hence our offspring] are the children of God: And if children, then heirs; heirs of God and joint-heirs with Christ."[12] If you accept the reality of a spiritual, as well as a physical, lineage, that we are descendants of the Father and the Son, then you cannot deny life to the Father and the Son in your child.

O women of America, mothers of the universe,[13] if you do not want your children, please, please love them to term, give birth to them in the joy of your Lord, who has made you a co-creator with him, and give them for adoption to those who will love them and provide them with the opportunity to once more live and laugh and play and sing and work together with their comrades on earth to fulfill their reason for being.

As you value your life, won't you and the one whose love you shared in this conception appreciate the awesomeness of the life of the soul aborning within you, this wonder of creation who is now flesh of *your* flesh and bone of *your* bones?

I have been speaking out against abortion since it was legalized in 1973. In an interview I gave at Camelot, our headquarters in Los Angeles, in January 1982 I said:

> Abortion is first-degree murder of God. Human government since Noah has existed to protect human life. The nation or the government that creates legislation allowing

murder is doomed to go down. It will go down by cataclysm; it will go down by economic collapse. But it *will* go down because it is not consistent with the laws of universal Life.

Now, that is a fiat of Almighty God. I didn't originate it but it has the power of the Holy Spirit. It will come to pass. And if America does not refute legalized, tax-supported murder, the judgment will come as surely as it came upon Israel and Judah and every other nation who has murdered its firstborn.[14]

Saint Germain said of that statement:

Out of the mouth of the Messenger I spoke this day, before a television camera, the pronouncement of God's judgment upon any nation that enacts a law authorizing murder through abortion. The nation that allows these laws to rest upon the books, and therefore to govern life itself, is judged. And unless it be overturned, cataclysm [will be, as it] has always been, the judgment upon those who have defended death, through their own selfishness and self-intent, rather than life in the sacrificial sense.[15]

On July 4, 1990, Saint Germain gave this prophecy about abortion in America:

I tell you, beloved, the turning of the decade does bring shortly to a close the remaining opportunity for the people of this nation to stand and hold fast in the defense of Life....

If the spiritual leadership of America does not cry halt to this massacre and this holocaust, then I tell you, you may count the number of July Fourths that will remain to be celebrated. [16]

On that occasion Saint Germain defined the exception as those "very specific cases of the danger to the life of the mother." He stated that "these cases are rare but the law should allow for them" and that "there should not be loopholes that allow for a broad interpretation, making excuses for abortion when there ought not to be abortion." [17]

Twenty-three million abortions, 23 million flames snuffed out in the United States since 1973 — this alone makes America vulnerable to all the prophecies I am speaking about. God help us! God forgive those who know not what they do! And God judge the wicked who do!

Jeremiah Challenges a Nation

Enter Jeremiah. Sent by the LORD to spark a spiritual revolution.

Sometime around 609 B.C., God directed Jeremiah to go to the entry of the Gate of the Potsherds toward the high place of Topheth in the Valley of Ben-hinnom, where the people of Judah practiced child sacrifice, and to speak these words:

Kings of Judah, citizens of Jerusalem! Listen to the word of the LORD! The LORD of Sabaoth, the God of Israel, says this: I am bringing down such a disaster on this place that the ears of every one who hears of it will ring.

This is because they have abandoned me, have profaned this place, have offered incense here to alien gods which neither they, nor their ancestors, nor the kings of Judah, ever knew before. They have filled this place with the blood of the innocent.

They have built high places for Baal to burn their sons there, which I had never ordered or decreed; which had never entered my thoughts.

So now the days are coming—it is the LORD who speaks—when people will no longer call this place Topheth, or the Valley of Ben-hinnom, but Valley of Slaughter.

Because of this place, I mean to drain Judah and Jerusalem of sound advice; I will make them fall by the sword before their enemies, fall by the hand of people determined to kill them; I will give their corpses as food to the birds of heaven and the beasts of earth.

And I will make this city a desolation, a derision; every passer-by will be appalled at it, and whistle in amazement at such calamity.

I will make them eat the flesh of their own sons and daughters: they shall eat each other during the siege, in the shortage to which their enemies, in their determination to kill them, will reduce them. [18]*

*This and remaining Bible quotes in this chapter are taken from the Jerusalem Bible.

Leaving the entry of the Gate of the Potsherds, Jeremiah went straight to the court of the Temple and before all the people pronounced the LORD's judgment:

The LORD of Sabaoth, the God of Israel, says this, "Yes, I am going to bring down every disaster I have threatened on this city and on all its outlying towns, since they have grown so stubborn and refused to listen to my words."[19]

No sooner had Jeremiah spoken than Pashhur, chief of the temple police, had him beaten and put in the stocks. The next day, when Pashhur released Jeremiah, the prophet said to him, "Not Pashhur but Terror is the LORD's name for you. For the LORD says this, 'I am going to hand you over to terror, you and all your friends; they shall fall by the sword of their enemies; your own eyes shall see it.'"[20]

Jeremiah's sermons caused an uproar and for a time he was barred from the Temple in Jerusalem. He was shunned and ridiculed. His friends deserted him and members of his family betrayed him. The people of his hometown threatened to kill him if he did not cease prophesying "in the name of the LORD."[21]

But the unpopular prophet would not relent. He was trying desperately to save the soul of a nation before it was too late.

Not only did Jeremiah rebuke the people for their pagan practices but he also called to task the nation's leaders—the kings, priests and prophets—for not setting a proper example. Of King Jehoiakim of Judah he said, "Doom for the man who founds his palace on anything but integrity, his upstairs rooms on anything but honesty....

"Your father...practiced honesty and integrity....You on the other hand have eyes and heart for nothing but your own interests."[22]

Of the prophets he said, "In the prophets of Jerusalem I have seen horrors: adultery, persistent lying, such abetting of evil men, that no one renounces his evil-doing; to me they are all like Sodom, its inhabitants all like Gomorrah."[23]

Despite Jeremiah's warnings, the people and their leaders continued their pagan practices while worshiping God in the Temple. They believed they would be protected from God's wrath by outer ritual. Jeremiah warned that their superficial performance of ritual was a sham that would never guarantee them God's protection. Sacrifices, he said, were no substitute for ethical conduct and obedience to God.

Standing in the gate of the Temple, Jeremiah declared:

> The LORD of Sabaoth, the God of Israel, says this: Amend your behaviour and your actions and I will stay with you here in this place. Put no trust in delusive words like these: This is the sanctuary of the LORD, the sanctuary of the LORD, the sanctuary of the LORD!...
>
> Yet here you are, trusting in delusive words, to no purpose!
>
> Steal, would you, murder, commit adultery, perjure yourselves, burn incense to Baal,

follow alien gods that you do not know?—

And then come presenting yourselves in this temple that bears my name, saying: Now we are safe—safe to go on committing all these abominations! Do you take this temple that bears my name for a robbers' den? I, at any rate, am not blind—it is the LORD who speaks.[24]

Jeremiah's most troublesome enemies were the false prophets of peace. They played a crucial role in bringing about the wholly unnecessary destruction of Judah.

What did the false prophets say? As Jeremiah lamented to his God:

Ah, Lord GOD, here are the prophets telling them, "You will not see the sword, famine will not touch you; I promise you unbroken peace in this place."[25]

The LORD through Jeremiah denounced their empty words:

For all, least no less than greatest, all are out for dishonest gain; prophet no less than priest, all practice fraud. They dress my people's wound without concern: 'Peace! Peace!' they say, but there is no peace.[26]

In Jeremiah's day the word *peace* meant much more than an absence of war; it also denoted well-being, success, spiritual as well as material prosperity.

Jeremiah was condemning the religious leaders who attempted to heal "the wound" of the people with shallow words and a false optimism. The nation's "wound"—their deep breach with God—could never be healed without going to the root of the problem, without a real change of heart.

The people, who wanted a shortcut to deliverance, refused to repent in the face of the judgment that Jeremiah had prophesied. They would not bend the knee before the law of their own karma and they were too proud to ask for God's mercy to intercede between themselves and that karma.

The "Evil from the North"

Jeremiah did not like prophesying war. But that is exactly what he saw. He said:

> Enemies are coming from a distant country, shouting their war cry against the towns of Judah; they surround Jerusalem like watchmen round a field because she has apostatized from me—it is the LORD who speaks.
>
> Your own behavior and actions have brought this on you. This is your fate! How bitter! How it pierces your heart!
>
> I am in anguish! I writhe in pain! Walls of my heart! My heart is throbbing! I cannot keep quiet, for I have heard the trumpet call and the cry of war. [27]

In 605 B.C. Babylon defeated Egypt and Judah became a Babylonian vassal. Jeremiah's prophecies spoke of Babylon as the instrument of "a great destruction" by which the LORD would punish Judah for her sins:

> Since you have not listened to my words, I will now send for all the clans of the North (it is the LORD who speaks—referring to Nebuchadnezzar king of Babylon, my servant) and bring them down on this land and its inhabitants . . . .
>
> The whole land shall be devastated and reduced to a desert, while they will stay in slavery among the nations for seventy years.[28]

About 599 B.C., King Jehoiakim of Judah made a bid for independence. He went against Jeremiah's advice, which was to submit and avoid destruction. In 598 Nebuchadnezzar sent an army to Jerusalem. Jehoiakim died or was assassinated before the Babylonians arrived. His son Jehoiachin surrendered without a fight.

Nebuchadnezzar stripped the Temple of ornaments, emptied the treasury, carried the king and 3,000 of Jerusalem's leading citizens into exile and placed Zedekiah, Jehoiachin's uncle, on the throne. By the standards of the time, Nebuchadnezzar was lenient with Judah.

But his invasion was not enough; Judah still had not learned her lesson. The people continued to listen to the false prophets of peace.

Rather than admit that Jeremiah had been right all along, the false prophets tried to show that this first phase of the Babylonian captivity was but a temporary setback by which God was testing the people. Promising a glorious future, they enflamed the people to revolt against Babylon, while Jeremiah told them to submit to Babylon as God's instrument of judgment upon them.

The people heard what they wanted to hear. They wanted reassurances of peace. So they listened to the prophets of peace.

As a symbolic gesture, Jeremiah placed a wooden yoke on his neck, saying that the people of Judah should serve the king of Babylon since God had appointed him to rule over them as punishment for their many sins.

Hananiah, a leading prophet and priest, openly challenged Jeremiah. He claimed that within two years the LORD would break the power of Babylon and restore the captives. He illustrated his point by taking the wooden yoke off Jeremiah's neck and breaking it.

Jeremiah rebuked Hananiah: "The LORD says this: You can break wooden yokes? Right, I will make them iron yokes instead! For the LORD of Sabaoth, the God of Israel, says this: An iron yoke is what I now lay on the necks of all these nations to subject them to Nebuchadnezzar king of Babylon."[29]

Jeremiah told Hananiah, "The LORD [I AM THAT I AM] has not sent you; and thanks to you this people are now relying on what is false."[30] Jeremiah prophesied that Hananiah would die that year. He died within two months.

In 589 B.C., King Zedekiah was pressured into joining a rebellion against Babylon. Nebuchadnezzar marched swiftly to Judah, destroyed all the fortified cities, and in 588 laid siege to the Holy City, Jerusalem. During the seige, which lasted for nearly one and a half years, "famine was raging in the city and there was no food for the populace."[31]

In 587, Babylonian soldiers entered the city. They killed Zedekiah's sons before his eyes, blinded him and led him and many of his people into exile. They burned the Temple of Solomon, the pride of Israel for nearly 400 years, and reduced Jerusalem and the walled cities of Judah to ruins.

God Is Prophesying in Your Heart

Today, as in the sixth century B.C., the world has gone after the prophets of peace. I have traveled around the world to deliver the message of Saint Germain; and in some of the places where I have spoken, to my astonishment, people have gotten up and left without even hearing what I had to say.

I am not attached—either to myself or to the message. But I am very attached to Saint Germain and to the saving of souls. I bring you this message because I love you and because I am concerned about you, each one.

You may wonder how I, not knowing you personally, can be sincere in my statement. I assure you that I can be and that I am. I feel a very real heart tie to everyone in whom there burns a desire to serve God. And you who have that sacred fire within your heart and that love of truth and freedom, *I know you, I am a part of you.* I meditate upon your hearts and souls daily. I pray for you and I have done so all of my life.

God is prophesying in your heart and in my heart. You are his instrument and you can hear his voice and listen to his message to you personally, if you will.

Sometimes when prophecies are dire and burdensome, we think that perhaps we have imagined them, that we have not heard the voice of God. We always have acquaintances who will allay our fears and tell us it isn't so. We push everything we do not want to face below the threshold of awareness. And we applaud our leaders who tell us peace is coming.

But I can tell you that peace is not coming until this nation achieves resolution at its very core.

I ask you, then, whether you agree or disagree with what you have read so far, to bear with me to the end. I don't ask you to accept it. I ask you only to consider it. I don't ask you to convert to my belief system but only to understand that I come as your sister on the Path and as your friend to give you this message that God has placed on my heart.

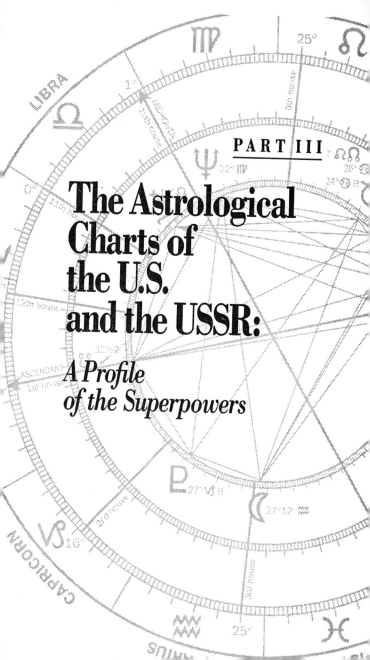

PART III

The Astrological Charts of the U.S. and the USSR:

A Profile of the Superpowers

CHAPTER 11

El Morya Unlocks the Mystery

Since I am going to be talking a good deal about the conjunctions of Mars, Saturn, Uranus and Neptune in Capricorn and other configurations in relation to the charts of the United States and the Soviet Union, I would like to introduce you to these charts.

In order to correctly interpret the astrological portents involving the United States and the Soviet Union, we must have the correct date and time for the birth of these nations. The first problem to be solved is: Which events marked the birth of each nation? The second: What is the precise hour of each event?

There is an ongoing debate among astrologers about the United States birth chart. Most astrologers assume that the United States was born on July 4, 1776, the day the Declaration of Independence was signed.[1] Since 1987 I have explained to my audiences that according to the Ascended Master El Morya, the Fourth of July is not the birth date of the United States but the date of her conception. The nation's birth date, El Morya told me, was the occasion of the inauguration of George Washington as our first president on April 30, 1789.

It is clear from the history of the American Revolution that the United States was not born at the signing of the Declaration, but conceived. It is a matter of record that the states did not intend to form a new nation concurrent with the adoption of the Declaration. The instructions the state legislatures sent to their delegates in Congress leave no doubt that the states intended to retain sovereignty and form a union later.

North Carolina, for example, authorized its delegates to vote for independence providing they reserved "to this colony the sole and exclusive right of forming a constitution and laws for this colony."[2] Virginia, in its instructions to its delegates, supported independence "provided that the power of forming government...be left to the respective colonial legislatures."[3] In fact, a company of militia volunteers from New Jersey initially refused to take an oath to the United States when they reported for duty to George Washington at Valley Forge on the grounds that "our country is New Jersey."[4] Men from other states felt the same.

In short, upon declaring their independence, the 13 states considered themselves to be—and were—separate countries that looked forward to a time when they would be united in a confederation. It was not until the Constitution had been framed and ratified and George Washington was inaugurated as the nation's first president that the United

States had a functioning national government.

Some astrologers even argue that other events that occurred days or years before the signing signified the birth. Helen Boyd and Jim Lewis claim the United States was born July 6, 1775, at 11 a.m., when Congress, sitting in Philadelphia, approved the Declaration of the Causes and Necessity of Taking Up Arms. Julian Armistead contends that the United States was born on July 2, 1776, when Congress adopted a resolution that read in part: "That these United States are, and, of right, ought to be, Free and Independent States..."[5] Both of these dates can be shown to be inaccurate on historical grounds.

Those who do see the signing of the Declaration as the birth of the nation disagree over the time of day it occurred. Official records were not kept for the times of key events in the birth of either the United States or the Soviet Union. The *Journals of the Continental Congress*, for example, do not record the time that resolutions were passed, the time debates began or ended, or even the time Congress commenced or adjourned. Because official records provide limited information, historians and astrologers have had to rely on unofficial records, such as letters and diaries, as well as circumstantial evidence to argue for various times of birth.

The proposed times of birth range from 2:13 a.m. to 5:13:55 p.m. and the proposed Ascendants (or rising signs) for the birth chart (what I call the conceptional chart) range from 7°14′ Gemini to

13°10' Sagittarius. Most astrologers believe that the July Fourth chart has either a Gemini or a Sagittarius Ascendant. But there is support for a Virgo, Libra and Scorpio rising as well.

British astrologer Ebenezer Sibly published the first-known astrological chart for the signing in 1787. As a contemporary of the signers, he was in the best position to research the time. Like many of the men who signed the Declaration, he was a Mason.

Astrologer Michael Baigent says that it is reasonable to assume that Sibly's Masonic brethren told him the time the document was signed.[6] (According to one source, 53 of the 56 signers of the Declaration were Masons.) Sibly said that the Declaration was signed at 5:10 p.m. Dane Rudhyar, a well-known twentieth-century astrologer, rectified Sibly's chart for 5:13:55. Both charts would give the United States conceptional chart a Sagittarius rising.

Having reviewed the arguments, I believe that the existing evidence, as well as the nation's character and response to transiting planets, strongly suggests a Sagittarius rising.

What time, then, *was* the Declaration of Independence signed? On November 14, 1989, I asked El Morya to solve the problem of the birth charts of the United States and the Soviet Union. The Master obliged by opening up the akashic records.

El Morya pegged the hour and the minute of the signing of the Declaration of Independence at exactly 5:13 p.m. on July 4, 1776. Therefore we know for certain that America's conceptional Sun is at 13°19′ Cancer, her conceptional Ascendant is at 12°59′ Sagittarius and her conceptional Moon is at 27°12′ Aquarius (fig. 2).

Now let us turn to the United States birth chart. Sometime before his inauguration, George Washington had been anointed by Saint Germain to wear the mantle of the Great White Brotherhood in the highest office in the land. Both as general and as president, Washington was destined to bear the flame of liberty for America.

Therefore, on April 30, 1789, by the vote of the people as well as by divine approbation, the Christed one George Washington was officially given the mantle of the leadership of the nation. America was truly born that day, and the people gained a sense of national unity through the man God had sent to embody all they had fought for and won under his leadership.

Although Washington was scheduled to take the oath of office at noon, the ceremony was delayed for at least an hour. Historians' estimates range from 1 p.m. to 1:30 p.m.

El Morya has confirmed that the time of the birth of the United States of America is 1:30 p.m., April 30, 1789. Knowing this, we can precisely calculate her birth chart: her natal Sun is at 10°46′ Taurus, her natal Ascendant is at 7°37′ Virgo, and her natal Moon is at 16°35′ Cancer (fig. 3).

Like the U.S. birth chart, the birth chart for the Soviet Union is subject to debate. Charts have been proposed for various hours of the day on the sixth,

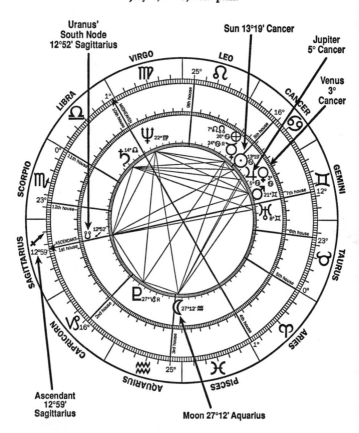

**The United States of America
Conceptional Chart
July 4, 1776, 5:13 p.m.**

Uranus'
South Node
12°52' Sagittarius

Sun 13°19' Cancer

Jupiter
5° Cancer

Venus
3°
Cancer

Ascendant
12°59'
Sagittarius

Moon 27°12' Aquarius

FIGURE 2   The United States was conceived at 5:13 p.m. local mean time (LMT), July 4, 1776, in Philadelphia, Pennsylvania, at the signing of the Declaration of Independence. The United States conceptional Sun is at 13°19' Cancer, her Moon is at 27°12' Aquarius and her Ascendant is at 12°59' Sagittarius. The Sun forms a conjunction with Jupiter at 5° Cancer and Venus at 3° Cancer, which finds expression in the expansive, maternal nature of the United States and her impulse to nurture and protect.

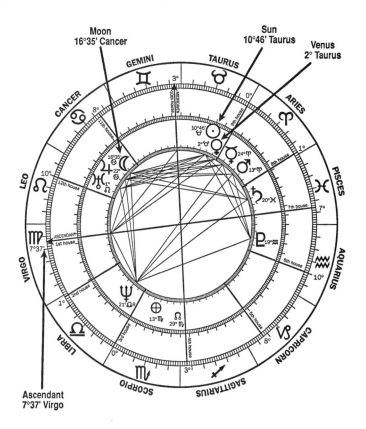

The United States of America
Birth Chart
April 30, 1789, 1:30 p.m.

Moon
16°35' Cancer

Sun
10°46' Taurus

Venus
2° Taurus

Ascendant
7°37' Virgo

FIGURE 3 The United States of America was born at 1:30 p.m. LMT on April 30, 1789, when George Washington took the oath of office as her first president at Federal Hall in New York City. The United States natal Sun is at 10°46' Taurus, her Moon is at 16°35' Cancer and her Ascendant is at 7°37' Virgo. The Sun is conjoined Venus at 2° Taurus sextile the Moon and trine the Ascendant. This configuration is the basis for a stable, practical government.

seventh, eighth and ninth of November 1917, the confused period when the Bolsheviks seized power over Mother Russia.

When El Morya opened up the akashic records to confirm the U.S. charts, he also revealed that the Soviet Union was born at 3 p.m., November 7, 1917. At that precise hour Lenin took the platform and delivered his famous speech proclaiming the triumph of the Bolshevik Revolution to the Petersburg Soviet with the words "Now begins a new era in the history of Russia, and this third Russian revolution must finally lead to the victory of Socialism.... Long live the worldwide Socialist revolution!"[7] The Soviet Union's Sun is at 14°33' Scorpio, her Moon is at 23°37' Leo, and her Ascendant is at 6°48' Aries (fig. 4).

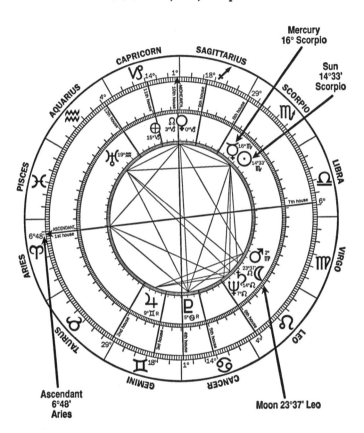

Union of Soviet Socialist Republics
Birth Chart
November 7, 1917, 3:00 p.m.

Mercury
16° Scorpio

Sun
14°33'
Scorpio

Ascendant
6°48'
Aries

Moon 23°37' Leo

FIGURE 4 The Union of Soviet Socialist Republics was born after a nearly bloodless coup at 3 p.m. eastern European time (EET) in Saint Petersburg, Russia, on November 7, 1917. The Soviet Union's Sun is at 14°33' Scorpio, her Moon is at 23°37' Leo and her Ascendant is at 6°48' Aries. The Soviet Union exhibits the inherently secretive nature of the unevolved Scorpio. It is a closed society whose leaders restrict the information that reaches their people and the outside world—even in the age of *glasnost*.

CHAPTER 12

The Portents of the United States Conceptional Chart

One of the notable features of the United States conceptional chart is the conjunction of the binary star Sirius to the Sun at 13° Cancer[1] (fig. 5).

Sirius, the brightest star in the night sky, was known by the ancients as the "Royal One." Its name may have derived from the Greek word for "sparkling" or "scorching." The Arabic name for Sirius, *Al Shi'ra*, is similar to its Egyptian, Persian, Greek, Phoenician and Roman names, suggesting that they have a common source. The nineteenth-century German astronomer Christian Ideler thought the origin of the name might have been the ancient Sanskrit *Surya*, meaning "the Shining One," "the Sun."[2]

When well-placed in a chart, Sirius gives honors, wealth, fame and commercial success. But it is also associated with danger and violence.

Sun-Jupiter-Venus Conjunction

The U.S. conceptional chart has several other distinguishing characteristics. Her conceptional Sun at 13° Cancer forms a conjunction with Jupiter at 5°

The United States Conceptional Sun Conjoined Sirius

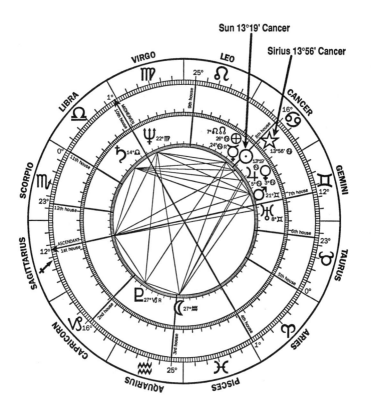

FIGURE 5 In 1776, Sirius, the brightest star in the night sky, was at 11°0′ Cancer conjoined the United States conceptional Sun at 13°19′ Cancer. Since fixed stars move forward in the zodiac at the rate of about 1° every 72 years, Sirius is now at 13°56′ Cancer and still conjoined the conceptional Sun. Sirius was known by the ancients as the "Royal One." Well-placed, Sirius gives honors, wealth, fame and commercial success. But it is also associated with danger and violence.

Cancer and Venus at 3° Cancer in the seventh house. The Sun, the most important body in the conjunction, gives life, identity, vitality and will power. In mundane astrology it is associated with the national identity and leadership. The sign of Cancer rules home, mother, family, land, food, the people, women and patriotism.

This conjunction finds expression in our country's expansive, maternal nature and the impulse to nurture, feed and protect. It explains the American people's deep attachment to the land of their birth, their strong patriotism and healthy concern for or not so healthy preoccupation with the material world. It also shows the potential for great wealth and abundance as well as extravagance, waste, indulgence and overexpansion.

The Sun-Jupiter-Venus conjunction in Cancer is the primary source of the strong American sense of home and family and the tendency to withdraw into home and family as a place of refuge in time of trouble.

The placement of the U. S. conceptional Moon in the evolutionary sign of Aquarius shows that the institution of the family and, more broadly, the concept of community was destined to evolve in America (Cancer rules the home and family, the Moon rules Cancer, and Aquarius rules community). We have seen this evolution in the family occur particularly as new technologies have made life easier, as women have gained greater social and political freedom, and as new legislation has affected the family both positively and negatively.

The Challenge of an Aquarius Moon

The conceptional Moon in Aquarius gives the United States the opportunity to create a new model or mode of expression for the family on a higher level. It shows the possibility of establishing Aquarian communities based on an evolved family unit. But such developments require much inner growth. Without spiritual development, the social innovations that are possible under the influence of the Moon in Aquarius could actually impede or reverse the evolutionary process and fragment the family.

Right now the family is under stress—if not assault. "Fifteen million American children, one quarter of the population under 18, are growing up today without fathers," writes social commentator Nicholas Davidson. "This is the greatest social catastrophe facing our country. It is at the root of the epidemics of crime and drugs, it is deeply implicated in the decline in educational attainment, and it is largely responsible for the persistence of widespread poverty despite generous government support for the needy."[3]

We are all aware of the symptoms of the besieged family—high divorce rates, teenage pregnancy, increased welfare, rising crime and drug abuse, battered wives, child abuse and so on. Throughout the eighties both political parties pledged to "save the family." But there has been no consensus about how to do it.

Some say that Congress (which is governed by

Aquarius and its ruling planet, Uranus) is partially to blame for the breakup of the family. According to Davidson, legislation that made divorce easier and welfare more accessible also increased the number of impoverished single women with children. Children who grow up without fathers are statistically more likely to get involved in drugs and crime and to demonstrate lower achievement in school than children from two-parent homes.

It is tempting to try to define the problems facing the family with an abundance of statistics and sociological rationales. But statistics measure effects, not causes. First and foremost, the problem of the family is spiritual. The astrology of the U.S. conceptional chart requires spiritual growth as a prerequisite to maintaining family health and cohesion while the family evolves.

And the challenges to the family are certain to increase. Pluto, transiting in Scorpio, begins to form a square to the conceptional Moon in Aquarius in January 1990. As the square grows tighter and becomes exact in 1994,* the family unit will be under far greater stress than we have seen thus far.

Jupiter, Ruler of the United States Conceptional Chart

The United States conceptional Ascendant is 12°59′ Sagittarius. The planet that rules the sign on the Ascendant is considered to be the ruler of the chart. Since Jupiter rules Sagittarius, it rules

*The square of transiting Pluto to the U.S. conceptional Moon will be exact on January 4, April 29, and October 31, 1994.

the U.S. conceptional chart. This greatly amplifies the Jupiterian/Sagittarian influence in the life of the nation.

Jupiter is a planet that tends to amplify or magnify whatever it touches. It rules philosophy, religion, higher education, the judiciary and legal theory, church-state relations, great wealth, ambassadors and foreign affairs.

A Sagittarius Ascendant indicates a temperament that is philosophical, religious and abstract, expansive and international, optimistic, just, prophetic, adventurous and freedom loving. If you take our national/international profile as individuals and as "Uncle Sam," that description fits.

Talking about the Sagittarius Ascendant in the U.S. chart, Dane Rudhyar says:

> The Sagittarian temperament is also usually considered to have the following characteristics: self-righteousness, the desire to be loved, dependence on intuition rather than on strictly intellectual logic, an outspoken, impulsive and demonstrative temperament, good fellowship, generosity, humanitarianism, joviality and philosophical optimism, love of sports and of distant journeys or adventures. Our ambitious schemes and passionate desire for expansion and for 'bigger and better' results [are Sagittarian].[4]

But the Sagittarius temperament can also be hypocritical, tyrannical, bigoted, hard-hearted, bombastic, blunt, undiplomatic and shortsighted.

Sagittarius gives the urge to develop one's world view and to live by it. Between 1760 and 1775, when an ideological revolution took place in America, this urge was a preoccupation. This period of philosophical ferment, and not the war, was the real revolution. "The Revolution," observed John Adams, "was in the minds of the people, and this was effected from 1760 to 1775, . . . before a drop of blood was shed at Lexington."[5]

Uranus and the Impulse for Freedom

For the most part, astrologers have been unsuccessful in discovering the astrological impulse for the American Revolution. Some have tried to explain the fervor for revolution by theorizing that the U.S. conceptional chart (they call it the birth chart) has Gemini rising. Then Uranus (the planet of revolution) would conjoin the U.S. Ascendant. But they disregard the fact that the Declaration of Independence would have had to have been signed between 2 a.m. and 4 a.m., when Congress was not even in session, for this to be correct.

In any case, we can find the drive for revolution right in the U.S. conceptional chart with a Sagittarius Ascendant. The heliocentric south node of Uranus is conjoined the U.S. conceptional Ascendant in Sagittarius. Uranus' heliocentric south node is now at 13°59′ Sagittarius. In 1776 it was at 12°52′ Sagittarius conjoined the U.S. conceptional Ascendant at 12°59′ Sagittarius. This conjunction combines the impulse for freedom, innovation and revolution (Uranus' south node) with the drive to externalize and expand a way of life built on a philosophical, religious and legal world view (Sagittarius).

Rudhyar writes: "When [a person's Ascendant is conjoined] to the line of Uranus' nodes there is an absolutely basic, karmic or structural identification between the person's individuality and Uranus. Indeed the individual person [or nation] is born indelibly stamped with Uranus' power, and fated to act as a transforming force in society, as an 'agent' of Uranus."[6]

Since Jupiter is the ruler of Sagittarius, which is conjoined Uranus' south node, it picks up the revolutionary impulse from the node. And since Jupiter is conjoined the Sun, representing the national identity, this revolutionary-philosophical influence is an integral part of the American identity. The Moon (ruler of Cancer, the sign where the Sun and Jupiter are placed in the U.S. conceptional chart) is in Uranus-ruled Aquarius, indicating that the impulse for freedom is an essential element of the political culture.

Jupiter-Sagittarius-Uranus'-South-Node Bungling

The influences of Jupiter, Sagittarius and Uranus' south node may not always be positively expressed. In their negative expression, they are associated with incompetent or militant foreign relations, religious intolerance, inflation, the misuse of foreign aid, an inflated sense of self-importance, inattention to detail, sudden, unpredictable, eccentric and tyrannical actions, anarchic or repressive behavior, radical ideology, guerrilla warfare and alliances of war.

The placement of Uranus' south node in Sagittarius also shows that the United States has the propensity to launch out in international matters—military, diplomatic and economic—without thinking through the details of her plan or the consequences of her actions.

It is easy to catalog modern U.S. military misadventures, from the conduct of the Vietnam War to Jimmy Carter's abortive rescue of U.S. hostages held in Iran to the Iran-Contra scandal. Even one of the most "successful" U.S. military adventures of the 1980s, the invasion of Grenada, was an embarrassing tangle of small disasters.

From start to finish, the invasion was typical of Jupiter-Sagittarius-Uranus'-south-node bungling. On October 25, 1983, the United States invaded the tiny island of Grenada. President Reagan told the nation, still feeling the effects of failed attempts to rescue Americans in Iran, that the armed forces "are standing tall again."[7] Yet 20,000 American soldiers had difficulty defeating a handful of Cubans and a small detachment of Grenadians.

To begin with, the entire operation was planned in four days. That in itself created considerable confusion. Because the CIA had no agents on the island, intelligence was thin. Furthermore, the military had no up-to-date maps. The U.S. Defense

Mapping Agency finally came up with a complete set on November 2, a week after the fighting ended. Soldiers fought with tourist maps and antiquated British charts. Vice Admiral Joseph Metcalf, a U.S. commander, used one dated 1895.

But this was not the only bungle. Troops were unable to communicate effectively because there were not enough batteries to run their secure voice radios. While U.S. troops were fighting, the Army couldn't talk to the Navy or the Air Force to the Marines. The commanders couldn't even communicate from land to ships they could see offshore. A shipment of batteries finally arrived after the fighting was over.

And then there was the problem of attacking the wrong targets. An A-7 attack jet destroyed an insane asylum, killing 17 people. Another A-7 mistakenly attacked a command post of the 82d Airborne Division, wounding 17 U.S. soldiers, one of whom later died.

But what borders on astonishing is that the military did not know the location of the 600 American students at St. George's University Medical School. This is almost beyond comprehension. Writer James Perry points out:

> President Reagan had told the nation the prime reason for the invasion was to safeguard more than 600 young Americans attending the island's St. George's University Medical School. The invading force was

informed that all these U.S. students were living at the school's Grand Anse campus. In fact, most of them were at the True Blue campus and living on the Lance aux Epines peninsula. Their parents knew that. A phone call could have confirmed it, for the school's switchboard was in full operation.[8]

Economic Influences in the U.S. Conceptional Chart

The United States has a number of indicators of material well-being and financial success in both her conceptional and birth charts. However, her astrology shows that her economy is subject to periods of boom and bust and to being dominated by a power elite.

The Sun-Jupiter-Venus conjunction in Cancer in the U.S. conceptional chart indicates an abundance of resources, a tendency to inflate the currency and a strong drive for material success and comfort. But it does not explain the American capacity to efficiently produce large quantities of crops through successfully harnessing technology. Nor does it explain her sophisticated business and financial structure. We find these in her birth chart. But the Sun-Jupiter-Venus conjunction is a good indicator of periods of boom and bust.

Saturn at 14° Libra is square to the Sun-Jupiter-Venus conjunction in Cancer. Saturn is the planet of crystallization and precipitation and provides the concrete element to this conjunction. It facilitates the physical precipitation of the potential wealth of the Cancer planets.

While the Sun-Jupiter-Venus conjunction in Cancer is expansive, it also shows that the nation is inclined to be somewhat impractical. But the square of Saturn helps make it practical and organized.

Saturn has the tendency to constrict flow, in this case of the nation's money and economic activity. At times the square of Saturn to these planets decreases or blocks the flow of abundance. Since Jupiter rules expansion and Saturn rules contraction, it is one of several indicators of the inflation-recession cycle.

Another indicator of U.S. economic affairs is her conceptional Pluto at 27° Capricorn in the second house of the nation's wealth, banks, stock exchanges and currency, opposed to Mercury at 24° Cancer in the eighth house of the national debt and interest rates. This is the principal indicator for domination of the economy by a power elite.

Pluto in Capricorn also has the capacity to reduce or destroy the nation's supply of money. Therefore, since Saturn rules Capricorn, the square of Saturn to Jupiter and the opposition of Pluto in Capricorn to Mercury in Cancer may at times interact to seriously reduce economic activity in the United States.

Understanding Saturn's square to Jupiter and its trine to Uranus is crucial to interpreting the economic dynamics and financial success of the United States (fig. 6). The square of Saturn (system and organization) to Jupiter (wealth and expansion) establishes a theoretical (Jupiter) and practical (Saturn)

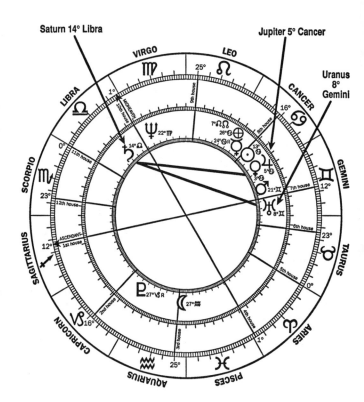

Saturn Square Jupiter and Trine Uranus in the United States Conceptional Chart

FIGURE 6 Saturn at 14° Libra, Jupiter at 5° Cancer and Uranus at 8° Gemini in the United States conceptional chart are the astrological foundation of the nation's political and economic systems. Saturn (system and organization) square Jupiter (wealth and expansion) creates a framework for producing wealth through a free-market economy (Uranus). Saturn (order) trine Uranus (freedom and innovation) is the basis for a new form of government that establishes political liberty and "a new order of the ages."

framework for a dynamic economic system capable of producing wealth through a free-market economy (Uranus) and property rights.

The Saturn-Uranus trine indicates innovations in the work place, a skilled labor force, technological development and advanced agricultural methods. It also holds the possibility of economic and political freedom for the working man.

A New Order of the Ages

When considering the organization of a national economy, it is important to remember that a nation's economic system is dependent on her political system. The form of the United States government is clearly described, in principle, by the U.S. conceptional Saturn in Libra square the Sun-Jupiter conjunction in Cancer and trine Uranus in Gemini. This configuration anticipates, and is the astrological underpinning for, the framing, adoption and activation of the Constitution as the supreme law of the land.

Saturn rules the national administration, political power and the form of government. In the conceptional chart it is placed in the tenth house, which it rules, and in the sign of Libra, where it is exalted. Since Libra rules the law, Saturn in Libra in the tenth house is a sign that the United States was destined to elevate and revere the law. As Thomas Paine said, "In America, the Law is King."[9]

Saturn, which has the capacity to precipitate, also has the power to limit, divide or separate.

Hence, we see the astrological matrix for the separation of powers, a concept imported from Europe (Jupiter in the seventh house) and applied (Saturn) for the benefit of the people (Cancer) in a practical (Saturn) legal (Libra) framework.

Libra rules equality, justice and cooperation. In simple terms, we are describing an equitable (Libra) system of government (Saturn, tenth house) that depends on checks (Saturn) and balances (Libra) in order to divide power and protect liberty—and where all are equal (Libra) before the law (Saturn in Libra).

Because Saturn rules order and Uranus rules newness, freedom and innovation, the Saturn-Uranus trine is the basis for a new form of government, a "new order" that establishes political liberty. The nation's founders inscribed the words *Novus Ordo Seclorum*, "A New Order of the Ages," under the unfinished pyramid that appears on the reverse side of the Great Seal of the United States.

The U.S. conceptional chart explains many aspects of the national life and personality, but it does not explain them all. For these we must look to the birth chart.

CHAPTER 13

The Portents of
the United States Birth Chart

The United States conceptional chart shows a
national temperament that is philosophical,
idealistic, revolutionary and freedom loving. The
United States birth chart, with its Sun at 10° Taurus,
shows a temperament that is stable, practical, patient
and materialistic (fig. 3, p. 147).

Venus rules the sign of Taurus, and the United
States Sun is conjoined Venus at 2° Taurus. Venus
and Taurus rule banks, stock exchanges, the nation's
currency, commercial affairs, trade, fertile fields
and grain. The conjunction of the Sun and Venus
in Taurus indicates a strong economy, equitable
distribution of wealth and budget surpluses.

The Sun-Venus conjunction also indicates
ardent appreciation and support for the arts and a
love of music. On the negative side, it shows a
propensity for government and nationally known
figures to become involved in sex scandals.

The United States birth chart carries forward
the potential for wealth found in the conceptional
chart and gives it practical expression. The natal
Sun at 10° Taurus conjoined Venus at 2° Taurus

sextile the Moon at 16° Cancer and trine the Ascendant at 7° Virgo forms the basis for a stable, practical government and a strong economy with intricate technology. It shows the nation's capacity to mobilize her agricultural, financial and commercial resources to generate great wealth. But it is also associated with conspicuous consumption, the concentration of wealth in a few hands, recessions or depressions, deficit spending and debt accumulation.

The U.S. natal Saturn at 20° Pisces (fig. 7) in the seventh house (of foreign affairs) is quincunx Neptune at 21° Libra in the second house (of money and banking). This is the basis for the nation's tendency to be cautious and isolationist as well as idealistic and compassionate in her relations with other nations, in contrast to influences in the U.S. conceptional chart that indicate a bold, opportunistic and internationalist approach to foreign affairs.

Saturn quincunx Neptune denotes American generosity to other nations; but it also shows that U.S. foreign policy tends to be bureaucratic and plagued by confusion, deception, false idealism and a lack of resolve. It indicates the potential to form alliances based on international trade and finance that serve the interests of the business community but not of the nation. And it shows false expectations related to the capacity of foreign aid to influence other nations.

The U.S. natal Neptune at 21° Libra in the second house (of money and banking) makes an opposition to Mars at 13° Aries and Mercury at 24°

Saturn Quincunx Neptune
in the United States Birth Chart

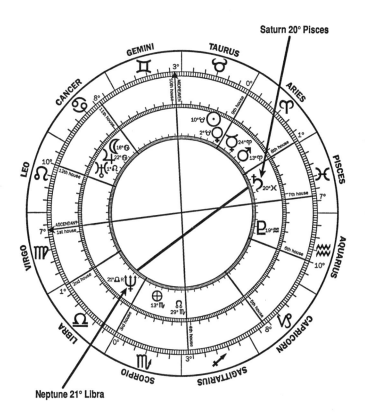

Saturn 20° Pisces

Neptune 21° Libra

FIGURE 7 The United States natal Saturn at 20° Pisces in the seventh house (of foreign affairs) is quincunx Neptune at 21° Libra in the second house (of money and banking). This aspect shows that U.S. foreign policy tends to be cautious and compassionate but plagued by confusion and deception. It also shows the potential to form alliances based on international trade and finance that serve the interests of the business community but not of the nation.

Aries in the eighth house (of taxes and interest rates). These planets square the Moon at 16° Cancer and Jupiter at 22° Cancer in the eleventh house (of Congress), forming a T-square (fig. 8).

This T-square shows an expansive economy and great wealth. But Neptune in the second house shows deception in the management of the nation's currency. And its square to Pluto in Capricorn in the U.S. conceptional second house shows that the nation's finances (and thus the government) could be dominated by a financial elite.

There are a few elements in the U.S. birth chart that indicate the potential for innovations in government that restrict freedom rather than enhance it. Even though the impulse for freedom exists in the conceptional chart—signaled by Uranus trine Saturn and Uranus' south node conjoined the Ascendant—it may not be expressed through the birth chart without enlightened leadership.

Uranus (which represents Congress) in the U.S. birth chart is at 1° Leo (which signifies political power) in the eleventh house (of Congress and legislation) square the Sun (which represents the president) and Venus in Taurus. Since hard aspects between the Sun and planets in Leo indicate power struggles, this placing points to conflicts between Congress and the president as well as the potential for a power-hungry Congress to pass oppressive legislation that increases the power of the federal government.

Pluto is at 19° Aquarius (the sign ruled by Uranus) in the sixth house (of the civil service, the

The Moon, Mercury, Mars, Jupiter and Neptune Form a T-Square in the United States Birth Chart

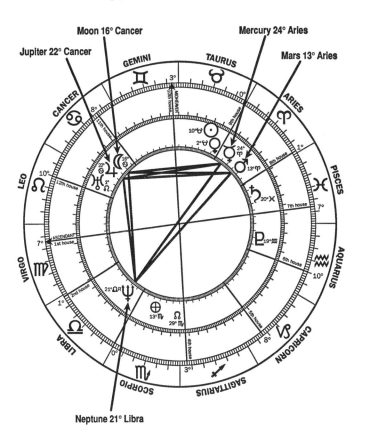

FIGURE 8 The United States natal Neptune at 21° Libra in the second house (of money and finance) makes an opposition to Mars at 13° Aries and Mercury at 24° Aries in the eighth house (of taxes and interest rates). These planets square the Moon at 16° Cancer and Jupiter at 22° Cancer in the eleventh house (of Congress), forming a T-square. The configuration shows an expansive economy and great wealth. But Neptune in the second house also shows deception in the management of the nation's currency.

armed forces, the labor force and the national food supply). Because Pluto is in the sign ruled by Uranus, there is a relationship between the two planets. This shows the potential for the loss of freedom through a congressionally created, unelected bureaucracy. With Pluto in the sixth house, Americans are apt to eat an unhealthy diet (witness junk food, sugar, alcohol and heavy meat consumption), which could thereby compromise a strong, decisive national identity.

Transiting Pluto in Scorpio is making a square to the U.S. natal Pluto at 19° Aquarius. The square will be exact on December 16, 1990; May 5, 1991; and October 13, 1991. As it grows tighter, we can expect to see an increase in labor unrest, food shortages or famine, and the destruction, disintegration or dismantling of our armed forces.

The Portents of the Birth Chart of the Soviet Union

The Soviet Union's natal Sun is at 14°33′ Scorpio, the sign that rules death and regeneration, science, engineering, military combat and joint economic relations. The behavior of the Soviet Union is typical of the unevolved Scorpio, which is inherently secretive. The Soviet Union is a closed society whose leaders restrict the information that reaches their people and the outside world. Even in the era of *glasnost*, Soviet leaders still release information selectively.

The Sun in Scorpio gives the Soviets a need both to dominate and to protect themselves from domination and inclines them to view all other nations as enemies to be conquered. Scorpio secrecy leads to deception, which the Soviets have fashioned into a state policy and raised to a fine art.

The Soviet Union's Neptune at 7° Leo, Saturn at 14° Leo and Moon at 23° Leo, all in the sixth house (of the work force, the armed forces and the national food supply), oppose her Uranus at 19° Aquarius in the twelfth house (of prisons, espionage and the secret police). These planets square the

Soviet Sun at 14° Scorpio conjoined Mercury at 16° Scorpio in the seventh house (of foreign affairs, treaties and war), forming a T-square (fig. 9).

This configuration shows that the Soviets are clever strategists and indefatigable propagandists but that they are unable to use their indigenous pool of scientific and engineering talent to establish a productive economy. It also shows the Soviet tendency to use political repression, espionage, secrecy, deception and military force to solve their economic and political problems.

Pluto, the planet of power and control, at 5° Cancer in the fourth house (of the people) indicates systematic domestic repression, the use of secret police, poor agricultural production and intentionally created famines.

The United States natal Sun at 10°46′ Taurus and the Soviet Union's natal Sun at 14°33′ Scorpio are in polarity (fig. 10). In astrological terms they form an opposition, an aspect that can show either union and cooperation or separation and conflict. Since this polarity involves the nations' Suns (representing national identity and leadership), it shows that at times the United States and the Soviet Union are cooperative and at other times they are not.

In general, however, the superpowers are likely to be cooperating *and* competing, at once friends *and* enemies, as Nostradamus prophesied.[1] For example, on October 24, 1973, during the heyday of détente, when U.S.-Soviet relations were the warmest they had been since the beginning of the Cold War,

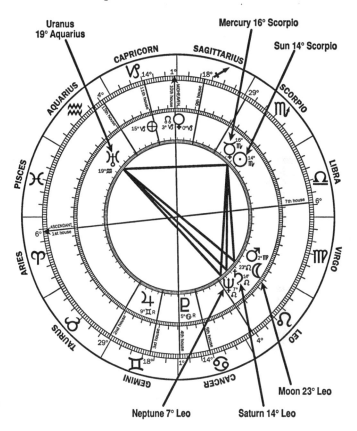

FIGURE 9 The Soviet Union's natal Neptune at 7° Leo conjoined her natal Saturn at 14° Leo and Moon at 23° Leo in the sixth house (of the work force) oppose her Uranus at 19° Aquarius in the twelfth house (of espionage and secret police). These planets square the Soviet Sun at 14° Scorpio conjoined Mercury at 16° Scorpio in the seventh house (of foreign affairs, treaties and war), forming a T-square. This shows a disorganized economy and a tendency to use repression, espionage and military force to solve economic and political problems.

The Soviet Union's Sun
Opposed the United States Sun

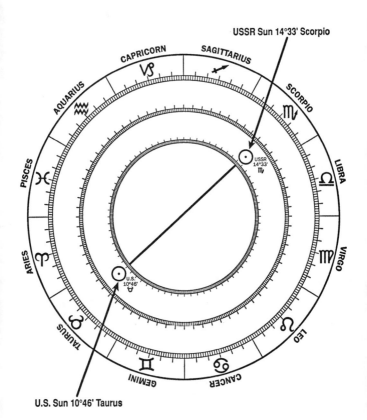

FIGURE 10 The United States natal Sun at 10°46′ Taurus forms an opposition to the Soviet Union's natal Sun at 14°33′ Scorpio, an aspect that can show either union and cooperation or separation and conflict. In general, the superpowers are likely to be cooperating and competing, at once friends and enemies.

the threat of direct Soviet intervention in the Yom Kippur War between Israel and a coalition of Arab states nearly provoked a nuclear exchange between the superpowers.

In the late 1980s and early 1990s, transiting planets will severely impact the charts of the United States and the Soviet Union, a subject we will take up in succeeding chapters.

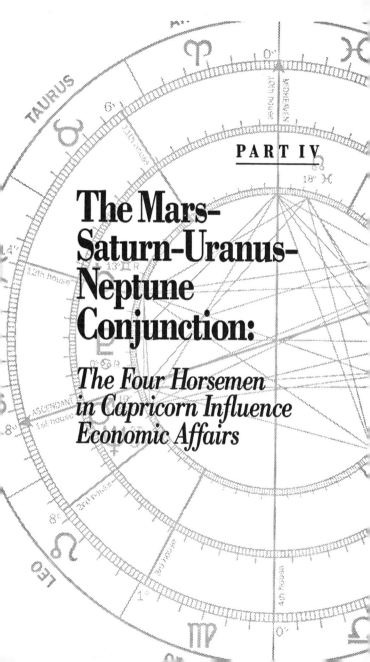

PART IV

The Mars–Saturn–Uranus–Neptune Conjunction:

The Four Horsemen in Capricorn Influence Economic Affairs

CHAPTER 15

A Capricorn Conjunction
Triggers the Great Depression

War often follows or is triggered by problems in the economies of nations. Therefore, let us return to our discussion of the February 22 and 23, 1988 conjunction of Mars, Saturn, Uranus and Neptune in Capricorn and follow the development of astrological influences in economic affairs.

This is not the first time a powerful Capricorn conjunction has strongly affected the United States. On December 30, 1929, Venus, Mars, Saturn, the Sun and the Moon formed a conjunction between 0° and 10° in Capricorn (fig. 11) just as the United States was sliding into the Great Depression. This conjunction spanned the same area of the zodiac (0°–10° Capricorn) as the conjunction of February 22 and 23, 1988 (0°–9° Capricorn).

Transiting Mercury compounded the depressing effect of the conjunction. Although it was not part of the conjunction, on December 31, 1929, Mercury was at 27° Capricorn conjoined the U.S. conceptional Pluto and opposed her conceptional Mercury at 24° Cancer.

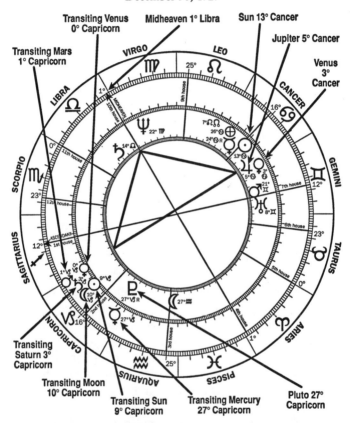

Conjunction of Five Planets in Capricorn Forms a T-Square in the United States Conceptional Chart
December 30, 1929

FIGURE 11 On December 30, 1929, Venus, Mars, Saturn, the Sun and the Moon formed a conjunction between 0° and 10° Capricorn. These planets opposed the U.S. conceptional Sun at 13° Cancer, Jupiter at 5° Cancer and Venus at 3° Cancer and formed a square to her Midheaven at 1° Libra. The next day, Mercury conjoined the U.S. conceptional Pluto at 27° Capricorn and opposed her natal Mercury at 24° Cancer. The effect of these configurations was to constrict the national economy, reduce personal wealth and create a state of psychological depression.

The Capricorn conjunction of December 30, 1929, also made an opposition to the U.S. conceptional Sun, Jupiter and Venus in Cancer. Neptune was in the earth sign Virgo at the time. The effect of this configuration was dramatic: it constricted the national economy, reduced personal wealth and created a state of psychological depression that prolonged the downturn. In this configuration we can also see the portent of the restructuring of the federal government in an increase and concentration of power. The New Deal legislation did just that.

The Capricorn conjunction of 1929 also influenced the Federal Reserve System (the Fed), which had been established by Congress on December 23, 1913, at 6:02 p.m. EST in Washington, D.C. (fig. 12).

The Fed's Sun at 1° Capricorn shows that the system is supposed to be prudent and provide long-term economic stability. But its Sun makes an opposition to Pluto at 0° Cancer in the twelfth house of deception and self-defeating behavior, which is indicative of the fact that the system was the secret creation of plutocrats and that the Fed periodically creates recessions and depressions.

The Capricorn conjunction of 1929 was conjoined the Fed's Sun and opposed its Pluto. This indicates the failure of the Fed to fine-tune the economy in order to forestall the Great Depression (if indeed it had any real intention of doing so). Instead, the Fed constricted the money supply at the wrong time, exacerbated the already dire financial situation and caused the economy to sink into the depression.

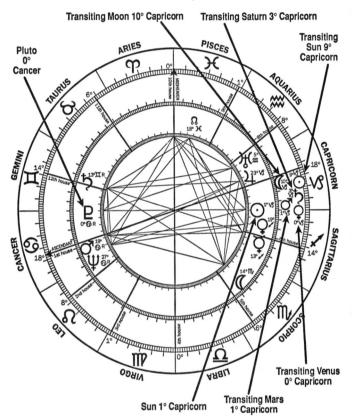

Conjunction of Five Planets in Capricorn
Activates the Federal Reserve System's Birth Chart
December 30, 1929

Transiting Moon 10° Capricorn

Transiting Saturn 3° Capricorn

Transiting Sun 9° Capricorn

Pluto 0° Cancer

Transiting Venus 0° Capricorn

Sun 1° Capricorn

Transiting Mars 1° Capricorn

FIGURE 12 The Federal Reserve System (the Fed) was established on December 23, 1913, at 6:02 p.m. EST in Washington, D.C. The Fed's Sun at 1° Capricorn opposed to its natal Pluto at 0° Cancer in the twelfth house of deception shows that the system was the secret creation of plutocrats and that the Fed periodically creates recessions and depressions. The Capricorn conjunction of December 30, 1929, activated this Sun-Pluto opposition. The Fed constricted the money supply and caused the economy to sink into the Great Depression.

As influential as the 1929 Capricorn conjunction was, it was not as powerful as the 1988 Capricorn conjunction. For one thing, the conjunction in 1929 had only one slow-moving, outer planet in it, Saturn. The conjunction of 1988 involved three slow-moving, outer planets—Saturn, Uranus and Neptune. Outer planets have more profound and longer-lasting effects than inner planets.

In addition, the February 1988 Capricorn conjunction followed two eclipses that were unprecedented in this century. On August 24, 1987, the Sun, Moon, Mercury, Venus and Mars were located between 0° and 5° Virgo (fig. 13). According to astroeconomist Arch Crawford, this was the tightest conjunction of any five planets in more than 100 years—possibly in 400 years.

Crawford used this conjunction to predict the date the stock market would reach its top. In the August 8, 1987 edition of *Crawford Perspectives* he wrote, "We pick the top for August 24, give or take 3 days. Then a horrendous crash into the eclipse of the Sun."[1] He meant the eclipse of the Sun that would occur on September 22.

August 25, the day after the conjunction, the Dow Jones industrial average reached its highest point at 2722 and started down, setting the stage for the record drops of October 1987, including the 508-point drop on October 19, known as Black Monday.

I don't know if Mark Twain was an astrologer, but he had some homespun wisdom on the subject: "October. This is one of the peculiarly dangerous

Five-Planet Conjunction in Virgo
August 24, 1987

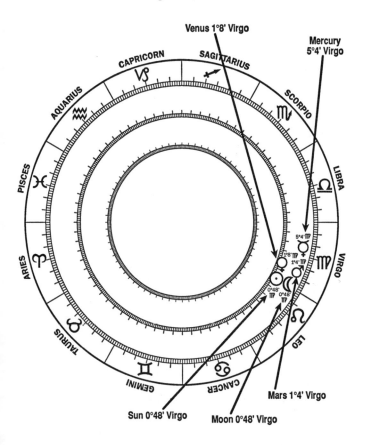

FIGURE 13 On August 24, 1987, the Sun, Moon, Mars, Mercury and Venus formed the tightest conjunction of any five planets in over 100 years. They were all between 0°48′ Virgo and 5°4′ Virgo. Astroeconomist Arch Crawford used this configuration to predict the date the Dow Jones industrial average would reach its peak. On August 25, the Dow reached its top at 2722 and started down, setting the stage for the record drops of October 1987, including the 508-point plunge on October 19, known as Black Monday.

months to speculate in stocks in. The others are July, January, September, April, November, May, March, June, December, August, and February."[2]

While we are on the subject of this August conjunction, I should like to add that Arch Crawford looked at the chart drawn for Dr. José Argüelles' Harmonic Convergence of August 16 and 17, 1987, and concluded as I did that there wasn't anything about those dates likely to herald an age of enlightenment. He believes as I do that Dr. Argüelles et al. picked the wrong day.[3]

While we're always hopeful for influences that could bring peace and enlightenment, we think the dates the Mayans must have calculated were August 22 to 24, not August 16 to 17, and that the portents were quite negative.

The September 22, 1987 Eclipse of the Sun

The decline in the economy since August 25, 1987, is only the first leg of its descent. The second leg will be related to the Capricorn conjunction of February 22 and 23, 1988, and to the eclipse of the Sun of September 22, 1987, at 29° Virgo or (as some astrologers prefer to designate it) 0° Libra.

That eclipse was destined to influence the economy, the government and the course of peace and war on the planet. It fell the closest to one of the equinox, or solstice, points of any eclipse in this century—a very powerful placing. This is quite probably the most intense eclipse of the century.

As a rule, the influence of eclipses can be felt

up to six months after they occur, sometimes longer. Since this eclipse fell close to an equinox point, its effects will be of indeterminate duration as it sets in motion self-perpetuating events. In addition, the eclipse point can be activated by future transits.

At 29° Virgo, the eclipse falls within 2° of the Midheaven of the United States conceptional chart at 1° Libra. The Midheaven rules the nation's government, purpose and reputation. This is why the eclipse affected the United States.

In the astrology of nations, eclipses often show a loss of power, a death or a disaster. An eclipse of the Moon conjoined Pluto was one of several influences that combined to trigger the Chernobyl disaster, as I demonstrated in Book Two, chapter 15, of *Saint Germain On Prophecy*.

Pluto is often associated with death and destruction. President John F. Kennedy's assassination on November 22, 1963, for instance, was preceded by a total solar eclipse opposed the U.S. conceptional Pluto at 27° Capricorn. That eclipse was exactly conjoined his natal Saturn at 27° Cancer in his tenth house of career and public standing.

In the fall of '87, prior to the stock-market crash, while I was on a speaking tour of the East Coast, I said:

> A solar eclipse falling on the U.S. Midheaven at a time when the nation is headed into progressively more difficult circumstances does not augur well. It could be extremely

detrimental to the nation's public standing and institutions, including the Congress and the office of the president—especially to Ronald Reagan. If played out to its extreme, it could lead to the fall of the government, the death of our form of government, the fall or death of the president, literally or figuratively, and the onset of a major economic catastrophe.

As we all know, the economic catastrophe, or at least the first part of it, took place on October 19. I believe that the other elements may soon play themselves out as the sequence of astrological events unfolds.

At the time of the solar eclipse of September 22, 1987, Neptune was at 5° Capricorn square to the eclipse and U.S. Midheaven in Libra. This indicates that things are not what they seem in the United States today. The potential for treachery and intrigue is exceptionally high. This eclipse puts every aspect of our nation at risk. In other words, the eclipse is the sign of the descent of karma.

The cyclic descent of karma often seems to belie the astrological times—degrees, minutes, seconds. For it would appear that if nothing happens on a given day and date, we're home free.

Not so. Astrology is precise, and so is the law of karma. Astrology tells us when the button of karma is pressed. But karma takes its time, moving invisibly yet inexorably: first through the etheric plane, then the mental, then the astral and finally the physical.

Like an avalanche, it appears as that "sudden destruction" that Paul wrote about, "as travail upon a woman with child." "And," the apostle added, "they shall not escape [their karma]!"[4]

As Paul observed the suddenness of the descent of karma in his time, so we, too, shall observe it in the decade of the 1990s.

CHAPTER 16

My Vision of the Four Horsemen

The Book of Revelation is God's gift to all who have answered his call to walk the path of initiation* unto Christhood in the footsteps of our Elder Brother Jesus Christ.

God gave his Revelation to Jesus Christ so that his servants might know beforehand "things which must shortly come to pass." Our Lord delivered this Revelation to his apostle John the Beloved, "sent and signified by his angel."[1]

The Book of Revelation reveals a path of initiation that each soul in her season must pass through if she would ascend to God. It is a study in the psychology of the soul and the testings that she must master on her homeward path leading to reunion with Alpha and Omega, the Father-Mother God.

Note: Read my forthcoming book *My Vision of the Four Horsemen* for updates on this vision.

*In *The Oxford English Dictionary*, *initiation* means "formal introduction by preliminary instruction or initial ceremony into some position, office or society." Here it is meant in its spiritual sense as a lesson that a soul must learn in order to evolve to the next stage of development. G. A. Gaskell describes *initiation* as follows: "Each stage, each step, each advance, each growth in grace corresponds to an initiation, which is a spiritual leading forth to a fuller life" (*Dictionary of All Scriptures and Myths* [New York: Julian Press, 1960], p. 391).

At any point in time and space in any century, the soul on the path of reunion with God may experience in sequence, one after the other, the initiations encoded in the 22 chapters of Revelation; these correspond to the symbology of the 22 letters of the Hebrew alphabet.

According to their soul pattern, evolution and attainment, Lightbearers of the world are experiencing all of the leaves of Revelation; and each of those leaves is tumbling in its time and space, though not necessarily in the same dimension, for we are multidimensional beings.

Revelation juxtaposes the soul and the collective planetary evolution with the forces of Light and Darkness engaged in Armageddon. The outcome of this warfare of the spirit is either the soul's resurrection unto eternal life or her final judgment. By free will the soul must choose either the path of initiation under the Lamb of God and his hosts or the path of Lucifer and the fallen angels in their rebellion against the LORD God and his Christ.

In Revelation we find an outline of these two paths and a prophecy of the outcome of freewill choices made—to be or not to be—each step of the way.

Through a preordained series of lifetimes God gives each soul the opportunity (1) to serve the Lord and glorify him in her members or (2) to deify the ego, the synthetic self and the carnal mind Paul spoke of when he said: "To be carnally minded is death; but to be spiritually minded is life and peace.

Because the carnal mind is enmity against God: for it is not subject to the law of God, neither indeed can be."[2] Those who take this path do swear enmity with God and his Christ and make war with the remnant of the seed of the Divine Mother.[3]

At the end of this cycle of opportunity, which extends over myriad incarnations on earth, the time comes when the soul "is judged according to his works."[4] The Keeper of the Scrolls reads the soul's record before the Ancient of Days, who sits on the great white throne at the Court of the Sacred Fire, and before the Four Beasts and the Twenty-four Elders.[5]

Who Are the Four Horsemen?

In the course of dealing with personal and planetary psychology and the karma of the cycles, the soul will encounter the Four Horsemen of the Apocalypse. They are initiators who provide karmic testing to all.

The subject of this chapter is their advancement on the world scene today and the vision God gave me of their doings (with Saint Germain at my side) in September 1986.

Let us read from chapters 5 and 6 of the Book of Revelation so that we can enter, as John the Revelator did, this prophecy and this path of our souls' initiation:

And I saw in the right hand of him that sat on the throne a book written within and on the backside, sealed with seven seals.

And I saw a strong angel proclaiming with a loud voice, Who is worthy to open the book, and to loose the seals thereof?

And no man in heaven, nor in earth, neither under the earth, was able to open the book, neither to look thereon.

And I wept much, because no man was found worthy to open and to read the book, neither to look thereon . . . .

And I saw when the Lamb opened one of the seals, and I heard, as it were the noise of thunder, one of the four beasts saying, Come![6]

And I saw, and behold a white horse: and he that sat on him had a bow; and a crown was given unto him: and he went forth conquering, and to conquer.

And when he had opened the second seal, I heard the second beast say, Come!

And there went out another horse that was red: and power was given to him that sat thereon to take peace from the earth, and that they should kill one another: and there was given unto him a great sword.

And when he had opened the third seal, I heard the third beast say, Come! And I beheld, and lo a black horse; and he that sat on him had a pair of balances in his hand.

And I heard a voice in the midst of the four beasts say, A measure of wheat for a penny, and three measures of barley for a penny; and see thou hurt not the oil and the wine.

And when he had opened the fourth seal, I heard the voice of the fourth beast say, Come!

And I looked, and behold a pale horse: and his name that sat on him was Death, and Hell followed with him. And power was given unto them over the fourth part of the earth, to kill with sword, and with hunger, and with death, and with the beasts of the earth.[7]

What is the seven-sealed book?

Well, first of all, in one sense *you* are the seven-sealed book! What's more, every continent is a seven-sealed book, and the inhabitants reflect it.

At the etheric level, you have seven spiritual centers called chakras. They are lined up from the base of the spine to the crown. These seven chakras are the seven sealed doors that open to the temple of being when the soul is ready for the initiations of Christhood. Only the Lamb of God can open the seven-sealed book.

When the Lamb opens the first four seals he shows John the Revelator the Four Horsemen, who go out one by one when the command, "Come!" is given by the Four Beasts in succession. These Four Cosmic Forces who guard the throne of God and the Lamb are described in chapter 4 of Revelation as the Lion, the Calf, the Man and the Flying Eagle.

Who are the Four Horsemen and their riders? They are the harbingers of personal and planetary karma. They come in every century to announce its imminent descent; in addition, they are the bearers of that karma and the literal embodiment of it. Hence, there is a sense of foreboding with the mere mention of their names.

The dread of their day is in the psyche of the race. For when their time is come, the opportunity for transmutation of world karma is no more. The mist has become the crystal; and at that point the violet flame does not mitigate or turn back the crystallized karma of a planetary evolution that did not act in time to restore balance to its inner and outer ecosystem. Even the LORD God does not abrogate his own laws of karmic retribution, which bear abundant mercy until the Lawgiver does declare to a recalcitrant mankind: "Thus far and no farther!"

My vision of the Four Horsemen is the sign that time is running out. Therefore, through prayer and dynamic decree we must make haste to intercede on behalf of those who know not what they do: "Father, forgive them! Father, forgive us!"

When God First Showed Me the Four Horsemen . . .

At the conclusion of the twentieth century, the signs in the heavens that portend the ride of the Four Horsemen are the four planets in Capricorn. Our study of the February 1988 Capricorn conjunction and related configurations as they impact the charts of the nations reveals the nature of the karma that these horsemen bear.

When God first showed me the Four Horsemen in September 1986, the thunder of their hoofbeats preceded them. They were moving toward me in a straight line. Those nearest me signified imminent karma; those at a greater distance signified that which was yet to be. I heard the awful roar of their approach, and it made me rise up and take notice that there was a great happening in our nation.

I had the impression that their crisscrossing of the United States would encompass a five-year period. But we know that the days of the Lord's prophecy can be shortened or lengthened for the elect's sake[8] by the Holy Spirit.

In this vision the Four Horsemen are cloaked. I cannot see their faces. They are leaning over their steeds, man and beast one as they gallop through the night. The night is bright. It is illumined by a full moon, whose magnetic pull on the emotions signifies that the astral bodies of mankind are vulnerable to their karma.

Although the night is bright, the riders are dark silhouettes against an age of spiritual darkness. The age is illumined only by the borrowed light of materialism, sensual pleasure, and a technology of which the people are not the masters.

The first horse I saw was not the white horse, as noted by John, but the black horse, the third in his sequence. I attribute this change in the order of their appearance to the fact that when I saw them the Four Horsemen were well on their way and had been for some time. John wrote his vision at the moment of the opening of the first, second, third and fourth seals.

So as I see them, they are descending from other dimensions into the nexus of history. Karmic history, rather than Revelation 6, now dictates the order of their appearing.

The black horse, an immense and awesome creature, was 12 feet from me, and his coat shone a black-silvery-green in the moonlight. The rider of the black horse is regarded as the one who delivers famine upon the earth, and so he does. Famine comes through economic problems as well as adverse weather conditions and improper food distribution. As I watched, Saint Germain told me that the role of this horseman is to deliver the karma for the abuse of the economies of the nations.

John's description of "a voice in the midst of the four beasts" sounds like an auctioneer in the marketplace. He is auctioning off our wheat, our barley and our grains, the staff of life: "A measure of wheat for a penny, and three measures of barley for a penny..." And the voice warns us to "hurt not the oil and the wine." We need both the wine of the Spirit (Father) for our spiritual life and the oil of the earth (Mother) for our material existence to keep the gears of civilization running.

The prices the "auctioneer" is quoting are famine prices. According to Professor Martin Rist, in the first century a measure of wheat for a penny would have been eight to 16 times the normal price and three measures of barley for a penny would have been "likewise far out of line."[9]

The prophesied scarcity of commodities shows that the value of the people's sacred labor, hence their self-worth, is being compromised. And who has compromised it?

Those whom I call the power elite, who know no allegiance to nation or law but who make merchandise of men, taking the profits that belong to the farmers, the laborers and the working people. (I can think of no more gross example of this than the current S&L scandal.)

So the black horseman delivers the karma created by the power elite through their manipulation of the economies of the nations and of the abundant life God gave us. The result of the manipulation of the "oil" and "wine" (and of the grain as well) is world famine.

The black horseman is the first to deliver his karma into the physical octave. The second and the third horsemen, the white and the red, follow close behind ready to deliver theirs. And the last in line, the pale horseman, is at a great distance. His karma is not yet due.

What do these four riders bring? Again, the black horseman brings economic debacle, "a pair of balances in his hand," weighing the commodities of nations and the karma of souls.

The white horseman brings war, with bow and crown, "conquering and to conquer." This rider represents (among other eventualities) the United States engaged in wars small and great outside her borders.

The red horseman, to whom is given "a great sword" and the power "to take peace from the earth," also brings war. The red rider represents (among other eventualities) the Soviet Union engaged in wars small and great outside her borders.

Death rides the pale horse and Hell follows. And Death is as Death does: the two kill with sword, famine and plague.

The Ride of the Black Horseman

On Thanksgiving 1986, one month after I received this vision, Saint Germain said:

Economic debacle is foreseen. Prepare. Setbacks will be sudden. Be not lulled by the heyday. Many Band-Aids upon the economy, the money system, the banking houses. These will not prevent the collapse of nations and banking houses built on sands of human greed, ambition and manipulation of the lifeblood of the people of God.

For they shall not prevail who have built their empires on the backs of the children of God who bear in their bodies the very Blood of Christ. . . .

The law of karma is inexorable, irrevocable, saving where the violet flame, the sacred fire, does consume [mankind's karma]. . . .

The mitigating factor in economic debacle, in nuclear war, in plague untold and death is the nucleus of Lightbearers and the quotient of sacred fire they invoke.[10]

As we moved forward into 1987, from time to time I would see the black horseman. One September evening in 1987 I was at the altar of our chapel at the Royal Teton Ranch in Montana. I was conducting a vigil of invocations and prayers for the healing of the economy.

I looked up and saw the black horseman directly in front of me. I raised my right hand and called to Almighty God to put his right hand over mine to stop the black horse, whereupon the black horse reared up on its hind legs and remained frozen in his stance by the Right Hand of God. That night I knew in my heart that the moment the horse came down, there would be a crisis in the economy.

I conducted a four-day conference in New York City from October 1 to 4, 1987. On the night of October 3, Saint Germain spoke regarding the ride of the black horse:

The "spiritual wickedness in high places" of this city...is a manipulation in money matters beyond conception.

And therefore I say, Woe! Woe! Woe! Let the judgments descend upon those who manipulate the abundant life of a people of God and subject them to a slavery untold far beyond that of the Egyptian taskmasters!...

I say unto all purveyors of drugs and all who poison the minds and souls and bodies of youth eternal everywhere:

Woe! Woe! Woe!

So the pronouncement of the judgment of Almighty God be upon you. So by the spirit of the Prophet does there descend now that karma upon those who are the destroyers in the earth![11]

When you hear the *Woe! Woe! Woe!*—the deprecatory woes—pronounced three times as they are in the Book of Revelation, this is the Lord's pronouncement of the descent of the karma of the people for their sins against the Father, the Son and the Holy Ghost. Remember, the word *judgment* means the release of mankind's karma after a period of grace under Jesus Christ, who has borne a certain weight (but not all) of world karma these past 2,000 years.

Whatever the people have done to violate the Light-Energy-Consciousness and the Power-Wisdom-Love of the Trinity is considered a sin against the divine spark, the threefold flame. This flame is the individualized focus of the Trinity that God placed within the hearts of his sons and daughters. When the karma descends, the three woes are the signal that humanity has gone too far and the threefold flame must be reduced in each lifestream proportionate to the severity of his karma.

In the very midst of the dictation from Saint Germain I heard these words pour from my lips as I delivered "The Speaking of the LORD God":

Hear me, people of earth! I say to you, bind, then, the oppressor! For the hour is come for the judgment of the fallen ones in the earth who would push you to the brink of war and economic collapse and famine and plague. . . .

And the golden-calf civilization does go down! And the Cain civilization is judged! For no longer is the Cain civilization protected by the mark of Cain. It is no more.

And therefore, let the fallen ones know that the hour is come that they must pay the price for the shedding of the blood of the holy innocents and of the sons of God and of the prophets and of the Christs. Therefore, let them tremble! For I come into their citadel of international power and moneyed interests. And I AM, of the LORD God, do declare unto you that through my Archangels they shall know the judgment. [12]

There was scarcely a delay factor from the spoken Word 'from on high' to the crystallization of these judgments. Three days after the dictation, on Tuesday, October 6, the Dow Jones industrial average fell a record 91.55 points, ending a five-year bull market.

On Wednesday, October 14, awakened in the

wee hours of the morning, I saw a change in the position of the black horse. His forelegs touched the ground and the sight of it sent through me a wave of terror. He touched the ground a number of times and reared up again. On that day the market dropped 95.46 points, the biggest daily drop since World War II. On Friday, October 16, the market dropped 108 points.

At 3 a.m. EST Monday, October 19, I was awakened by Saint Germain. I saw the black horse come down on all four hooves, race around me and go beyond me, the white horse galloping after. There was no stopping either of them. I knew that the karma of the economies of the nations had descended. And that war would be next.

That day the Dow dropped 508 points, the biggest drop in history. On the night of October 19, I was lecturing in Toledo, Ohio, and I received this prophecy:

> This day does mark, surely, a turning point in the nations.
>
> Can there be a regrouping of forces? Can there be a rise again? Yes, there can be a rise again, beloved, but never as steady as before.
>
> Thus, the sudden setbacks are experienced. Prepare, then, for there is truly a way and a path to endure and to survive unto thine own ascension in the Light. Therefore, seek the path of reunion with God.[13]

After October 19, 1987, the market rallied and even exceeded its pre-crash highs. But, as I discussed in chapter 6, the Dow Jones industrial average has separated from the economy in general. Regardless of the rise, the signs of the times and the handwriting on the wall do not augur well for the economy.

The long-standing debt problems have not been and almost certainly will not be solved. In the United States an arsenal of debt bombs is waiting to go off at any moment: the farm debt, the energy debt, the consumer debt, the corporate debt—and especially the national debt.

In 1990, people have started to admit that a recession is likely. But it's been on its way for a long time, prophesied in the skies for anyone to read.

God has not left us comfortless in the face of returning karma. He has written his signs of warning in the heavens, in our hearts and in our souls. He has sent his angels to warn us. He has given us a way out—the invocation of the violet transmuting flame. And for those who heed the warning from none of the above, he has established the office and the mantle of the "Prophet-Messenger" for them to contend with.

The Four Horsemen, then, are moving toward the present, each in his turn. As the days pass and the sands in the hourglass fall, we must prepare ourselves to face the karma they will surely deliver according to the commands of the Four Beasts.

There is a cycle when the horsemen can be held back and there is a cycle when they cannot.

Day by day the moving vision of the Four Horsemen is before me. When I tell people what I see, they don't seem to comprehend what I am saying. They have already been lulled into a false peace. I call it karma stupefaction.

If they feel uneasy, they cover it over with their pleasures, their businesses, their livelihoods, their concerns and their families. And, I am sorry to say, the Lightbearers are not galvanized.

They sit around and talk about past lives instead of getting together to call on the name of the LORD. They try to solve their problems with subliminal programming instead of going out to challenge injustice with the zeal of the ancient prophets.

People ask me if I am concerned, if I feel that the situation is "really intense." I am profoundly concerned. And it *is* intense. This is why I am delivering this message at my "stumps" across North America and Europe. I will speak it wherever people will hear me.

CHAPTER 17

How the February 1988 Conjunction Affects the United States

The conjunction of Mars, Saturn and Uranus at 0° Capricorn and Neptune at 9° Capricorn on February 22 and 23, 1988, will dramatically affect the United States.

It opposed the U.S. conceptional Sun at 13° Cancer, conceptional Jupiter at 5° Cancer and conceptional Venus at 3° Cancer. The Capricorn conjunction also squared the U.S. conceptional Midheaven at 1° Libra and the point of the solar eclipse of September 22, 1987, at 29° Virgo, completing a T-square (fig. 14). This T-square inaugurated the second leg of the economic downturn that began with the October 1987 stock-market crash.

The Saturn-Uranus conjunction at 0° Capricorn, which occurred as part of the larger conjunction, is particularly noteworthy. A Saturn-Uranus conjunction alone can ignite international political and economic upheaval, even without any of the complicating and amplifying factors in this configuration. As I pointed out earlier, a Saturn-Uranus conjunction is a primary indicator of war.

Conjunction of Mars, Saturn, Uranus and Neptune Forms a T-Square in the United States Conceptional Chart
February 22 and 23, 1988

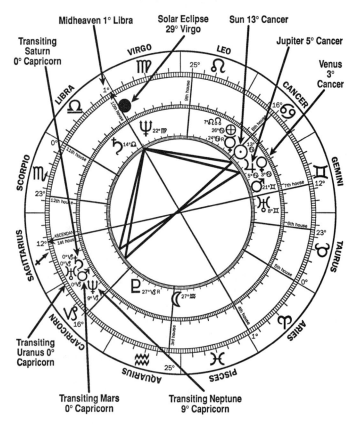

FIGURE 14 On February 22 and 23, 1988, Mars, Saturn and Uranus at 0° Capricorn and Neptune at 9° Capricorn conjoined each other and opposed the United States conceptional Sun at 13° Cancer, Jupiter at 5° Cancer and Venus at 3° Cancer. These planets squared the conceptional Midheaven at 1° Libra and the solar eclipse of September 22, 1987, at 29° Virgo, completing a T-square. This T-square inaugurated the second leg of the economic downturn that began with the October 1987 stock-market crash.

The Federal Reserve System has an opposition between its Sun at 1° Capricorn and its Pluto at 0° Cancer and therefore will also be powerfully influenced by the February 1988 Capricorn conjunction. This Capricorn conjunction was conjoined the Fed's Sun and opposed its Pluto. All of these planets squared the U.S. conceptional Midheaven at 1° Libra conjoined the eclipse of the Sun of September 22, 1987, at 29° Virgo, forming a T-square.

T-squares are dynamic configurations. This one indicates that the Federal Reserve System has been acting, and will probably continue to act, in a manner that is harmful to the nation and ultimately harmful to itself, even though what the Fed is doing may be of immediate value to those who created it— the financial and industrial powers of this nation.

The records show that one cause of the October 1987 crash was the Fed's tight money policy. Under the heavy Capricorn influence since February 1988, the Fed has continued to follow a generally deflationary policy, which has pushed the economy into a recession.

The 1989 Saturn-Neptune Conjunction Accelerates the Economic Downturn

As part of the Saturn-Uranus-Neptune conjunction that began in 1988, Saturn and Neptune made three exact conjunctions. The final one took place on November 13, 1989, at 10°22′ Capricorn opposed to transiting Jupiter at 10°29′ Cancer. This configuration accelerated the economic downturn already in process in the United States.

The opposition of transiting Saturn and Neptune to transiting Jupiter will affect more than the New York Stock Exchange and other stock, bond and commodity markets. It was a critical factor in triggering major debt liquidation and could lead to the dissolution of much of the Western banking system. It could even precipitate an economic crisis so severe as to provoke revolution or lead to the dissolution of the U.S. government.

On November 13, 1989, transiting Jupiter, Saturn and Neptune also squared the U.S. conceptional Saturn in Libra, forming a T-square (fig. 15). Saturn, which represents the federal government and the Constitution, is the focal point of the T-square. This is another indication that the government as well as the Constitution that gave it life could be strained to the point of collapse by national and international karma coming to bear upon the people.

Although these portents may sound far-fetched, they are a lot more plausible today than they were two years ago. The banking crisis has appeared, right on schedule.

ABC "World News Tonight" reported on July 17, 1990, that since 1987, 718 commercial banks have closed nationwide, which is more than at any time since the Great Depression. Dan Brumbaugh of Stanford University said, "We are in the midst of a commercial banking crisis which, if it were not for the thrifts [S&Ls], would itself be a national emergency."

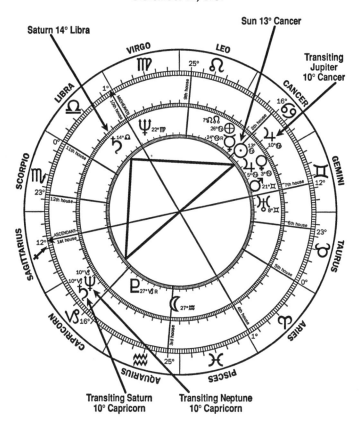

**Transiting Saturn, Neptune and Jupiter
Form a T-Square in the United States Conceptional Chart**
November 13, 1989

FIGURE 15   On November 13, 1989, transiting Saturn and Neptune formed a conjunction at 10° Capricorn and an opposition to transiting Jupiter at 10° Cancer conjoined the United States conceptional Sun at 13° Cancer. These planets squared the U.S. conceptional Saturn at 14° Libra. This configuration activated major debt liquidation in the United States. Early signs of the liquidation: the savings and loan bailout and the big drop in the stock market on October 13, 1989.

Brumbaugh says that some of the nation's biggest commercial banks are close to insolvent. This includes Chase Manhattan Bank, Chemical Bank, Manufacturers Hanover Trust Company, Citibank, Bank of America and Bankers Trust.

But the Federal Deposit Insurance Corporation (FDIC), which protects consumer deposits, has only $13 billion in its bank insurance fund, not nearly enough to pay for the potential losses. Therefore the taxpayer will again have to carry the load. And Brumbaugh says that the government is hiding this fact from the American people. "I believe we are in the midst of the largest government cover-up of a financial scandal ever in the country's history," Brumbaugh said on "Nightline" on July 31, 1990.

In addition to the S&Ls that have failed, about 200 commercial banks have failed each year for the last two years, the most bank failures since the Great Depression. Another 200 are expected to collapse in 1990.

But the figure could be higher. Brumbaugh said that 460 commercial banks have had losses every year since 1986 and that they "will exhaust their net worth on an accounting basis this year." But he said that few people are aware of the problem "because the accounting method we use in this country covers up true market insolvency when these institutions get to the end of their rope. That's exactly what happened with the savings and loan crisis. And its happening all over again with commercial banks."[1]

It's surprising that even that much is on the news. It's the tip of the iceberg of the scandalous manipulation of the economy and the money of this nation.

How big could a potential commercial bank bailout be? Perhaps the biggest bailout ever. Frank Anunzio, chairman of the House Banking Subcommittee, said on "Nightline," "The FDIC is not only in bad shape, it is in horrible shape. Without a massive transfusion of money, it will die very shortly and the taxpayers will have to pay for the funeral. And it will be the most expensive funeral in the history of any country of the world."[2]

CHAPTER 18

Capricorn Conjunctions in 1989, 1990, 1991 and 1994

The conjunction of February 22 and 23, 1988, is the first in a series of major groupings of planets in Capricorn that will unfold over the next several years. So our Capricorn initiations have only begun.

On December 27, 1989, the Sun, Moon, Mercury, Saturn, Uranus and Neptune were in Capricorn, with the Sun and Moon at 6° Capricorn making a close conjunction to Uranus at 5° Capricorn and a looser conjunction to Neptune at 11° Capricorn and Saturn at 15° Capricorn.

This conjunction had a profound effect on the Soviet Union. The Sun and the Moon were conjoined Uranus in the Soviet Union's tenth house (of the nation's leaders) and opposed the Soviet Union's Pluto at 5° Cancer conjoined transiting Jupiter in the Soviet Union's fourth house (of the people). Transiting Venus at 6° Aquarius and Mars at 6° Sagittarius were each quincunx the Jupiter-Pluto conjunction, forming a Finger of God, which was bisected by the Sun-Moon-Uranus conjunction (fig. 16).

The Finger of God put extraordinary pressure on the Soviet leadership. The Uranus-Pluto opposition,

Capricorn New Moon Forms a Bisected Finger of God in the Soviet Union's Birth Chart

December 27, 1989

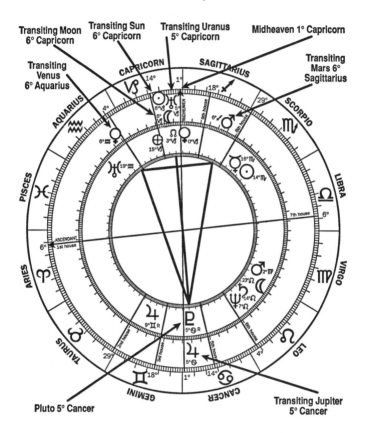

FIGURE 16 On December 27, 1989, the Sun and Moon at 6° Capricorn conjoined transiting Uranus at 5° Capricorn in the Soviet Union's tenth house (of the nation's leaders) and opposed the Soviet Pluto conjoined transiting Jupiter at 5° Cancer in the Soviet Union's fourth house (of the people). Transiting Venus at 6° Aquarius and Mars at 6° Sagittarius were quincunx the Jupiter-Pluto conjunction, forming a Finger of God. This put extreme pressure on Soviet leaders from unstable political and economic conditions.

the backbone of the configuration, was the driving force behind the upheaval that occurred in Romania, Bulgaria, Azerbaijan, East Germany, the Baltic Republics and the Ukraine in late 1989 and early 1990.

In late December 1990, there will be six planets* in Capricorn: the Sun, Mercury, Venus, Saturn, Uranus and Neptune. Even though these planets do not form a conjunction, they will tend to have a depressing effect on the government, the economy and the people. Economist Ravi Batra, in his book *The Great Depression of 1990*, uses well-established U.S. economic cycles to argue convincingly that we are due for a "great depression" beginning in 1990 that will last for seven years.[1]

On February 6, 1991, Saturn, the planet that rules Capricorn, will leave Capricorn and enter Aquarius. This will lighten the load somewhat, but with Uranus and Neptune remaining in Capricorn there will still be a major Capricorn challenge.

On January 11, 1994, seven planets—Mars, Venus, Neptune, the Moon, the Sun, Uranus and Mercury—will form a tight "megaconjunction" between 17° and 26° Capricorn (fig. 17). The unusually large number of planets in one sign and their proximity to each other gives this conjunction extraordinary power.

But what makes this conjunction even more intense than the ones I have already discussed is that at the same time, Saturn at 28° Aquarius will form a

*Astrologers acknowledge that the Sun and Moon are not planets, but they sometimes refer to them as such for convenience.

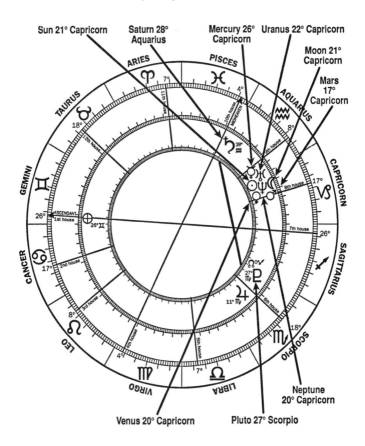

Megaconjunction of Seven Planets in Capricorn
January 11, 1994

FIGURE 17 On January 11, 1994, Mars, Venus, Neptune, the Moon, the Sun, Uranus and Mercury will form a tight "megaconjunction" between 17° and 26° Capricorn. A nearly exact square of Saturn (the ruler of Capricorn) at 28° Aquarius to Pluto at 27° Scorpio is likely to intensify the conjunction's negative potential. This conjunction could trigger economic and military challenges, the establishment of dictatorships, widespread plague and famine and danger from radioactivity, possibly from nuclear war.

tight square with Pluto at 27° Scorpio. This will increase the potential for the negative Capricorn characteristics to manifest. Under this conjunction we could experience extreme economic and military challenges.

In addition to heralding war and depression, this megaconjunction portends major earthquakes. Further, we are apt to see the dramatic loss of political liberty in the United States and throughout the world, the establishment of dictatorships, an increase in spy and secret police activity, widespread plague and famine, the rise and fall of nations and power blocs, and danger from radioactivity, possibly from nuclear war.

These negatives will not be the sudden result of this conjunction only. Should they appear, they will be the logical manifestation of influences that began on the portentous day of February 13, 1988.

The Correlation between the Sunspot Cycle and the Onset of Wars and Earthquakes

There are other indicators of war for the 1990s. First, there is a correlation between the sunspot cycle, which peaks about every 11 years, and the onset of wars. The term "sunspot cycle" refers to the cyclic increase and decrease in the number of sunspots on the surface of the sun. A cycle peaks about every 11 years. Biologist Marsha Adams, an expert on the relationship between sunspots and earthquakes, compared the outbreak of wars with sunspot cycles going back to the 1700s. She found that wars tend to occur about three years after the peak of a sunspot cycle, although they occasionally occur before.[2]

Adams also found that two years after a sunspot cycle peaks, very large-magnitude earthquakes (those eight and above on the Richter scale) occur for a two- to three-year period.

Scientists believe the current sunspot cycle peaked in July 1989. However, it will be at least another year before they are sure. It could begin to rise again and peak sometime in the future. This cycle rose faster than previous cycles and is one of the three largest on record.

The Cyclical Index

There are other astrological cycles that indicate a high probability of war in the late 1980s and early 1990s. French astrologers Henri-Joseph Gouchon and Claude Ganeau discovered three major cycles of peace and war based on the zodiacal proximity of the five outer planets, Jupiter through Pluto, to each other.

As astrologer Charles Harvey explains, Gouchon "found that by calculating the total angular separation between each of the pairs of the outer planets" (Jupiter-Saturn, Jupiter-Uranus, Jupiter-Neptune, Jupiter-Pluto, Saturn-Uranus, Saturn-Neptune, Saturn-Pluto, Neptune-Pluto) on an annual basis "and then plotting the results on a graph, the resulting curve showed a striking correspondence with the main periods of international crisis and, most impressively, major and sustained 'lows' for the period 1914–18 [coinciding with World War I] and 1940–45 [coinciding with World War II]."[3] Astrologer André Barbault called this the "Cyclical Index." The Korean War, the Suez Crisis and the Vietnam War also correlate with a negative slope on the graph.

Ganeau developed two cycles—the "Index of Cyclic Equilibrium" and the "Index of Cyclical Variation"—which are variations of the Cyclical Index. All three indexes have successfully predicted positive periods of harmony, growth, optimism and peace and negative periods of destabilization, disruption and decay. In the late 1980s and early 1990s these indexes are in the depths of their negative cycle, indicating the potential for conflict of the magnitude of past world wars.[4]

CHAPTER 19

The Great Neptunian Delusion

In the 1990s the United States will face major challenges from Neptune, the planet of illumination and illusion.

First of all, Neptune plays an important role in the United States conceptional solar return for 1990. A person's solar return tells him the karmic challenges he will face from this year's birthday to the next.

On July 4, 1990, Neptune at 13°11′ Capricorn was only eight minutes of arc removed from an exact opposition to the U.S. conceptional Sun at 13°19′ Cancer. This configuration in the U.S. conceptional solar return shows that the United States will have to come to grips with the negative side of Neptune—illusion and delusion—throughout the year ending July 3, 1991.

Neptune made an exact opposition to the U.S. conceptional Sun on February 5, 1990, and a second exact opposition on June 30. On December 10 it makes its last exact opposition to the U.S. conceptional Sun for about the next 164 years (fig. 18). But the Neptunian challenge will continue, remaining

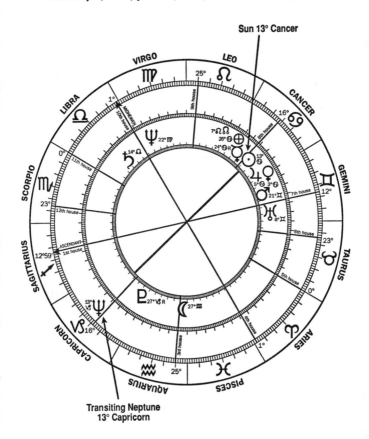

**Transiting Neptune Opposed
the United States Conceptional Sun**
February 5, 1990, June 30, 1990, and December 10, 1990

Sun 13° Cancer

Transiting Neptune
13° Capricorn

FIGURE 18 Transiting Neptune at 13° Capricorn made an exact opposition to the U.S. conceptional Sun at 13° Cancer on February 5, 1990, and a second exact opposition on June 30. On December 10 it makes its last exact opposition to the U.S. conceptional Sun for about the next 164 years. While under its influence, the United States will have to come to grips with the negative side of Neptune—illusion and delusion.

strong while transiting Neptune is in close opposition to the U.S. conceptional Sun through January 1993. The Neptunian influence will taper off and end about February 1994.

Let's look at the popular perception of things as they were on July 4, 1990. The nation was at peace, the Dow Jones industrial average was at an all-time high, and President Bush had a high approval rating, despite his proposal for a new tax.

Things were looking up. The Cold War had ended, which would enable us to cut back on military spending and put more effort into solving the problems of education, the environment and the homeless.

True, we had our problems. But maybe George Bush's one thousand points of light wasn't such a bad metaphor after all. We had our lives, families, careers, music, sports, causes and hobbies. The American Dream was alive and well and Americans felt good about themselves.

This euphoria stems from the influence of Neptune. Many Americans think they are living the Great American Dream. But in actuality they are lost in the Great Neptunian Delusion.

On the upside, an opposition of Neptune to the Sun can spark illumination, refinement and spirituality. On the downside, it can bring illusion, intrigue and unreality, resulting in an inability of the government or the people to recognize or respond to danger.

It is almost as if much of America is saying at

the subconscious level: "I'm tired of the search for reality. What I'm looking for is a good fantasy."

Neptune's transit in the earth sign Capricorn tends to ground or crystallize either illumination or illusion. My fervent desire and prayer is that it will crystallize Cosmic Christ illumination from the heart of the World Teachers.

And I think about it with every breath I breathe— how the awake people of America and the world are going to bring the great Christic illumination to this and every nation. I believe that if together we tap the illumination of the universal Mind of God, we *can* have a resurrection and a new birth on every continent. But the awake people have to want it. And we have to want it bad enough to make it happen.

What we have to do when faced with the portents of any aspect in our personal chart or the charts of our family, friends, business or nation is to call upon the Lord for the precipitation of the positive qualities that can be expressed under that aspect and for the mitigation and transmutation of their antithesis. And then do our part in daily determined effort.

Many people today indulge in illusion. This indulgence is a deadly form of psychological denial. Denial of what? Denial of their accountability in the returning cycles of personal and planetary karma. In some people, the denial takes the form of unconscious anger. In others, it takes the form of escape into the euphoria of drugs or alcohol or sugar or anything else people take to numb themselves to the inner voice of God. All this against a background of endless rock music that drowns out the music of the spheres.

Transcendence or Disintegration

The transit of Neptune opposed to the U.S. conceptional Sun also indicates the potential for the nation to weaken at the center and disintegrate at the periphery.

I sometimes see before me scenes of a city that represents the United States. It is a beautiful, peaceful city of ultramodern buildings, neatly manicured parks and broad avenues with suburbs of middle- and upper-class neighborhoods as far as the eye can see. The people are well-fed, smartly dressed and self-satisfied, with solutions for every problem. It's almost too perfect, like the last days of Atlantis.

Then I look under the street and sidewalks and I see that everything is in a state of decay.

The message is unmistakable: the foundations of Western civilization are rotting from beneath, and the surface dwellers are unaware of it.

When something rots from underneath— whether termites are eating away at it or the cement is crumbling or the earth itself is eroding—the collapse is sudden. And when it comes, you go through the floor, boom!

Under the influence of the Neptune-Sun opposition, the United States should be going through a process of spiritual transcendence. If we do not elect to take this path, the negative elements of Neptune will fill our spiritual vacuum and take over to diffuse and dissipate the areas of life represented by the Sun: our national identity, the office of the president and our vital energies. This somewhat unconscious loss of our life-force will leave us vulnerable to external forces.

Without a true, liberated spirituality, the nation cannot help but be in psychological bondage and could find itself, as a result, in physical bondage. The enemy within works against us through our psychological problems and the enemy without works through the stimuli that we use to dull our senses to those very problems.

So we must be alert. We must know our true selves and the enemy within and without.

Environmental Problems

Under the influence of Neptune, the United States could see an intensification of problems related to chemical and petroleum products—from oil spills to difficulties with chemical or toxic wastes—and the danger of chemical and biological warfare. These portents began to take concrete form after Iraq's invasion of Kuwait.

Environmental problems can be expected to grow more acute while the nation's ability to define the problems and formulate plans of attack to solve them may suffer from Neptunian confusion and illusion. These characteristics of Neptune are also negative traits of the sign of Cancer. And since the U.S. conceptional Sun is in Cancer, we are more vulnerable to the negative side of Cancer.

Drugs and the Economy

Neptune is associated with all methods of avoiding or escaping reality. The ultimate, of course, being drugs. The nation can anticipate continued difficulty in coming to grips with the drug epidemic and may even move closer to legalizing some illicit drugs.

Another way to avoid reality is simply to ignore problems. Over the past two years, Americans have done their best to avoid dealing with the grave problems in our economy, from the S&L bailout to the crash of the junk-bond market to a collapsing real-estate market.

We know these problems, and more, are there. But we refuse to look at them—until one fine day the termites eat through to the surface, the beams give way, the cement and the earth collapse, and we fall through the floor, boom!

Other Neptunian Portents

While transiting Neptune at 13° Capricorn is opposed to the U.S. conceptional Sun, it is also square to the U.S. conceptional Saturn at 14° Libra, forming a T-square. Transiting Neptune also makes a square to the U.S. natal Mars at 13° Aries. Together, these four planets form a combination T-square/grand square (fig. 19).

The Sun deals with vitality, Mars with action, Neptune with delusion and Saturn with depression. Their combined influence could leave many people in a daze akin to sleepwalking.

Transiting Neptune Forms a T-Square/Grand Square in the United States Charts

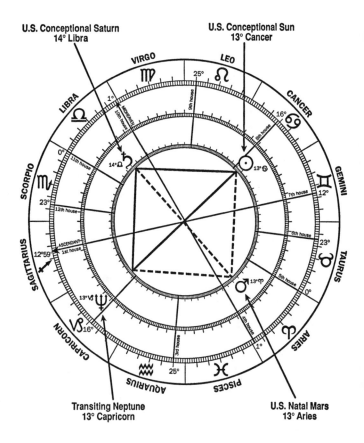

FIGURE 19   While transiting Neptune at 13° Capricorn is opposed to the U.S. conceptional Sun, it is also square to the U.S. conceptional Saturn at 14° Libra, forming a T-square. Transiting Neptune also makes a square to the U.S. natal Mars at 13° Aries. Together, these four planets form a combination T-square/grand square. This configuration shows, among other things, danger from espionage and indirect methods of warfare.

Saturn and Mars tend to intensify and crystallize Neptune's delusions. This configuration shows, in addition to the Neptunian delusions I have discussed, danger from espionage and indirect methods of warfare. It also shows the possibility of confused, escapist and self-defeating behavior by the president, the Congress and the Supreme Court.

In the U.S. conceptional solar return for 1990, transiting Neptune forms a quincunx to transiting Venus at 12° Gemini. This aspect can trigger the following: the unseen depletion or disintegration of financial resources; an acceleration of personal and corporate bankruptcies; illusion and deception related to the stock market; loss through drugs and alcohol; epidemics, possibly related to sexually transmitted disease; scandal; and loss through confused diplomacy and the treachery of one's enemies.

Neptune in Capricorn can sustain the illusion that the status quo is going to be maintained. But the nation has gotten, and will continue to get, wake-up calls from Uranus, the planet of abrupt and unexpected change.

CHAPTER 20

Uranus—the Great Awakener

We have been roused from our national slumber by the Great Awakener—the planet Uranus. Uranus conveys the impulse to freedom and governs representative political bodies; social organization and the relationship between groups in society; scientific invention, computers and high technology; the wise or unwise use of nuclear energy; and explosions.

In the political sphere, Uranus rules revolution and ideologies that promote either freedom or repression, strikes and political agitation. But first and foremost, Uranus rules change—sudden, unpredictable and explosive change.

There is an old adage in astrology: Jupiter makes the law, Saturn preserves the law, and Uranus breaks the law. Ideally, we would like Uranus to assist us in breaking the law of our karma, thereby opening the way for divine mercy, mitigation and the true rapprochement of our souls with Jesus Christ.

If the configuration portends karmic reckoning, repentance is the first order of business. We must call on the law of forgiveness, imploring the mercy of God for our disobedience to his laws. And since the Holy Spirit has given us the violet flame for the alchemy of the New Age, we can and ought to apply our violet flame decrees to transmute our misqualifications of God's energy. This will insure that all changes descending upon us through Uranus will have a positive resolution, according to God's will.

In order to get on the right side of Uranus, we must forsake all our negative vibrations. For under the Uranus placements I am about to discuss, the minus factors of our karma will surely boomerang as the negative elements of Uranus—the elements of anti-freedom in self and society.

As I said in chapter 19, every planet and configuration has a positive and a negative side. When faced with a challenge from a particular planet, we can choose to take the high road or the low road. Free will is the x factor in every chart.

If we are going to benefit from the positive energy of Uranus, we must have already embraced the will of God as *the* guiding star of our lives and come to the conclusion that, no matter what it takes, we desire to right all past wrongs and pursue change for the better.

Each one of us can achieve this change as we align ourselves with our Inner Teacher (our Holy Christ Self), pursue our personal walk with God, and know Jesus Christ as our Lord and Saviour. Accepting his grace and his salvation, we must nonetheless be willing to take responsibility for our karma and come to grips with it by practical and spiritual means.

If people are not ready and willing to change their ways, if they are relentless in violating the laws of God instead of preparing to meet their God, then the impact of Uranus will be the triggering of a karma, long held in abeyance by Opportunity's hand, whose time has come. For the day of the Lord's justice "cometh as a thief in the night," as Paul said.[1] Of this spiritual cataclysm Peter also wrote:

> But the day of the Lord will come as a thief in the night; in the which the heavens shall pass away with a great noise, and the elements shall melt with fervent heat, the earth also and the works that are therein shall be burned up.
>
> Seeing then that all these things shall be dissolved, what manner of persons ought ye to be in all holy conversation and godliness, looking for and hasting unto the coming of the day of God, wherein the heavens being on fire shall be dissolved, and the elements shall melt with fervent heat?
>
> Nevertheless we, according to his promise, look for new heavens and a new earth, wherein dwelleth righteousness.
>
> Wherefore, beloved, seeing that ye look for such things, be diligent that ye may be found of him in peace, without spot, and blameless.[2]

Yes, Uranus is the thief that comes in the night to strip from us all ill-gotten gains, to leave us naked before our God. And if we do nothing to get ready for his appointed round, we will awaken to a world without options—only karmic toil by the sweat of the brow.

Uranus will have a different effect on each of us, depending on how it aspects our birth chart and whether we have made our peace with God and man. How we experience Uranus will also depend on whether we have the will to embrace our karma, the courage to see it through and the bulldog tenacity to come out on the other side with balanced accounts.

The day of the reckoning of our karmic accounts is at hand. And we have to wake up to the fact that the universe isn't going to carry our accounts for us! Unfortunate indeed are those who expect it to. It is our cumulative momentum of nonaccountability that makes the signs of this astrology so serious, demanding our attention. And if we don't give these signs our attention today, they will command it tomorrow.

Uranus can bring change for the better just as easily as it can bring change for the worse. The upcoming Uranus configurations could turn you around, get you out of your slump and put you back on the track before you knew what happened.

"There is a tide in the affairs of men, which, taken at the flood, leads on to fortune."[3] In this case, if you want to take the tide in your astrological affairs at its flood, you shouldn't waste a minute in getting on the right side of every planetary configuration in your chart.

Uranus often triggers a situation that can liberate a person or a nation from a limiting condition in a swift and unsettling manner, such as an accident or disaster, the loss of a job, a divorce, a strike or a revolution.

We can see in Uranus the hand of the Guru or the heart of the Cosmic Christ that strips from us, even in a painful way, those things that could kill the body or destroy the soul in hell.[4] Like surgery for cancer— the sacrifice of an organ so that the body itself will survive—or the dissolution of a dangerous alliance.

Such swift, sudden changes of Uranus bespeak the intercession of a power greater than our own, without which we may not experience the resolution of our souls with God.

There is almost always a freedom-producing silver lining associated with Uranus-triggered events—if you look for it, if you humbly assimilate the lesson and go on. One thing is certain about Uranus: it will never fail to get your attention.

Uranus Opposed the U.S. Conceptional Jupiter Brings Dramatic Reversals

In the 1990s, Uranus will dramatically affect the United States in both foreign and domestic matters.

On January 3, 1990, Uranus at 5° Capricorn made an exact opposition to the U.S. conceptional Jupiter at 5° Cancer (fig. 20). It made two more exact oppositions to Jupiter in 1990, one on August 16

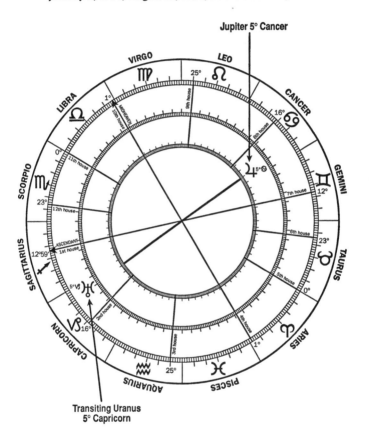

**Transiting Uranus Opposed
the United States Conceptional Jupiter
January 3, 1990, August 16, 1990, and October 12, 1990**

Jupiter 5° Cancer

Transiting Uranus
5° Capricorn

FIGURE 20   On January 3, 1990, transiting Uranus at 5° Capricorn made an exact opposition to the U.S. conceptional Jupiter at 5° Cancer. It made two more exact oppositions to Jupiter in 1990, one on August 16 and the other on October 12. Uranus will not return to that position in the zodiac for another 84 years. Since Jupiter is one of several planets that governs business activity and prosperity in the United States charts, this opposition will shake up the U.S. economy.

and the other on October 12. Uranus will not return to that position in the zodiac for another 84 years.

Jupiter is one of several planets that governs business activity and prosperity in the United States. Thus, the oppositions of Uranus to Jupiter could lead to sudden, dramatic economic reversals and events related to finance, productivity and debt liquidation. Large financial institutions (such as savings and loans), international banks, insurance companies and very wealthy individuals will be most affected. This opposition could lead to the loss of status and wealth for the rich and famous. No doubt the American people will be alarmed by the economic events triggered by Uranus.

Jupiter rules both trust and hypocrisy. As Uranus makes its oppositions to Jupiter, people may become disillusioned with the power elite for their financial and political machinations of the past decade and century. Many may feel betrayed and lose trust in large public or private financial institutions. Since confidence is the glue that holds our economy together, a loss of trust could spark economic turmoil, with revolutionary or pre-revolutionary consequences.

Uranus made its last opposition to the U.S. conceptional Jupiter on October 12, 1990. The rule of thumb for transits is that the last of a series of aspects is the most powerful. I have been anticipating economic disruptions for the fall of 1990 and following. The cumulative weight of increasingly bad economic news is already having political and social consequences. As the S&L scandal unfolded in the summer of 1990, Americans became more and more distrustful of the nation's bankers and Congress, who failed to safeguard their assets.

Jupiter also rules law. It governs the process whereby broad legal principles are derived from philosophical ideas. In mundane astrology, Jupiter governs the nation's courts, especially the Supreme Court. Adding Uranus' element of change, the Uranus-Jupiter oppositions tell us that the Supreme Court could be changed in some way or could issue rulings that radically alter the course of American society.

Just three weeks from an exact Uranus-Jupiter opposition, the Supreme Court went through the first of perhaps a number of changes when Justice William J. Brennan, Jr., resigned on July 20, 1990. Brennan was the most persuasive advocate of the liberal point of view and it is widely expected that Supreme Court rulings will shift to the Right, particularly on key issues such as abortion.

Since transiting Uranus is opposed the U.S. conceptional seventh house, which rules foreign relations, we can also expect surprising and probably divisive developments in relations with our traditional allies. We can expect unforeseen difficulties with past treaties and sudden reversals in relations with friends and enemies alike.

Uranus Shakes Up the U.S. Government

Transiting Uranus will make three oppositions to the U.S. conceptional Sun in 1991, on March 15, May 23 and December 25 (fig. 21). Having shaken the

Transiting Uranus Opposed
the United States Conceptional Sun
March 15, 1991, May 23, 1991, and December 25, 1991

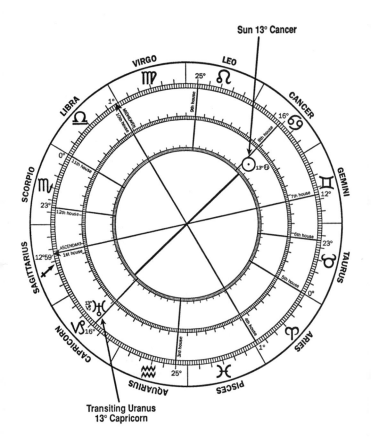

FIGURE 21 Transiting Uranus will make three oppositions to the U.S. conceptional Sun in 1991, on March 15, May 23 and December 25. Uranus will bring its revolutionary impulse into direct polarity with the federal government and the president (represented by the Sun).

economy and social and financial institutions, Uranus will bring its revolutionary impulse into direct polarity with the federal government and the president.

Uranus challenges the status quo. Unpredictable political, economic and social events, as well as an increase in the number of sudden disasters, will start to break the Neptunian bubble of illusion on an individual and national basis. What was once a pre-revolutionary situation could mature into a state of revolution.

It is hard to imagine a state of revolution in this country, but it wouldn't take much to ignite it—just economic chaos. When people do not have enough to eat and their financial security is wiped out, society is ripe for anarchy and revolution.

Violent revolution under these Uranus configurations is not inevitable. Revolution, should it come, could take the form of a dramatic but peaceful transformation of society such as occurred during the New Deal in the 1930s.

We pray God that violent revolution will not happen, and we will be praying throughout the 1990s. I am bringing you the portents of this cycle of the ride of the Four Horsemen of the Apocalypse so you can comprehend the serious nature of the karmic challenges we face, pray for their mitigation, and adopt measures at the national and international level that may, by God's grace, forestall them entirely.

Whether or not there is widespread violence, we can expect strikes and sudden political and social realignments. There could be political fragmentation and social upheaval.

In addition to ruling sudden changes Uranus rules attractions and repulsions as well as charisma or the lack of it. As Uranus opposes the U.S. conceptional Sun (which represents the president), the chief executive's charisma could suddenly rise or fall. The president could find himself either suddenly attractive to more and more voters or suddenly rejected by them.

Thus, the transit of Uranus in 1991 will be a great turning point for the president. In extreme circumstances, he could be either driven from office or ride the Uranus transit to great popularity.

Uranus-Neptune Conjunction: Progress or Revolution

Transiting Uranus follows directly in transiting Neptune's track. As I have explained, Uranus can awaken and thereby liberate people from their Neptunian delusions. Uranus and Neptune will form exact conjunctions three times in 1993: February 2 (at 19° Capricorn) and August 19 and October 24 (both at 18° Capricorn).

Uranus-Neptune conjunctions are generally considered to be beneficial; they coincide with periods of scientific and spiritual progress. But Uranus-Neptune conjunctions can also intensify illusion and social unrest, particularly as they aspect the U.S. charts. The two planets can amplify each other's negative influences.

Since Uranus rules revolution, eccentric

behavior and unreasonable demands for freedom, and Neptune rules intrigue, deception and mass movements, we could see unstable, treacherous and potentially violent mass movements transform our political system and nation. We could also see monumental foul-ups in complex technical systems such as the telecommunications network, an increased number of air and sea disasters, and major earthquakes.

Uranus in President Bush's Chart

As I prepare this book to go to press, world events have taken a sudden turn for the worse with Iraq's invasion of Kuwait. In a lecture I delivered on July 7, 1990, I gave the following portents:

President Bush's natal Uranus is at 21° Pisces. It is located in his seventh house, which is the house of treaties, foreign nations and war. It makes an exact square to his natal Sun and the U.S. conceptional Mars at 21° Gemini (fig. 22).

As you know, Mars is the planet that in its negative aspect represents war; Uranus is the planet of sudden and explosive events. The close square between the president's natal Uranus and the nation's conceptional Mars creates a dangerous and unstable situation.

During Bush's term in office, there is the potential for unexpected wars and battles. The portent for war is especially strong since the U.S. conceptional Mars falls in the seventh house of warfare.

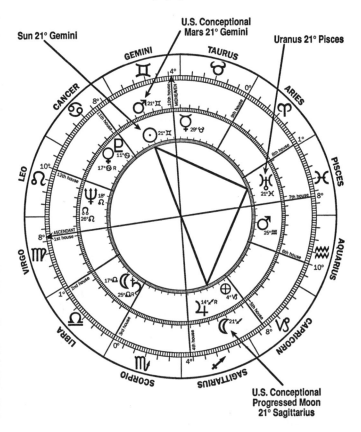

**U.S. Progressed Conceptional Moon
Forms a T-Square in George Bush's Birth Chart
July 4, 1990**

Sun 21° Gemini

U.S. Conceptional
Mars 21° Gemini

Uranus 21° Pisces

U.S. Conceptional
Progressed Moon
21° Sagittarius

FIGURE 22 President Bush's natal Uranus is at 21° Pisces in his seventh house (treaties, foreign nations and war). It makes an exact square to his natal Sun and the U.S. conceptional Mars at 21° Gemini. On July 4, 1990, the U.S. conceptional progressed Moon at 21° Sagittarius turned the square of Bush's natal Sun and Uranus and the U.S. conceptional Mars into a T-square. This shows the potential for unexpected wars and battles during Bush's term in office.

This square between Bush's Uranus and the U.S. conceptional Mars is now being activated by the U.S. conceptional progressed Moon for July 4, 1990, at 21° Sagittarius, which forms a T-square with Bush's natal Sun and Uranus and the U.S. conceptional Mars.

This configuration could coincide with the sudden use of U.S. military force—perhaps a series of battles or confrontations. It could also inaugurate a cycle of events leading to major military conflict. It could even spark conflict between the president and the electorate.

This T-square will be at its most powerful for about three months on either side of July 4, 1990.

On August 2, 1990, Iraq invaded Kuwait. And the rest will be history.

Transiting Uranus Ignites Power Struggles in the U.S. Government

In 1991, transiting Uranus will form a T-square in the U.S. conceptional chart. It will be exact on March 15, May 23 and December 25. Transiting Uranus at 13° Capricorn will oppose the U.S. conceptional Sun at 13° Cancer and square the U.S. conceptional Saturn at 14° Libra (fig. 23).

This T-square shows that there is likely to be a history-making power struggle between the president and Congress. The Constitution could be amended

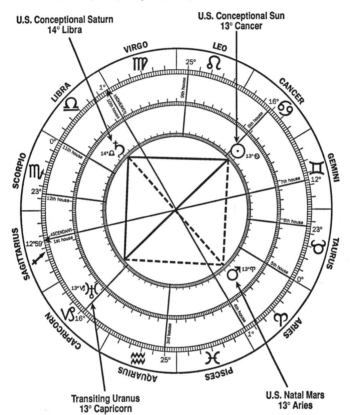

FIGURE 23 In 1991, transiting Uranus will form a T-square in the U.S. conceptional chart. It will be exact on March 15, May 23 and December 25. Transiting Uranus at 13° Capricorn will oppose the U.S. conceptional Sun at 13° Cancer and square the U.S. conceptional Saturn at 14° Libra. The T-square shows that the structure of checks and balances in the U.S. government could be changed. The U.S. natal Mars at 13° Aries turns this T-square into a grand square, increasing the possibility that change in the United States during 1991 could be violent.

or reformed and the distribution of power between the branches of government and between the government and the people will most likely be altered.

Let's examine the dynamics of this configuration to see why it could create such a crisis.

In mundane astrology, the Sun represents the president and Uranus represents the Congress. In the U.S. conceptional chart, Uranus is in Capricorn and the Sun is in Cancer, two signs related to the acquisition and use of political power. This opposition could show harmony and cooperation between the president and Congress. But that would require an adroitness that neither branch of the government has shown for as long as anyone can remember. Therefore, the opposition tends to indicate a power struggle.

Since transiting Uranus is in the U.S. conceptional first house of self-expression, which has an Aries substructure, Congress may want to assume some of the powers of the president, or at least take a stronger leadership role.

The powers and the responsibilities of the three branches of the federal government are spelled out in the Constitution. As I noted in chapter 12, the formation of a political document with the characteristics of the Constitution was prefigured in the U.S. conceptional chart by a trine between Saturn at 14° Libra and Uranus at 8° Gemini.

Saturn in Libra in the tenth house describes a constitutional form of government with checks and balances such as a separation of powers. Since Saturn is trine Uranus, it shows that the system can produce political freedom and innovation.

In the T-square we are discussing, transiting Uranus is square the U.S. conceptional Saturn in Libra and opposed the U.S. conceptional Sun. Uranus' revolutionary influence shows the possibility that the system of checks and balances established by the Constitution could be fundamentally changed while Congress is engaged in a power struggle with the president.

But the U.S. natal Mars at 13° Aries adds another dimension to this T-square. It turns it into a grand square (fig. 23, p. 242). The T-square/grand-square combination increases the possibility that change in the United States during 1991 could be violent.

Since Mars represents aggression, we can anticipate physical danger to the president and members of Congress, violent strikes and political action, an increase in the number of disasters and catastrophes of national significance (including the likelihood of a nuclear disaster), the disruption of our alliances and the threat of war.

Eclipse of the Sun Conjoined Uranus and Neptune Portends Reform or Anarchy

The process of Uranus-driven change will come to a head in 1992. On January 4, 1992, there will be an eclipse of the Sun at 13°51' Capricorn, almost exactly conjoined transiting Uranus at 13°55' Capricorn. Transiting Neptune will be nearby at 16° Capricorn (fig. 24). This eclipse will explosively

Eclipse of the Sun, Transiting Uranus and Neptune Form a T-Square in the United States Charts
January 4, 1992

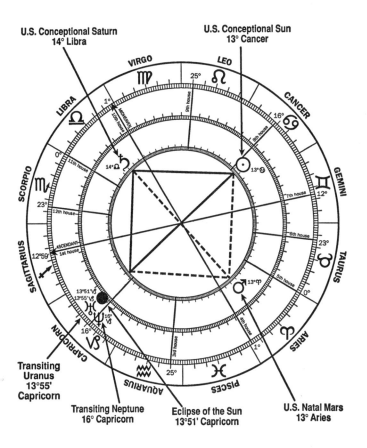

U.S. Conceptional Saturn 14° Libra

U.S. Conceptional Sun 13° Cancer

Transiting Uranus 13°55′ Capricorn

Transiting Neptune 16° Capricorn

Eclipse of the Sun 13°51′ Capricorn

U.S. Natal Mars 13° Aries

FIGURE 24 On January 4, 1992, there will be an eclipse of the Sun at 13°51′ Capricorn, almost exactly conjoined transiting Uranus at 13°55′ Capricorn. Transiting Neptune will be nearby at 16° Capricorn. This eclipse will explosively amplify the power of the Sun-Saturn-Uranus-Mars T-square/grand square.

amplify the power of the T-square/grand square we have been discussing.

This will be a moment of truth or consequences for the United States, the president, the Congress and our form of government. We could experience a period of reform that gives us greater freedom. Or we could witness a breakdown of the social order, the loss of political freedom, anarchy or chaos. The effect of the eclipse will last for about six months, but events stemming from the eclipse will have long-term consequences for America.

CHAPTER 21

The Power Elite and
Their Hidden Agenda

The Federal Reserve System is a unique fixture in the United States government. With no Congressional supervision, the Fed can, through its power to set interest rates and expand or contract the supply of money and credit, unilaterally create economic policy. Responsible only to itself, the Fed is omnipotent.

The U.S. conceptional Pluto at 27° Capricorn in the second house of money and finance (fig. 25) shows the probability of a powerful banking elite dominating the nation's finances and thereby the government. This is exactly what has happened.

The plan for the Federal Reserve System was worked out in November 1910 at a secret meeting of bankers held at J. P. Morgan's estate on Jekyll Island, Georgia. Their plan became law when Congress passed the Federal Reserve Act on December 23, 1913.

Thus, on behalf of the banking and business community, Congress turned over to a private corporation the nontransferable money powers granted to it in Article I, Section 8, of the Constitution:

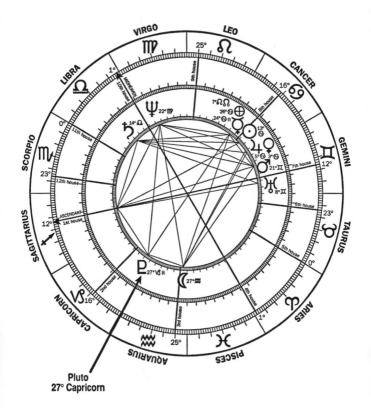

Pluto in the Second House
of the United States Conceptional Chart

Pluto
27° Capricorn

FIGURE 25 Pluto (secrecy, power from wealth) is at 27° Capricorn (political power) in the United States conceptional chart in the second house (of money and banking). This is the principal indicator for domination of the economy by a powerful banking elite. On December 23, 1913, Congress created the Federal Reserve System and gave it the money powers granted to Congress by the Constitution. The Fed now unilaterally creates economic policy on behalf of big business and the banking establishment.

"The Congress shall have Power To . . . coin Money, regulate the Value thereof, and of foreign Coin, and fix the Standard of Weights and Measures."

The Federal Reserve System, under the guise of acting in the public interest, institutionalized the bankers' control of America's finances. The framework was in place for an unscrupulous power elite to influence virtually every aspect of life in America.

How does the Federal Reserve System work? It consists of 12 regional banks supervised by a seven-man Board of Governors, who are appointed to 14-year terms by the president and confirmed by the Senate.

The Fed has several ways to manipulate the economy. But the tool that it uses most is its unlimited ability to buy and sell securities, mostly U.S. government securities such as Treasury bills, through the Federal Open Market Committee. These purchases and sales influence interest rates and the quantity of money in circulation, hence the rate of inflation or deflation and the general state of the economy.

Congress has no authority to oversee Fed policy. According to Joe Cobb, Republican staff director of the Joint Economic Committee of Congress, "The only opportunity for oversight is during the confirmation hearings for the Board of Governors members,"[1] and that is tantamount to no oversight at all.

Legislation passed in 1979 requires the Fed's chairman to report to Congress twice a year. But the chairman can tell Congress as much or as little as he wants and, says Cobb, his report is "very, very opaque."

According to Cobb, this situation is not likely to change soon. "Most people in Congress don't understand the Fed," he says. "They know that monetary policy is important and can cause recessions or recoveries, but they don't know why or how. The Fed is able to insulate itself from any real oversight by maintaining this cult of mystery so that members of Congress are afraid to take it on."

The public accepts the Fed's supposed right to manipulate the economy because, like Congress, they do not understand monetary policy or its consequences. "They just know that it's terribly dangerous, terribly important and terribly technical," says Cobb. And so, they defer to the experts.

The Power Elite

Just who are the power elite, anyway?

By definition, a nation's leadership is an elite. It is when this elite becomes self-serving that problems arise. A *power* elite is one that dominates a nation's political and economic systems for personal gain.

Prior to and during the Revolutionary War (1776–83), the American elite was composed largely of civic-minded individuals. Sociologist C. Wright Mills, in his influential study of the American ruling class, *The Power Elite*, writes that from the years spanning the Revolution through the beginning of the nineteenth century, America's elite were "political men of education and of administrative experience, and, as Lord Bryce noted, possess[ed] a certain 'largeness of view and dignity of character.'"[2]

Mills writes that during the next period of time, roughly from Jefferson to Lincoln (1801–65), "no set of men controlled centralized means of power; no small clique dominated economic, much less political affairs. . . . For this was the period. . . when the elite was at most a loose coalition."[3]

Nevertheless, a power elite had some control over the government even prior to the Civil War. In 1933 President Franklin Roosevelt, a bona fide member of the Establishment, wrote to Col. Edward House (a Kissinger-like figure), "The real truth of the matter is, as you and I know, that a financial element in the larger centers has owned the Government ever since the days of Andrew Jackson [who was president from 1829 to 1837]."[4]

Few people remember that one of the primary battles President Abraham Lincoln fought during the Civil War was with Northern bankers and businessmen who tried to use the war to get control of the nation's financial system.

Lincoln's assassination in 1865 set the stage for the power elite to use the government to increase their wealth and power. According to Mills, "the supremacy of corporate economic power began, in a formal way, with the Congressional elections of 1866."[5]

It is hard to imagine just how unethical this new elite was. Mills, summarizing the words of several of their most severe critics, writes:

> The robber barons, as the tycoons of the post-Civil War era came to be called, descended upon the investing public much as a

swarm of women might descend into a bargain basement on Saturday morning. They exploited national resources, waged economic wars among themselves, entered into combinations, made private capital out of the public domain, and used any and every method to achieve their ends. They made agreements with railroads for rebates; they purchased newspapers and bought editors; they killed off competing and independent businesses, and employed lawyers of skill and statesmen of repute to sustain their rights and secure their privileges. There *is* something demonic about these lords of creation; it is not merely rhetoric to call them robber barons. Perhaps there is no straightforward economic way to accumulate $100 million for private use; although, of course, along the way the unstraightforward ways can be delegated and the appropriator's hands kept clean. If all the big money is not easy money, all the easy money that is safe is big. It is better, so the image runs, to take one dime from each of ten million people at the point of a corporation than $100,000 from each of ten banks at the point of a gun. It is also safer.[6]

The financial moguls of the late nineteenth and early twentieth centuries recognized that if they were to gain great wealth, they must control the nation's political system in order to neutralize or circumvent the constitutional and legal barriers to their activities.

There emerged a set of unspoken rules by which they operated that were, oddly enough, written down in 1906 by financier Frederick Clemson Howe in his book entitled *Confessions of a Monopolist:*

> These are the rules of big business. They have superseded the teachings of our parents and are reducible to a simple maxim: Get a monopoly; let Society work for you: and remember that the best of all business is politics, for a legislative grant, franchise, subsidy or tax exemption is worth more than a Kimberley or Comstock lode [these were fabulously rich diamond and silver lodes, respectively] since it does not require any labor, either mental or physical, for its exploitation. . . .
>
> Mr. Rockefeller may think he made his hundreds of millions by economy, by saving on his gas bills, but he didn't. He managed to get the people of the globe to work for him.[7]

Professor Antony C. Sutton comments on the modus operandi of the power elite in his book *Wall Street and FDR:*

> Old John D. Rockefeller and his 19th century fellow-capitalists were convinced of one absolute truth: that no great monetary wealth could be accumulated under the impartial rules of a competitive laissez-faire society,

[that] the only sure road to the acquisition of massive wealth was monopoly: drive out your competitors, reduce competition, eliminate laissez-faire, and above all get state protection for your industry through compliant politicians and government regulation. This last avenue yields a legal monopoly, and a legal monopoly always leads to wealth.

This robber baron schema is also, under different labels, the socialist plan. The difference between a corporate state monopoly and a socialist state monopoly is essentially only the identity of the group controlling the power structure. [8]

Howe recognized that there was a profound difference between free-market capitalism and the capitalism he and his fellow capitalists practiced. He wrote:

This is the story of something for nothing—of making the other fellow pay. This making the other fellow pay, of getting something for nothing, explains the lust for franchises, mining rights, tariff privileges, railway control, tax evasions. All these things mean monopoly, and all monopoly is bottomed on legislation....

...Monopoly and corruption are cause and effect. Together, they work in Congress, in our Commonwealths, in our municipalities. It is always so. It always has been so. Privilege gives birth to corruption, just as the poisonous sewer breeds disease. Equal chance, a fair field and no favors, the "square deal" are never corrupt. They do not appear in legislative halls nor in Council Chambers. For these things mean labor for labor, value for value, something for something. This is why the little business man, the retail and wholesale dealer, the jobber, and the manufacturer are not the business men whose business corrupts politics.[9]

The Federal Reserve Act Compromises the Plan of the Founding Fathers

By the end of the nineteenth century, the power elite were in control of many aspects of American finance. They were now ready for the ultimate move: control of the money supply. Why was this so important? Sutton explains in *Wall Street and FDR:*

In modern America the most significant illustration of society as a whole working for the few is the 1913 Federal Reserve Act. The Federal Reserve System is, in effect, a private banking monopoly, not answerable to Congress or the public, but with legal monopoly control over money supply without let or hindrance or even audit by the General Accounting Office. It was irresponsible manipulation of money supply by this Federal Reserve System that brought about the inflation of the 1920s, the 1929 Depression, and so the presumed requirement for a Roosevelt New Deal.[10]

As I said earlier, the Fed was based on a secret plan formulated by the banking elite at Jekyll Island, Georgia, in November 1910. In his book *The War on Gold*, Sutton describes the seminal meeting:

> Senator Nelson Aldrich, bankers Frank Vanderlip (president of National City Bank and representing Rockefeller and Kuhn Loeb interests), Henry P. Davison (senior partner of J. P. Morgan), and Charles D. Norton (president of Morgan's First National Bank), met in secret to decide how to foist a central bank system on the United States. Others at the meeting were Paul Moritz Warburg, the German banker, and Benjamin Strong (a Morgan banker who later became first Governor of the Federal Reserve Bank of New York).
>
> Out of the Jekyll Island cabal came the basic bill passed by Congress and signed into law by President Woodrow Wilson as the Federal Reserve Act of 1913. Under the earlier sub-Treasury system, bankers had no control over the money supply in the United States and, even less to their liking, none over currency issues.[11]

Thus, from these masterminds meeting behind closed doors we have inherited the central banking system.

Jekyll Island participant Frank Vanderlip, in his autobiography, *From Farmboy to Financier*, had no compunctions about revealing the purpose of the Jekyll Island meeting. He wrote:

> Our secret expedition to Jekyll Island was the occasion of the actual conception of what eventually became the Federal Reserve System. The essential points of the Aldrich Plan [Senator Aldrich's proposed legislation for a central banking system] were all contained in the Federal Reserve Act as it was passed. [12]

The power elite came to dominate both the Republican and Democratic parties. They elected and defeated presidents, especially in the post–Civil War days, and simply bought senators and judges. They gained control of the media and set the national agenda and the tone of the debate on the issues.

But ultimately, it was the American people who were at fault. They allowed these men to control them instead of electing those who would follow the principles of the Founding Fathers.

America, if we allow the power brokers to decide the life or death of our nation, it may be suicide by proxy, but it will still be suicide. If the United States of America is destroyed by others because we do nothing, it will be just the same as if we destroyed it ourselves. If we want to fulfill our destiny, it's time we realize who the real culprits are and stop allowing them to manipulate the people of planet earth!

The transfer of Congress' nontransferable money powers through the Federal Reserve Act was the compromise of a nation sponsored by Saint Germain. The Founding Fathers placed the power over money in the hands of the people because they wanted to ensure economic freedom. But the power elite effectively circumvented their careful measures, aborting the dream of Saint Germain.

Looking back to the birth of this nation, we see the light of Aquarius becoming America through the Master-disciple relationship. We see the Master choosing the Founding Fathers and calling them to be his initiates. We see the movement of people from the 13 colonies across a continent. We see coming to life the green shoot of a new hope for millennia of freedom by the power and presence of Saint Germain.

Yet in the shadows, not perceived, there are lurking those who have not that original light, have no heart tie to Saint Germain and are not sponsored by him, for they do not bear the kindling light of freedom. These are the power elite, who reincarnate across the centuries in every nation. They are not of any particular race or creed and have no national loyalties. Money is their god and they are the betrayers of the people. You will recognize them when you see them, for Jesus gave us the key: "By their fruits ye shall know them."[13]

No matter whom they pay lip service to, they affirm, "We are the law, we bow to no other." Such as these have no direct access to the Light of the I AM THAT I AM, for they long ago extinguished the divine spark in their absolute rebellion against

Almighty God and the Christ flame he placed in the hearts of his offspring.

They see the people of Light coming from all over the world impelled by the Spirit of Freedom. They see them bearing the flame of the I AM Presence to America's shores to fulfill a grand experiment in freedom. They see them becoming a part of the great tapestry of America, stitch by stitch, life by life, hard won.

They watch and wait and they move in—to control, to subjugate, to elevate themselves once again. They assume the posture of a royal dynasty, not as *noblesse oblige* but as *mon droit*, my right—an elitist corps. They think they are a privileged class. They think they own the so-called common people.

They have come to enslave their souls, knowing that it is the light of the people that produces and multiplies the wealth and the health of the economy. They have come to live off of that light and to make all Americans pawns in their monopoly games. Their hidden agenda is world control by the supreme power that money confers upon them.

CHAPTER 22

"How Are the Mighty Fallen!"

The chart of the Federal Reserve System has Pluto at 0° Cancer in the twelfth house of hidden influences, making an opposition to its Sun at 1° Capricorn. This shows that the Fed was created surreptitiously to serve the interests of hidden power blocs.

The Fed's Neptune (the planet of deception and illusion) is at 27° Cancer, forming an exact opposition to the U.S. conceptional Pluto (the planet of secrecy, power and control) at 27° Capricorn in the second house (of money and banking) (fig. 26). This again shows the hidden but critical tie between the Fed and the power elite. But since Neptune also rules the process of dissolution, the power elite's hold on the economy is potentially tenuous, and the Federal Reserve System could well dissolve if the financial elite should lose their power.

And it looks like there's a good chance of that happening. Configurations in the 1990s show that the power of the financial elite may come to an end or be greatly diminished. Unfortunately, the influences that could cause the demise of the power elite

The Federal Reserve System's Neptune Opposed Pluto in the United States Conceptional Chart

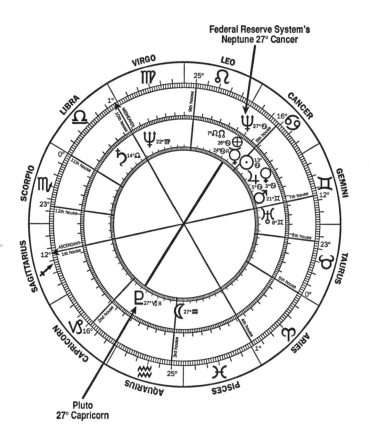

FIGURE 26 The Fed's Neptune (deception and illusion) at 27° Cancer forms an exact opposition to the United States conceptional Pluto (secrecy, power and control) at 27° Capricorn in the second house (of money and banking). This shows the hidden tie between the Fed and the power elite. Four eclipses between 1990 and 1996 form hard (stressful) aspects to the U.S. conceptional Pluto and could "eclipse" the financial elite's power.

could also cause the destruction of the U.S. economy, so intertwined are they. "How are the mighty fallen!"[1]

A Solar Eclipse Eclipses the Power Elite

Take the eclipse of the Sun at 29° Cancer that occurred on July 21, 1990. This is the first of a series of eclipses between now and 1996 that could cumulatively "eclipse" the power of the power elite. It formed a nearly exact opposition to the U.S. conceptional Pluto at 27° Capricorn in the second house. Pluto rules hidden or deceptive behavior and governs the use and abuse of financial, social and political power by plutocrats. Plutocrats are those who exercise power and influence by virtue of wealth.

Astrologer Barbara Watters explains that Pluto governs "cartel or other secret agreements between businesses or corporations to fix prices or defraud the public."[2]

The second house rules the nation's resources. This includes income, the gross national product, buying power, banks, stocks and bonds, and the status of the nation's currency. Therefore it also governs the money supply and its impact on the economy. Capricorn rules institutional authority and governmental power.

That is why Pluto in the second house of the U.S. conceptional chart indicated from the beginning the potential for a powerful banking elite to dominate the nation's money, economy and, finally, the government.

The eclipse of the Sun at 29° Cancer on July 21, 1990, made a conjunction to the Fed's Neptune at 27° Cancer. It falls in the U.S. conceptional eighth house. The eighth house rules public income, taxes, the national debt, foreign investment, multinational corporations, interest rates and financial organizations such as insurance companies. The eighth house is also related to the process of death and regeneration and karmic or involuntary circumstances.

At the least, the eclipse will sharpen the debate over debt and taxes; it could also cause confusion at the Fed, in the banking community and throughout the economy wherever matters of debt, finance and interest rates are important.

Neptune rules dissolution or the dissolving of entities. When applied to financial matters, it governs bankruptcy. Since this eclipse is conjoined the Fed's Neptune, the pace of debt liquidation and bankruptcy could accelerate in the United States.

The World's Largest Debtor Nation

In the last several years, problems with debt have crept up, seemingly out of nowhere, and become so large that they threaten to engulf the entire U. S. financial system.

Until 1983 the United States was the world's largest creditor nation. We have now become the world's largest debtor nation.

This process coincided with the transits of Saturn, Uranus and Neptune in Capricorn, starting with the entry of Neptune into Capricorn in 1984. I pointed out on February 13, 1988, that Neptune's entry into Capricorn signaled the beginning of the end of the era of international financial growth related to oil and unrealistic monetary expansion.

On July 3, 1990, *The Wall Street Journal* reported:

> America's foreign debt swelled again last year, further miring the nation in its rank of the world's largest debtor.
>
> During the year, foreign holdings in the U.S. grew nearly twice as much as U.S. holdings abroad, the Commerce Department said. As a result, the U.S. was left shouldering a net debt burden—the difference between U.S. holdings abroad and foreigners' holdings here—of $663.75 billion."[3]

That means that as of 1989, we owe foreign nations $663.75 billion more than they owe us. That's nearly 25 percent higher than in 1988. We are in debt—not up to our ears, not up to our eyebrows but well over our heads.

The *Journal* story continued:

> The report was the latest chapter in America's stunning decline from the world's largest creditor nation in 1983 to the world's largest debtor nation.
>
> A continued surge in foreign investment

in everything from New York office towers to Treasury securities to entire U.S. companies, hoisted foreigners' assets in the U.S. to $2.076 trillion last year from $1.797 trillion in 1988. That swamped the growth in U.S. investment abroad, which lifted U.S. foreign assets to $1.413 trillion from $1.266 trillion in 1988.

Not only was the report grim news for the U.S. government, but it also brought some embarrassing chiding of the Commerce Department. For the first time, the department decided not to publish the bottom-line debtor positions of the U.S.—the $663.75 billion figure—in its report on international investment, although it provided enough information to calculate the number.[4]

In other words, the Commerce Department was caught red-handed in keeping from the people the facts they need to know. They tried to eclipse the figure from the public eye, right in the shadow of the July 21 eclipse.

This eclipse also shows the prospect for increased financial trouble in the savings and loan and commercial banking industries. Commercial banks may find that they can no longer dodge the consequences of their foreign or domestic debt. As I discussed in chapter 17, this could start the process of debt liquidation in the commercial banking industry that the S&Ls have already experienced, setting the stage for another massive bailout.

However, growing public disgust with the S&L bailout may make it politically untenable to directly tax the people to pay the bankers' debts. But a government bank bailout could be disguised so that it does not look like the taxpayers are footing the bill.

The president and Congress may try to find an indirect method of saving the banks. They might rely on the Fed to create money and credit and inflate their way out of the problem. But whatever method they adopt to deal with the banks' debts, this eclipse is likely to unleash forces that could create financial chaos.

Here's the dilemma: If the Fed increases the money supply to help offset business losses and bankruptcies, it will spur fears of inflation and inflation itself, which could lead to a panic. If the Fed decreases the money supply or increases it at low levels, it will accelerate the process of debt liquidation and push the nation deeper into a recession or even into a depression.

In either case, astrology shows that the Fed can be expected to take deceptive action on behalf of the nation's financial interests. They're not worried about saving the people, they're worried about saving the power elite and the banks, in that order.

The Fed may also make some big mistakes. It could adopt a course of action that is destructive or self-defeating. Remember, in the 1930s the Fed contracted the money supply when it should have expanded it, thereby hastening the onset of the Great Depression.

In the coming months and years the Fed may be seen as a financial saviour. But this eclipse could lift the veil of secrecy that shrouds the Fed, making the American people aware of the Fed's financial manipulations on behalf of the power elite. They could lose confidence in the Fed and demand that it be accountable to Congress.

This eclipse could affect the economy in other ways. Tax policy is apt to be the focus of an intense power struggle. Dealings between foreign nations and the United States are likely to change significantly. Foreign sources of capital may dwindle or dry up. The United States may become increasingly vulnerable to food shortages, epidemics, natural disasters and war.

Other Configurations Threaten the Power Elite

During the next eight years, a series of eclipses will fall in close aspect to the U.S. conceptional Pluto at 27° Capricorn, which represents the power elite.

I already discussed the solar eclipse at 29° Cancer on July 21, 1990, opposed the U.S. conceptional Pluto. On January 15, 1991, a solar eclipse at 25° Capricorn will conjoin the U.S. conceptional Pluto; a lunar eclipse at 25° Libra on April 15, 1995, will square it; and a solar eclipse at 28° Aries on April 17, 1996, will also square it. These could further eclipse the power elite's power.

Then, in 1995, transiting Uranus (the planet of freedom and violent and unpredictable change) will make exact conjunctions to the U.S. conceptional Pluto at 27° Capricorn on February 5, August 14 and November 25. This transit will shake and perhaps break the power elite's grip on the U.S. economy (fig. 27). The nation's financial system could be destroyed or perhaps restructured along more enlightened lines—of, by and for the people.

Finally, in 1997, on January 20, August 31 and November 14, after Uranus has shaken up the financial powers that be, transiting Neptune will make exact conjunctions to the U.S. conceptional Pluto at 27° Capricorn (fig. 27) and oppositions to the Federal Reserve System's Neptune at 27° Cancer.

During this transit, the nation's financial system stands to dissolve (if it hasn't already under the influence of Uranus) and with it the power of the financial elite. It is at this time that the Federal Reserve System is also likely to be restructured or dissolved, depriving the financial elite of their most powerful mechanism of control over the government and economy, hence the people of the United States.

The Fed is both the fulcrum and the Achilles' heel of the power elite's control of this nation's money system.

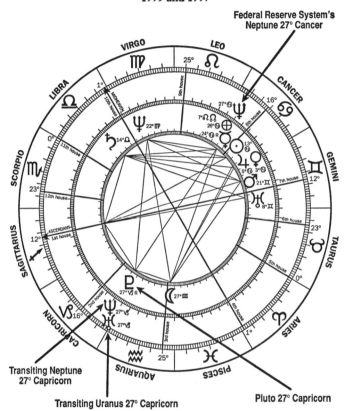

**Transiting Uranus and Neptune
Conjoin the United States Conceptional Pluto
1995 and 1997**

Federal Reserve System's
Neptune 27° Cancer

Transiting Neptune
27° Capricorn

Transiting Uranus 27° Capricorn

Pluto 27° Capricorn

FIGURE 27 On February 5, August 14 and November 25, 1995, transiting Uranus (freedom and unpredictable change) will make exact conjunctions with the United States conceptional Pluto (power) at 27° Capricorn in the second house (of money and banking) and may break the power elite's grip on the U.S. economy. On January 20, August 31 and November 14, 1997, transiting Neptune (dissolution) will make conjunctions with the U.S. conceptional Pluto and oppositions to the Fed's Neptune at 27° Cancer. This could dissolve the nation's financial system and the power of the financial elite.

CHAPTER 23

Opportunity Knocks

The 1990s bring hope as well as challenge. When you consider negative astrological portents, you must keep in mind that negative astrology represents opportunity. And we can choose self-transcendence over destruction. That is the great gift God has given to us.

In addition, the cycles of importunity we have been discussing are concurrent with two important cycles of opportunity.

First, we are in the midst of Pluto's 20-year transit inside the orbit of Neptune. This happens only once in Pluto's 248-year orbit around the Sun. Pluto entered Neptune's orbit on January 21, 1979, and will not leave it until March 14, 1999. During this period, Pluto is actually closer to the Sun than Neptune.

This is no ordinary event. Pluto's orbit inside Neptune's orbit has coincided with epochal events, including the birth of Jesus; the baptism of Clovis, the first king of France, into the Christian church about A.D. 498; and the discovery of America by Christopher Columbus in 1492.

The second cycle of opportunity we see on the horizon will come with the Uranus-Neptune conjunction of 1993. These conjunctions take place every 172 years and are associated with new phases of history that have a scientific and mystical character and can lead to greater freedom, innovation and enlightenment.

As I noted in chapter 20, Uranus and Neptune will make three exact conjunctions in 1993, two at 18° Capricorn (August 19 and October 24) and one at 19° Capricorn (February 2).

There is still time for we the people of planet Earth to get on top of the Uranus-Neptune conjunction and ride it to a golden age of peace and enlightenment. And we can start by doing our very best to make the golden age happen in the small corner of Terra each one of us occupies.

The Archeia Hope said in her dictation of January 2, 1987:

> Do you know one thing that you have absolute and complete control over? It is this— that the golden age *can* manifest in this hour *where you are!* Where the individualization of the God flame is in you, the golden age can already be in session and progress in your aura.[1]

In a dictation I delivered on April 4, 1983, beloved Gautama Buddha brought us the hope of a new day of opportunity:

> I would remind you, lest any fear, that all prophecy concerning Light and Darkness may fail. It may fail for a very good reason.

For the people of God have made strides and accelerated; and therefore, the dark cloud has been dissolved and a new day of opportunity is born. . . .

We desire, therefore, to reinforce in your heart that whatever you may have interpreted as prediction of cataclysm, worldwide or specifically here or there, must not remain in your mind as something that has been stated with ultimate definition or finality by any of our bands but only as a reading of world karma and as a reading of the consequences of world karma.[2]

Saint Germain said in his dictation of May 28, 1986:

The prophecy that is written in Revelation and in the Old and New Testament, that is written in the very sands and in the ethers which may be perceived, is not final! This is my cry to the age!

You are mediators between mankind (who are in a state of ignorance and rejection of the truth of the teachings of Jesus Christ we bear) and the oncoming karma returning. *You* as anointed ones [Christed ones], by choosing this calling and election, may form a Body of Light that does indeed become the manifestation of the all-consuming flame of God.

And that karma can be transmuted, beloved. And remember, the requirements are few. Ten righteous men could save an entire city by their righteousness,[3] proving that the power of God in manifestation is far greater than millions engaged in the blasphemy of the anti-Light and the desecration of the innocence of the child.[4]

Opportunity knocks. Opportunity is the name of Portia, the twin flame* of Saint Germain. Aquarius is not only an age of freedom, it is an age of opportunity. Opportunity is Divine Justice returning to us the opportunity we deserve (because we have given it to others) to serve to set life free.

By the very law of karma that mandates our astrology, we also have the opportunity to undo our past mistakes and make things right where we've wronged or been wronged. Opportunity is an open door that we can choose to walk through to help our planet and our people survive this "time of trouble," prophesied by Daniel, "such as never was since there was a nation."[5]

Beloved Lightbearers of the world, the handwriting is in the skies. But there is another handwriting in our hearts and it's a Valentine from Saint Germain and from our Father. It simply says, "I love you." And because God loves us, we have this opportunity to move through that purple fiery heart of Saint Germain. Yes, to move through our beloved Master's heart and to win!

---

*Your twin flame is your "other half," the soul who was born out of the same "white fire ovoid" as you. Your twin flame shares your blueprint of identity. When twin flames descend into form, one assumes the masculine polarity and one assumes the feminine polarity.

Some years ago Saint Germain penned a Valentine of greatest hope to his students. It read in part:

> Your heart is indeed one of the choicest gifts of God. Within it there is a central chamber surrounded by a forcefield of such light and protection that we call it a "cosmic interval." It is a chamber separated from Matter and no probing could ever discover it. It occupies simultaneously not only the third and fourth dimensions but also other dimensions unknown to man.
>
> This central chamber, called the altar of the heart, is thus the connecting point of the mighty silver cord of light that descends from your God Presence to sustain the beating of your physical heart, giving you life, purpose and cosmic integration.
>
> I urge all men to treasure this point of contact that they have with Life by giving conscious recognition to it. You do not need to understand by sophisticated language or scientific postulation the how, why and wherefore of this activity.
>
> Be content to know that God is there and that within you there is a point of contact with the Divine, a spark of fire from the Creator's own heart called the threefold flame of Life. There it burns as the triune essence of Love, Wisdom and Power.

Each acknowledgment paid daily to the flame within your heart will amplify the power and illumination of Love within your being. Each such attention will produce a new sense of dimension for you, if not outwardly apparent then subconsciously manifest within the folds of your inner thoughts.

Neglect not, then, your heart as the altar of God. Neglect it not as the sun of your manifest being. Draw from God the power of Love and amplify it within your heart. Then send it out into the world at large as the bulwark of that which shall overcome the darkness of the planet, saying:

> I AM the Light of the Heart
> Shining in the darkness of being
> And changing all into the golden treasury
> Of the Mind of Christ.
>
> I AM projecting my Love
> Out into the world
> To erase all errors
> And to break down all barriers.
>
> I AM the power of infinite Love,
> Amplifying itself
> Until it is victorious,
> World without end!

With this gift of infinite freedom from God's own heart this Valentine season, I close this epistle with a never-ending promise to assist you to find your immortal freedom as you determine never to give up and never to turn back. Remember that as long as you face the Light, the shadows are always behind. And the Light is there, too, to transmute them all.

Keep your gaze toward "the City" and be not overcome of evil but overcome evil with Good.[6]

AQUARIUS ♒

VŚ

PART V

The U.S. and the USSR– Antagonists in War:

An Analysis of Current Events in Light of Prophecy

TAURUS ♉

CHAPTER 24

The Astrology of War between the Superpowers

Now is the time to ask the overwhelming question: Who will engage in the wars prophesied in the handwriting in the skies?

First let us recapitulate the configurations that point to war: the Saturn-Uranus conjunctions of 1988, including Saturn and Uranus conjoined the Galactic Center; Mars, Saturn, Uranus and Neptune in Capricorn on February 22 and 23, 1988 (fig. 1, p. 100); and the Capricorn megaconjunction on January 11, 1994 (fig. 17, p. 215). To this we can add the sunspot cycle and Gouchon's and Ganeau's cycles of peace and war.

The astrology of nations analyzed in light of the worldwide military and political situation shows that a great many nations are likely to be engaged in some kind of conflict in the next decade. But few people want to think about the unthinkable. They do not want to read the prophecy written in the handwriting in the skies: that the two nations that have the power to affect the entire planet—the United States and the Soviet Union—are prime candidates for a major war in the near future.

Many Americans believe that war is out of date. And some in the New Age movement think we are about to enter a golden age and that we have come too far for God to allow the earth to be destroyed by war or cataclysm. In the present context of who are the players on the world stage and what are the prophecies of the stars, I believe this is wishful thinking.

The United States conceptional Mars at 21° Gemini makes a nearly exact square to her conceptional Neptune at 22° Virgo (fig. 28). This configuration shows that despite a generally practical nature, the American people have a propensity to engage in illusory thinking and self-deception, particularly in matters related to other nations, foreign affairs and war.

In all areas of national life, things are not what they seem. Neptune, the planet of illumination and refinement, is also the planet of illusion and deception. Since Neptune is afflicted by Mars in both the U.S. conceptional and birth charts, we must be on guard against illusion, especially the illusion that if we "think peace," we will have peace.

I will discuss *glasnost* and the "end of the cold war" in the next chapter. But first I will explore the astrological influences that indicate a high probability of war between the United States and the Soviet Union.

The Opposition between the U.S. and Soviet Suns

I pointed out earlier that the U.S. natal Sun at 10° Taurus forms an opposition to the Soviet Union's Sun at 14° Scorpio. This aspect can show either

Mars Square Neptune
in the United States Conceptional Chart

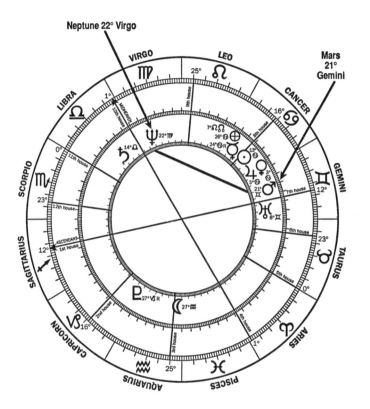

FIGURE 28 The United States conceptional Mars at 21° Gemini is square her conceptional Neptune at 22° Virgo. This configuration shows that despite a generally practical nature, the American people have a strong tendency to engage in illusory thinking and self-deception, particularly in matters related to other nations, foreign affairs and war. Since Neptune rules drugs and Mars rules war, this configuration shows that foreign nations could wage drug warfare against the United States.

union and cooperation or separation and conflict. It suggests that the superpowers are likely to be both friends and enemies at the same time.

Since I am, as far as I know, the only one who is using the Inauguration Day of George Washington, April 30, 1789, as the birth date of the United States, I would suspect that I am the only one who is drawing these conclusions from the relationship of the U.S. and Soviet natal charts.

The incomplete and incorrect knowledge of the astrology of the superpowers is giving the American people a false picture of the karmic forces at play, just as the misinterpretations of Nostradamus have done so. (If you want to know what's wrong with popular interpretations of Nostradamus, read *Saint Germain On Prophecy*.)

There is nothing so dangerous as an incorrect astrological chart, and no one in greater danger than he who follows it and his preferred illusions.

Pluto Conjoined the Soviet Sun Presents Mortal Challenges

For the first time since the Soviet Union was born 70 years ago, Pluto is making a conjunction to the Soviet Sun at 14° Scorpio and an opposition to the U.S. Sun at 10° Taurus (fig. 29). This occurs between January 1988 and October 1991, when Pluto is transiting between 12° and 19° Scorpio. While the conjunction is operative during the entire period, it was most powerful during Pluto's exact conjunctions with the Soviet Sun at 14°33' Scorpio

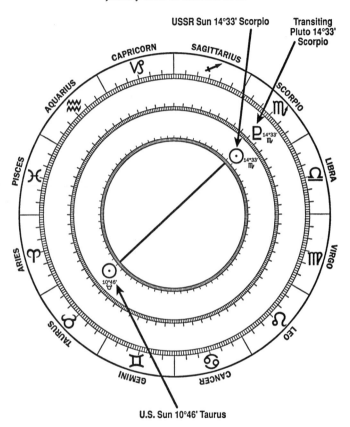

**Transiting Pluto Conjoined the Soviet Union's Sun
and Opposed the United States Sun**
January 1988 to October 1991

FIGURE 29 As Pluto crosses between 12° and 19° Scorpio from
January 1988 to October 1991, it makes three exact conjunctions
with the Soviet Union's Sun at 14° Scorpio opposed to the United
States natal Sun at 10° Taurus. Pluto transits in hard aspect to the
natal Sun are associated with the outbreak of wars and with mortal
challenges. Even if the superpowers do not go to war, they will face
severe challenges that could include economic problems, power
struggles, civil unrest and terrorism.

on December 31, 1988, April 5, 1989, and October 24, 1989.

In mundane astrology, the transits of Pluto in hard aspect to the natal Sun or other important planets are associated with the outbreak of wars and with mortal challenges.

This configuration could trigger war between the superpowers, but not necessarily right away. Since Pluto is a slow-moving planet that takes 248 years to orbit the Sun, the effect of a Pluto conjunction can take anywhere from a few months to several years to appear.

Transiting Pluto conjoined the Soviet Sun and opposed the U.S. Sun tells us that even if the superpowers do not go to war, they will face severe challenges. These could include economic problems, nuclear power accidents, power struggles, civil unrest, terrorism and a challenge to both governments' grip on power. Since I first gave these portents in February 1988, we have already seen most of them come to pass in the Soviet Union.

I would like to give you an idea of what to expect from a Pluto transit across a natal Sun. Pluto was transiting across the U.S. natal Sun at 10° Taurus during the American Civil War (1861–65). As the war began on April 12, 1861, Pluto was at 8° Taurus. By the war's end on April 9, 1865, it had crossed to 12° Taurus.

It is difficult to imagine a more serious national challenge than the Civil War; it could easily have resulted in the end of the United States of America had it not been for enlightened leadership. The challenges we are facing today are equally serious. But we face them with popularity seekers and poll watchers for leaders.

Transits That Could Trigger War

While Pluto transits can set the stage for war, often the transits of Mars (the planet of war) light the fuse.

On February 14, 1989, transiting Mars at 15° Taurus conjoined the U.S. natal Sun at 10° Taurus and opposed the Soviet Sun at 14° Scorpio, which was conjoined transiting Pluto at 15° Scorpio. This is an explosive placing, capable of igniting a war. As Mars continues its transits during the time that Pluto is conjoined the Soviet Sun, it could initiate conflict between the two nations every time it makes a conjunction, square or opposition to the U.S. and Soviet natal Suns.

For example, on November 26, 1989, Mars, the Moon and Pluto were conjoined at 15° Scorpio within one and a half degrees of the Soviet Sun at 14°33′ Scorpio (fig. 30). This conjunction of Mars, the Moon and Pluto with the Soviet Sun formed an opposition to the U.S. natal Sun at 10°46′ Taurus.

It followed the November 13, 1989 Saturn-Neptune conjunction in Capricorn opposed the U.S. conceptional Jupiter in Cancer, which initiated major debt liquidation in the United States and could lead to the fall or paralysis of the U.S. government.

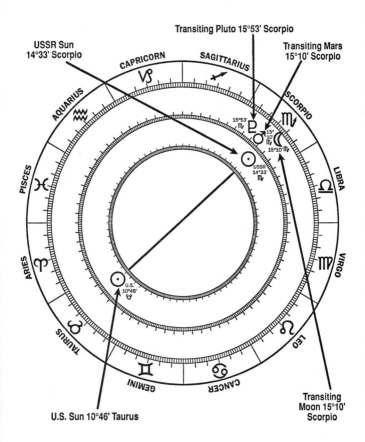

Transiting Pluto, Mars and Moon Conjoined the Soviet Union's Sun and Opposed the United States Sun
November 26, 1989

Transiting Pluto 15°53' Scorpio

Transiting Mars 15°10' Scorpio

USSR Sun 14°33' Scorpio

CAPRICORN

SAGITTARIUS

AQUARIUS

SCORPIO

15°53' ♏ ♇

15°10' ♏ ☿

15°10' ♏ ☽

USSR 14°33' ♏

PISCES

LIBRA

ARIES

U.S. 10°46' ♉

VIRGO

TAURUS

LEO

GEMINI

CANCER

Transiting Moon 15°10' Scorpio

U.S. Sun 10°46' Taurus

FIGURE 30 On November 26, 1989, Mars, the Moon and Pluto were conjoined at 15° Scorpio within one and a half degrees of the Soviet Sun at 14°33' Scorpio. This conjunction formed an opposition to the United States natal Sun at 10°46' Taurus.

As Mars continues its transit, it forms a series of hard aspects to the U.S. and Soviet Suns conjoined transiting Pluto:

On July 28, 1990, Mars at 10° Taurus conjoined the U.S. natal Sun. On August 3, 1990, Mars reached 14° Taurus and formed a direct opposition to the Soviet Sun. The following day, Mars, transiting at 15° Taurus, opposed transiting Pluto at 15° Scorpio.

In June 1991, Mars transiting in Leo will form a series of squares to the U.S. and Soviet Suns and transiting Pluto. On June 13, transiting Mars will be at 10° Leo square the U.S. Sun at 10° Taurus. On June 19, Mars will be at 14° Leo square the Soviet Sun at 14° Scorpio. And on June 25, Mars will be at 17° Leo square transiting Pluto at 17° Scorpio.

Finally, in November 1991, Mars, transiting in Scorpio, will make a series of aspects that mirror image its positions during the summer of 1990. On November 1, transiting Mars will be at 10° Scorpio opposed to the U.S. Sun at 10° Taurus. On November 6, the day before the Soviet Union's 74th birthday, transiting Mars will conjoin the Soviet Sun at 14° Scorpio. And on November 15, transiting Mars will conjoin transiting Pluto at 20° Scorpio.

The U.S.-Soviet Grand Square

When we take a closer look at the relationship between the natal charts of the United States and the Soviet Union, the intensity of the Pluto transit between January 1988 and October 1991 becomes even more clear. Critical planets in the birth charts of the two

nations form a grand square: The U.S. Sun at 10°
Taurus is square the U.S. Pluto at 19° Aquarius,
which is conjoined the Soviet Uranus at 19° Aquarius. The U.S. Pluto and the Soviet Uranus square
the Soviet Sun at 14° Scorpio conjoined the Soviet
Mercury at 16° Scorpio, both of which square the
Soviet Saturn at 14° Leo (fig. 31).

This grand square indicates that the relationship between the nations can be violently explosive. The opposition of the U.S. and Soviet Suns
shows that the grand square influences the life of
both nations. The conjunction of the U.S. Pluto
and the Soviet Uranus suggests an unforeseen break
in relations accompanied by danger from the destructive use of nuclear energy, violence arising out
of reform, and war. The Pluto-Uranus conjunction
opposed to the Soviet Saturn shows that interactions
between the superpowers could unexpectedly cause
the death of one or both nations or, at the very least,
widespread death and destruction.

Grand squares, however, tend to be static. It
would take intense pressure to release the energy
locked up in this grand square. The current transit
of Pluto across the Soviet Sun could provide the
necessary pressure.

In addition, in 1990 there were two lunar
eclipses in close aspect to every planet in the U.S.-
Soviet grand square. The first eclipse took place on
February 9, 1990, at 20° Leo (fig. 32). This could
trigger a U.S.-Soviet conflict much in the same
way a lunar eclipse triggered the Chernobyl disaster.

United States–Soviet Union Grand Square
in Their Combined Birth Charts

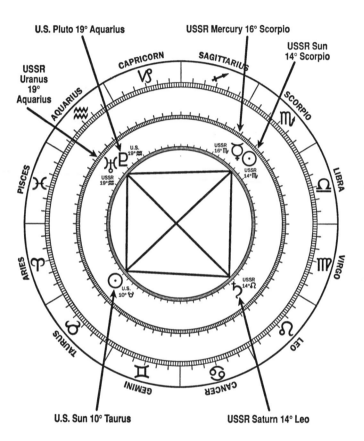

FIGURE 31 Key planets in the birth charts of the United States and the Soviet Union form a grand square. The opposition of the U.S. and Soviet Suns shows that the grand square influences the life of both nations. The conjunction of the U.S. Pluto and the Soviet Uranus suggests an unforeseen break in relations and danger from nuclear energy, violence arising out of reform, and war.

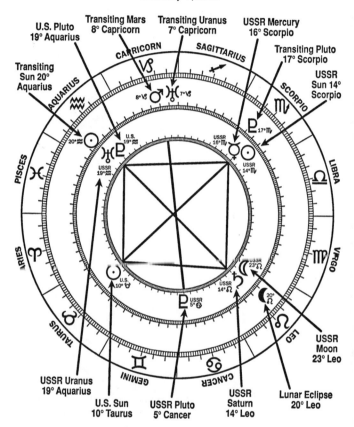

Eclipse of the Moon in Leo
Activates the United States–Soviet Union Grand Square
February 9, 1990

FIGURE 32   On February 9, 1990, there was a lunar eclipse at 20°
Leo in close aspect to every planet in the United States–Soviet
Union grand square. It occurred about five hours after an exact
conjunction of transiting Mars and Uranus at 7° Capricorn opposed
the Soviet Pluto at 5° Cancer. This Mars-Uranus-Pluto opposition
could trigger a U.S.-Soviet conflict. It links the planets of war
(Mars), unpredictable events (Uranus), and widespread death and
destruction (Pluto).

The eclipse occurred about five hours after an exact conjunction of transiting Mars and Uranus at 7°57′ Capricorn opposed to the Soviet Pluto at 5° Cancer.

This Mars-Uranus-Pluto opposition links the planets of war (Mars), unpredictable events (Uranus), and widespread death and destruction (Pluto). When combined with the effects of the eclipse of the Moon, the results could be disastrous.

The second eclipse took place on August 6, 1990, at 13° Aquarius (fig. 33). Even if it had not been in close aspect to the U.S.-Soviet grand square, this eclipse would have been capable of igniting a war anywhere on earth. At the time of the eclipse, four transiting planets—the Sun, Moon, Mars and Pluto—formed a grand square in the heavens.

The August 6 eclipse, along with one on July 21, 1990, triggered Iraq's invasion of Kuwait (see chapter 29). But it also activated the U.S.-Soviet grand square. At the time of the eclipse, Pluto was at 15° Scorpio conjoined the Soviet Union's natal Sun at 14° Scorpio. Mars was at 16° Taurus conjoined the U.S. natal Sun, and the progressed U.S. conceptional Sun was at 15° Aquarius conjoined the eclipse point.

I don't expect and haven't expected war on the dates of eclipses and exact conjunctions. I have often mentioned that an eclipse remains active for about six months and sometimes longer. Even though there were no hostilities between the superpowers on or around August 6, the eclipse could

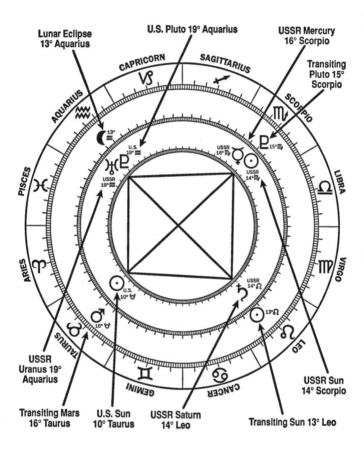

**Eclipse of the Moon in Aquarius
Activates the United States–Soviet Union Grand Square
August 6, 1990**

Lunar Eclipse 13° Aquarius

U.S. Pluto 19° Aquarius

USSR Mercury 16° Scorpio

Transiting Pluto 15° Scorpio

USSR Uranus 19° Aquarius

Transiting Mars 16° Taurus

U.S. Sun 10° Taurus

USSR Saturn 14° Leo

Transiting Sun 13° Leo

USSR Sun 14° Scorpio

FIGURE 33 On August 6, 1990, there was a partial eclipse of the Moon at 13° Aquarius. Even if it had not been in close aspect to the U.S.-Soviet grand square, this eclipse would have been capable of igniting a war anywhere on earth. The August 6 eclipse, along with one on July 21, 1990, triggered Iraq's invasion of Kuwait.

cause the buildup of tension that will intensify the ultimate release of the power of the U.S.-Soviet grand square at some future date. That future date could be any day between now and April 22, 2002. (I will discuss in *My Vision of the Four Horsemen* why the date April 22 is significant.)

The energy of the August 6 eclipse could also manifest as accidents, altercations, fires, emotional and financial difficulties and a host of other problems at a personal level, depending on where it fell in your chart.

We always say "could" because we know that negative prophecy is meant to fail. When God tells us what will happen if we don't change our ways, we can pray to him for the merciful mitigation of prophecy. And we can ask him to give us the opportunity to balance that planetary karma which the Great Law will allow to be transmuted by the violet flame released from the Holy Spirit in answer to our prayers.

The influences of eclipses are not uniformly negative. An eclipse can literally "eclipse" the negative influences associated with a configuration and catalyze the positive potential. More often, it activates the positive and negative potential simultaneously. When dealing with nations or other large entities whose astrology is based on mass phenomena, the negative portents of the eclipse usually manifest to a greater degree.

The Pluto transit across the Soviet Sun concludes in October 1991. Once we get past it (with or without a war), it does not mean that the rest of the century will be peaceful. The Capricorn megaconjunction of January 1994 is fully capable of igniting war (see chapter 18). And at the close of this century and the beginning of the next, we will have three exact Saturn-Uranus squares.

The first of these squares will occur on July 17, 1999, when Saturn will be at 15° Taurus square to Uranus at 15° Aquarius (fig. 34). Not only does this Saturn-Uranus square indicate war but it also activates the grand square in the combined birth charts of the United States and the Soviet Union, showing that there is the prospect for a major war between the nations during the 18 months before and after July 17, 1999.

The other two exact Saturn-Uranus squares will also activate the U.S.-Soviet grand square. These will occur on November 14, 1999 (when Saturn will be at 13° Taurus square to Uranus at 13° Aquarius) and on May 13, 2000 (when Saturn will be at 20° Taurus square Uranus at 20° Aquarius).

The Saturn-Neptune Cycle—
A Catalyst for the Growth of Communism

In chapter 17, I discussed the Saturn-Neptune conjunction of 1989 as it relates to economic problems. Saturn-Neptune conjunctions also correlate with the growth and development of socialism and Communism.[1]

Saturn and Neptune conjoin each other about every 36 years. The Saturn-Neptune conjunction

Transiting Saturn Square Transiting Uranus
Activates the United States–Soviet Union Grand Square
July 17, 1999

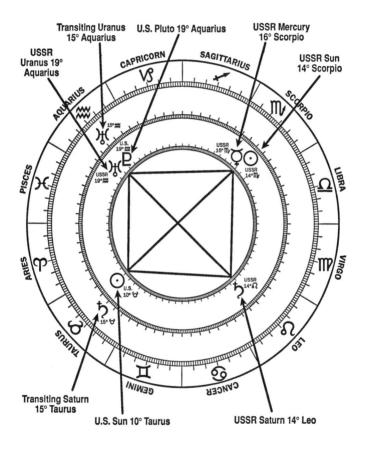

FIGURE 34 On July 17, 1999, Saturn at 15° Taurus will form an exact square to Uranus at 15° Aquarius. Not only does this Saturn-Uranus square indicate war but it also activates the U.S.-Soviet grand square, showing the prospect for a major war between the nations during the 18 months before and after July 17, 1999.

of 1846 was followed by the publication of *The Communist Manifesto* by Karl Marx in 1848. The next Saturn-Neptune conjunction, in 1882, coincided with the establishment and growth of the main European socialist parties. The next two conjunctions of Saturn and Neptune coincided with the Bolshevik Revolution in 1917 and with Stalin's death and Soviet expansion into the Third World in 1953.

Saturn-Neptune squares have also coincided with the expansion of Communism. When Saturn squared Neptune in 1979, the Soviet Union invaded Afghanistan and became embroiled in a crisis in Poland, and the Sandinistas came to power in Nicaragua and established a Soviet beachhead in the Americas.

Given the strong correlation of Saturn (the planet of organization, planning and centralized control) and Neptune (the planet of glamour, illusion, deception and impractical idealism) with the growth of socialism, it is not surprising that some people were taken in by the promises of socialism.

Socialism is an economic theory based on government ownership of the means of production and distribution of goods. Although socialism is commonly thought of as a political system, or a political *and* economic system, Marx, Lenin and other seminal theorists insisted that it was first and foremost an economic system. They argued that a nation's prevailing method of economic organization was the foundation of her political life; if one altered the economic system, the political system would reflect the change.

Communism, according to Marx and Lenin, is a hypothetical, or utopian, stage of socialism characterized by a classless, stateless society and the equal distribution of goods. The Soviet Union and other socialist states claim to be working to establish a communist society through centralized economic planning and rigid control of the economy, a one-party state and limited individual liberties.

But socialism has never worked. Socialist economies are disorganized (Neptune) and plagued by low levels of production, shortages and the maldistribution of goods (Saturn). Since socialism is not a viable economic system, Soviet leaders have been forced to do two things to stay in power: (1) create a police state, (2) take control of other nations and siphon off their wealth. Case in point: Eastern Europe.

The Saturn-Neptune conjunction of 1989 marks a crucial turning point in Soviet Communist development and thus world history. We the people who read the handwriting on the wall can take the flame of freedom and use it to prevent the prophecy of the expansion of World Communism from taking place. We can fulfill Nostradamus' prophecy that another "law of More"[2] will supersede the totalitarian Communist governments. I believe this will be a worldwide communion of the Mystical Body of God in the Holy Spirit.

I have demonstrated that Saturn-Neptune

conjunctions are related to the expansion of Communism. Some astrologers say the Saturn-Neptune conjunctions of 1989 portended the dissolution of borders rather than the expansion of Communism. They note that East Germany opened the Berlin Wall on November 9, 1989, just four days before the Saturn-Neptune conjunction opposed Jupiter.

They fail to take into account that the dissolution of borders could just as easily imply Soviet expansion, not contraction.

Saturn-Neptune conjunctions can also show the organization, crystallization or implementation of a deception. The British Broadcasting System reported on May 30, 1990, that the KGB and Czech secret police helped engineer the Czech revolution. Ted Koppel took note of these reports on "Nightline" on June 14, 1990. Joseph Douglass, Jr., an expert on Soviet strategy, says the KGB also helped overthrow Romanian dictator Nicolae Ceausescu.[3]

Are the revolutions in Eastern Europe genuine or are they a Soviet deception? The answer is that they are both.

The revolutionary forces in Eastern Europe are real. But the Soviets are making a determined effort to manipulate them to their own ends in order to maintain power.

Will Communism expand or contract in Europe? The outcome has not yet been decided, but consider this:

The current Saturn-Neptune conjunction could touch off international economic turmoil. During this cycle, Soviet aggression and Western economic chaos will be interrelated.

The Soviets are increasingly dependent on Western money and technology to keep their civilian economy afloat and their empire cohesive. As economic conditions in the Soviet bloc grow worse, the need for Western loans will reach crisis proportions.

If economic problems squeeze the amount of available loan money, Western nations may no longer be able to support the Soviet economy. Economic hardship has already pushed the Soviet republics to the brink of civil war. Further crisis could push them over the brink.

Then the Soviet leaders may have no choice but to go to war in order to save their economy—and stay in power. And all the glad promises of all the king's horses and all the king's men will not be able to put the Humpty Dumpty of a shattered *glasnost* and a shattered *perestroika* back together again in the face of this realpolitik.

CHAPTER 25

Haven't You Heard the Cold War Is Over?

"Haven't you heard the Cold War is over?" It is impossible not to have heard. The media has told us the Cold War is over so often that *Newsweek* columnist Meg Greenfield complained: "The confusion over Lithuania is what we get for going around telling ourselves and anyone else who will listen that 'the cold war is over.'"[1]

Never mind little inconsistencies like the Soviets' refusal to give Lithuania independence. The prevailing view in Congress and among experts is that the Cold War is over—and we've won.

President Bush is reticent to gloat over the victory, but he also says the Cold War is over. Soviet president Gorbachev agrees, although he says there was no winner. Even the leaders of the North Atlantic Treaty Organization (NATO), the military alliance formed in 1949 to resist Soviet aggression in Europe, have declared that the Cold War is over.

In the London Declaration, a historic communiqué issued July 6, 1990, NATO leaders proposed signing a joint declaration with their former enemies in the Warsaw Pact, the Soviet Union's version of NATO, that would say: "We solemnly state that we are no longer adversaries." NATO leaders said it was necessary to "reach out to the countries of the East which were our adversaries in the cold war and extend to them the hand of friendship."

If the leaders of NATO (those old cold warriors) said it, who is to argue?

And so I am frequently asked, as if I am the *only* person in the West who has not gotten the message, "Haven't you heard the Cold War is over?"

Just what is the Cold War? Political scientists, historians, journalists, and intelligence and foreign-policy experts disagree. Some say that the Cold War was American resistance to Soviet expansion into Western Europe following World War II. Others believe it was a period of indirect warfare between the superpowers that took the form of proxy wars, economic warfare, espionage and propaganda.

Some hold that the Cold War was a sustained period of *peace* (direct war did not break out between the superpowers). Others say that there was no Cold War. The *Encyclopaedia Britannica* says, "It is analytically uncertain what the Cold War was about."[2]

But for the average American the issue is clear. The Cold War was a tense, often irrational state of relations between the superpowers that threatened to escalate into nuclear war. In essence, the term *Cold War*, as it is currently used, is a code phrase for "threat of nuclear war between the superpowers."

But now, we are told, things are different. The Soviet Union has entered an era of irreversible change. The Soviets are liberalizing their society, becoming more democratic and trying to implement a market economy. The Berlin Wall, quintessential symbol of the Cold War, has come down. The Soviet Union has lost its Eastern European empire and is itself on the verge of disintegration.

For the first time the Soviets are telling the truth about what is going on inside their borders and it's worse than almost anyone imagined. The Soviet Union is broke, demoralized, ideologically bankrupt, polluted, hungry and racked by strikes and ethnic violence.

Of greatest importance, the Soviets say they have abandoned their drive for control of the Eurasian land mass (and the world) and have changed their offensive military strategy to a defensive one. And a visionary, Mikhail Gorbachev, the exponent of *glasnost* and *perestroika*, is behind it all.

What else is there to say? The threat of nuclear war is a thing of the past. The Soviets don't want one. Besides, they are too weak, preoccupied or disorganized to fight. Based on their new outlook, they are reducing their military forces. Even if they didn't want to, they are being forced to shift resources from their military to their consumer economy.

So why worry? The Cold War is over.

Military Reductions?

The Cold War, however you define it, may or may not be over. But before you decide that the threat of nuclear war has passed, let me tell you a few things that George Bush knows but that he finds politically inexpedient to tell the American people.

When Gorbachev came to power on March 11, 1985, it was the consensus in the West that the Soviets needed to redirect their resources from a military to a civilian economy. On that assumption, since 1985 the Soviets have been allowed to borrow tens of billions of dollars from Western banks and Western governments.[3] But in 1990 the Soviet civilian economy is in much worse shape than it was in 1985. In fact, for the first time since the Bolshevik Revolution there have been shortages of bread in Moscow.

Where did the money go? Certainly not into the civilian economy. The only sector of their economy that has shown signs of life is the military.

A study by John M. Collins, senior specialist in national defense at the Library of Congress, reveals the extent of the Soviet military buildup under Gorbachev. From 1985 to 1989 the Soviets produced 468 new intercontinental ballistic missiles (ICBMs) and submarine-launched ballistic missiles (SLBMs) with 2,152 new warheads, 9 ballistic missile submarines, 95 bombers, 5,300 tanks and 9,700 armored personnel carriers.[4]

Collins' figures for ICBM warheads and tanks are conservative compared to the Pentagon's estimates. The Pentagon estimates that under Gorbachev the Soviets have built 1,100 ICBMs and SLBMs and 14,800 tanks. No matter whose figures you accept, Gorbachev's five-year buildup exceeds

Reagan's eight-year buildup in every category except ballistic missile submarines (the U.S. produced 10).

It has long been argued that once the Soviets reached nuclear parity (equality of nuclear forces) with the United States, they would stop building. While parity has never been precisely defined, in the 1980s the Soviets reached parity with the United States in terms of the number of nuclear warheads—and then went right on building. During the 1980s the Soviets deployed about 900 ICBMs while the U.S. deployed 50 (the MX). As of 1989, the U.S. had only 83 percent of the warheads that the Soviets had.[5]

This is not to dispute the rightness or wrongness of building more nuclear weapons. It is merely to show that the Soviets have not stopped building nuclear weapons—either for economic reasons or because they have reached parity. And there is every indication that the Soviet buildup is continuing.

A classified CIA-Pentagon study completed in July 1990, whose conclusions were leaked to journalist Peter Samuel, says the Soviets are rapidly increasing their inventories of mobile ICBMs[6]— just the kind of weapons they would use to attack the United States if war broke out.

The study estimates that the Soviets are expected to *double* the number of their rail-mobile SS-24 missiles and launchers and their road-mobile SS-25 missiles by the end of 1990. The SS-24 carries 10 highly accurate warheads and the SS-25 carries one large warhead.

In September 1989, the Soviets had 20 mobile SS-24s and 170 SS-25s. According to the CIA-Pentagon study, by the end of 1990 they are expected to have 70 mobile SS-24s and 300 SS-25s, raising the number of warheads deployed on these missiles from 400 to 1000. The SS-24 also has a rapid reload capability for several more missiles, potentially doubling or tripling the SS-24 force.

The SS-24s and SS-25s are part of an enormous Soviet nuclear missile modernization program that is rapidly making the already formidable Soviet first-strike capability even more deadly. But the increase in mobile missiles is only one part of the Soviets' modernization program.

The centerpiece of the Soviet nuclear strike force is a heavy silo-based ICBM designated the SS-18. The fourth model of this ICBM, the Mod 4, carries 10 powerful, accurate warheads (some experts think it can carry as many as 30 warheads). The Soviets have deployed 308 SS-18 Mod 4 missiles.

With the SS-18s alone, the Soviets can target all U.S. silo-based ICBMs and bases for strategic nuclear submarines and still have thousands of warheads on their other 1,000 ICBMs available to attack other targets in the United States.

The SS-18 Mod 4 is the most deadly weapons system ever deployed. Yet the Soviets are replacing the Mod 4 with the Mod 5, which is 20 percent larger and even more reliable and accurate! The SS-18 Mod 5 is qualitatively so much better than the Mod 4 that Dr. Joseph Douglass, Jr., an expert on nuclear strategy, says the Mod 5 gives the Soviets "more than a twofold improvement on a 1-to-1 replacement" of the Mod 4.[7]

When considering the mind-boggling power of the SS-18 Mod 5s, the SS-24s and SS-25s, all of which have been deployed since Gorbachev came to power, remember that nuclear weapons are expensive. And the Soviets are producing them in the midst of a prolonged economic crisis.

It's not just ICBMs that the Soviets are building. A new Pentagon study, *NATO and Warsaw Pact Weapons Production Report 1980–1989*, says that the Soviets are also increasing their production of cruise missiles.

In the first half of the 1980s—before Gorbachev came to power in 1985—the Soviets produced about 1,400 cruise missiles a year. But the estimated production of Soviet cruise missiles rose to 1,600 cruise missiles in 1987, 1,800 in 1988 and 2,000 in 1989.[8] Not bad for a country in financial ruins.

On top of this, the Soviets are currently producing three sophisticated, supersonic jet bombers, the Bear H, the Backfire and the Blackjack. In 1989, the year the Berlin Wall came down, they commissioned more tonnage of warships than in any year in two previous decades. Political scientist Joseph K. Woodard points out that Soviet naval forces "are growing at an accelerating rate."[9]

The Soviet Union (traditionally a land power) is building surface warships faster than the United States (a sea power) and submarines twice as fast as the United States. Woodard says that the Soviet naval deployments reflect their desire to "use their fleet" for economic gain, especially in the Pacific:

> Beyond the mouth of the Amur River lie Japan and South Korea, with all of the industrial capacity and technological might needed for the development of still-empty Siberia. The Soviet Pacific fleet has grown even faster than their navy as a whole; it now comprises more than a third of Soviet naval strength. . . . This represents the transfer of the largest, most advanced Soviet warships to the Pacific. Equally troubling, most of the KGB's Krivak III-class frigates have also gone east.
>
> Increasingly blatant incursions by Soviet bombers into Japanese airspace have been answered by increasing Japanese eagerness to invest in the industrial development of Soviet Siberia. New military agreements have been signed with the ever-stronger North Koreans, and the Soviets invest in bases in Vietnam even as the Americans may be divested of their bases in the Philippines. Most worrisome, the Russians have been practicing large-scale, amphibious assault operations. All of this seems to suggest that, in the Pacific at least, the Soviet Union is preparing simply to take what it wants. [10]

The July 1990 CIA-Pentagon study says that in addition to building new offensive systems, the

Soviets are enhancing their massive civil-defense system. It reports new and ongoing construction of deep underground nuclear-war stations, leadership command posts, offices, military repair facilities, and warehouses for defense equipment.

In light of the continuing buildup, we must consider the Soviet Union's military capability separately from its stated intent. Intent can change overnight with a change of circumstances or leaders.

But there is another way of looking at the situation. The Soviet Union has amassed the most powerful conventional *and* nuclear forces on the planet at a time when it has no serious external enemies. And it is continuing to improve those forces, at great expense, even though it is in the midst of a deep depression.

Under these circumstances, capability is tantamount to intent: Why spend a fortune on big-ticket weapons if you're not planning to get a return on your investment?

Experts often argue that the Soviets can have either "guns" (military goods) or "butter" (consumer goods), not both. Now that the Soviets are broke, they are supposedly being forced to choose butter, not guns. But they are doing just the opposite.

The implication is that the Soviets intend to use their military forces to take what they want from the prosperous nations in the West and on the Pacific rim. Guns can compel butter.

Is this what the Soviets have in mind? Or have they really adopted a defensive strategy? That's what a distinguished group of retired U.S. military leaders and civilian experts wanted to know.

Face to Face in Moscow

From January 24 to 26, 1990, top U.S. and Soviet experts met in Moscow for a no-holds-barred discussion of the U.S.-Soviet strategic balance. The conference was cosponsored by the International Security Council, a private Washington think tank, and the Academy of Sciences of the USSR in collaboration with the Central Committee of the Communist Party of the Soviet Union and the General Staff of the Armed Forces of the USSR.

The American delegation was headed by Dr. William R. Van Cleave, senior research fellow at the Hoover Institution and director of the Center for Defense and Strategic Studies, Southwest Missouri State University. American participants included Donald H. Rumsfeld, former U.S. secretary of defense; retired Adm. Elmo R. Zumwalt, Jr., former chief of Naval Operations; retired Gen. Paul X. Kelley, 28th Commandant, U.S. Marine Corps; retired Maj. Gen. George J. Keegan, Jr., former chief of U.S. Air Force Intelligence; Dr. Leon Gouré, Soviet studies editor for *Strategic Review*; Dr. Steven S. Rosefielde, professor of economics at the University of North Carolina; and Dr. Joseph Churba, president of the International Security Council.

The Soviet delegation was led by Gen. Lt. Viktor P. Starodubov, division head of the International Department of the Central Committee. Soviet participants included retired Adm. Nikolai N. Amelko, former deputy chief of the General Staff of the Armed Forces; Gen. Maj. G. Fedosov, Ministry of Foreign Affairs; Gen. Maj. A. F. Goloborodov, division head of the General Staff, Strategic Research Center; and retired Gen. Lt. Mikhail A. Milshtein, Institute of the U.S.A. and Canada.

The Americans confronted the Soviets with the particulars of their military buildup—the SS-18s, SS-24s, SS-25s, the strategic bombers, their naval program, and their civil and strategic defense programs—and the evidence that the Soviets have a much bigger military budget than they have admitted. "We went fully determined to have a face-down confrontation on these issues and facts, and we did,"[11] says General Keegan.

Citing the Soviets' continued buildup of offensive nuclear weapons, the Americans challenged the Soviet premise that they have ruled out the use of nuclear weapons in warfare and adopted a defensive posture. A summary of the meeting published in *Global Affairs* says:

> The Americans argued that [nuclear weapons] is another area in which Soviet actions invalidate Soviet words. The Soviet participants insist that the Soviets rule out the use of nuclear weapons in warfare, . . . but the Soviets continue to design, produce, and deploy the same kinds of weapons that they did when Soviet military writings acknowledged

that the aim was to be able to wage nuclear war successfully, to fight and hopefully win nuclear wars.[12]

Most of the American challenges were met with denials. The Soviets claimed that the Americans were misinterpreting the data and produced a few maps and charts in an unsuccessful effort to prove their case. Keegan says that some American challenges were met with nothing more than "dumb silence."[13]

But as the conference went on the Soviets changed their stance, at least informally. Rosefielde says, "For the first two days they tried the usual dog-and-pony show. But they saw we weren't buying it. After that they were quite candid." They admitted, in ways both direct and indirect, he says, that the Americans were correct. "They knew we knew. There was no serious attempt at protesting."[14]

Numbers Games

What, it may be asked, about all the reported Soviet military *cuts*? It is clear that the Soviets are not cutting their strategic nuclear forces or naval forces. They are not cutting their civil or strategic defenses. In fact, under Gorbachev Soviet military spending has steadily increased and, according to senior Defense Intelligence Agency (DIA) analyst William Lee, is now about 25 percent of the Soviet Union's gross national product (GNP).[15]

The Soviets have not been candid with the

West about how much they are spending on their military, despite *glasnost*. In the beginning of 1989 the Soviets claimed they were spending 20 billion rubles a year on their military. Then in June of 1989, Soviet Prime Minister Nikolai Ryzhkov said emphatically that the real figure was no more than 77 billion rubles a year. By July 5, 1990, the Soviets said they were spending 120 billion rubles a year.[16]

Other analysts say that figure is still too low. Rosefielde, an expert on the Soviet economy, says it is difficult to put a precise figure on total Soviet military spending. He believes it is in excess of 20 percent of their GNP and says that it may be as high as 40 percent.[17]

Lee, who analyzes the Soviet military budget for the DIA, estimates that Soviet military spending has been increasing at an annual rate of about 6 to 8 percent.[18] While that seems like a very high rate of growth, it was confirmed by no less a figure than Mikhail Gorbachev. In a little-reported speech at a Soviet tank factory, Gorbachev said that the current five-year plan provided for a 45 percent increase in military spending, which comes out to a 7.7 percent annual increase.[19]

No matter whose figures you accept, the fact is the Soviets did not produce their weapons in the last five years by rubbing Aladdin's lamp. Real men and women working in real factories built them. Which means they cost money. It is a mathematical impossibility for the Soviets to have been increasing weapons production while cutting their defense budget.

The Soviets have made some cuts in manpower, but they are not what most people think. "Most of the widely applauded '500,000-man cut,'" says intelligence analyst Stephen Cole, "was accomplished by redesignating non-combat military units (labor, railroad, border guards) as civilians."[20] About 200,000 military railway workers were made civilians and about 300,000 military border guards were transferred to the Ministry of the Interior. They do the same job and wear the same uniform as before. But they have been "cut" from the military.

John Collins says, "The cuts look good on paper. But the implication of troop reductions is not as straightforward as one may think. The Soviets will reduce the size of their armed forces in significant ways by removing whole segments that were unessential."[21]

The Soviets cut probably less than 50,000 real military troops.[22] But this cut does not significantly alter their fighting ability, considering that the Soviets had about 5 million men in their armed forces with 8 million in reserve (the U.S. has 2 million active with 1.5 million in reserve).[23]

Nor does the recent decrease in tank production change much of anything. After a five-year period of record tank production during which the Soviets produced as many as 3,500 tanks annually, they finally cut production to 1,500 top-of-the-line tanks in 1989.[24]

But the Soviets do not *need* any more tanks to defend their homeland. Tanks are used to seize and hold ground or to destroy other tanks. Since no nation (or alliance) has the capability, much less the intent, to invade the Soviet Union, the size of their inventory (63,000 tanks) and their annual rate of production (1,500 tanks) strongly suggests that the Soviets still have an offensive strategy.

When all is said and done, the Soviets have done nothing to decrease their military capabilities and much to enhance them. As the International Security Council recently pointed out:

> In April the Defense Intelligence Agency issued a report to Congress that could support a conclusion very different than the official line [that the Soviet military threat has irreversibly collapsed]. Among its findings: Huge stockpiles of Soviet arms remain in Eastern Europe and are being increasingly updated;... conversion of military plants to civilian industry remains virtually non-existent; "no major weapons development program appears to have been stretched out or canceled;" and the Soviets continue to deliver $17 billion a year in military support to their Third World clients (interestingly enough, about the level of the proposed Western aid package to the Soviet Union.)[25]

In the final analysis, the evidence of a gargantuan Soviet offensive military buildup belies all their public statements of a defensive strategy and a desire for peace.

The leaders of the West are aware of the Soviet

military buildup. They know that it can't be sustained without money. The question we should ask is: Why are Western banks and governments lending billions of dollars to the Soviets when it's clear the money isn't benefiting the Soviet consumer economy?

Are Western leaders afraid that if they don't keep pouring in money, the Soviet Union will use its military to take what it wants?

CHAPTER 26

Have the Soviets
Lost Eastern Europe?

It seems obvious that the Soviet Union has lost its Eastern European empire. The Berlin Wall came down and popular revolutions toppled the Communist governments of Eastern Europe and installed democratic regimes.

But were these really popular revolutions? And has the Soviet Union really lost control of its former satellites?

Dr. John Lenczowski, former director of European and Soviet Affairs at the National Security Council, is one of a number of experts who is not so sure the Soviet Union has lost Eastern Europe. He points out that the agendas of some of the new leaders of Eastern Europe are almost identical to Gorbachev's. On January 11, 1990, he wrote:

> Do we know enough to dismiss the possibility that the changes at the top of almost all of these countries may have come at the instigation of the Kremlin, and that these countries' party leaders are simply following the party line as usual, only this time, the Gorbachev line?[1]

Lenczowski was aware that in 1984 Anatoliy Golitsyn, a high-ranking defector from the KGB (the Soviet secret police) had predicted a "false liberalization" in Eastern Europe and probably in the Soviet Union, whose "spectacular" reforms would dazzle, blind and incapacitate the West. Golitsyn said these would include the "exhibition of spurious independence on the part of the regimes of Romania, Czechoslovakia and Poland."[2]

The false liberalization, he said, would be part of a "final, offensive phase of the long-range policy, entailing a joint struggle for the complete triumph of communism," which would be "marked by a major shift of Communist tactics in preparation for a comprehensive assault on the West."[3] Golitsyn's warning appeared in *New Lies for Old*, a book published in 1984 but based on a manuscript completed in 1968.

Golitsyn's statements cannot be easily discounted for two reasons. First, Golitsyn was an expert in counterintelligence and was thoroughly familiar with the long-range Soviet plans. From 1955 to 1959 he was assigned to the KGB Institute, where he was privy to the inner workings of the KGB and intelligence operations related to overall Soviet strategy. From 1959 to 1960 he served as senior analyst in the NATO section of the KGB's Information Department while the KGB was being reorganized and a new aggressive long-range policy was being developed.

Second, most of Golitsyn's predictions came true. It is almost as if he had been reading from a script. The "script," based on Golitsyn's knowledge of Soviet strategy, sounded like pure fantasy in 1984, when a lot of Americans still thought the Soviet Union was the Evil Empire.

Golitsyn's predictions included the formation of a coalition government in Poland made up of the Communist Party, Solidarity and the Church; the return to power of Alexander Dubcek and his associates in Czechoslovakia; the inclusion of Andrei Sakharov in the Soviet government; the Soviets' condemnation of the war they had waged in Afghanistan; and the "reform" of the KGB.

Golitsyn also predicted the reunification of Germany and the "demolition of the Berlin Wall,"[4] an enduring symbol of the Cold War, at a time when no one expected it to come down. And yet it came down so suddenly. Or did it?

Harold Rood, a professor at the Center for Defense and Strategic Studies at Southwest Missouri State University, suggests that the Soviets actually may have taken steps to dismantle the wall as early as 1984. Rood says that the Soviets "started removing the anti-personnel land mines and taking automatic shotguns out of the fence along East Germany and West Germany toward the end of 1984 and the beginning of 1985."

Rood walked up and down the fence dividing East and West Germany among the watchtowers and pillboxes in 1985 and observed these changes. Now, in retrospect, he asks, "Was that the first hint that the Berlin Wall was coming down?"[5]

The Hard Evidence Surfaces

In January of 1990, when Lenczowski and others questioned whether the changes in Eastern Europe could be taken at face value, there was not much evidence to suggest that the revolutions of Eastern Europe started in the Kremlin. There were only Golitsyn's predictions and a lot of suspicious coincidences.

But on May 30, 1990, the BBC broadcast a documentary called *Czech-Mate: Inside the Revolution*, which revealed that the KGB and the Czech secret police jointly engineered the Czech revolution. According to a May 31, 1990 Associated Press summary of the documentary, "Secret police leaders in both the Soviet Union and Czechoslovakia conspired to bring down the hard-line Communist leadership in Prague because it rejected Mikhail Gorbachev's reforms in the Soviet Union."

In the documentary, John Simpson, the BBC foreign affairs editor, said that a KGB-Czech secret-police ploy ignited one of the major demonstrations that started the revolution. On November 17, 1990, a Czech student was supposedly killed during the demonstration. The documentary reported that the "student" was actually Lt. Ludek Zivcak, a member of the Czech secret police who had infiltrated the student movement, and that he was apparently not killed.

The AP summary said, "In the days that followed [the feigned death], people poured into

Wenceslas Square in the heart of the capital to mourn the death and the protests grew.... The mass protests finally brought about the downfall of hard-line President Gustav Husak's government."

The Czech "revolution" was not an isolated case. On June 14, 1990, Barrie Dunsmore, ABC's chief diplomatic correspondent, gave his assessment of the revolutions in Eastern Europe. He said that with the exception of Romania, the revolutions were instigated by Communist leaders rather than by the people. Dunsmore said that the events of Eastern Europe were to some extent "a revolution from above," which "came first of all from Mikhail Gorbachev but then from other leaders within Poland, within Czechoslovakia, within Hungary."[6]

Dunsmore said he believed that the revolution in Romania was a popular revolution. But David Funderburk, United States ambassador to Romania between 1981 and 1985, writes, "It is obvious that the shadowy hand of Gorbachev can be seen behind the developments in Romania and other East European countries."[7]

For years, Western analysts have viewed Romania as a "maverick" Communist state, which generally did not cooperate with Moscow. Funderburk, however, claims that Romania was never a maverick. "Ceausescu was not independent from Moscow," he writes; Romania and the Soviet Union collaborated "behind the scenes in terms of military maneuvers and troop transit, intelligence (KGB-Securitate) coordination and economic-trade ties."[8]

It is well known that Ceausescu did not tolerate dissent and that the Securitate, the Romanian secret police, crushed any signs of political activity hostile to the regime. Yet Ceausescu did not crush the National Salvation Front, the opposition group that eventually replaced him, even though it was formed six to eight months before the revolution.

This suggests to Funderburk that the Front "was protected and encouraged by a power such as Moscow." Supporting the thesis that some of Eastern Europe's new leaders are Gorbachev's men, Funderburk writes: "It is more than coincidental that [Ion Iliescu, the new Communist president of Romania,]...studied at Moscow University and served as the President of Foreign Students when Gorbachev was President of Russian Students."[9]

Romania's largest newspaper, *Adevarul*, which has been the voice of the ruling National Salvation Front, confirmed the essence of Funderburk's thesis. *FPI International Report* said that on August 23, 1990, *Adevarul* "backed a view that the overthrow and execution of dictator Nicolae Ceausescu in December was a coup by other government officials and was not a people's revolution."[10]

The KGB started the revolution in Czechoslovakia. There is evidence that other Eastern European revolutions were orchestrated from the top. They were not "democratic"; they were closer to purges carried out under the cover of crowds. It is impossible for Mikhail Gorbachev not to have known of and approved these doings. Considering this along with Golitsyn's predictions, I can reach no other conclusion than that Gorbachev was behind the revolutions in Eastern Europe.

What was his purpose? To get rid of hard-line leaders cast in the Stalin-Brezhnev mold and to bring in so-called moderate Communist regimes that reflected his "new thinking" and image.

But did Gorbachev expect the revolutions to go as far as they did? He knew that the peoples of Eastern Europe were dissatisfied with their Communist governments. The Kremlin strategists made an effort to direct these pent-up feelings against the "Old Guard," men like Erich Honneker in East Germany, Todor Zhivkov in Bulgaria and Nicolae Ceausescu in Romania.

What Gorbachev and the KGB apparently weren't aware of was the depth of the peoples' desire for freedom. Once their aspirations were unleashed, the people took the revolutions further than anyone in the Soviet hierarchy had anticipated.

Control from Behind the Scenes

When Gorbachev set in motion the events that led to the Eastern European revolutions, he never intended to free the nations from Moscow's control. Despite cosmetic changes at the top, Moscow-aligned Communists still control the essential sectors of society.

Ted Koppel observed on "Nightline," "Perhaps the reason that it all seemed too easy and too good to be true is that it was. After 45 years of Communist control throughout Eastern Europe, it may have been expecting too much to believe that the Communist infrastructure would just collapse and go away."[11]

Since the Soviets apparently started the revolutions, it is reasonable to assume that they took steps to control Eastern Europe after the revolutions were over. In the case of Bulgaria and Romania, the new methods of Soviet domination are the old methods. Although the leaders have changed, both nations are still Soviet satellites and it's business as usual.

In Romania, Gorbachev's old friend, Ion Iliescu, is in power. "What happened in Romania was a great success for Gorbachev," says James Sherr, a specialist on Soviet defense and security policy at Oxford University who is associated with the Soviet Studies Institute of Military Defense in Britain. "What happened there is pretty much what he wanted to happen everywhere else in Eastern Europe."[12]

In Bulgaria, the Communists renamed their party the "Socialists" and won the first free elections in 40 years. Anti-government forces say the election was rigged; the government says the election was fair. In any case, Communists friendly to Moscow are in power.

But the other revolutions seem to have gotten out of control. The new Czechoslovakian president, Václav Havel, a playwright and former dissident, is no Iliescu. And in East Germany, Hungary and Poland as well, the Communists no longer hold the top positions in government.

Nevertheless, in each of these nations Communists loyal to or controlled by Moscow still control the instruments of coercive power: the military, the secret police, the intelligence services and the courts.

Intelligence and defense experts say that even where the Communists don't control the top leadership positions, they control the government bureaucracies. For example, *U.S. News and World Report* noted on September 10, 1990, that Poland "remains stuck with a rigged assembly, Communists in positions of influence and the general who instigated martial law in 1981 as head of state."[13] *Newsweek* reported that "ten months into the Czech revolution, communist state planning remains almost intact."[14]

That gives Communists the power to frustrate the initiatives of inexperienced top officials like Havel. It also gives Communists the power to carry out their own agendas. As Sherr explains:

> You've got a reverse of the situation that existed in Russia in the 1920s during the NEP [New Economic Policy] period when the Communists decided to keep control of the commanding heights but give up control of everything else in society. Now the Communists have decided to surrender control of the commanding heights, but they are still in the woodwork and under the floorboards everywhere.[15]

This phenomenon has gone largely unnoticed in Eastern Europe. But it is more noticeable in Nicaragua. On August 20, 1990, *Time* magazine reported that even though Violeta Chamorro is the democratically elected president of Nicaragua, the Soviet-backed Sandinistas still control the government:

> After 100 days of ruling Nicaragua, what power does the Violeta Chamorro government actually wield? Not much, according to State Department officials, who believe that the ousted Sandinistas still run the country. "The civilians hold the offices, but the Sandinistas have all of the muscle, and they monitor phone calls at will," says a U.S. diplomat just back from Nicaragua.
>
> Humberto Ortega, brother of the ex-President and Chamorro's army chief, earns grudging American respect as the most politically adroit figure in the country. Chamorro gets a harsh assessment. "Even her friends call her 'Rag Doll,'" says the U.S. official. "She's basically apolitical and wants Nicaragua to be a big happy family. Not surprisingly, nobody respects her. Ministers ignore the orders she signs."[16]

And that's the way it goes when a nation tries to reverse the course of a Communist takeover. Where totalitarianism is concerned, there is nothing new under the sun.

CHAPTER 27

The KGB Handle on Eastern Europe

After World War II, the Soviet Union created, organized and trained the secret police and intelligence services of the East bloc nations. They exercised such tight control over them that they were virtually extensions of the KGB. Through them, the Soviets spied on the West and subjugated the peoples of Eastern Europe.

If there had been real reform in Eastern Europe, the Soviets would no longer be able to control the Eastern European secret police forces and intelligence services. But KGB control is still so complete that when the new governments of Czechoslovakia and Hungary tried to cut their ties with the KGB they discovered they were powerless to do so. Instead, they signed new long-term cooperative agreements between the KGB and their intelligence services.[1]

The Czechs have complained about the "heavy presence" of the KGB in Czechoslovakia.[2] They also have openly acknowledged that they are having a hard time getting control of their own intelligence service.

The problem, explains defense consultant and political scientist Dr. Avigdor Haselkorn, is that large parts of the Czech intelligence service were funded from outside of normal government channels by the KGB. "The Czech government not only does not have any control over parts of their intelligence service," he says, "they possibly don't have any knowledge that part of their operation is simply funded and operated by outside forces."[3]

The Stasi Comes Back to Life

In East Germany, the picture is more complex. The Stasi, or East German secret police, was one of the largest and best-run intelligence services in the world. It had 85,000 full-time employees and an additional 150,000 full-time informers. But the Stasi was disbanded shortly after the revolution.

Intelligence analysts say that when the Stasi was dismantled, low-level Stasi agents were "hung out to dry." But, according to Charles Via, chairman of the Center for Intelligence Studies, "the senior East German intelligence [Stasi] officers were evacuated to Moscow. The East German intelligence networks are now functioning under direct KGB control."[4] In short, the supposedly moribund Stasi has come back to life—under Soviet control.

On August 12, 1990, *The New York Times Magazine* published a remarkable story by Steven Emerson about former Stasi chief Markus Wolf. Emerson wrote:

> Although officially defunct, Markus Wolf's organization continues to show remarkable signs of life. . . .

After the Stasi was disbanded, the wiretapping of Western diplomats in East and West Germany suddenly stopped. But two months later, intelligence officials believe they found evidence that it had begun again—this time, they claim, from Soviet military bases in East Germany, suggesting that Stasi agents may have turned over their operation to the Russians, whose military bases will remain in East Germany for another five years.[5]

No one knows exactly why the Soviets decided to permit the reunification of Germany. Some say it became too expensive for the Soviets to keep East Germany and they decided to let the West solve East Germany's horrendous economic and environmental problems.

Others say that Gorbachev never intended to let East Germany go. Egon Krenz, the East German leader who succeeded Honnecker in October 1989, was Gorbachev's man. He was a Gorbachev-like "attractive reformer" (and former head of the secret police).

But the revolution in East Germany took on a life of its own and got out of hand. Krenz was ousted as head of state after only 44 days and replaced by Hans Modrow. Gorbachev couldn't have stopped the revolution without the use of force. And he was loathe to do that because Soviet troops might have had to fight the East German people and elements of the

East German army. If that had happened, the West German army might have stormed across the border to help them, creating a major fiasco for the Soviets.

Others argue that the Soviets favor a reunited Germany for geopolitical reasons. A reunited Germany and the Soviet Union could become close allies and dominate Europe. There are almost as many theories as there are theorists.

Whatever happens, it may be a moot point: numerous Stasi moles, still under Soviet control, have infiltrated and are influencing the highest levels of the West German government. As Emerson reported:

> West German intelligence officers estimate that there are some 5,000 [Stasi] operatives in West Germany today, 500 of them "top agents." Eighty of those are thought to have penetrated the highest echelons of the military and Government, West German officials say, including intelligence agencies.
>
> Despite dramatic political changes in Europe, West German intelligence officials fear that not all these spies have changed their loyalties. Highly disciplined and still undercover, some are still collecting and relaying information to Soviet intelligence organs, the West Germans believe. Others, they suspect, are simply biding their time, waiting to be activated.[6]

Through domestic spying organizations, the Soviets also maintain a significant measure of control over the other Eastern European nations. In Hungary, Poland and Czechoslovakia, the internal security forces were disbanded and then immediately reconstituted.

For example, 20,000 out of 24,000 officers of the SB, the Polish secret police, were transferred to the police force. But Jan Rokita, a Solidarity deputy involved with police reform, says this is a deception. The same people are doing the same job. "Only the signs on the doors have been changed,"[7] he says. According to Tadeusz Kowalczyk, a Solidarity member of parliament, people are still afraid.[8] The Polish Minister of Internal Affairs, General Czeslaw Kiszczak, recently resigned when the press reported that he was not only getting orders from the KGB, but getting *written* orders.[9]

A hallmark of the Cold War was the East-West spy games. One would expect that with the end of the Cold War, espionage would diminish. There was a brief lull in spying following the revolutions of 1989. According to West German and Austrian intelligence, agents were told to stay in place and keep quiet. But then the Eastern European intelligence services, under KGB control, actually increased hostile activities against the West.[10]

CHAPTER 28

Is the Warsaw Pact Finished?

Is the Warsaw Pact defunct? Have the revolutions of 1989 dealt the Soviet Union a cataclysmic military defeat? That's the view from Washington, and a lot of other places as well.

The Warsaw Pact was formed in 1955 by the Soviet Union and Eastern Europe as a counterweight to NATO, an alliance formed by the United States and her allies after World War II. Soviet troops stationed in Eastern Europe are considered to be part of Warsaw Pact forces.

For an organization supposedly on its last legs, the Pact shows remarkable signs of life. The Warsaw Pact conducted joint naval maneuvers in the Baltic sea in June 1990.[1] The new Polish defense minister, who assumed office on July 7, 1990, under a Solidarity-led government, swore allegiance to the Warsaw Pact.[2]

The Soviets have 99 divisions assigned to the Warsaw Pact. Despite reported withdrawals, they are planning to leave a large number of troops in Eastern Europe. And Soviet troops being removed from Poland and Czechoslovakia are being reassigned to East Germany.[3]

In addition, the Soviets have huge stockpiles of supplies in each Eastern European country. For example, in Poland, where the Soviets have two divisions, they have supplies for five more divisions.[4] These two Soviet divisions, which are expected to stay in Poland, have tactical nuclear weapons.[5]

Furthermore, intelligence experts say that the armies of the Eastern European nations are still under Soviet control. The methods of control are the same as before—the KGB, the GRU (Soviet military intelligence), and the allegiance of the officer corps to the Warsaw Pact and Moscow.

The alleged death of Soviet military power in Europe doesn't appear to have affected Soviet conduct at the negotiating table. The agreement reached between West German chancellor Helmut Kohl and Mikhail Gorbachev, announced July 16, 1990, shows that the Soviets are negotiating from a position of strength, not weakness.

The agreement will allow the Soviet Union to keep about 400,000 Soviet soldiers and more than 3,000 nuclear warheads in eastern Germany for four years after Germany is reunited. And the West German government will *pay* the Soviet Union about $7.6 billion in hard currency over the four-year period. After Germany is reunited, the Soviet military will occupy some 8,000 square miles (or 20 percent) of eastern Germany—an area about the size of Massachusetts.

The accord was part of a broad range of agreements between West Germany and the Soviet Union that included a $2.98 billion loan from West Germany, the largest single credit ever granted to the Soviet Union.

In return for all of this, Germany gets to stay in NATO. As Harold Rood observes, "That's the kind of deal you would cut with the Mafia if you didn't have any choice and you wanted to keep your laundry open."[6]

None of this makes it sound like the Warsaw Pact is dead or that the Soviets have left Eastern Europe with their tails between their legs. And even if the alliance does formally disband, it might just be a ruse.

That's the opinion of Jan Sejna, a man who ought to know. Sejna was once a general major in the Czech army, chief of staff at the Ministry of Defense and secretary of the Czech Defense Council, the highest decision-making body in Czechoslovakia. He is also the highest-ranking military figure to defect from the Soviet bloc.

Sejna says that plans were made in the 1960s so that even if the Warsaw Pact alliance formally ceased to exist, the armies of the Pact nations would still cooperate and function as an alliance. "The Soviets knew that one day the Warsaw Pact would come to an end formally," he says.[7]

Does It Matter if the Warsaw Pact Disbands?

But suppose the Warsaw Pact *is* through. Suppose the plans Sejna is familiar with were scrapped. The question remains: Does it really matter?

There is growing evidence that the Soviets do

not regard the military changes in Eastern Europe
as a great strategic loss, even in the worst-case
scenario. When building their alliance, the Soviets
had other things in mind than the offensive potential of the Eastern European armies.

Soviet specialist James Sherr says that the reason the Soviets established the Warsaw Pact was to
prevent the Eastern European nations from hinder-
ing Soviet operations in, or passage through, their
territories. The armies of the Eastern European
nations were trained and structured so that it would
be difficult for them to defend themselves against
the Soviets. "The purpose of the Warsaw Pact all
along," says Sherr, "has been to deny those countries military sovereignty."[8]

Sherr says that if the Soviets play their cards
right, they could disband the Warsaw Pact and
come out ahead. "The Soviets have realized for
some time that it would be a greater advantage to
them to actually destroy NATO than to strengthen
their own alliance system," he explains. "Therefore,
if they were to give up their own alliance system and
the United States gave up its alliance system in
exchange, they would be the beneficiaries."[9]

Since NATO is presently without a purpose,
having extended the hand of friendship to its "former adversaries" in the Warsaw Pact, it could disband or become an empty shell in the foreseeable
future, especially if the Warsaw Pact disintegrates.

And the demise of the Warsaw Pact would not
necessarily limit the Soviets' ability to launch an

offensive war in Europe. The Eastern European armies—those of Bulgaria, Czechoslovakia, East Germany, Hungary, Poland and Romania—make up only 19 percent of the total Soviet and East European forces. The Soviet Union has about 200 divisions of its own, composing the most powerful and heavily armed ground forces in the world. And they don't have to cross the Atlantic to use that force in Europe as the United States would.

Sherr says that the Soviets could "withdraw most of their forces, remove any appearance of an offensive force structure, and still retain an offensive capability based mainly upon forces deployed in the western military districts in the USSR."[10]

The Train Jumps the Tracks

The real question of our time is not whether the Cold War is over but whether the Soviet Union will use its military to solve its problems.

Look at the facts. The Soviet Union is still increasing its military power. The Soviet Union apparently started the revolutions of Eastern Europe and still retains control of the instruments of coercive power: the secret police, the intelligence services, the military and the courts.

Anatoliy Golitsyn predicted a period of false liberalization in the Soviet Union and Eastern Europe culminating with a Communist assault on the West. The evidence we have suggests that Golitsyn's theory (or a close variant) describes the operative Soviet strategy.

But everything did not go as planned. Mikhail Gorbachev unleashed a revolution of rising expectations throughout the Soviet Union and Eastern Europe—and lost control. The train jumped the tracks.

Not only did the revolutions in Eastern Europe get out of hand, the Soviet republics themselves began demanding independence. The crisis is exacerbated by the nonfunctioning Soviet consumer economy. Now the Soviets are faced with an unstable situation and are forced to improvise on a day-to-day basis.

Where will it all end up? That remains to be seen. But there are some likely options: civil war, the breakup of the Soviet Union, or a declaration of martial law and the reimposition of an imperialistic empire.

In any case, the Soviet government will almost certainly have to use force. It has no real diplomatic or economic leverage. Military might is the Soviet Union's only claim to superpower status and its one effective instrument of statecraft. Sooner or later it may have to use it. The alternative is death of the existing order, the largest empire in history. But empires do not willingly roll over and die. And totalitarian regimes, by definition, do not pass the torch of freedom.

And so my answer to the question "Haven't you heard the Cold War is over?" is "Yes, I've heard that it's over." I've heard it a thousand times. But the real question we should be addressing is: "Is the Hot War about to begin?"

CHAPTER 29

The Astrology of
Iraq's Invasion of Kuwait

This is a tale of two eclipses, two superpowers and one invasion that turned the world upside down. It's a story that doesn't have an end—at least not yet.

The action began on July 21, 1990, when Iraq began to mass troops on its border with Kuwait. The word from the Bush administration was that this was nothing to worry about—Iraq's president Saddam Hussein was just bluffing.

So strongly was this belief held in official Washington that, as one inside story goes, when James Schlesinger—former head of the CIA, the Pentagon and the Department of Energy—wrote to Brent Scowcroft, Bush's national security adviser, and told him that Iraq might be on the march, Scowcroft wrote back and told him he disagreed and not to bother him anymore.

Top Washington officials did not err because of a lack of information. They knew from satellite photos and other means how many tanks Iraq had in position. In fact, they had such detailed intelligence that they knew, as one defense expert said facetiously, how many fillings occupied the teeth of

Iraqi soldiers camped on the border. Moreover, the CIA issued repeated warnings to the White House and the State Department that Iraq would attack.

The real reason Washington was caught flat-footed was because of flawed conceptional thinking. As former Assistant Secretary of State Richard Murphy observed, "There was a mind-set on the part of experts inside and outside the administration . . . that assumed an invasion would not happen."[1]

In the early morning hours of August 2, 1990, Saddam "the Bluffer" invaded Kuwait with 100,000 troops and suddenly became "the Butcher of Baghdad."

For those who remember the moment in Jimmy Carter's presidency when the Soviet Union invaded Afghanistan, it was déjà vu. In late 1979, U.S. intelligence watched as Soviet tanks and troops massed on the Soviet-Afghanistan border. The Carter administration had some inkling what those troops were for. They warned the Soviets at least five times not to invade. And Carter thought they would not.

On December 27, 1979, when the Red Army barreled into Kabul, Carter found out just how wrong he had been. Once again, a lack of information wasn't the problem. Intelligence on troop movements, on the construction of a satellite communications station near the Afghan border, and on motorized divisions being placed on alert status had been passed along to the president and his cabinet. Inability (or refusal) to see the obvious was the culprit.

The moral: the conventional wisdom may often be nothing more than wishful thinking. It is vital that we learn this lesson quickly. There is yet another dangerous popular misconception to be wary of in the Iraq crisis. But before we examine it, let's talk about the astrology of Iraq's invasion of Kuwait.

Chart for the Republic of Iraq

Iraq has a long and complex history. The Tigris-Euphrates valley, located within Iraq, is the site of the oldest known civilization. Sumerian city-states flourished there as far back as 4000 B.C., followed by the great empires of Assyria and Babylonia.

Persia conquered Babylon in 538 B.C. and dominated the area until superseded by the Greeks, the Arabs, the Mongols and Turks. The British invaded Iraq during World War I and in 1920 received a League of Nations mandate to rule it.

On August 23, 1921, Britain recognized Iraq as a kingdom. Iraq became fully independent in 1932 when the League of Nations mandate expired. Mundane astrologer Nicholas Campion says, "The horoscope for this date deserves to be taken as a national chart in view of the fact that an entirely new state was being recognized for the first time."[2]

Most astrologers, however, use a chart set for Baghdad at 5:00 a.m. on July 14, 1958, as Iraq's birth chart. That was the place, time and date that a military junta carried out a lightning coup. They overthrew the pro-Western monarchy, installed a socialist military dictatorship and established the

Republic of Iraq. The chart for this coup describes recent events better than any other chart proposed for Iraq.

The Republic of Iraq has its Sun at 21° Cancer, its Ascendant at 19° Cancer and its Moon at 17° Gemini. But the most important feature of this chart is a T-square formed by Mars at 25° Aries opposed to Jupiter at 22° Libra, both square to the Sun at 21° Cancer (fig. 35).

This planetary pattern shows the propensity for Iraq's leaders (Sun) to take decisive (Aries) military action (Mars) against anyone or anything that threatens their domestic security (Cancer) or international (Jupiter) ambitions (Aries).

It also shows far-reaching (Jupiter) territorial (Cancer) ambitions (Mars in Aries). These are likely to be pursued by military conquest since Mars is in the sign it rules (Aries) and Jupiter, which acts as a multiplier, is in Libra, which rules warfare.

Oil has made Iraq a wealthy country. Iraq has about 100 billion barrels of proven underground petroleum reserves. When it invaded Kuwait it seized control of nearly another 100 billion barrels of oil. Only Saudi Arabia, with 257 billion barrels, has greater reserves.

Saudi Arabia and other oil-rich Persian Gulf states, such as Kuwait and the United Arab Emirates, have used their oil reserves to buy a better life for their citizens. But true to its T-square, Iraq has spent its money on weapons. Not only does Iraq manufacture many of its own weapons, but over the

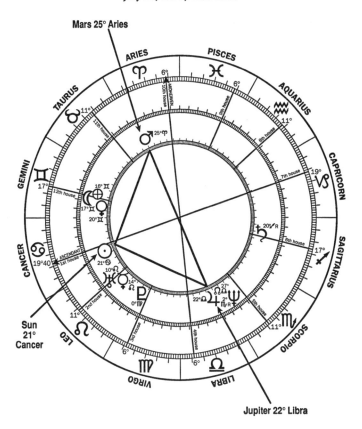

Republic of Iraq
Birth Chart
July 14, 1958, 5:00 a.m.

Mars 25° Aries

Sun
21°
Cancer

Jupiter 22° Libra

FIGURE 35 The Republic of Iraq was born at 5:00 a.m. Baghdad time (BGT), July 14, 1958, when a military junta overthrew the pro-Western monarchy. Iraq's Sun is at 21° Cancer, its Moon is at 17° Gemini and its Ascendant is at 19° Cancer. The T-square formed by Mars at 25° Aries opposed to Jupiter at 22° Libra and square to the Sun at 21° Cancer shows that Iraq's leaders would have a propensity to take decisive military action against anyone or anything that threatens their domestic security or international ambitions.

past 12 years Iraq has been the world's largest importer of armaments. Iraq now has the world's fourth largest military and an extensive military infrastructure.

Iraq and Hussein

What is the relationship between Iraq and Saddam Hussein? The way President Bush and the State Department have been talking, it sounds like the current crisis is of one man's making. The implication is that if we simply get rid of Hussein, our problems with Iraq will be over.

But that is not the case. Iraq's astrology and history show that with or without Hussein the nation is a force to be reckoned with. Should the United States fulfill its undeclared goal of toppling Hussein, Iraq would still have powerful conventional forces (a million-man army, 5,500 tanks, 800 surface-to-surface missiles and 550 combat aircraft) and a growing arsenal of chemical and biological weapons.

American and Israeli intelligence experts believe that Hussein's successor could be at least as bad as Hussein himself and that the threat of Iraq starting a nuclear war in the near future will persist. As an Israeli expert told *The New York Times*, "The [Iraqi] army is now led by young Turks [hotheads], and a change from Hussein would probably be a change for the worse."[3]

Iraq currently has medium-range ballistic missiles and, according to a new U.S. intelligence assessment, could have nuclear weapons in two years or less. It is only a matter of time before they make the leap from medium-range to intercontinental ballistic missiles capable of reaching the United States. In other words, the United States must deal with Iraq *and* Hussein, not just Hussein.

Madman or Rational Risk-Taker?

Even though Hussein is not indispensable to Iraq, he has just the right kind of astrology to express the most militant and aggressive aspects of Iraq's chart.

Since his invasion of Kuwait, Hussein has often been described as a madman. This is in sharp contrast to his previous image as a force of moderation in the Arab world and an ally against the hated regime of Iran's Ayatollah Khomeini.

During the Iran-Iraq war the United States helped Iraq. The U.S. reestablished diplomatic relations with Iraq in 1984 (Iraq had broken them off in 1967 in response to the Arab-Israeli Six-Day War), sold Iraq huge quantities of grain as well as materials for its missile and nuclear-weapons programs, and turned a blind eye to its use of chemical weapons.

The Reagan administration shrugged off Iraq's unprovoked attack on the USS *Stark* on May 17, 1987, which killed 37 American seamen. It accepted Iraq's claim that the attack was an accident when there was evidence to the contrary, and then swiftly took action against *Iran*.

The U.S. Navy attacked Iranian patrol boats in the Persian Gulf that had been harassing Kuwaiti oil tankers. (Kuwaiti oil was financing the Iraqi war effort.) As *Newsweek* reported, "Kuwaiti oil, which had been sold to finance Saddam's military effort, proceeded safely to market. The American move, coming when Iranian troops were advancing, may have saved Iraq from defeat."[4]

When the Iran-Iraq war ended in 1988 and Iraq failed to demobilize and began making increasingly bellicose statements, the White House, the State Department and some members of Congress tried to appease Hussein. On April 12, 1990, Senator Howard Metzenbaum (D-Ohio), in Baghdad with a delegation of senators, actually told Hussein, "I am now aware that you are a strong and intelligent man, and that you want peace."[5]

Since he came to power in 1979, Hussein has turned Iraq into a brutal police state where spying, imprisonment, torture and death are a way of life. He appears to have no qualms about killing anyone—friend or foe—who gives the slightest indication of threatening his power or authority.

He has used chemical weapons on Kurdish women and children and rockets on Iranian civilians. He has killed cabinet members, military officers, and reportedly even two of his relatives. According to one account, Hussein drew his revolver and shot and killed one of his generals who told him that a certain plan would cause many Iraqi soldiers to die in battle.

Hussein is brutal. But is he a madman?

Hussein was born on April 28, 1937, in the Iraqi village of Tikrit. Since his time of birth is unknown, I use a solar chart set for noon on his date of birth as his natal chart (fig. 36). A solar chart is one drawn for the date but not the time of birth The time can be arbitrarily set for noon or dawn. It is valuable to set the solar chart of a leader for noon because a noon chart puts the Sun in the tenth house of career and public standing and reveals the nature of his public life.

Hussein's Sun is at 7° Taurus closely conjoined Uranus at 9° Taurus. This conjunction indicates that he is practical, innovative and capable of surprising and unexpected action. He also has great determination and staying power. U.S. leaders may seriously miscalculate if they think they are going to simply "get rid" of Hussein.

Hussein's Sun-Uranus conjunction shows his potential to be a dictator. The Sun rules the use of power to lead or to bully. Uranus, the planet of freedom, in its negative mode can be expressed as anti-freedom, or tyranny. Astrologers Charles Jayne and David Williams say that Uranus is the planet of dictators since it indicates the capacity to rule by whim.

Hussein's Sun-Uranus conjunction does not necessarily show a drive for military conquest but he has a T-square that does. His natal Jupiter at 26° Capricorn is opposed to his Pluto at 26° Cancer, and both are square to his Venus at 21° Aries. This T-square resonates with the T-square in Iraq's chart, showing that Hussein is apt to express the most brutal attributes of Iraq's T-square.

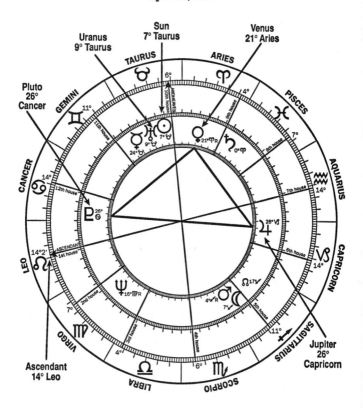

Saddam Hussein
Birth Chart
April 28, 1937

FIGURE 36 Saddam Hussein was born on April 28, 1937, in Tikrit, Iraq. Since the time of his birth is unknown, the chart has been drawn for noon. Hussein's Sun is at 7° Taurus conjoined Uranus at 9° Taurus. This conjunction indicates that he is practical, innovative and capable of surprising and unexpected action. The T-square formed by Jupiter at 26° Capricorn opposed to Pluto at 26° Cancer and square to Venus at 21° Aries shows that Hussein has a tendency to engage in large-scale power struggles and that he is politically ruthless.

Hussein's T-square shows a tendency to engage in large-scale power struggles (Jupiter-Pluto) that cause the death (Pluto) of many (Jupiter) people (Cancer). It also shows Hussein to be politically ruthless (Jupiter-Pluto). At times Hussein will be financially well off (Jupiter-Venus); at other times he will be either in dire financial straits or seized by the lust for wealth (Pluto-Venus).

The placement of Jupiter in a chart is a key to a person's "luck" and his willingness to gamble or take a chance. Hussein's Jupiter is in Capricorn, the sign that governs political, organizational or social power. His Jupiter-Pluto opposition reveals that the areas in which he is likely to take risks will involve large-scale life-and-death power struggles over political and economic power that could cost him or others their lives.

The Pluto-Jupiter opposition in Cancer-Capricorn shows that Hussein's need for power vastly outweighs his sensitivity to the suffering of others—if he has any sensitivity to others at all. In this area of his life he tends to see things in terms of absolutes and acts to accrue or preserve power no matter what the cost or risk.

It is important to note, however, that what others see as Hussein's reckless behavior may in fact be calculated behavior. Hussein has a very different set of values than others. He is willing to do things—gas, torture, kill, bully, et cetera—that most people could or would not do. When he takes risks, he counts on the discrepancy between his values and others' to skew the odds in his favor.

Hussein's natal chart shows him to be a risk-taker but not mad or irrational. Although he is not a military genius, he has a lifetime of paramilitary and military experience, he understands the ways of the Middle East, and he studied law. What he lacks in brilliance he makes up for with cunning and audacity. "He is an extremely shrewd, cold-blooded, clever thug,"[6] a senior British diplomat who has dealt with Hussein told *Time* in August 1990.

Hussein's T-square and Iraq's T-square both show the capacity for war, conquest and repression. Hussein's chart makes other important contacts with Iraq's chart, showing that under his leadership Iraq will express its warlike characteristics. Hussein's Pluto at 26° Cancer conjoins Iraq's Sun at 21° Cancer. His Venus at 21° Aries conjoins Iraq's Mars at 25° Aries. And his Jupiter at 26° Capricorn squares Iraq's Jupiter at 22° Libra.

Iraq at the Crossroads

In 1990, the Republic of Iraq had its solar return on July 13, the day before its 32nd birthday. A chart drawn for the solar return gives an astrologer an idea of the opportunities and challenges that can be expected during that year.

July 13, 1990, was also the day that transiting Jupiter at 22° Cancer made an exact opposition to transiting Saturn at 22° Capricorn. To have such an opposition on a solar return is significant. Jupiter and Saturn are a planetary pair that rule opposite characteristics. Jupiter rules space; Saturn rules time.

Jupiter shows where expansion is likely; Saturn shows where crystallization will occur. Jupiter is philosophical; Saturn is practical.

Jupiter and Saturn make their oppositions only once every 20 years. The ancients believed major Jupiter-Saturn aspects governed the course of history. Since 1840, Jupiter-Saturn conjunctions have been associated with the death of U.S. presidents. During a Jupiter-Saturn opposition, an existing trend can be reinforced and given the impetus to either continue for another 10 years or be reversed.

Iraq went to war with Iran on September 22, 1980, as Jupiter and Saturn were forming their conjunction. Now, when the planets are opposed, it is again in formation for war—400,000 troops strong in Kuwait!

On July 13, 1990, transiting Jupiter and Saturn were in close aspect to Iraq's T-square (fig. 37). They activated the T-square and turned it into a grand square. Transiting Jupiter at 22° Cancer conjoined Iraq's Sun at 21° Cancer. These planets opposed transiting Saturn at 22° Capricorn and squared Iraq's Mars at 25° Aries and Iraq's Jupiter at 22° Libra.

There is no set astrological interpretation for a configuration like this. To be sure, the activation of the T-square made war and the quest for territorial gain likely; the formation of a grand square indicates complex events with long-term consequences.

But the Jupiter-Saturn opposition falling so close to Iraq's Sun indicates that Iraq is at a crossroads.

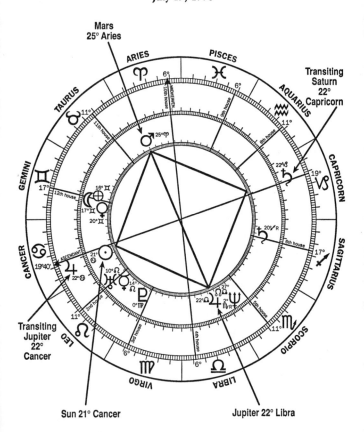

**Jupiter and Saturn Form a Grand Square
in Iraq's Natal Chart
July 13, 1990**

Mars
25° Aries

Transiting
Saturn
22°
Capricorn

Transiting
Jupiter
22°
Cancer

Sun 21° Cancer

Jupiter 22° Libra

FIGURE 37 On July 13, 1990, the day of Iraq's solar return, transiting Jupiter at 22° Cancer conjoined Iraq's Sun at 21° Cancer opposed to transiting Saturn at 22° Capricorn and squared Iraq's Mars at 25° Aries and Iraq's Jupiter at 22° Libra. This formed a grand square, which indicates complex events with long-term consequences. Jupiter and Saturn also activated Iraq's T-square, making war and the quest for territorial gain likely. Jupiter conjoined Iraq's Sun is a fortunate placing for Iraq.

If Iraq is successful in its aggression and expansion, it could grow in power and continue to be a force to be reckoned with for a long time. If it is not successful, it could be reduced in power or destroyed.

The grand square has several other influences including the increased likelihood of economic difficulties. Saturn (restriction) is opposed to the conjunction of the Sun and Jupiter (expansion) in Cancer (sustenance). It also suggests the possibility of economic warfare that could take the form of a blockade or embargo, and it indicates that actions taken by Iraq could tax the financial strength of other nations.

Returning to Iraq's solar return, I would like to point out that transiting Jupiter at 22° Cancer conjoined Iraq's Sun at 21° Cancer is a "lucky" placing because of Jupiter's fortunate and protective influence. It is also in the first house, where its beneficial influence is amplified. As astrologer Barbara Watters points out, "In mundane charts concerning war, Jupiter's placement may indicate which side will be victorious."[7] Jupiter well-placed in Iraq's solar return means Iraq is poised for victory. It has already conquered and absorbed Kuwait.

Saturn, the significator of defeat, is in the seventh house of Iraq's enemies. This could indicate defeat or a stalemate for the United States. But the outcome is not predestined. If the U.S. meets all of Saturn's requirements, i.e., timing, planning, organization and practicality, this Saturn initiation could lead to victory for the United States.

Iraq Mobilizes for Attack

Iraq and Hussein have the astrological drive to conquer. Iraq's solar return for 1990 indicates it might get into a major war. But what triggered Hussein's troop mobilization and invasion? The answer: Two eclipses.

The first was the eclipse of the Sun at 29° Cancer that I mentioned in chapter 22. It took place on July 21, 1990, the day that Iraq started massing troops and tanks on its border with Kuwait.

This eclipse hit Hussein's Jupiter-Pluto opposition (at 26° Capricorn-Cancer), inflaming his ambition (Capricorn) and desire for power (Pluto) and land (Capricorn) and increasing his chances for success (Jupiter). It also activated Hussein's Jupiter-Pluto-Venus T-square, his mechanism for calculated power struggles, which in turn activated Iraq's Mars-Jupiter-Sun T-square, its mechanism for attaining power and territory by military conquest.

But this eclipse also indicated that any military adventure would be a high-stakes (Pluto) gamble (Jupiter) with serious long-term consequences. Under Jupiter's influence there was the potential for Hussein to overreach or be overly optimistic.

On the March

The eclipse of the Moon at 13° Aquarius on August 6, 1990, set Iraq marching. The invasion began at about 2 a.m. on August 2, when the eclipse was waxing.

On August 4, there was an exact opposition of Mars at 15° Taurus to Pluto at 15° Scorpio, one of the most dangerous of all aspects since it combines the influences of the planet of war (Mars) with the planet of widespread death and destruction (Pluto). The eclipse of the Moon at 13° Aquarius and the transiting Sun at 13° Leo squared the Mars-Pluto opposition, forming a grand square.

This grand square brings together the body that rules life, power, vitality, leadership and identity (Sun) with the body that rules the material world, the people and emotions (Moon) with the planet of war (Mars) and the planet of hidden action and widespread death and destruction (Pluto).

As I said in chapter 24, this grand square is so explosive that it could ignite a major war. I also noted that the eclipse energized the grand square in the combined natal charts of the United States and the Soviet Union. It also formed a grand square in Iraq's progressed chart for August 6, 1990 (fig. 38). Iraq's progressed Ascendant at 13° Leo conjoined progressed Uranus at 12° Leo and the Sun at 13° Leo and opposed the eclipse of the Moon at 13° Aquarius. All of the above were square transiting Pluto at 15° Scorpio and transiting Mars at 16° Taurus conjoined Iraq's progressed Mars at 14° Taurus.

The square of Iraq's progressed Ascendant and Uranus to progressed Mars is a strong indication of sudden aggression and power plays. The conjunction of transiting Mars with Iraq's progressed Mars in the tenth house (reputation and public standing)

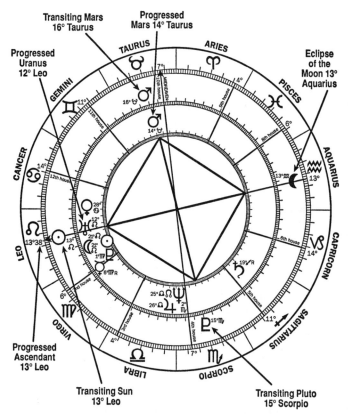

Transiting Mars, Pluto and the Eclipse of the Moon Form a Grand Square in Iraq's Progressed Chart
August 6, 1990

FIGURE 38   On August 6, 1990, the eclipse of the Moon formed a grand square in Iraq's progressed chart. The eclipse of the Moon at 13° Aquarius opposed Iraq's progressed Ascendant and the transiting Sun at 13° Leo, which conjoined Iraq's progressed Uranus at 12° Leo and squared transiting Pluto at 15° Scorpio, which was conjoined Iraq's progressed Mars at 14° Taurus and transiting Mars at 16° Taurus. The Mars-Mars conjunction in the tenth house heightened the potential for war and signified that Iraq would be almost universally seen and condemned as the aggressor.

heightened the potential for war and signified that Iraq would be almost universally seen and condemned as the aggressor.

This configuration shows that while Iraq's serious economic problems are important, they were not the primary reason for the invasion. Hussein invaded Kuwait for power and glory.

The conjunction of Iraq's progressed Uranus with the transiting Sun in Leo during the eclipse made it easy for Hussein, who has a natal Sun-Uranus conjunction, to express his identity by invading Kuwait.

Leo indicates a sudden power play and shows that the invasion was not merely an attempt to overpower Kuwait, but an effort to bully the entire Arab world, intimidate Israel, and change the global balance of power.

Crash and Burn

The August 6 lunar eclipse also formed a grand square in Hussein's natal and progressed charts (fig. 39). The eclipse of the Moon at 13° Aquarius fell on his seventh-house cusp (war) opposed his natal Ascendant at 14° Leo conjoined the Sun at 13° Leo.

All of these squared Hussein's progressed Moon at 22° Scorpio, which conjoined his progressed Mars at 19° Scorpio and transiting Pluto at 15° Scorpio and opposed transiting Mars at 16° Taurus, Hussein's progressed Venus at 13° Taurus, his progressed Uranus at 12° Taurus and his natal Uranus and Sun at 9° and 7° Taurus.

The Eclipse of the Moon Forms a Grand Square in Saddam Hussein's Natal and Progressed Charts
August 6, 1990

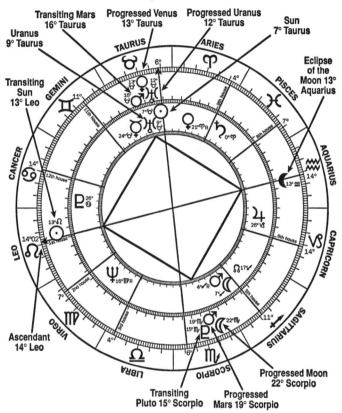

FIGURE 39 The lunar eclipse of August 6, 1990, formed a grand square in Saddam Hussein's natal and progressed charts. The eclipse of the Moon at 13° Aquarius opposed the transiting Sun at 13° Leo and squared Hussein's progressed Moon at 22° Scorpio, progressed Mars at 19° Scorpio and transiting Pluto at 15° Scorpio and squared six planets: transiting Mars at 16° Taurus, Hussein's progressed Venus at 13° Taurus, progressed Uranus at 12° Taurus, and natal Uranus and Sun at 9° and 7° Taurus. This configuration indicates the unbridled use of military force in the pursuit of power.

Note: Transiting and progressed planets are shown on outer ring; natal planets on inner ring.

This configuration spotlights some of Hussein's strengths and weaknesses. It indicates, for example, the unbridled use of aggression in the pursuit of power. It shows that Hussein is driven by great anger and what, under less dangerous circumstances, would be a ludicrous sense of self-importance.

It shows that in addition to the will to conquer, Hussein has a deep-seated desire to destroy. The linking of Mars, Uranus and Pluto shows the sudden and devastating use of military force, including the potential use of chemical and biological weapons—and even nuclear weapons—perhaps by the United States.

The conjunction of the Moon, Mars and Pluto in Scorpio can be not only aggressive but also self-destructive. In short, Hussein could crash and burn. Scorpio self-destructivity is often a frightening phenomenon. The Scorpio death wish can inflict terrible punishment on those in the vicinity when the person self-destructs. Thus, Hussein's threats to fight to the death should not be taken lightly.

Quicksand?

There are three configurations that show that things are not what they seem in terms of U.S. intervention in Saudi Arabia and her future conflict with Iraq.

First of all, the grand squares in Iraq's and Hussein's charts are a sure sign of hidden power plays and deadly subterranean machinations.

Secondly, the current opposition of transiting Neptune at 13° Capricorn to the U.S. conceptional

Sun at 13° Cancer (fig. 18, p. 220) shows treachery, intrigue and confusion, especially surrounding Neptune-ruled oil.

Thirdly, the interaction of the U.S. conceptional Neptune with the T-square in President George Bush's chart (fig. 22, p. 240) indicates deception. In chapter 20, I said that this T-square indicated a high probability of military confrontation, battles, or war three months on either side of July 4, 1990. I also said it "could inaugurate a cycle leading to major military conflict."

The T-square is made up of Bush's Sun at 21° Gemini conjoined the U.S. conceptional Mars at 21° Gemini opposed to the U.S. conceptional progressed Moon at 21° Sagittarius, all square to Bush's natal Uranus at 21° Pisces. The U.S. conceptional Neptune at 22° Virgo opposed to Bush's Uranus extends this configuration into a grand square, indicating that the military conflict could be related to oil and intrigue (both Neptune-ruled). In short, it shows that something dangerous is going on beneath the surface.

Fusion

There is an astrological link between the events now unfolding in the Middle East and a potential future confrontation between the United States and the Soviet Union.

The grand squares formed by the August 6 eclipse of the Moon at 13° Aquarius in Iraq's progressed chart and in Hussein's natal and progressed charts are almost identical, hence fused, to the grand square in the combined charts of the United States and the Soviet Union (fig. 31, p. 289). And I said in chapter 24 that the August 6 eclipse has the potential to ignite a war between the superpowers (pp. 291–93).

If these three grand squares (fig. 33, p. 292; fig. 38, p. 354; and fig. 39, p. 356) were superimposed, the following planets would be either conjoined, square or opposed to each other: the transiting Sun, U.S. natal Sun, Soviet natal Sun and Saddam Hussein's natal Sun; transiting Pluto and the U.S. natal Pluto; the Soviet natal Uranus, Saddam Hussein's progressed Uranus and Iraq's progressed Uranus; and transiting Mars, Saddam Hussein's progressed Mars and Iraq's progressed Mars.

Thus, these three grand squares link the national identities of the U.S., the Soviet Union and Iraq with the planets of mass death and destruction (Pluto), unpredictable events (Uranus) and war (Mars). They show that Iraq's invasion of Kuwait will affect both the United States and the Soviet Union and could be a fuse for U.S.-Soviet conflict.

CHAPTER 30

Dangerous Liaisons

Did Moscow know that Iraq was going to invade Kuwait? The story being circulated by Washington is that Soviet Foreign Minister Eduard A. Shevardnadze was genuinely surprised by the invasion.

On August 1, 1990, Secretary of State James Baker was in Irkutsk, Siberia, with Shevardnadze. According to published reports, Baker told Shevardnadze that he was concerned that Iraq, a long-time Soviet client, was poised to invade Kuwait. "We hope you'll try to restrain these guys," he said as they drove to lunch.[1] Shevardnadze, so the story goes, was confident that they did not plan to invade. "The Iraqis are just posturing," he said. "They are not going to do it."[2]

On August 2, Baker got word at 7:45 a.m. that the CIA was convinced the invasion would take place within hours. Baker promptly told Shevardnadze. *Newsweek* reported that "this time Shevardnadze gave Baker the impression that Saddam had assured the Soviets that he would not attack. 'The crisis is being defused,' Shevardnadze insisted."[3]

Perhaps an unhealthy reliance on Soviet promises led the Bush administration to conclude that Iraq would not invade.

Baker was meeting with Shevardnadze when the invasion took place. According to Morton Kondracke, senior editor for *The New Republic*, "Baker got the word from his policy planning chief, Dennis Ross, in a men's room during a break in his talks with Shevardnadze. When Baker told Shevardnadze, aides say, the Soviet official was 'clearly surprised.'"[4]

Newsweek, in a more dramatic rendition of these events, said, "When Baker told Shevardnadze, the Soviet Foreign Minister was stunned—and embarrassed. 'We haven't heard anything about it,' he said. Turning to an aide, Sergei Tarasenko, he ordered: 'Look into this immediately.'"[5]

The next day, August 3, the United States and the Soviet Union held a joint press conference in Moscow and condemned "the brutal and illegal invasion of Kuwait." Moscow suspended arms deliveries to Iraq and both superpowers urged the nations of the world to cut off "all arms supplies to Iraq."[6]

During the conference Shevardnadze admitted that he had been mistaken about Iraq. Kondracke reported that "Baker aides . . . were astounded that a Soviet foreign minister . . . would confess to his own press and public that American information was better than his own."[7]

The not-so-hidden message of this episode from "Scenes in the Lives of Diplomats" is that no one in the Kremlin expected Iraq's invasion. In fact, these confidential details were released to convince people of just that. According to Kondracke, "This sequence of events is being cited around the Bush administration to refute claims from outside critics... that the Soviet Union is playing a perfidious double game in the Iraq crisis—pretending to be part of the 'new world order' that the administration is trying to put together, while at the same time keeping up its ties with Iraq."[8]

Reality Check

What's wrong with this picture? Almost everything—starting with the fact that it is virtually impossible for Shevardnadze, the former KGB chief in Soviet Georgia, to have been surprised by the invasion.

Let me be blunt: Despite Shevardnadze's Oscar-caliber performance, the Soviets had to have known that Iraq was going to invade Kuwait. And there is substantial evidence that they helped plan the invasion and have continued to support Iraq militarily ever since.

This view is very much at odds with the popular mythology that the Soviet Union is our ally on this one. After all, the Soviets issued a joint statement with the U.S. condemning the invasion, supported United Nations resolutions for sanctions against Iraq, and attended a snap superpower summit in Helsinki, where presidents Bush and Gorbachev issued an extraordinary statement that said "aggression cannot and will not pay."[9]

This "crime does not pay" message plays well on the evening news. But the Bush administration is being taken for a ride—or, more likely, the Bush administration is taking itself for a ride. In either case, the administration should know that something is terribly wrong with its reading of events.

What Did They Know? When Did They Know It?

Could Iraq have invaded Kuwait without Soviet approval? There has been considerable discussion in recent weeks of the military assistance provided to Iraq by France, Brazil, West Germany and the United States. Nevertheless, the Soviet Union is unquestionably Iraq's biggest military supplier.

The Soviets sold Iraq about $17 billion in arms between 1983 and 1988 alone, including advanced T-72 tanks, Scud-B ballistic missiles, anti-aircraft missiles and MiG fighters—even Moscow's most advanced model, the MiG-29. And after the Iran-Iraq war ended in 1988, the Soviets helped Iraq rearm.

Iraq has been a Soviet client since 1958. The Soviets have organized, trained and equipped Iraq's military and intelligence service. They have helped build and still help run Iraq's military industrial complex. They have even set up production lines in Iraq for Soviet T-72 tanks and MiG-29 fighter aircraft. Given the history of Soviet-Iraqi collaboration, intelligence experts say it is highly unlikely or impossible that Iraq would have invaded Kuwait without Soviet approval.

The Soviets have thousands of military advisers in Iraq. Experts differ over the numbers (the estimates range from 1,000 to 8,000). These advisers must have known what Iraq was up to since, as intelligence expert and author Edward Jay Epstein notes, they were "attached to the helicopter, tank, logistic, and radar units used for the invasion."[10]

Foreign policy analyst Peter Schweizer points out that "among these [Soviet military] personnel are several senior officers who are reported to be members of the closest circle of military advisers to the Iraqi strongman, Saddam Hussein."[11]

In addition, intelligence sources say that the KGB has "penetrated every aspect of Iraqi government life to the highest levels."[12] And it is almost certain that the KGB and GRU (Soviet military intelligence) were intercepting Iraqi radio traffic and diplomatic messages. Intelligence analyst Charles Via says that the Soviet Union probably sold Iraq their encryption and decryption equipment, which would make it relatively easy for the Soviets to break Iraq's codes.[13]

Could the Soviet military advisers in the field, or those close to Hussein, have failed to report to Moscow what Baghdad was planning? Could the KGB agents who have penetrated the upper reaches of Iraq's government have neglected to mention the most important development in the Middle East in a decade? Could the Soviet intelligence analysts, who were no doubt reading Iraq's radio traffic, also have dropped the ball?

Not likely. But should there have been a catastrophic failure of Soviet intelligence, the Soviets had plenty of opportunity to *ask* the Iraqis why they were massing troops on the Kuwait border.

On July 27, 1990, Iraq's minister of state, A. Al-Zibari, was in Moscow for a Soviet-Iraqi Friendship Festival, where, according to *Izvestia*, he was received by the Soviet deputy minister of foreign affairs, A. M. Belonogov. *Izvestia* reported that Al-Zibari and Belonogov "had a thorough discussion during which key questions of Soviet-Iraqi relations and the situation in the Middle East region was touched upon."[14]

Surely the topic of Iraqi troops massing on Kuwait's border came up in conversation. The Soviets knew they were there since they had changed the orbit of their Cosmos-2086 spy satellite on July 28 while Al-Zibari was still in Moscow. The new orbit enabled the satellite to make a low-altitude pass over Kuwait daily.[15]

By that time Iraq had more than 30,000 troops and a large number of tanks on its border with Kuwait, and Hussein was threatening Kuwait and Saudi Arabia with dire consequences if they didn't comply with his demands.

Iraq's "grievances" with Kuwait and the other Gulf states were no secret. They were aired for months in Arab diplomatic circles and were discussed openly in the press—along with Hussein's thinly veiled threat of military action if the disputes were not resolved to his satisfaction.

Nor was Hussein reticent to discuss the subject with U.S. Ambassador April C. Glaspie. On July 25, 1990, Hussein summoned Glaspie for a meeting. In a lengthy discussion of U.S.-Iraq relations, oil and war, Glaspie told Hussein that the United States was concerned about the massive troop deployment and that she had instructions to ask him about his intentions.

Hussein said Iraq was running out of patience and raised the possibility of an invasion. But he told Glaspie, "Assure the Kuwaitis and give them our word that we are not going to do anything until we meet with them. But if we are unable to find a solution, then it will be natural that Iraq will not accept death."[16]

Hussein discussed the use of force with the Arabs and Americans. Can we believe that the subject of mobilization never came up in discussions between Iraqi diplomats and their Soviet benefactors?

Soviet Shadows

Iraq's invasion of Kuwait was a model of Soviet tactics. Iraq, which did not perform well offensively against Iran, executed a well-timed and coordinated nighttime air, land and sea blitzkrieg against Kuwait.

What could have been behind this sudden quantum improvement in Iraq's offensive abilities? For one thing, on July 17, 1990, Colonel General Albert Makashov arrived in Baghdad for a several-week tour of duty as the Soviet military counsellor to

Iraq. According to Schweizer, Makashov "held a series of private meetings with the Iraqi Foreign Minister."[17]

Makashov's visit strongly suggests not only that the Soviets knew about the invasion but also that they played a major role in planning it.

Makashov is one of the Soviet Union's best field officers and a protégé of General Nikolai Orgarkov, former Soviet chief of staff and an advocate of lightning-fast offensive operations. *Pravda* recently described Makashov as a man who believes that "military might and military victories are the only means of maintaining national security."[18]

Makashov is a remarkable figure. As *Insight* magazine reported:

> The published Soviet military biographies of Makashov leave significant holes in his curriculum vitae from 1971 to 1980. This indicates that he was either carrying out clandestine military assignments (for example, in Angola or Ethiopia) or was attached to the GRU, the Main Intelligence Directorate of the Soviet General Staff. He then served in the Afghanistan war. In 1982, he won the gold medal of the Soviet General Staff Academy.
>
> In addition to his superior performance at the academy, Makashov always has excelled as a field officer. He was made deputy commander, then promoted to commander of the Soviets' Third Shock Army, one of the two

armies that would lead an attack on Western Europe. This is a plum posting, one of the most highly desired commands in the army.

Makashov became commander of the Transcaucasus Military District and was in Yerevan in Armenia in 1988 to suppress nationalist demonstrations. Subsequently he was promoted to commander of the Volga-Urals Military District. This would be the wartime headquarters of the Soviet General Staff, embedded in the granite massif at Kuybyshev on the Volga River.[19]

Makashov has just the kind of military experience the Iraqis needed to plan their invasion of Kuwait. So what was he doing in Baghdad?

According to Moscow, he was in the doghouse. A week before Iraq invaded Kuwait, Soviet officials sought out Western reporters to inform them that Makashov was sent to Baghdad as a punishment for criticizing Gorbachev's reforms.

At the most recent Communist Party Congress, held in Moscow in June 1990, Makashov did unleash a scathing denunciation of *perestroika*. He attacked the "new thinking in international affairs" as a "falsification of Leninist doctrine" and accused Gorbachev and other reformers of "ideological surrender" to the West.[20]

But if Makashov were truly out of favor, why would the Soviets send him to a strategically important hot spot that was getting hotter every moment?

Only the most loyal Soviet officers are allowed to travel abroad.

Can it really be a coincidence that Makashov arrived in Baghdad just before the Iraqi military executed a large-scale operation using the kinds of tactics in which he specializes?

The Moscow Connection

One day after the invasion, the Soviet Union announced the cutoff of all arms shipments to Iraq and, in a joint statement with the United States, urged all other nations to do the same.

Discussion of this historic event and other diplomatic "signals" that the superpowers have sent to Iraq have all but eclipsed one significant fact: The Soviets are still shipping arms to Iraq.

On August 7, 1990, five days *after* the invasion, the Soviet Union delivered a critical military shipment to Baghdad. Peter Schweizer, who broke this story in *The New York Times* on August 22, 1990, says his contacts in the Defense Intelligence Agency told him that the shipment consisted of several thousand tons of spare parts for tanks and aircraft— mostly aircraft. "Eleven of the 17 wings of the Iraqi air force are Soviet aircraft," explains Schweizer. "You're looking at a shipment that would sustain those 11 wings for about six months."[21]

Spare parts are essential to any army and are considered to be Iraq's Achilles' heel. By delivering these spare parts, which are shipped semiannually and could have been withheld by simply ordering the transport ship to return home, the Soviet Union guaranteed that Iraq would be able to fight at full strength if necessary.

But the Soviets have done more than simply deliver spare parts that were already in the pipeline. On August 18, 1990, two Soviet transport ships, believed to be carrying arms and spare parts for the Soviet-built Mi-17 Hip helicopters and military troop transports, docked at the Jordanian port of Aqaba; the supplies were then driven overland to Iraq.[22]

There may have been other Soviet arms shipments to Baghdad as well. On September 6, 1990, just three days before the Bush-Gorbachev summit, The Washington Times reported, "U.S. intelligence officials said the Soviets continued to send military equipment to Iraq after Moscow announced a cutoff of such supplies...and have extended new financial credits for the Baghdad regime worth more than $150 million for new arms purchases."[23]

The Soviets were not the only ones to send arms to Iraq. Libya and North Korea conducted a massive airlift of spare parts to Iraq shortly after the U.N. naval embargo against Baghdad went into effect. This is tantamount to a Soviet arms shipment: Soviet clients were sending Soviet equipment to Iraq's Soviet-supplied army and the Soviets did nothing to stop them. In addition, informed sources suspect that Soviet transport planes were used to augment the Libyan and North Korean airlift capacity.

"They're Only Advisers"

Moscow did not just turn over a lot of technologically advanced military equipment to the Iraqis and then leave them to figure out how to use it. They provided thousands of experts, technicians and military advisers to make sure everything worked.

From almost the first days of the Iraqi invasion, there were reports of Soviet military advisers in Kuwait. They were suspected of advising Iraqi combat units and operating the sophisticated Soviet electronics equipment that was being used to jam U.S. AWACS reconnaissance planes in Saudi Arabia. There were also indications that the Soviets were providing the Iraqis with crucial intelligence on U.S. naval and troop deployments in Saudi Arabia and the Persian Gulf.

Intelligence assessments suggest that the Soviets played a key role in the invasion. As Jed Snyder, a consultant to the Pentagon, put it, "A withdrawal of Soviet military advisers and technical support personnel would cripple any sustained Iraqi military effort."[24]

Soviet military advisers in Iraq presented the Bush administration with a serious *military* problem. But they saw it more as a threatening *political* problem.

It appears that Bush, in fact, would have preferred that word of the Soviet advisers in Iraq had never gotten out. Soviet cooperation with the United States is the cohesive element in the coalition of nations that Bush had forged to oppose Iraq's aggression. White House spokesman Marlin Fitzwater underscored that point when he said that "the Soviet Union has been supportive in five U.N. sanctions that have, in effect, made this world unity possible."[25]

Bush has maneuvered himself into a dangerous position: his popularity is tied to his handling of the Iraq crisis. And since superpower unity is the centerpiece of his diplomatic efforts, public perception of Soviet behavior directly affects Bush's political fortunes—a fact that cannot have escaped Gorbachev.

The threat of war in the Persian Gulf has been a political godsend for Bush. It has kept the public from thinking too much about the deteriorating U.S. economy, the budget mess, and the role that his son Neil played in the failed Silverado Savings and Loan.

Bush received a high approval rating for his initial handling of the Iraq crisis. The last thing anyone in the White House wanted was something that could destroy the appearance of superpower unity.

But the Soviets themselves raised the issue at a press conference on August 22, 1990, when Colonel Valentin Ogurtsov told reporters that there were 193 Soviet experts in Iraq. These experts, said Ogurtsov, were completing their "contractual obligations" to the Iraqis, which included showing them how to operate and maintain sophisticated Soviet fighters, tanks and missiles. Prior to Ogurtsov's press conference, there had been minimal discussion of the Soviet advisers in the media. But with the cat out of the bag, the Bush administration was forced to respond.

Rather than express outrage that the Soviets were honoring "contractual obligations" when the rest of the world had closed ranks against Iraqi aggression, and demand that those advisers leave at once, the State Department meekly suggested that the presence of Soviet advisers in Iraq might be a violation of the U.N. sanctions. "It is inappropriate to provide any form of military assistance to Iraq,"[26] said State Department spokesman Richard Boucher.

Critics said the Soviets were playing a "double game." Senator William Cohen (R-Maine), vice chairman of the Senate Intelligence Committee, said that for the Soviets to "insist that contracts have more intrinsic value and interest than the interest of world peace is a deception masquerading as principle."[27]

Dollars for Diplomacy

Bush was not damaged by the disclosure of Soviet advisers in Iraq. The subject surfaced periodically in the media, but was never a major issue. Even after Ogurtsov's press conference, news reports on the Iraq crisis continued to concentrate on the "unparalleled level of cooperation" between the United States and the Soviet Union.

Nevertheless, by late August there was a collection of problems that threatened to torpedo Bush's policy. Some members of Congress and the media started asking, "Who lost Kuwait?" The media reported that U.S. forces were suffering from sand and boredom and might be forced to fight with defective weapons. The high oil price was taking its toll on a weakened domestic economy. And there was some concern about the unresolved issue of the Soviet military advisers.

It was said with increasing frequency that Bush was using the Gulf crisis to avoid domestic problems. It was also said that Bush's popularity could vanish overnight if things took a turn for the worse in the Middle East.

Bush needed Gorbachev's help to maintain the appearance that his policies were effective. No doubt that's what Bush thought he was buying when he called a snap summit for September 9, 1990, in Helsinki.

On September 5, 1990, just four days before the Bush-Gorbachev summit, *The Washington Times* reported, "Administration officials said the White House is willing to overlook the fact that the Soviets have some 6,000 economic and military advisers stationed in Iraq . . . in return for continued diplomatic support from the Kremlin."[28]

The White House minimized the role played by the advisers and, as the *Times* reported, "suggested the Kremlin should be rewarded for helping President Bush form a worldwide coalition to isolate Iraqi President Saddam Hussein."[29] Marlin Fitzwater said, "I think it's fair to say that the Soviet cooperation in the [Persian] Gulf has impressed us to the point that we are even more interested in being supportive economically if we can be."[30]

The new "unity" made Bush a political sweepstakes winner. As Fitzwater admitted, "it would have been very difficult to have done what we've done so far if we had to worry about the Soviet Union lining up against us."[31]

The Bush administration seems to be handling the superpower relationship like a TV game show—something like "Dollars for Diplomacy." As long as the Soviets smile and give the right answers, the United States will award them cash prizes. After all, the president's popularity depends on it. Gorbachev, desperately in need of cash and aware that other contestants on "Dollars for Diplomacy" have won big money (Turkey, for example, received $2 billion in Western loans) is more than willing to play.

At a press conference following the summit meeting, Bush reiterated the theme of U.S. dollars for Soviet diplomatic assistance. He said that based on "the common stand that the Soviet Union and United States have taken at the United Nations... we should be as forthcoming as we possibly can in terms of economics, and I plan to do that."[32]

Gorbachev, when asked if he planned to withdraw Soviet military advisers from Iraq, said the number of their experts in Iraq is being reduced. "Whereas at the beginning of the conflict, I think there were still 196 of them, there are now some 150 of them," Gorbachev said.[33] Bush said that "it would facilitate things" if Soviet advisers were withdrawn, but added that they are "not a major irritant."[34]

In reality, Soviet advisers are a lot more than an irritant. Less than a week after the summit, the CIA completed a report that said there are about 1,000 Soviet advisers—not 150—attached to the Iraqi military who are assisting Iraq with intelligence, air defense, and electronic warfare. The report, the contents of which were leaked to journalist Peter Samuel, also said that there are 6,000 Soviet technicians at work in Iraq's defense industry helping the Iraqis manufacture tanks and jet fighter planes.[35]

About the same time the CIA completed its assessment, the House Republican Research Committee published its own report called "The Soviet Union's Support for the Iraqi Invasion." Its conclusions were similar to the CIA's but went even further.

The Republican report points out that Hussein has created a vacuum of power in the Iraqi officer corps. Officers who have failed in battle are often executed even when the circumstances were beyond their control. Few of the remaining officers are willing to accept responsibility. The empty spaces have been filled by Soviet advisers.

As a result, Soviet advisers are now staffing the headquarters of Iraq's elite units such as the Republican Guards. They are also integrated into the strategic planning staff in the Iraq Ministry of Defense.

So terrorized are the remaining Iraqi officers that only units led by Soviet officers are likely to do well in battle. The report goes on to say:

These Soviet officers not only were able to plan operations, advise on their conduct and correct mistakes, but probably no less important, stand up to the Saddam Hussein headquarters.... In the present confrontation, the presence of Soviet military experts can make a great difference in the ability of the Iraqi armed forces to conduct large scale offensives and especially to react to sudden changes in the theater and on the battlefield.[36]

The composite picture of Soviet military assistance to Iraq is that the Iraqi army is very nearly a clone of the Soviet army. Iraq's army was organized and trained by Soviet advisers. It is now led by Soviet advisers. It also uses Soviet weapons and tactics and is guided by Soviet intelligence.

If fighting breaks out between the United States and Iraq, American soldiers will die fighting a Soviet-cloned army. Even worse, American soldiers are likely to be killed by Soviet advisers and Soviet advisers are likely to be killed by American soldiers.

That's a sobering thought. Direct confrontation between U.S. and Soviet forces is the stuff world wars are made of. At the very least, it gives a new meaning to terms like U.S.-Soviet "cooperation" and "unity."

Winners and Losers

Suppose, for a moment, that the Soviet Union did help Iraq plan its invasion of Kuwait. Why would they do it? One obvious answer is that whether Iraq wins, is utterly annihilated by the United States, or breaks even, Moscow makes a fortune. Here's why.

The Soviet Union is the world's biggest exporter of energy. As Edward Jay Epstein writes:

> The Soviet Union...exports 3.3 million barrels of crude oil a day (about the same as Saudi Arabia) and, in addition, sells Europe almost an equivalent amount of natural gas, the price of which is contractually tied to the price of a barrel of oil ... . It has also been quietly negotiating a deal under which Japan would develop gas fields in eastern Siberia and build a pipeline across the Sakhalin peninsula to the northern Japanese island of Hokkaido. If the crisis goes on for a year or so, Japan reasonably can be expected to sign up for Soviet gas.[37]

There have been a number of reports in the media about how the Soviets cannot really take advantage of the rising price of oil because its production is declining. While Soviet oil production *is* going down (it will decrease about 5 percent this year), the Soviet Union pumps 12 million barrels a day and is still the world's biggest oil producer.

Thus, despite the decline in production, the rising oil price gives the Soviets fantastic windfall profits. Experts differ in their estimates, but the Soviets make an additional $1 billion to $2 billion per year for every dollar increase in the price of a barrel of oil.

Oil was about $16 a barrel before the invasion. It is almost $40 as of this writing. The World Bank says that it could go to $65 a barrel if war breaks out. Other estimates go as high as $100 a barrel.

If oil goes from $16 to $66 a barrel and the Soviets make $1 billion per year for each dollar increase in the price of a barrel of oil, then the Soviets will make an additional $50 billion a year. That's not counting their extra income from natural gas sales to Europe and from the high price of gold, another major Soviet export commodity. The price of gold increased more than $50 an ounce following the invasion.

The longer and hotter the conflict is in the Persian Gulf, the richer the Soviets will become.

On the other hand, the United States loses money every day the crisis continues. The U.S. is the world's largest importer of energy. As Epstein points out, "Each dollar increase [in the price per barrel of oil] drains more than $2 billion a year from the U.S. economy."[38] If oil stays at $40 or $50 a barrel for any length of time—let alone at $65 or $100 a barrel—it could trigger a deep depression in the United States.

The U.S. has few options. It must quickly destroy Iraq's war-making capability and keep the oil flowing out of the Persian Gulf. No one doubts that the United States could defeat Iraq. But does it have the will to do so?

The Joint Chiefs of Staff estimate that about 20,000 to 30,000 Americans could die in a war with

Iraq in a matter of weeks (as compared with 58,000 American deaths in the Vietnam war over a period of about nine years).[39] How many deaths will the American public tolerate before they demand a negotiated settlement?

And a negotiated settlement will not end the matter. Neither will a halfhearted military effort. Even if the U.S. forces Iraq out of Kuwait (what's left of it) or topples Hussein, it will still have to deal with Iraq's armed forces in the future. If the United States does not destroy Iraq's nuclear, chemical and biological warfare capability, its missile production facilities and its military-industrial complex, it will have to face a more powerful and threatening Iraq in just a few years.

How long would it be before Iraq, angered by a U.S. attack (or emboldened by U.S. appeasement) and armed with nuclear weapons, attacked American cities such as Washington or New York?

This brings to light another reason the Soviets may have planned or encouraged Iraq's invasion— to catch the United States in a strategic trap that it won't be easy to get out of.

Other reasons for the Soviet involvement in Iraq will no doubt become apparent as the conflict develops. But we can be certain of one thing: this chapter reveals only the tip of the iceberg of the intrigue and deception prophesied in U.S. astrology.

CHAPTER 31

What Are We Going to Do About All Those Nuclear Weapons?

Iraq has taught us the obvious. A lot of nations have, or will soon have, nuclear, biological and chemical weapons and ballistic missiles to deliver them.

This has been reported for a long time. But the threat to U.S. troops in Saudi Arabia brought the point home. It was one thing when Iraq and Iran used chemical weapons on each other. Or when Iraq used chemical weapons on their restive Kurdish minority. But it is another thing when "the Butcher of Baghdad" threatens American soldiers with deadly chemical weapons delivered by Soviet-supplied Scud-B missiles.

Welcome to the 1990s.

At this moment, at least seven nations have nuclear weapons: the United States, the Soviet Union, Great Britain, France, China, India and Israel.

Twenty other nations could have nuclear weapons in the next decade. These include Pakistan, Libya, Iraq, Argentina, South Africa, North Korea, Cuba and Afghanistan.

These 20 nations already have short- or intermediate-range ballistic missiles capable of carrying conventional, nuclear or chemical warheads but they do not have the nuclear warheads.* Although at this moment their ballistic missiles cannot reach the United States, given the right ingredients they could develop long-range missiles in this decade. Defense expert James Hackett writes, "The 1990s promises to be the decade of the ballistic missile, and some are likely to have chemical and even nuclear warheads."[1]

Nuclear-weapons technology is a genie that escaped from the bottle in 1945 and isn't going to get back inside. As intelligence analyst Charles Via notes, "Anybody with a scientific base comparable to what the Germans had in 1945 is capable of building an ICBM. Iraq clearly, Egypt clearly, Israel, Brazil, Taiwan. The list is endless."[2]

Hackett says that India and Brazil already have the capability of producing ICBMs. He says that during the 1990s "the more technologically advanced Third World nations may well be able to develop a 1,000-mile missile" accurate to within 50 meters.[3]

Iraq may be first in line. Gary Mulhollin, director of a team at the University of Wisconsin that is researching technology transfers to Saddam Hussein, says that a Brazilian team is "now in Iraq, helping Iraq make ballistic missiles." He says the team could also help Iraq make nuclear weapons.[4]

*A ballistic missile is one that is boosted up at a high-arch trajectory by its engines. The engines then shut down and it falls to its target. There are short-range, intermediate-range and long-range (or intercontinental) ballistic missiles. They may carry nuclear, conventional or chemical warheads.

As I noted in chapter 29, a U.S. intelligence assessment says that Iraq could produce nuclear weapons in two years or less. Iraq purchased 27.5 pounds of enriched uranium from France in 1980.[5]

Arms control has not stopped nuclear proliferation. Iraq is a signatory of the Nuclear Nonproliferation Treaty, yet it is frantically trying to build nuclear weapons. And both Iran and Iraq, who have used chemical weapons on each other, are signatories of the Geneva Protocol of 1925, which prohibits the use of chemical weapons.[6]

There *is* a solution to nuclear proliferation—strategic defense (i.e., methods of stopping incoming missiles) and civil defense (fallout and blast shelters). But since the 1960s, the United States has sat back benignly, believing that the very threat of its nuclear arsenal would forever prevent any other nation from attacking it. Thus it has spent its money almost exclusively on offensive weapons instead of a mix of offensive and defensive weapons.

Strategic Defense in the 1990s

One week after Iraq invaded Kuwait, an important test launch took place in Israel. The Arrow antiballistic missile, under joint development by the U.S. and Israel, was launched from a site south of Tel Aviv and landed in the Mediterranean Sea. The missile is a timely reminder that the Iraqi arsenal of intermediate-range Scud-B missiles can be countered by defensive weapons. But the Arrow will not be ready to deploy until 1992 at the earliest.[7]

Antiballistic missiles (ABMs) are nothing new. The Arrow is simply the latest development in ABM technology. The United States has been able to shoot down intercontinental ballistic missiles (ICBMs) since 1962, when a Nike Zeus ABM based on Kwajalein atoll in the Pacific successfully destroyed dummy warheads fired from Vandenberg Air Force Base in California.[8]

The U.S. deployed an ABM system called Safeguard in 1975 but it was dismantled almost immediately as directed by Sen. Ted Kennedy's amendment to the 1976 defense budget. Kennedy argued that since Safeguard's 100 interceptor missiles would be ineffective against a full-scale Soviet attack, it shouldn't be deployed at all. Furthermore, the prevailing logic was that the superpowers were deterred from aggression by mutual terror and therefore no defense was necessary.

The United States needs systems to defend itself against the threats of the 1990s—bombers, cruise missiles, ICBMs and submarine-launched ballistic missiles (SLBMs). It also needs to defend its military bases abroad against air attack and short- and intermediate-range ballistic missiles.

Systems exist today that can defend against all of these weapons.

For starters, there's the Patriot surface-to-air missile (SAM) that can defend against aircraft. It has recently been upgraded to defend against ballistic missiles like the Iraqi Scud-B. It is deployed in Saudi Arabia and Israel. But there are no Patriots or any other kind of SAM defending the borders of the United States. The U.S. dismantled its extensive air defense under the Johnson, Nixon and Carter administrations since it was thought to be unnecessary. Today, Cuba could bomb Miami with a cargo plane!

Strategic Research Initiative

Many Americans think that Ronald Reagan's Strategic Defense Initiative did everything possible to protect us against incoming nuclear warheads. And that there wasn't much that could be done.

On the contrary, we could have done a lot if Reagan had set a goal of deployment. But he didn't. He started a research program.

In his March 23, 1983 speech that launched the initiative, Reagan said, "I am directing a comprehensive and intensive effort to define a long-term research and development program to begin to achieve our ultimate goal of eliminating the threat posed by strategic nuclear missiles."[9]

Reagan's program focused on futuristic technologies at the expense of the systems that use off-the-shelf technology and could be ready to deploy soon if a commitment were made to deploy them. As defense expert Angelo Codevilla writes, "The SDI program has spent some $20 billion, in large part to pay for research into questions unrelated to the destruction of ballistic missiles and warheads."[10]

Reagan's fuzzy concept allowed Congress to restrict SDI to a research program by limiting its budget. Nothing can be deployed unless Congress approves funds for it. Most Congressmen aren't ready to see their pet defense programs cut in favor of strategic defense. Without a mandate from the president or the people, strategic defense will never be more than a research project.

In addition, development of "low-tech" systems such as ABMs has been further delayed by a restriction from the Joint Chiefs of Staff that says that near-term systems can be developed only if high-tech systems such as particle-beam weapons are developed at the same rate. This has effectively cut in half the amount of money available for developing near-term systems.

What We Can Do

Three promising systems that have been delayed by such restrictions are HEDI, ERIS and Brilliant Pebbles. We need to deploy all three systems as a three-layered defense.

HEDI, the High Endoatmospheric Defense Interceptor, is a non-nuclear, heat-seeking missile that intercepts and destroys nuclear warheads after they reenter the atmosphere. It could defend both cities and military bases against ICBM and SLBM warheads.

ERIS, the Exoatmospheric Reentry-vehicle Interceptor Subsystem, is a long-range ABM that reaches out into space to destroy warheads before they enter the atmosphere. ERIS could defend much of North America against ICBMs from a single site in the center of the country. If we added two more sites on the coasts, ERIS could defend against SLBMs as well.

At the same time, we could begin deploying a space-based defense. The most promising space-based system is called "Brilliant Pebbles." It would consist of thousands of small, non-nuclear missiles about three feet long and weighing about 100 pounds each.

They would orbit the earth and spring into action upon detection of a missile launch. They would home in on the missile and knock a hole in it solely by kinetic energy. The missile would disintegrate as it reentered the atmosphere, harming no one.

Brilliant Pebbles could stop most kinds of intermediate-range ballistic missiles and all long-range missiles. In fact, it could stop any missile with a range of over 200 miles (trajectories of missiles with ranges under 200 miles are too low for Brilliant Pebbles). Brilliant Pebbles are purely defensive since they could not be used to attack any targets on the ground.

A system of 4,000 Brilliant Pebbles and 300 ERIS interceptors, along with the necessary radars, sensors and command, control and communications network, would cost about $55 billion. HEDI would cost about $18 billion. This is a pittance when you consider that Americans spend $100 billion a year buying "recreational" drugs!

The final component of the system could be the Patriot or another SAM as an air defense. The SAMs could link up with the ABM radars, sensors and command, control and communications network.

Why Not Deploy?

There are three main arguments used against deployment of such a system. First, it would violate the 1972 ABM Treaty between the United States and the Soviet Union, which limits the number of ABMs that each side can deploy to 100.

Second, since it might not be able to stop 100 percent of incoming missiles, a strategic defense would give the U.S. false hope of surviving a nuclear war. It might even make war more likely by destabilizing the superpower relationship.

And third, if there were a war with the Soviet Union, it wouldn't work; even if only 5 percent of the warheads got through, the U.S. would be destroyed. Therefore, the argument goes, it is better to stick with arms control to solve the problem of nuclear weapons.

As I have already shown, we cannot count on arms control to stop nuclear proliferation. Furthermore, advances in technology have blurred the distinction between ABMs and SAMs.

For example, the Soviets have deployed 1,700 SA-10 SAM launchers, each of which can fire four missiles for a total of 6,800 SAMs. The SA-10 can intercept cruise missiles and some kinds of ballistic missiles.[11] In other words, some SAMs have an ABM capability. As Hackett writes, "The ABM Treaty has been rendered obsolete by technological advances in both offensive and defensive weaponry."[12]

In 1987, the George C. Marshall Institute studied the effectiveness of a proposed strategic defense system consisting of 3,000 HEDI interceptors, 10,000 ERIS interceptors, and 11,000 space-based kinetic-kill vehicles (an earlier version of Brilliant Pebbles).

It found that such a system would be more than 93 percent effective against a full-scale Soviet ICBM attack.[13] Such a high degree of effectiveness would be likely to prevent the Soviets from ever launching an attack since they would know that almost none of their missiles would get through.

But even if the defense were only 50 or 30 percent effective, it would strengthen deterrence. The Soviets see nuclear weapons as a means to gain military advantage by destroying other nuclear weapons. If your object is to destroy nuclear weapons, you cannot afford to have 50 or even 30 percent of your missiles prevented from reaching their targets.

By destroying Soviet confidence in their ability to carry out their strategy, even an imperfect defense would deter an attack. And even a limited strategic defense would deter an attack by a Third World nation since these nations would possess only a small number of warheads in the foreseeable future.

However, it doesn't seem likely that a strategic defense system of any sort will be deployed in the near future.

A majority in both houses of Congress opposes deployment. Since 1983, the SDI budget has consistently been cut in committee, even though it makes up only 1 percent of the $300 billion defense budget. In 1990, the House cut in half

President Bush's $4.66 billion fiscal 1991 budget request for SDI—to $2.3 billion. The Senate version of the budget cut it to $3.7 billion.

Lawmakers like Sen. Sam Nunn rationalize that if we continue SDI as a research program, it will be available as a "hedge" against a future Soviet SDI or a Soviet breakout from the ABM Treaty. But, as I will show in chapter 33, the Soviets may already be breaking out of the ABM Treaty and deploying a strategic defense.

If people like Nunn have their way, we may find out the hard way that it's a lot more expensive to buy a new country than it is to defend an old one.

CHAPTER 32

Why I Believe We Can and Should Survive a Nuclear War

The odds are that there's a good chance of nuclear war or an accidental nuclear launch sometime in the next decade. So it's about time you started thinking about having a fallout shelter.

Shelters are becoming a more sensible option every day. Not only because of nuclear proliferation but also because of the ever-present threat of a nuclear power accident like Chernobyl. Unless we want our genetic material and that of our children permanently damaged by fallout from a nuclear power accident, we should protect ourselves against fallout.

Poets, singers, authors, scientists and politicians in the latter half of this century have given nuclear war an almost supernatural status, on a scale with the apocalyptic last days prophesied in the Bible. The subject of nuclear war is so tangled with emotion that it is difficult to view it in a rational manner.

Of course, a nuclear war would be more terrible than anything we have experienced in our lives. But nuclear weapons do have measurable effects that can be studied, analyzed *and survived.*

Richard Pipes, a Harvard history professor who served at the National Security Council as director of East European and Soviet affairs, attempts to put the issue in perspective. He writes:

> In the view of much of humanity, nuclear weapons are not weapons in the ordinary meaning of the word but instruments of cosmic destruction, the expectation of which forms part of what Carl Jung called mankind's "collective unconscious." It is an unsettling but by no means unusual experience in the 1980s to attend professional symposiums at which so-called conventional war, which from 1939 to 1945 claimed 50 million lives, is calmly discussed as an acceptable alternative to nuclear war.[1]

Pipes goes on to say that because doomsday legends are prevalent in nearly every religion, "the expectation of an inevitable final holocaust has embedded itself deeply in the human psyche; it is a classic archetype with which argument is powerless to contend." Once "the bomb" had made its appearance, he writes, it "filled a role that had awaited casting for thousands of years."[2]

The advent of nuclear weapons has made the prospect of an apocalyptic end of the world worse because our future is in error-prone human hands rather than divine hands. Pipes writes:

> Following the general decline of belief in God and the afterlife, man is left with the

appalling prospect that his fate has passed into human hands; the unleashing of the holocaust, once the prerogative of God or gods, is now the prerogative of a few mortals with fingers on the 'button.'. . . Thus, agnosticism intensifies an anxiety that has its origins in religious beliefs, leaving the horror but robbing it of hope. It produces an overpowering sense of helplessness that the unscrupulous exploit for their own political ends.[3]

The End of the World?

Opinion makers, either unscrupulous or misinformed, have introduced serious misconceptions about nuclear war into the minds of the general public, based on rumor, exaggeration and myth rather than scientific fact.

For example, many people in the United States believe that nuclear war means the end of civilization and human life on earth. This misconception stems from the way Americans approach nuclear war—we try not to think about it. We can only relate to it emotionally.

That explains how one work of fiction could shape our views about nuclear war. In 1957, a novel called *On the Beach* by Nevil Shute became the number-one best-seller. The story is set in Australia, about a year after a global nuclear war has ended.

The war, which was fought with cobalt bombs,* was started by Albania. It escalated to involve

---

*A cobalt bomb can theoretically be made by coating a hydrogen bomb with cobalt, producing more dangerous fallout.

England, the United States, the Soviet Union
and China. The cobalt bombs and the radioactive fallout killed everyone in the Northern
Hemisphere.

Now no one can escape the deadly poison that
is creeping to the south, and eventually everyone on
earth will die. In southern Australia, they are waiting to die. They figure they have about six months
left. The story describes how the Australians in
Williamstown, the naval dockyard of Melbourne,
deal with the prospect of human extinction (some
try to drink up the 3,000 bottles of vintage wine
remaining in the cellars of an exclusive club; others
have wild parties every night).

Toward the end of the novel, the last Australian Grand Prix is held, and everyone who ever
dreamed of racing cars enters the race. Because the
drivers know they are to die sooner or later, they
show no mercy to themselves or each other. Many
drivers are killed that day.

At one point in the book, three naval officers
contemplate their imminent fate. They are returning from an expedition by submarine to northern
Australia, where they were able to glimpse the shore
through the periscope. All the people in the towns
were dead, but the trees, flowers and buildings still
stood in apparent tranquility.

> "It's—it's the end of the world," [said
> Peter Holmes, the liaison officer]. "I've never
> had to imagine anything like that before."

John Osborne laughed. "It's not the end of the world at all," he said. "It's only the end of us. The world will go on just the same, only we shan't be in it. I dare say it will get along all right without us."

Dwight Towers raised his head. "I suppose that's right. There didn't seem to be much wrong with Cairns, or Port Moresby either." He paused, thinking of the flowering trees that he had seen on shore through the periscope, cascaras and flame trees, the palms standing in the sunlight. "Maybe we've been too silly to deserve a world like this," he said.[4]

The novel ends as the main characters, stricken with the first signs of radiation sickness, bid each other farewell and swallow suicide pills issued by the Australian government.

Those who didn't read the book could watch on the big screen the lifelike portrayal of the emotional aftermath of a nuclear war. The film *On the Beach* was made in 1959, starring Gregory Peck and Ava Gardner.

Shute's novel is high on drama, plot and emotion, and low on fact or rational analysis of a probable nuclear-war scenario. But then, it was not meant to be an exegesis on the capabilities of atomic weapons, or on a realistic outcome of global nuclear war. Perhaps that's why it was so popular.

Nuclear strategists coined a term from Shute's novel—one "beach," or one "Death of Earth," referred to as one DOE. One beach represents the total megatonnage required to wipe out the human race.

In 1960, scientists, political scientists and weapons specialists gathered in Dedham, Massachusetts, for a discussion called the "Summer Study on Arms Control." They referred to the figure of 500,000 megatons as "roughly one-half of a beach." In other words, one million megatons is regarded as a "Death of Earth."

The total U.S. nuclear megatonnage is about 3,000 megatons. The total Soviet megatonnage is about 5,800 megatons.[5] In a nuclear war, assuming that both sides delivered their entire capability without destroying any of the other side's capability, which is highly unlikely, the megatonnage released would be roughly 1 percent of one beach.

Overkill

One of the reasons given for why it is impossible to survive a nuclear war is "overkill." Simply stated, overkill is the alleged capacity of each of the superpowers to kill the entire civilian population of the other 5, 10 or even 20 times over.

There is only one problem with this analysis. It's wrong.

A typical overkill argument says that just one 5-megaton bomb has more explosive power than all the bombs dropped during World War II. While that may be true, one 5-megaton bomb does not have the destructive power of all the bombs dropped during World War II.

Explosive power becomes less effective when concentrated in larger bombs. Five megatons of explosive power distributed over thousands or millions of conventional bombs in World War II had far greater destructive power than a single 5-megaton bomb. This has to do with a physical principle known as the inverse square law, which says that the amount of radiation received at a distance from a source is inversely proportional to the square of that distance, i.e., it drops off rapidly.

The second reason why one 5-megaton bomb would not have the destructive capacity of the bombs dropped in World War II is simple logistics. You could not gather up all the cities that were damaged in World War II and put them under a 5-megaton bomb. Mount Saint Helens exploded with the force of an 8-megaton bomb, about 500 times the size of the bomb dropped on Hiroshima (about 16 kilotons).* Yet the volcano killed only about 100 people. Why? There weren't any more people around to kill.

Journalist Edward Zuckerman in his book *The Day After World War III* quotes federal civil defense researcher Dr. Conrad Chester on the "myth of overkill":

> As nearly as we can tell, this myth originated in an article in the *Bulletin of Atomic Scientists* in which the casualties per kiloton in

*A kiloton is approximately the amount of energy that would be released by the explosion of 1,000 tons of TNT. A megaton is 1,000 kilotons, approximately the amount of energy that would be released by the explosion of 1,000,000 tons of TNT.

Hiroshima and Nagasaki were multiplied by the number of kilotons in the world's arsenal. This misleading calculation implies that some means can be devised to collect the entire target population into the same density as existed in Hiroshima and Nagasaki, and keep them in a completely unwarned and hence vulnerable posture. A statement of identical validity is that the world's inventory of small arms ammunition, or, for that matter, kitchen knives, can kill the human population several times over.[6]

The idea that the population could be killed many times over assumes that all nuclear weapons are meant to attack cities. Cities are not the superpowers' primary targets; military installations are. Nuclear war in the 1990s is not a 10-megaton bomb exploding on top of New York or Los Angeles. The trend in nuclear weapons is toward smaller, more accurate warheads that can be used to attack military targets. In fact, three warheads may be assigned to destroy a single missile silo.

According to William C. Martel and Paul L. Savage, authors of *Strategic Nuclear War: What the Superpowers Target and Why*, the Soviets would allot over 5,000 warheads to target U.S. ICBM fields, bomber and submarine bases, and command and control centers such as NORAD. For example, they would likely assign 550 SS-18 warheads (about one-sixth of their SS-18 force) just to destroy the Minuteman IIIA missile field at Grand Forks, North Dakota.[7]

This strategy of using nuclear weapons to attack other nuclear weapons is known as counterforce; the strategy of attacking cities is known as countervalue.

During the 1980s, both superpowers phased out most of their ICBM warheads in the megaton range and replaced them with smaller, more accurate warheads. The U.S. phased out the Titan II ICBM, which carried one 9-megaton warhead accurate within eight-tenths of a mile* in favor of the MX ICBM, which carries 10 300-kiloton MIRVs (multiple independently targetable reentry vehicles). Each MX warhead is accurate to within one-twentieth of a mile. The purpose of the MX is to target Soviet nuclear weapons.

The Soviet SS-18 carries 10 500-kiloton warheads. They are accurate to within about one-tenth of a mile. They are powerful and accurate enough to destroy U.S. Minuteman and MX missile silos.

In sum, the argument that it is impossible to survive a nuclear war relies on the scenario of cities being attacked by large warheads. In such an attack, people would be killed by blast and heat, by collapsing buildings, breaking glass and falling debris.

Given what we know about nuclear strategy, the reality is that very few Americans would come within the blast radius of a Soviet attack on U.S. nuclear weapons. Thus most Americans would have to contend with fallout, not blast. And they could survive if they were in fallout shelters.

---
*All accuracies are given in terms of nautical miles.

Nuclear Winter

In 1983, five scientists collectively known as TTAPS (for the first letters of their last names) announced the theory of nuclear winter. They contended that a large nuclear war (5,000 megatons) would produce 225 million metric tons of smoke and 65 million metric tons of dust, which would block out almost all sunlight. Temperatures would plunge to subfreezing levels and remain there for months, causing crop failure and mass starvation. The prolonged period of darkness could disrupt the aquatic food chain, and various unforeseen disturbances of the global ecosystem could make future agriculture impossible. Acting synergistically, these effects could cause earth's population to be reduced to prehistoric levels and human beings could become extinct.

Carl Sagan, a member of TTAPS, postulated a "threshold" of smoke production which, if surpassed, would trigger human extinction. Sagan says that even a "small" war which targeted 100 major cities could surpass this threshold. His conclusion is based on the assumption that the nuclear explosions would ignite fires in the centers of those cities. The fires would burn profusely, creating enough smoke to push the earth over the edge.[8]

But the nuclear winter theory has been challenged. Another study, conducted in 1985 by the National Center for Atmospheric Research (NCAR) in Boulder, Colorado, suggests that "nuclear winter" may actually be more like "nuclear fall" and that the smoke released in an all-out nuclear war would not cause the end of life on earth. NCAR scientists Starley L. Thompson and Stephen H. Schneider point out several flaws in the TTAPS study:

> The [TTAPS] model was one-dimensional; that is, it did not take into account north-south and east-west directions, but instead treated the earth as a homogeneous all-land sphere having a temperature that depended only on the up-down direction (atmospheric altitude). Thus, the model had no geography, no winds, no seasons, instantaneous spread of smoke to the hemispheric scale, and no feedback of atmospheric circulation changes on the rate of smoke washout by rainfall.[9]

In other words, the TTAPS model is over-simplified. The global model developed by NCAR is a sophisticated three-dimensional model that looks at more variables.

Smoke production, for example, is difficult to estimate from looking at old nuclear test data. The NCAR scientists believed that TTAPS' smoke estimate of 225 million tons was excessive. The NCAR model uses three different amounts of smoke: 20 million, 60 million and 180 million tons.

The NCAR study calculated that in the 180-million-ton scenario, temperatures in the Northern Hemisphere would drop an average of 22 degrees Fahrenheit for only a few weeks.[10] It would be colder than normal but life on earth would not cease.

Thompson and Schneider give three reasons for the moderation of temperature compared to TTAPS calculations:

> First, the oceans have a large heat capacity, which ameliorates the cooling over land. Second, about three-fourths of the smoke is removed from the model's atmosphere over the course of 30 days. Third, the infrared "greenhouse" effect of the smoke, which was not included in earlier three-dimensional models, does produce a significant mitigation of the surface cooling.[11]

Summarizing their findings, Thompson and Schneider write: "Despite the continued potential for serious nuclear winter effects, there does not seem to be a real potential for human extinction; nor is there a plausible threshold for severe environmental effects."[12]

How can two studies produce such opposite conclusions? Computer models reflect the bias of their creators. Computers can only interpret data based on parameters set up by the scientist. In other words: nuclear winter in, nuclear winter out.

Does Civil Defense Work?

Can a person survive a nuclear war in a fallout or blast shelter? To answer that question we should analyze the effects of a nuclear explosion. A nuclear bomb releases three primary forms of energy: blast, heat and nuclear radiation.

The strength of the blast varies with the height

at which the weapon is detonated and the size of the weapon. The blast creates changes in air pressure, called overpressure, as well as high winds.

In a 1-megaton airburst, overpressure of 20 pounds per square inch (psi) and winds up to 470 miles per hour would occur within .8 mile of ground zero;* this would level reinforced concrete structures.

At 4.4 miles from ground zero, overpressure would be 5 psi and winds would be 160 mph; this would level a typical house. Most of the people who would be killed in the 20-psi to 5-psi range would be crushed by collapsing buildings or flying objects.

Overpressure would be reduced to 1 psi at 11.6 miles from ground zero. One psi would damage some houses and create winds up to 35 miles per hour. At least 75 percent of the people in this range would survive the blast.

The heat of a nuclear blast can cause flash-blindness and skin burns. In a 1-megaton explosion, people who are exposed to the heat would receive third-degree burns at a distance of 5 miles from ground zero and first-degree burns at a distance of 7 miles from ground zero. The heat could also ignite kindling material like newspapers and leaves, causing fires. Fires could also be ignited by damage to power lines and gas lines.

Fallout is the most far-reaching effect of a nuclear explosion. It is produced when the nuclear fireball sucks particles of dirt high into the atmosphere, contaminating them with radioactivity. The particles are carried by wind and eventually fall back

*The surface area directly below the point of detonation of a nuclear bomb.

to earth, beginning one or more hours after detonation and continuing for weeks or months. Many of the radioactive particles will decay after two weeks so the most dangerous time for fallout is within two weeks of a nuclear explosion. The area covered by fallout can be large or small, depending on wind speed, wind direction and rainfall.

More fallout is created by weapons detonated at the earth's surface than by nuclear weapons detonated in the air. A surface burst (used to attack military targets) digs a large crater and could destroy an underground missile silo. The dirt blasted out of the crater becomes fallout. An airburst (used to attack cities) spreads the energy of the blast over a wider area but does not suck up as much dirt.

Since the superpowers target each other's nuclear weapons, let's take a look at the likely effects of a Soviet attack on U.S. nuclear weapons.

The object of the attack would be to destroy U.S. ICBM bases, command and control centers, strategic (long-range) bomber bases and strategic submarine bases. Therefore the weapons would be detonated at the surface, creating a smaller blast radius but a huge quantity of fallout.

The 1-psi blast radius of a 500-kiloton warhead (the standard warhead in the Soviet ICBM arsenal) is 5.8 miles. This means that someone who is 5.8 miles away would experience 1 psi of overpressure. Thus anyone who does not live within 5 or 10 miles of a nuclear-weapons base would need to be primarily concerned with fallout, not blast.

A study by the Office of Technology Assessment of the U.S. Congress concluded that a Soviet counterforce attack "would produce relatively little direct blast damage to civilians and to economic assets; the main damage would come from radioactive fallout."[13] The study said that roughly two million Americans would be killed by the direct effects of the nuclear weapons but an additional 20 million would be killed by fallout.[14] Those 20 million people could be saved if they had fallout shelters.

There are two other kinds of likely nuclear attack scenarios: (1) A rogue nation or terrorist detonates one or more nuclear bombs on American cities. (2) The Soviet Union or another nuclear power accidently launches an ICBM or SLBM targeted at either a military base or a city. While blast casualties could be high in both cases, many more people would be at risk from fallout; thus fallout shelters would also be useful in such scenarios.

Blast protection is possible; it is just more complicated and expensive than fallout protection. A 1957 experiment showed that it is possible to survive the explosion of a bomb about the size of the one dropped on Hiroshima in a blast shelter less than a mile from ground zero.

Edward Zuckerman described the experiment. In the Nevada desert, civil defense researcher Walmer E. (Jerry) Strope sat in a blast shelter and waited for an atomic bomb to explode less than a mile away. The bomb, called "Diablo," was a 17-kiloton weapon, perched on a 500-foot tower. Zuckerman writes:

Strope...was a little upset the day before the shot to find that construction workers had not buried the shelter he was going to be sitting in—an arched, corrugated-steel structure—quite as deep as it was supposed to be. Nevertheless, he and seventeen other volunteers climbed in at midnight to begin their wait. They sat on the floor, back to back, away from the walls, as the final countdown began just before dawn. They could hear it on a public-address system wired into their shelter. Five, four, three, two, one. Zero.

Nothing happened. While scientists on the surface tried to figure out what had gone wrong, concluded that Diablo was not about to go off at any moment, and, finally, recruited a brave soul to drive over to the tower and disconnect the wires, Strope and his colleagues waited underground. They were finally let out of the shelter late that night.

Two months later they were back—in the shelter, on the floor, back to back, away from the walls. The countdown went to zero, and this time Diablo exploded. "We started counting," Strope recalls. "At four the blast wave came. It sounded exactly like you were inside a garbage can and somebody slammed the cover. Suddenly dust was very visible. The blast wave bounced it up. We got a double pulse on our buttocks and our feet. The first was the direct ground shock. The second was where the ground shock hit the underlying rock and bounced back up. . . .

"It was," Strope concludes, "very interesting."[15]

Experiments such as these have proven that survival in a blast shelter is possible, yet I still hear people avow that nuclear war means the extinction of the human race. If survival weren't possible, the Soviet Union and 13 other nations would not have invested so much money in blast and fallout shelters.

Civil Defense in 14 Nations

The Soviets have built blast shelters for more than 60 percent of their urban population and fallout shelters for an even larger percentage.[16] The Soviet Union spends 5 percent of its defense budget on civil defense and 100,000 people work full-time on civil defense in peacetime. They produce masks and radiation suits and conduct regular drills at schools and factories. The Soviets also have a large industrial and agricultural protection program.

The Soviet Union is not the only nation that has civil defense. Seven Eastern European countries— East Germany, Czechoslovakia, Hungary, Bulgaria, Poland, Romania and Yugoslavia—have civil defense programs modeled on the Soviet Union's program. Six other nations—China, Switzerland, Sweden, Norway, Denmark and Finland—have provided varying levels of civil defense for their populations.

The People's Republic of China has built what some experts say is the most effective urban civil defense system in the world. In the event of a nuclear attack, Beijing's nine million residents, as well as residents of other major Chinese cities, can reach the safety of underground tunnels in a matter of minutes.

Switzerland has blast shelters for 85 percent of its citizens. Every building constructed is required by law to have a blast shelter able to withstand the blast of a 1-megaton bomb from as close as one and one half miles. The shelters must be stocked with the necessary supplies for survival.[17]

Sweden has developed an elaborate system of huge underground shelters capable of protecting 5.5 million people, or 65 percent of its population. The Swedes also have a comprehensive industrial defense plan.

Why the United States Has No Civil Defense

The United States has no effective civil defense program for its population. There are two reasons for this:

1. The leadership has not been willing to spend the necessary money.

2. The prevailing theory has been that fallout shelters are unnecessary since mutual terror prevents nuclear weapons from ever being launched.

During the Eisenhower administration, the government seriously considered implementing a national civil defense plan. Zuckerman writes that in 1956 federal civil defense officials proposed a national system of blast and fallout shelters at a projected cost of more than $20 billion:

President Eisenhower was taken aback by the proposal—the *total* federal budget in 1956 was only $66 billion—and he appointed a blue-ribbon panel that came to be known as the Gaither Committee to undertake an exhaustive study of the problem of protecting civilians in a nuclear war. The committee recommended a nationwide fallout-shelter program costing $22.5 billion. "This seems the only feasible protection for millions of people who will be increasingly exposed to the hazards of radiation...," the committee's report said. "We are convinced that with proper planning the post-attack environment can permit people to come out of the shelters and survive."[18]

Eisenhower was reluctant to approve the shelter plan because of its cost. His secretary of state, John Foster Dulles, strongly opposed civil defense with the argument that, in Zuckerman's words, "American security was best served not by attempting to reduce the damage that would be caused by a nuclear attack but by maintaining the power to retaliate devastatingly against any attacker and thus discourage an attack from being launched in the first place."[19]

At a White House meeting, according to Eisenhower's memoirs, Dulles said, "For our security, we have been relying above all on our capacity for retaliation. From this policy we should not deviate now. To do so would imply we are turning to a 'fortress America' concept."[20] In that meeting, Eisenhower vetoed the shelter plan.

In 1961, when tensions between the superpowers flared up over the erection of the Berlin Wall, President John F. Kennedy renewed national interest in civil defense. He wrote a message in the September 1961 issue of *Life* magazine addressed to "my fellow Americans" as the introduction to a special section on fallout shelters. "I urge you to read and consider seriously the contents of this issue of *Life*," he wrote. "In these dangerous days... we must prepare for all eventualities. The ability to survive coupled with the will to do so therefore are essential to our country."[21]

A fallout-shelter boom swept the country. In December 1961, the Department of Defense began the National Fallout Shelter Survey, which eventually identified more than 250,000 existing structures that could offer some fallout protection to 238 million people. Many were stocked with food and water.

But enthusiasm for civil defense died away by 1963. The public, amid skepticism and confusion, raised questions about the life-saving potential of fallout shelters. Congress cut the funds for the construction of new fallout shelters and civil defense disappeared from the public eye.

Which brings us to where we are today. Those

public fallout shelters are no longer stocked and many do not have adequate ventilation. Furthermore, hardly anyone knows where they are.

How You Can Survive a Nuclear War

After World War III, will the living envy the dead? It depends on how they survive. Without civil defense, the survivors will be those who have somehow managed to live, barely, through the blast itself, through flying debris, through direct nuclear radiation, through thermal radiation, through fires, and through fallout.

If America were to fall victim to a nuclear attack tomorrow, many of the survivors would first envy, then become, the dead. However, with an effective civil defense, most of the population would have a good chance of surviving.

But the belief that no one will survive a nuclear war may become a self-fulfilling prophecy. In today's political and budgetary climate, I am not hopeful that the U.S. government will provide a national civil defense. If we want to survive a nuclear war, it is up to each of us to provide our own fallout shelter.

Cresson Kearny, who has been involved in civil defense research since the 1960s, gives detailed instructions on how to survive a nuclear war in his book *Nuclear War Survival Skills*. Kearny, who graduated *summa cum laude* from Princeton in civil engineering and earned two degrees at Oxford as a Rhodes scholar, has studied the civil defense systems of Switzerland, Sweden, the USSR and China.

In his book he gives do-it-yourself instructions on how to build the makeshift shelters he has field-tested. These include expedient fallout shelters and expedient blast shelters. He also gives instructions for permanent fallout shelters.

Kearny addresses problems such as food, ventilation, protection against fires and carbon monoxide, fallout radiation, and surviving without doctors. He even gives instructions on how to build a homemade ventilating pump and fallout radiation meter. Using his directions, families and college students have built shelters in 34 to 48 hours.

Most basements and root cellars can easily be converted to fallout shelters. Twelve inches of concrete or 18 inches of earth between you and the fallout would reduce radiation to one-tenth of that outside; double the thickness would reduce radiation to one-hundredth of that outside.

Under most attack scenarios, you would not have to stay in your shelter full-time for more than two weeks. The time could vary depending on the type of nuclear attack, time of year and weather patterns. Kearny says that after two weeks, occupants of most shelters could come out either for good or for an hour or two, depending on radiation levels. He writes:

> Exceptions would be in areas of extremely heavy fallout such as might occur downwind from important targets attacked with many weapons, especially missile sites and very

large cities. To know when to come out safely, occupants either would need a reliable fallout meter to measure the changing radiation dangers, or must receive information based on measurements made nearby with a reliable instrument.[22]

Thomas F. Nieman, a civil defense researcher, writes:

Generally after about 7 hours, the fallout has lost about 90 percent of its strength. In two weeks, 99.9 percent of its strength is gone. Nevertheless, if the radiation at the beginning were high enough, the *remaining 0.1 percent could be extremely dangerous.* A person must stay under protection until radiation is measured and safety levels are established.[23]

In addition to a fallout shelter, you also need at least a year's supply of food, provision for pure water, and basic survival equipment. You can find good instructions for what you need and how to get it in *Nuclear War Survival Skills* by Cresson Kearny and *Life After Doomsday* by Bruce Clayton.[24]

Choose Life, Not Death

All of the available evidence shows that it is possible to survive a nuclear war.

When confronted with this evidence, some people switch to the tack, "But who would want to survive? I can't do without _____." Fill in the blank. Television, radio, city life, dishwashers, sports cars, CDs, the Super Bowl, Big Macs, golf, the Miss America Pageant—you name it.

Others say that the very notion of trying to survive a nuclear war when millions of other people will die is immoral. For the life of me, I can't figure out this mentality. A large percentage of Americans take out insurance policies in case of all kinds of eventualities—accident, fire, earthquake, flood, et cetera. Do they believe that it's immoral for them to have insurance when other people don't?

It would be nice if the government would provide everyone in America with fallout insurance— a shelter. But since it hasn't, why shouldn't each person start with himself and then help others?

I am not saying that surviving a nuclear war would be easy. Should a war come (God forbid), survival would be the hardest thing that we in our comfortable lives have ever known.

But we have a responsibility to survive because we have a responsibility to ensure the survival of the human race. Souls will need to reembody so they can have the chance to balance the karma that they can only balance on earth. And we ourselves need to survive so that we can fulfill our karma and our reason for being and ascend back to God. If we do not survive, we will have to reembody on earth to balance our karma. And how can we be sure that God will be able to find us parents whose genetic material has not been damaged by fallout?

Not to make plans to survive a nuclear war is to

surrender the will to live. In the last sermon Moses preached to the children of Israel, he said:

> I call heaven and earth to record this day against you, that I have set before you life and death, blessing and cursing: *therefore choose life, that both thou and thy seed may live:*
>
> That thou mayest love the LORD thy God, and that thou mayest obey his voice, and that thou mayest cleave unto him: for he is thy life, and the length of thy days: that thou mayest dwell in the land which the LORD sware unto thy fathers, to Abraham, to Isaac, and to Jacob, to give them.[25]

I believe Moses admonished us to choose life because God places a portion of himself, a divine spark, in our body temples. He has breathed upon us the breath of his life. And we have no right to allow the divine spark to be extinguished or the sacred breath to be withdrawn.

If I am in the path of an oncoming train and I do not move out of the way, I am committing suicide. If I perceive a potential threat of nuclear war and I do not build a bomb shelter, I am allowing myself to die—I have chosen death. By not having civil defense and not having defense against incoming missiles, I believe that we the people of the United States of America have committed ourselves, our posterity and this land God gave us to national suicide.

Instructions for an Expedient
Four-Person Basement Shelter

These shelter instructions are condensed from *Better Read than Dead* by Thomas F. Nieman (out of print). You should obtain more detailed instructions before attempting to build this shelter.

The way to build an emergency shelter in your home is to increase the fallout protection factor of a small area (about 6' × 6' for four people) rather than trying to fallout-proof an entire room.

1. Select a corner of your basement (or a portion of your house where the exterior walls are sheltered by earth) as far away from windows as possible. The two walls that meet at the corner will be the first and second walls of your shelter.

2. Arrange furniture such as dressers, cabinets and bookshelves to form the third and fourth walls of your shelter.

3. Remove some interior doors of your house to use as a roof.

4. Lay the doors across the top of the furniture to form the shelter roof.

5. Pile objects such as dirt, books and concrete blocks around the walls and on top of the shelter to provide radiation shielding. Be careful that the material does not overload the roof of the shelter.

6. Pile dirt and objects on the floor of the room above the shelter and outside the basement walls for additional protection. Be careful that the heavy material does not overload the floor.

Note: These two sets of instructions are for emergency shelters, not permanent shelters.

7. Cover the basement windows with dirt or packed snow to block radiation.
8. Stock the shelter with food, water, a first-aid kit and other items needed for survival.

Expedient Four-Person Door-Covered Trench Shelter

These shelter instructions are condensed from *Nuclear War Survival Skills* by Cresson Kearny. You should purchase Kearny's book before attempting to build the shelter.

1. Assemble the following tools and materials:
   - Four doors (solid core preferred)
   - Three sheets of ¾" plywood (4' × 8')
   - Three two-by-fours (4' long)
   - Plastic, burlap or canvas bags sturdy enough to hold dirt
   - Plastic waterproof materials (such as shower curtains)
   - Shovels, picks, hammer, nails, tape measure, buckets
2. Select a site in an area outside of drainages or low-lying terrain that will not be flooded by heavy rains and where firm, cohesive soil at least 4½' deep exists. Avoid a site with non-cohesive, sandy soil. Dig a test hole below the topsoil to check for soil type and stability.
3. Dig a main trench approximately 4' wide × 8' long × 4½' deep. Carefully observe the excavation to ensure that the soil type is consistent, that the walls remain stable and that no groundwater is apparent.

4. On the two narrow ends of the main trench, dig a level adjoining trench approximately 18″ wide × 36″ long × 30″ deep, one for the entry and one for ventilation.

5. Place excavated soil into six or seven canvas bags. Pile the remaining soil on both sides of the main trench at least 3′ away from the edges.

6. Line the two vertical main trench walls with one plywood sheet apiece.

7. Place another plywood sheet on the bottom of the trench so that it is firmly wedged between the vertical plywood sheets.

8. To hold the vertical plywood sheets apart at the top, install three two-by-four braces at the top edge of the vertical plywood walls—one at each end and one in the middle.

9. Stack the dirt-filled canvas bags around three sides of the entry and ventilation trenches.

10. Slope the ground around the shelter away from the shelter so that water can't run into the shelter.

11. Place the four doors flat side by side over the trench as a roof.

12. Mound excavated earth over the doors so that the soil is 12″ deep over the center of the door and slopes to 2″ deep at each end of the door. Spread waterproof materials over the mound and add a second mounded 12″-deep layer of dirt.

13. Dig drainage ditches around the shelter.

14. Stock the shelter with food, water, first-aid kit and other items needed for survival.

CHAPTER 33

Why I Believe the Soviet Union Intends to Launch a Nuclear First Strike

There are three reasons why I believe the Soviet Union intends to launch a surprise first-strike nuclear attack on the United States.

1. Saint Germain has warned us that we have every reason "to believe, to be concerned, and to be prepared" for a first strike by the Soviet Union.

2. Czechoslovakian General Jan Sejna, the highest-ranking member of the Soviet military apparatus ever to defect, says that a nuclear first strike on the United States is the cornerstone of Soviet strategy.

3. The Soviet nuclear forces are structured to launch a first strike. (U.S. nuclear forces are structured for a retaliatory strike.)

A first-strike capability means being able to destroy most of the enemy's nuclear weapons before they are launched and being able to shoot down or absorb a retaliatory strike.

Prerequisites for a credible first-strike capability are:

1. Enough counterforce weapons to destroy most or all of the enemy's nuclear weapons.

2. A strategic defense to stop most or all of the enemy's retaliatory strike.

3. Civil defense to protect the leadership and the population against any warheads that might leak through the defense.

If you also have enough nuclear weapons in reserve after a first strike to threaten the enemy's cities and thus frighten him into not retaliating at all, the first-strike capability is even more credible.

It doesn't take a prophet to tell you that the Soviets are working towards a first-strike capability.

The Soviet Union has most of the prerequisites and may soon have all of them. It also has a reserve of nuclear weapons to deter the United States from retaliating.

The Rarefied Concept of MAD

During the 1960s, when the Soviets first developed ICBMs, the United States tried to convince them that mutual security lay in both sides restricting themselves to a retaliatory capability against the other side's population. Neither side was to attempt to target the other's nuclear weapons.

Robert S. McNamara, Kennedy's secretary of defense, codified this philosophy into the strategy of the avoidance of war through the threat of "mutual assured destruction" (MAD).

MAD was based on the belief that peace would be kept if the United States and the Soviet Union maintained the capability to destroy each other with nuclear weapons. If both sides knew that they would both be destroyed if either attacked, they would conclude that nuclear war is unwinnable and neither side would be tempted to push the button.

McNamara said that a U.S. capability to "destroy, say one-fifth to one-fourth of [the Soviet] population and one-half of her industrial capacity"[1] would be an adequate deterrent to Soviet attack.

Under MAD, both sides are supposed to build weapons to kill the maximum number of civilians and destroy as much of the enemy's economic resources as possible. Neither side is supposed to build antiballistic missiles or any other kind of system to prevent the missiles of the other from having a free ride to their targets. Likewise, neither side is supposed to build civil defense to protect its citizens. Under MAD, it is considered "bad" to try to defend yourself because that will make you less vulnerable and may make your enemy conclude that you plan to attack.

MAD, reduced to an axiom, is: defense is offense, offense is defense; killing people is good, killing weapons is bad. Translated, this Orwellian jumble means: A defense against nuclear weapons would allow a country to have an offensive strategy since the country could attack without fear of annihilation. Therefore, no countries should build defenses; they must build only offensive weapons in order to insure that no nation will ever be irrational enough to attack, knowing that attack would mean its own death as well as that of its enemy.

Stability lies in being able to kill the population

of the opposing side but not its weapons. If one nation targets the other's weapons, the other may decide to attack first to save his weapons. Thus, being able to kill people promotes stability and being able to kill weapons promotes instability.

As barbaric and immoral as it sounds, this philosophy was meant to keep the peace for generations to come. But it would not work unless the Soviets bought into it.

McNamara made certain that the U.S. could not target Soviet missile silos. As defense expert Angelo Codevilla, a senior research fellow at the Hoover Institute, writes, "Against the will of the Joint Chiefs of Staff at the time, he made new U.S. missiles incapable of striking Soviet missiles. He oriented American targeting toward populations."[2]

The 1972 ABM Treaty was meant to insure that the weapons of both superpowers could not be stopped from hitting their targets. During the negotiations, U.S. arms-control negotiators tried to inculcate the principles of MAD in the minds of the Soviet team.

But the Soviets weren't ready for such rarefied concepts. They signed the ABM Treaty, which limited them to two ABM sites (later reduced to one) with 100 launchers each. And they signed the SALT I Treaty, which limited each side's ICBM launchers to those already built or under construction. Soviet academics have even paid lip service to MAD. But their actions show that they never adopted it as their nuclear strategy.

Between 1972 and 1982, they deployed 6,000 counterforce ICBM warheads capable of destroying U.S. missile silos and other military targets (this was considered bad, or destabilizing, under MAD). The Soviets got around the treaty provisions by MIRVing their missiles—i.e., putting more than one warhead on each missile. Such a massive counterforce capability was the very thing that SALT I was designed to prevent.

During the 1970s, the U.S. stuck to MAD. It chose to rely on its aging fleet of strategic submarines, whose missiles were capable only of annihilating Soviet cities (considered good under MAD) and did not build counterforce weapons that could attack Soviet missile silos (considered bad under MAD).

When President Jimmy Carter came to office in 1977, he saw the handwriting on the wall. The Soviets hadn't accepted MAD so the U.S. had better get out of it too. In 1980, Carter issued Presidential Directive #59, which officially changed the U.S. strategy. It made Soviet missile silos the number-one priority targets and removed civilian areas from the target lists altogether.

But PD-59, as it is called, is an empty document. The United States simply does not have enough counterforce warheads to destroy Soviet ICBM silos, some of which are hardened to withstand a pressure of 7,200 pounds per square inch.[3]

Strategy must be based on capability. Most U.S. nuclear weapons can only attack cities. So, despite PD-59, we are still living under mutual assured destruction. I said in chapter 32 that the superpowers target weapons, not cities. This is true; but unlike the Soviets, the U.S. has not built enough weapons to carry out its targeting strategy.

The 50 MX Peacekeeper ICBMs with 10 warheads apiece and 48 Trident II D-5 SLBMs with 8 warheads apiece deployed between 1986 and 1990 can destroy Soviet missile silos. But they do not constitute a first-strike capability since they have a total of 932 warheads, which could destroy only about 450 of the 1,100 Soviet ICBM silos (2 warheads allotted per silo) and none of the 20 rail-mobile SS-24s and 220 road-mobile SS-25s.

The 6,000 Soviet counterforce warheads show that the Soviet Union remains committed to a counterforce strategy and does not accept MAD. The Soviet military has not changed its position, even under *glasnost*.

In chapter 25, I mentioned a conference held in Moscow from January 24 to 26, 1990, where top U.S. and Soviet military leaders and civilian experts met to discuss the strategic balance. During the discussions, Soviet military leaders made clear that they do not believe in MAD. As *Global Affairs* reported:

> Contrary to what some Soviet and Western civilian analysts have urged, the Soviet speakers condemned both a MAD posture and any strategic force reduction to levels that would leave the United States and USSR no other option than to target cities. Such

postures were characterized as "anti-people" and "immoral."[4]

Soviet Strategic Defense

As I said, the prerequisites for a first strike are a counterforce capability and strategic and civil defense. The Soviets already have a counterforce capability. And for the last 20 years, they have been zealously pursuing strategic defense, i.e., ways to stop our missiles from hitting their targets. They may be very close to nationwide deployment.

The Pentagon concluded in its publication *Soviet Military Power 1988* that the Soviets' strategic defense efforts "suggest that the USSR may be preparing an ABM defense of its national territory."[5] The Pentagon is reluctant to categorize Soviet ABM developments as a "breakout" from the ABM Treaty. To do so would be to admit that the defense policy of the last 20 years, including the Reagan years, has been flawed. But others, who are outside the defense establishment, are not afraid to call it a breakout.

The Soviets have already deployed around Moscow the 100 ABMs allowed under the treaty. But what a number of intelligence sources have claimed is that the Soviets are mass-producing these ABMs and the mobile radars that "see" for them and could deploy them around the country at any time.

Angelo Codevilla says that in 1984 Lawrence Gershwin, the CIA's national intelligence officer for Soviet strategic forces, gave a briefing to the Senate

Armed Services Committee on Soviet antimissile developments. As summarized by Codevilla, Gershwin said that the smaller ABM radars and the interceptor missiles that are deployed around Moscow are "in full production."[6]

Codevilla's summary of the briefing continues:

Since all [of the missiles and radars] are small enough to be moved by trucks, we do not know how many the Soviets have produced, or where they are. If the Soviets were producing these components seriously, and were storing them with a view to deployment, only a few months would pass between the time when the U.S. could notice that open deployment had started and the full operational capability of a very serious nationwide ABM system.[7]

Codevilla concluded that "together, the Soviet devices would stand a good chance of intercepting most, if not all, warheads from a U.S. attack."[8]

The Soviets could also link their surface-to-air missiles to their ABM network. The 6,800 SAMs on the Soviets' 1,700 SA-10 SAM launchers can shoot down cruise missiles and some ICBM warheads. Last year, the Soviets reportedly increased the power of their air-defense radars, making each SA-10 launcher capable of defending 310 square miles.[9]

The Soviet SA-12 SAM can also shoot down ICBM warheads at altitudes of between 10 and 20 miles and can defend an area with a radius of about

30 miles.[10] As of 1989, the Soviets had deployed about 70 SA-12s.

The Soviets have built nine large phased-array radars that blanket the most populated areas of the Soviet Union. They are well-suited to battle management of a nationwide ABM network. Taken together, the SAMs, ABMs, small mobile radars and large phased-array radars could handle most of the warheads from a retaliatory strike by any U.S. submarines that survived a Soviet counterforce strike.

Gorbachev's Star Wars

The Soviets are also moving forward with high-tech strategic defense systems. After bitterly attacking the American Strategic Defense Initiative as aggressive and destabilizing, on November 25, 1987, Mikhail Gorbachev admitted for the first time that, "practically, the Soviet Union is doing all that the United States is doing, and I guess we are engaged in research, basic research, which relates to these aspects which are covered by the SDI of the United States."[11]

This admission was shocking but inadequate. The Soviets are doing far more than we are. They are spending $20 billion a year on their strategic defense system[12] while in 1990 we spent $3.57 billion on ours.

Furthermore, it is now generally known that they are winning the race for space. But most people don't know that 90 percent of Soviet space operations are for military purposes and that a number of

Soviet space achievements are necessary components of a space-based defense.[13]

Thomas Krebs, who worked as the Pentagon's expert on Soviet space warfare capabilities, says that the Soviets' immediate goal is to put up a space-based missile defense system. And they are rapidly developing the prerequisites. The Soviet Energia rocket is capable of carrying large numbers of satellites, which would be a key component of any space defense.

The Soviets also have the world's only operational space-based anti-satellite weapon, capable of destroying our early-warning and reconnaissance satellites in orbit. And they have ground-based lasers at Sary Shagan in south central Russia and in the remote Nurek region near the Soviet border with Afghanistan that may be able to damage U.S. satellites. The ability to blind early-warning satellites strengthens a first-strike capability since it makes it unlikely that the enemy would be able to quickly respond to an attack.

Taken together, Soviet strategic defenses are further proof that they are working toward a first-strike capability. And we may not know when they have reached it. Or we may find out when it's too late to do anything about it.

Their civil defense, the third prerequisite for a first strike, is perhaps more complete than their strategic defense. Civil defense for the leadership and industry includes hardened command centers for 175,000 key party and government personnel, reserves of vital economic supplies stored in hardened underground structures, and even underground factories. For civilians, there are blast shelters for 60 percent of the urban population, fallout shelters for almost everyone else, and mandatory civil defense training for the entire population.[14]

Since, by their actions, the Soviet leadership has shown that they believe that it is possible to fight and win a nuclear war, what we are really living under is unilateral assured destruction.

Americans have a difficult time understanding why the Soviet leaders would attempt to achieve the capability to "win" a nuclear war. That is because Americans view nuclear war as the unthinkable and we assume that the Soviets do the same.

Sadly, nothing could be further from the truth. Much as we would like to think that Soviet leaders share our views (and our fears) of nuclear war, they do not. The Soviet *people* may share our hopes and concerns, but they are not the ones with their fingers on the button.

I think it's time we faced reality. The Soviets have a vastly different view of nuclear weapons and their purpose than do Western strategists. And they have fully integrated these weapons into their military strategy.

A Surprise Attack

Gen. Jan Sejna, who, as I said, is the highest-ranking military official ever to defect from the Soviet bloc, has some interesting revelations about

Soviet strategy. He was a member of the Czechoslovakian Central Committee, the National Assembly and the Administrative Organs Department.

Dr. Joseph Douglass writes, "The Administrative Organs Department...is the most important department [of the Central Committee] insofar as defense, intelligence, and deception are concerned."[15] Sejna was also assistant secretary of the Czech Defense Council, which is the chief military decision-making body in the country. (Mikhail Gorbachev is head of the Soviet Defense Council.) Douglass writes that "Sejna met regularly with the highest officials in the Soviet Union and other communist countries."[16]

Sejna says that since 1963, Soviet military strategy has been to launch a surprise nuclear attack on the United States simultaneously with a conventional invasion of Europe. In 1987, I interviewed Sejna on my talk show, *Summit University Forum*. He said:

> Until 1963, the Soviets concentrated on defending their territory because they thought they were not strong enough to attack. They were behind in nuclear weapons and those things.
>
> Marshal Malinovsky, who was at that time minister of defense, visited Czechoslovakia and other satellites. And he said, "Comrades, we have to change our preparation. We have to change our tactic from

defense to offense. For the next war, we have three possibilities. First, the NATO missiles will be first in the air. Second, our missiles and NATO's will meet in the air. And third, our missiles will be first in the air. The first two possibilities are not acceptable to us."

Since then, all of the Soviet preparations have been for a surprise nuclear attack.[17]

Let's look at the prospect of a surprise attack. The United States military does not accept the possibility. Most military planners believe, almost as an act of faith, that any Soviet attack would come after an escalating crisis.

The United States believes that even in the worst case it will have at least several hours' warning of a nuclear attack during which bombers could be loaded and alerted and submarines in port could be put to sea. This is folly for four reasons:

1. *Surprise attack is an integral part of Soviet strategy.*

Soviet military strategy is characterized by preemptive, surprise attacks, often in peacetime and often accompanied by deception (such as military exercises or ongoing negotiations) to disguise their activities.

2. *The United States has a history of being surprised because it is unwilling to believe the warning signals.*

For example, America was unwilling to accept and act on available data that indicated a Japanese attack on Pearl Harbor. As a result, the Japanese achieved complete surprise, catching the bulk of the U.S. Pacific Fleet in harbor. Things haven't changed much. Despite warning signals, the Bush administration refused to believe that Iraq was about to invade Kuwait.

3. *The Soviets have a big incentive to pull off a surprise attack.*

According to a 1987 study by defense expert William Van Cleave, in a surprise attack the Soviets could destroy about 7,500 U.S. warheads by catching our ICBMs and bombers on the ground and our submarines in port. That's two-thirds of our warheads. In an attack following a period of generated alert, they could destroy only about 3,700 warheads since more of our submarines would be at sea and decision makers would be ready to launch our ICBMs and bombers on warning.[18]

Thus the Soviet incentive for surprise attack is about 3,800 warheads. In other words, in a surprise attack they could destroy almost twice as many warheads as they could if they warned us ahead of time.

4. *The United States is not prepared for a surprise attack.*

Our military leaders think that a surprise attack would be too complicated for the Soviets to carry out and too difficult for them to conceal.

Although General Sejna says the Soviets plan a simultaneous surprise nuclear attack on the United States and conventional invasion of Europe, some

U.S. intelligence experts have concluded that as a result of recent political changes in Eastern Europe, we are likely to have a month or more of warning of a conventional attack in Europe.

However, Van Cleave says, "The Soviets probably would forego attack preparations that might improve their military strength if those preparations would also deny them the element of surprise. At the very least, the Soviets should be expected to conceal or obscure such preparations by a combination of political and military deception."[19]

After a surprise first-strike attack, what would our options be? The surviving U.S. bombers would still have to outmaneuver the Soviet air defense. And that's not likely.

The Pentagon recently admitted that the 90 brand-new B-1B bombers deployed from 1986 to 1988 have "a limited capability to penetrate heavily defended targets within the Soviet Union."[20] The weapons on the 18 or so surviving submarines (except for the Trident II D-5s) could not be used to attack Soviet military targets. Furthermore, an undetermined number of SLBM warheads could be stopped by the Soviet strategic defense I already outlined.

What do all these figures boil down to? Quite simply, following a first strike the president of the United States would have the choice of (1) surrender or (2) retaliation by destroying innocent Soviet civilians and submitting to Soviet retaliation on U.S. cities.

If the president attacked Soviet cities, the Soviets

would still have over 5,000 warheads in reserve with which to annihilate undefended U.S. cities. America would be worse off if he retaliated than if he did nothing. If the U.S. did retaliate, the extensive Soviet civil defense would reduce their casualties considerably.

For the last 20 years, the Soviet Union has devoted itself to achieving a first-strike capability. Now that it is nearly complete, the question is: Will they use it?

For one thing, the way the Soviets have spent their money reveals their strategy. If they have built a first-strike capability, we had better act like they plan to use it.

We should take General Sejna's warning seriously. And since conditions in the Soviet Union are rapidly deteriorating, the Soviet leadership may soon conclude that a first strike against the United States, while highly dangerous, is preferable to watching their empire disintegrate when they are at the pinnacle of military power.

Saint Germain's Warning—Preparedness Is the Key

Given this equation, my conclusion is that the only sane thing for United States citizens to do is to provide themselves with civil defense. And that is just what Saint Germain has recommended that we do. On Thanksgiving 1986, he said:

> You have every reason to believe, to be concerned, and to be prepared for a first

strike by the Soviet Union upon these United
States....

Therefore, secure the underground shelters, preserve the food, and prepare to survive.
And if it be an exercise proven unneeded,
then bless God that it did not go unheeded.
For, beloved, my word and your response,
your very preparedness, is the one condition
that can prevent the almost inevitable scenario of nuclear war.[21]

On February 13, 1988, the day I gave my
address on the astrology of the 1990s, Saint
Germain said:

The preparedness at a personal and national level has never been more paramount.
Your preparedness in your life can be complete in a matter of months. When you are
fully prepared and determined to survive
physically in the earth, come what may in all
of these predictions and those you have heard
elsewhere, you are then a free agent of Saint
Germain and you may give your life and
heart to this very cause of stopping those
conditions in their tracks before they are outpictured, therefore rendering your preparations only a safety valve, a security net, a
lifeboat, if you will.[22]

Saint Germain recommends for everyone in
America a simple fallout shelter, a food supply for

seven months to a year, and provision for uncontaminated water. But he asks us to see it as an insurance policy rather than a preparation for an inevitable scenario. On October 8, 1989, he said,

> I, Saint Germain, shall never predict with absolute certainty that this war and holocaust shall occur. . . . If you can see the realism of the world geopolitical configuration in this hour, then you, too, must surely see that the chances that this will occur are as great as, or greater than, they are that you will have a fire in your house or you will have robbers or you will have an accident or you may have a death in the family. And all of these probabilities are the reasons why you have taken out insurance policies.[23]

That same day, however, Saint Germain warned us that even as we look for the mitigation of prophecy, so we cannot count on its complete mitigation. Concerning the possibility of war with the Soviet Union, he said that we must consider events already set in motion that will be outplayed to a greater or lesser extent:

> For this war not to occur it would take the complete undoing of the military strategy of the Soviet Union this day. It would take the healing of their economy. It would take the resignation of the entire Politburo and leadership to the idea that the people of the

Communist world are determined to be free!

If the Soviets do not go to war, they will have on their hands a wholesale war and revolution of the people, as you can see in the events passing every day in Eastern Europe. And there is only one reason why they do not stop their satellite nations from moving toward greater freedom. It is because, beloved, they have another agenda. And the activities of their satellites and their activities in *glasnost* simply play into their hands to keep the people in a stupor, to keep them asleep so that the Soviets will have the advantage in a greater surprise attack. [24]

On Wesak 1989, Gautama Buddha spoke to us about the need to be practical and realistic when we think about what may happen in the 1990s. He reiterated Saint Germain's call to be physically prepared:

Do not fear to face the future or what is coming upon the earth, but take heed to be in preparedness, as we have told you. For when you are in the physical body you are subject to physical conditions. Therefore, if you go out in subzero weather, you may take cold or pneumonia unless you are one of the few yogis in the high Himalayas who may sit naked in the ice and snow untouched.

Remember, you are subject to the forces of this world, to the chemistry, to the poisons, to the diseases, to all of the threatening woes and that which is delivered as karma of the earth through the Four Horsemen of the Apocalypse.

Understand this, beloved, and do not confuse by your metaphysics the absolute God-Reality of your Higher Self with the mutable lower self as so many in the past have done in their self-idolatry. And therefore they have not met the challenges of the times because they have refused to bend the knee to acknowledge the laws that govern time and space. [25]

Once again, then, I urge you to heed the warning and to be prepared.

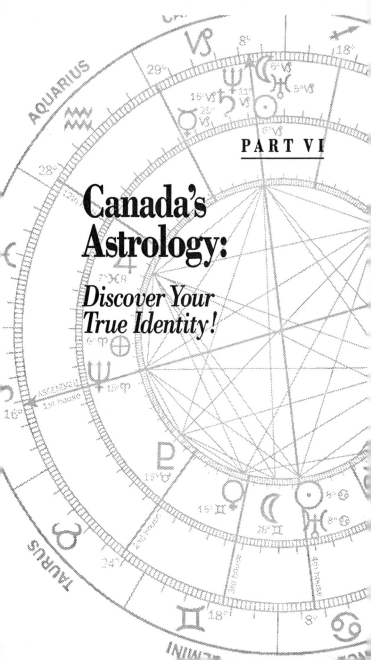

PART VI

Canada's Astrology:

*Discover Your
True Identity!*

CHAPTER 34

The Positive Portents in Canada's Birth Chart

How does Canada fit into the framework of coming astrological events?

Canada was born at midnight, July 1, 1867, the day and hour she became a Dominion. In the chart drawn for this date (fig. 40), Canada's natal Sun is at 8° Cancer in the fourth house. A fourth-house Sun usually shows material success. Uranus, also at 8° Cancer in the fourth house, makes a nearly exact conjunction with the Sun. This aspect marks Canadians as a unique people.

A Sun-Uranus conjunction gives the stimulus to freedom and individuality and is a catalyst for genius. It endows Canadians with the capacity to be individualistic and innovative. It shows that Canada should prosper through developing the genius of her people.

This could come about in cutting-edge technologies, such as electronics, aviation, computers and mass communications, and in new methods of developing human and natural resources, especially primary economic activities such as farming, fisheries, forestries and mining. The Sun-Uranus conjunction

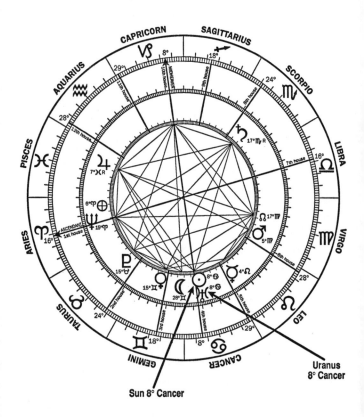

**Dominion of Canada
Birth Chart
July 1, 1867, 12:00 a.m.**

Sun 8° Cancer

Uranus
8° Cancer

FIGURE 40   The Dominion of Canada was created by the British
North America Act, which took effect at midnight on July 1, 1867,
in Ottawa, Ontario. Canada's Sun is at 8° Cancer in the fourth
house (of agriculture, mining and real estate). A fourth-house Sun
usually shows material success. The nearly exact conjunction of the
Sun and Uranus at 8° Cancer marks Canadians as a unique people.
It also gives the stimulus to freedom and endows Canadians with
the capacity to be highly individualistic and innovative.

could also give the impulse for the development of an Aquarian or New Age social order.

This conjunction makes beneficial trines with Saturn at 17° Scorpio and Jupiter at 7° Pisces, the planetary pair that governs the coordinates of the physical universe. Saturn rules time and Jupiter rules space. Canada is fortunate to have Jupiter and Saturn trine her Sun and Uranus (fig. 41).

The ancients called Jupiter and Saturn "the great chronocrators," or rulers of time, because the cycles of conjunctions between the two planets subdivide time into large units with observable political and economic cycles.

Saturn, in addition to governing time, rules the government, the constitution and the laws. Saturn rules people who are employed by national, state and local governments. It rules the ability to organize, to crystallize aspirations and to take practical action leading to the fulfillment of long-term goals. It rules tradition, prudence and stability, and land, agriculture and resources. It also rules karma, delays and restrictions. In sum, Saturn is a yang force.

Jupiter is a yin force. In addition to governing space, Jupiter rules the capacity to grow and expand spiritually and materially. It rules optimism, good judgment and honest character; people and places associated with law, religion and education, judges and the judiciary; ministers and churches; lawmakers and elected assemblies; and teachers and educational institutions. Jupiter also rules foreign and cultural relations and good fortune. All of these

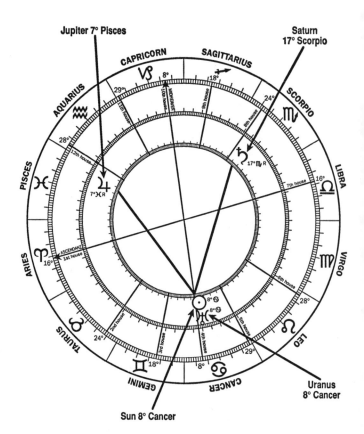

FIGURE 41 Canada's Sun-Uranus conjunction at 8° Cancer makes beneficial trines with Saturn at 17° Scorpio and Jupiter at 7° Pisces. These four bodies provide the framework for Canada to be an economic, cultural, political and spiritual world power. Saturn's trine to the Sun and Uranus shows that Canada has an obligation to play a responsible and evolutionary role in world affairs. Jupiter's trine shows that Canada has a mission to use her resources for the benefit of her own people and those of other nations.

areas that Saturn and Jupiter rule are at a keen level of development in Canada.

Saturn is essentially conservative; Jupiter is liberal. Having these planets in harmonious aspect to the Sun and Uranus brings about the conditions necessary for a harmonious, integrated expression of all the elements that we have discussed thus far.

Jupiter is in the twelfth house of spiritual resources and Saturn is in the seventh house of other nations. Jupiter in Pisces in the twelfth house trine the Sun shows that Canada has the capacity and mission to use her material and spiritual resources for the benefit of her own people and for the betterment of the people of other nations. Saturn in Scorpio in the seventh house trine the Sun and Uranus shows Canada's ability and obligation to play a responsible and evolutionary role in international and economic affairs.

These four planets—the Sun, Uranus, Jupiter and Saturn—provide the framework for Canada to be an economic, cultural, political and spiritual world power.

Remember, astrology is not predestination. Astrology shows opportunity. If you are to realize the potential greatness in your chart, you must have the will and determination to make it happen. Sometimes we see in wealthy families that the founder who built the company was successful because he took nothing for granted except hard work. Succeeding generations, taking everything for granted, accomplish less and less and finally end up with nothing.

Canadians have a great inheritance from their Higher Consciousness and their momentums of attainment from their past lives. Having the riches of the Spirit and abundant material resources, they must be careful to forge their identity and build their beloved country on a solid foundation of Christ Truth, year upon year.

We must all learn the eternal lesson: Never take for granted the abundance of opportunity that is the gift of God, but ride it—ride the proud wave of your heritage to your victory!

CHAPTER 35

The Challenges in Canada's Birth Chart

L et's take a look at the astrological challenges to Canada's expression of her vast potential.

First, Canada's natal Neptune at 15° Aries in the twelfth house (of spiritual impulses) is conjoined her Ascendant at 16° Aries. Both are square to her Sun and Uranus at 8° Cancer in the fourth house (of national sentiment) (fig. 42).

This square has a number of effects. It can increase the national level of intuition, idealism, and religious and artistic inspiration. It can intensify the impulse of enlightened democratic rule. And it can refine and elevate all aspects of national life.

However, the positive qualities of Neptune are difficult for a person or nation to accurately express. They appear only to the degree that the person or the nation is spiritually developed and grounded.

Unless she fully integrates the positive aspects in her chart, Canada is likely to experience problems under the influence of this square. She could have difficulty understanding who and what she is, and thus be unable to act effectively to fulfill her reason for being.

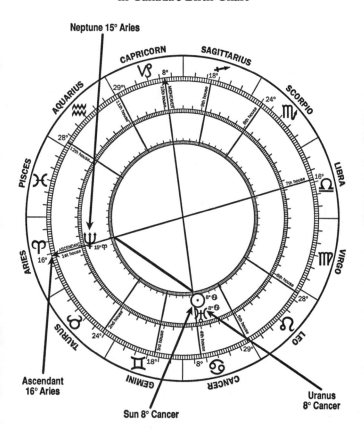

FIGURE 42 Canada's Neptune at 15° Aries conjoined her Ascendant at 16° Aries makes a square to the Sun and Uranus at 8° Cancer. This aspect can increase the national level of intuition, idealism and religious and artistic inspiration. But the positive side of Neptune manifests only to the degree that the nation is spiritually developed. Without a strong spiritual foundation, Canada is likely to experience an identity crisis accompanied by illusion, confusion and the inability to formulate practical goals.

The problem of an identity crisis goes back to a shortage of spiritual luminaries among the people. Every nation must have a quota of those who know who God is and that he abides within their temples, who in humility understand the glorious nature of the indwelling Presence.

Where does anyone find identity if it's not in the divine spark centered in the heart? What other identity is permanent about ourselves except the God flame? *That* must be the fount of our fiery destiny.

An identity crisis arising from a square such as Canada's Sun-Uranus-Neptune-Ascendant square is often accompanied by illusion, confusion and diffusion of energies and the inability to formulate practical goals. Without vision the people perish. They cannot agree on national purpose. They are unable to solve their problems.

This square could also activate peculiar problems that block goals or delay their fulfillment, the tendency to fantasize and dream instead of act, opposition from hidden enemies, as well as an undeservedly bad reputation and social unrest.

Finger of God Bisected by a Saturn-Pluto Opposition

Other configurations amplify the effects of this square in Canada's chart. One of these is a Finger of God formed by Neptune at 15° Aries sextile Venus at 15° Gemini, both making a quincunx to Saturn at 17° Scorpio in the seventh house (fig. 43). This Finger of God shows Canada's obligation to crystallize her true

Finger of God Bisected by Pluto
in Canada's Birth Chart

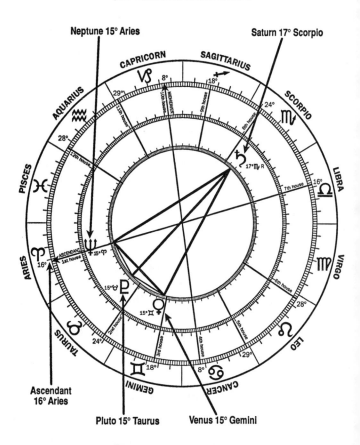

FIGURE 43 Canada has a Finger of God formed by Neptune at 15° Aries and her Ascendant at 16° Aries, Venus at 15° Gemini and Saturn at 17° Scorpio. It can extend Neptunian confusion and deception into economic affairs and foreign relations. The Finger of God is bisected by the opposition of Pluto at 15° Taurus to Saturn. This opposition is indicative of an obnoxious bureaucracy and shows the potential for domestic and international power elites to oppose the will of the people.

identity and conduct an enlightened foreign policy based on practical spiritual principles.

On the downside, this configuration could extend Neptunian confusion and deception into domestic and international economic affairs and foreign relations. It could generate anxiety about Canada's fuzzy self-image, social standing and reputation. It could also disorganize Canada's economy, block the formulation and passage of sound domestic and international economic policy and lead to periodic recessions and depressions.

The Finger of God is bisected by an opposition between Saturn at 17° Scorpio in the seventh house and Pluto at 15° Taurus in the first house. This opposition makes it difficult for Canada to fulfill the karmic obligations indicated by her Finger of God. It tends to block the expression of the true will and personality of the body politic.

This Saturn-Pluto opposition shows the intrusion of domestic and international power elites. It is also indicative of an obnoxious bureaucracy, delays and difficulties in the government, and constitutional crises. It was directly related to the long delay in repatriation of the Canadian Constitution, which I will discuss in chapter 36.

Saturn-Pluto oppositions are often associated with mass destiny and serious karmic problems such as the outbreak of wars. Since this opposition is nearly exact and falls in the first and seventh houses of other nations and war, it could lead to the cataclysmic destruction of the government through war or economic crisis. As I will discuss in the next chapter, transiting Pluto recently activated this opposition.

Canada also has a Mars-Jupiter opposition in her natal chart. Mars at 5° Virgo in the sixth house (of the work force) opposed to Jupiter at 7° Pisces in the twelfth house (of institutions) shows, among other things, a talented labor force but one that is aggressive and inclined to go on strike even when it is not warranted or in the interests of the nation.

This opposition, along with the one between Saturn and Pluto, can also tend to give some Canadians an aggressive, harsh, vindictive, combative, blindly ambitious and acquisitive nature.

A Third-House Moon—
Skill in Communication and Separatism

Canada's natal Moon is at 28° Gemini in the third house of communication and education. On the positive side, a Gemini Moon in the third house shows skill in all forms of communication and the ability to unify diverse aspects of the people into a productive, healthy body. It is also indicative of bilingualism.

Canada's Moon is generally well aspected. But the negative elements of Gemini, the loss of energy and inability to achieve goals due to divisiveness, are clearly evident. The divisions in Canadian society go back to the square of Neptune at 15° Aries to the Sun and Uranus at 8° Cancer. The Moon rules Cancer and therefore the afflictions of the Sun and Uranus can be transferred to the Moon.

When the Sun, which represents national identity and will, is weakened by the square of Neptune, the center of gravity of the nation is weakened. Consequently, the parts of the whole break into nonintegratable pieces.

The individuality of Canadian ethnic groups, which should be expressed in their unique Christhood, instead becomes separatism. This denies the larger profile of all citizens as Canadians first, which is essential in coalescing national unity and purpose. This effect is amplified by the opposition of Pluto to Saturn, which reduces the ability of the people to focus and express their true personality.

But let's not see these aspects as "obstacles." Let's see them as the creative tension that tests the mettle of a man, a woman, a child, and compels us to become our best and highest self. There's always a creative tension that is a part of the birth process—whether of a nation or of a child from its mother's womb.

And so, along with the good aspects come the testers and teasers of your karma that you must overcome in order to fulfill your nation's destiny and your own. You have to summon all of your strength, your self-knowledge, your experience, your will and that sacrificial staying power to be sure that you win—when the Fates are betting on your winning and when they're not.

If the forces of Antichrist were to meet in council to determine how to defeat the Christhood of the people of Canada, the first thing they would do is study the astrological charts of the nation and of her citizens to determine the national, individual and collective points of weakness, which I call their karmic vulnerability. Then they would work to break down the leadership as well as the rank and file wherever they could.

If you are going to defeat the Fates, you must ferret out those weaknesses in your personal chart and the chart of your nation. Then you must determine how you will overcome the karma that caused them. Only thus can you and your nation move forward to victory.

CHAPTER 36

Canada's Future

The series of Capricorn conjunctions that began with the February 23, 1988 conjunction of Mars, Saturn, Uranus and Neptune in Capricorn will challenge Canada. She will be affected by the global economic, political, environmental and military crises of the next decade. And she will have her own set of problems.

The Capricorn conjunctions fall in Canada's ninth house, tenth house and on her Midheaven at 8° Capricorn. The ninth house rules foreign affairs, higher education, cultural affairs and religion. The tenth house rules the nation's chief executive, government, constitution, the party in power, the nation's reputation and public standing, and its honor, ideals and achievement.

The Midheaven, or tenth-house cusp, is a concentrated expression of tenth-house affairs. More than any other point in the chart, it reveals a nation's reason for being and her mission.

For the first time in Canada's history, on January 8, 1988, transiting Neptune in Capricorn conjoined Canada's Midheaven at 8° Capricorn and opposed her Sun and Uranus at 8° Cancer (fig. 44). This means that Canada is entering a new and crucial phase of her life and development.

Canada is meant to come of age as a nation and play a leading role on the world stage. What makes these transits even more significant is that they coincide with a time of momentous world changes.

Canada must come of age spiritually, and the enlightened among her citizenry must lead the way! She must crystallize her identity, her true Christhood. She must demonstrate the correct uses of power, transcend the Neptunian conditions in her birth chart that have partially incapacitated her, and allow her highest spiritual impulses to direct the course of government policy. The consequences of Canada's failure to do so could be severe.

Saturn, Uranus and Neptune formed the backbone of the six-planet Capricorn conjunctions of late 1989 and 1990 (fig. 45). As I said in chapter 7, conjunctions of these three planets are extremely rare. They set in motion forces that change the course of history. Their immediate influence may last decades; their long-term influence, centuries. These conjunctions could have a depressing effect on the government, economy and people of Canada and the rest of the world, unless they have worked diligently to build their nations on a foundation of reality.

November 13 T-Square Challenges Canada's Identity

On November 13, 1989, Saturn and Neptune made an exact conjunction at 10° Capricorn in

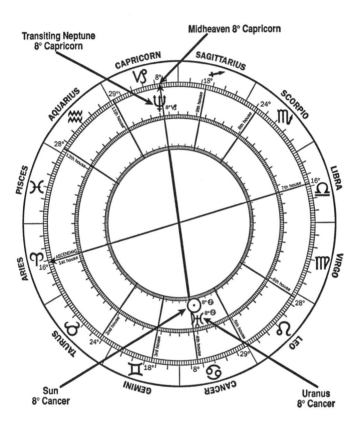

Transiting Neptune Conjoined Canada's Midheaven and Opposed to Canada's Sun and Uranus
January 8, 1988

FIGURE 44 On January 8, 1988, Canada entered a new and crucial phase of her development. Neptune (spiritual growth) conjoined Canada's Midheaven (national policy, purpose and reputation) at 8° Capricorn and opposed her Sun and Uranus conjoined at 8° Cancer. Canada is due to come of age and play a leading role on the world stage, but in order to do so she must come of age spiritually.

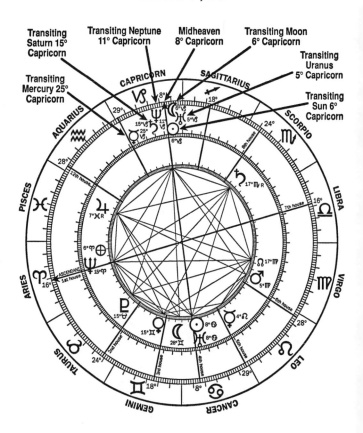

FIGURE 45 The first of several six-planet conjunctions in Capricorn that took place in 1989 and 1990 occurred on December 27, 1989. The planets in these conjunctions are close to Canada's Midheaven and are likely to have a depressing effect on her government, economy and people. Saturn, Uranus and Neptune form the nucleus of the six-planet Capricorn conjunctions. Saturn-Uranus-Neptune conjunctions are extremely rare and set in motion forces that change the course of history.

Canada's tenth house conjoined her Midheaven at 8° Capricorn (fig. 46). This configuration opposed Canada's Sun-Uranus conjunction at 8° Cancer conjoined transiting Jupiter at 10° Cancer in the fourth house. All of these planets, plus the Midheaven, squared Canada's Neptune at 15° Aries conjoined her Ascendant at 16° Aries, forming a T-square.

On April 16, 1988, I said to an audience in Toronto:

> By November 13, 1989, Canada should have completely integrated into her national psyche the positive elements of the trines of Jupiter in Pisces and Saturn in Scorpio that are in her birth chart and be capable of expressing the highest attributes defined in her chart.
>
> If Canada is unable to do that, the November 13, 1989 configuration, which could eventually cause the dissolution of the economy, stock market and even the government of the United States, could have a similar but more powerful effect in Canada.
>
> There could be social, economic and political cataclysm of considerable duration. At the very least, the government in power will be threatened. More likely, the Canadian form of government could be drastically and unpredictably altered for the worse.

The T-square of November 13, 1989, could mark the onset of a major economic downturn for

Transiting Saturn and Neptune Form a T-Square in Canada's Birth Chart
November 13, 1989

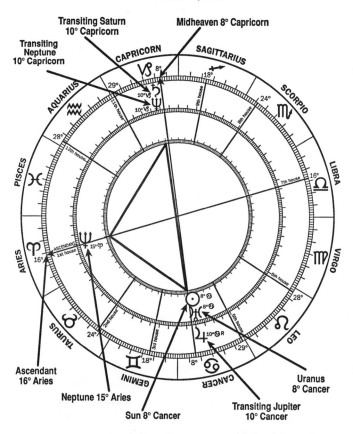

FIGURE 46 On November 13, 1989, Saturn and Neptune made an exact conjunction at 10° Capricorn. They conjoined Canada's Midheaven at 8° Capricorn and opposed her Sun and Uranus at 8° Cancer and transiting Jupiter at 10° Cancer. All of these planets, plus the Midheaven, squared Canada's Neptune at 15° Aries conjoined her Ascendant at 16° Aries. This configuration indicates that Canada could experience social, economic and political cataclysm and that her government could be drastically altered for the worse.

Canada and political changes leading to a loss of individual freedom. If the negative elements of international karma associated with this configuration break through into the physical, it will be difficult to solve the problems that may arise. It may even be too late.

There are a number of reasons for this. Capricorn is ruled by Saturn and its effects are long-term. On November 27, 1989, transiting Mars was conjoined transiting Pluto at 15° Scorpio and Canada's Saturn at 17° Scorpio, which exacerbated the negative potential of the Saturn-in-Capricorn configuration enough to call into question the continued existence of Canada as we know her today.

In addition, between December 1987 and February 1995, transiting Neptune in Capricorn squares Canada's natal Neptune at 15° Aries in the twelfth house. Neptune square Neptune can precipitate problems that are difficult to solve. (Israel, for example, which has been unable to formulate a workable policy for the occupied territories, is currently beset by a square of transiting Neptune in Capricorn to her natal Neptune at 10° Libra.)

Prospects for Violence and War

If the previously mentioned configurations were not enough, in February, June and December of 1990, transiting Uranus conjoined Canada's Midheaven at 8° Capricorn and opposed her Sun and Uranus at 8° Cancer, creating T-squares in her birth chart similar to the Saturn-Neptune T-square of November 13, 1989 (see fig. 46).

The first of these three T-squares was particularly explosive. It took place February 11, 1990, when transiting Mars at 9° Capricorn conjoined transiting Uranus at 8° Capricorn and transiting Neptune at 13° Capricorn, and all three squared Canada's natal Neptune at 15° Aries and opposed her natal Sun and Uranus at 8° Cancer. In its most extreme expression, this T-square could lead to a violent overthrow of the government.

The Neptune squares show a mounting force from within of treachery and intrigue by hidden enemies and possibly by agents from foreign governments as well. The Capricorn challenges will go on, but I think you get the point.

As I pointed out in chapter 24, there are powerful astrological indicators of war in the next few years: the Saturn-Uranus conjunctions of 1988, including Saturn and Uranus conjoined the Galactic Center; Mars, Saturn, Uranus and Neptune conjoined in Capricorn on February 22 and 23, 1988; the Capricorn megaconjunction of 1994; the peaking sunspot cycle; and Gouchon's and Ganeau's cycles of peace and war.

Transiting Pluto in Scorpio conjoined the Soviet natal Sun at 14° Scorpio and opposed the U.S. natal Sun at 10° Taurus shows that the United States and the Soviet Union are likely to be combatants during this time of extreme tension.

If the superpowers go to war, Canada will almost certainly be a participant. Canada and the

United States are physically close to each other; they share common values and a common defense.

But even if the United States and the Soviet Union do not go to war, Canada's astrology is such that she herself could go to war or experience a mortal challenge equal to war. One indicator of this is the Pluto-Mars conjunction of November 27, 1989 that I mentioned on page 461. It took place at 15° Scorpio, only two degrees from Canada's Saturn at 17° Scorpio in the seventh house and opposed Canada's natal Pluto at 15° Taurus in the first house (fig. 47). Since Pluto was moving quickly at that time, it made an exact conjunction with Canada's Saturn at 17° Scorpio on February 13, 1990 (fig. 48).

A Mars-Saturn-Pluto combination in Scorpio and Taurus can trigger long-term, life-and-death battles. Since the conjunction falls in Canada's seventh house, which rules war, the prospect for international battles is even higher.

Pluto was already conjoined Canada's Saturn on February 11, 1990, the day when transiting Uranus formed a T-square almost identical to the November 13, 1989 T-square. And it will be part of other intense placings that indicate a high probability of war, including two other conjunctions with Canada's Saturn on October 25, 1990, and June 13, 1991.

These configurations make it evident that Canada will be profoundly influenced by the karmic challenges affecting the United States and the rest of the world in the 1990s.

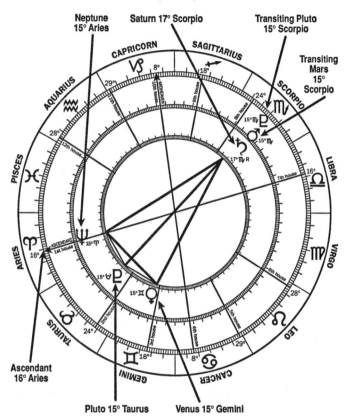

FIGURE 47 On November 27, 1989, transiting Mars (the planet of war) and transiting Pluto (the planet of widespread death and destruction) formed an exact conjunction at 15° Scorpio. This conjunction activated Canada's bisected Finger of God formed by Saturn, Pluto, Venus, Neptune and the Ascendant. The conjunction of transiting Mars and Pluto fell only 2° from Canada's Saturn (the planet of karmic circumstances) at 17° Scorpio in the seventh house (of war) and opposed Canada's Pluto at 15° Taurus in the first house (of the nation as a whole).

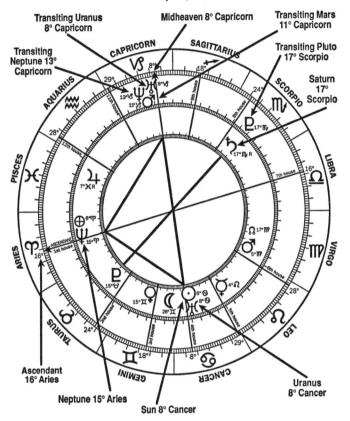

**Transiting Pluto Makes an Exact Conjunction
with Canada's Natal Saturn
February 13, 1990**

FIGURE 48 On February 13, 1990, transiting Pluto formed an exact conjunction to Canada's Saturn at 17° Scorpio and an opposition to her Pluto at 15° Taurus. This occurred just two days after transiting Uranus exactly conjoined Canada's Midheaven at 8° Capricorn with Mars at 11° Capricorn and Neptune at 13° Capricorn close by. These planets formed a T-square with Canada's Sun and Uranus at 8° Cancer, her Neptune at 15° Aries and her Ascendant at 16° Aries. The combined effect of the two configurations has the potential to ignite a war.

A *Nation Divided*

The challenges to the continued existence of Canada's form of government became apparent in June 1990. That is when the latest battle over Canada's constitution ended with the failure of all of the provinces to ratify the Meech Lake accord.

The accord would have secured Quebec's approval of the 1982 constitution. But since the document included conditions promoting Quebec's "distinct society" status, other provinces would not ratify it. Now the next move is Quebec's—and it remains in question whether she will secede or attempt reconciliation with the other provinces.

The battle over the Meech Lake accord brought to a head controversy over Canada's two recurring historical problems. First, the provinces have traditionally fought the federal government in Ottawa for greater autonomy and more power over their internal affairs. Second, Quebec has always seen herself as a conquered nation that has not received enough powers of her own and that has not been given her rightful status.

The story began in 1759 during the Seven Years War between France and England. As recounted in *Maclean's* magazine, "On September 13, 1759, British Maj.-Gen. James Wolfe captured Quebec from the Marquis de Montcalm....The 15-minute battle was fierce. Both generals died. Four years later, King Louis XV quietly ceded Canada to Britain."[1]

With the British North America Act of 1867, Nova Scotia, New Brunswick, Quebec and Ontario formed the Dominion of Canada. Manitoba joined in 1870, and British Columbia followed a year later. Prince Edward Island joined in 1873; Alberta and Saskatchewan in 1905. Newfoundland was the last to join, in 1949.

The British North America Act of 1867 was Canada's primary constitutional document up until 1982, even though England had freed her dominions with the Westminster Statute in 1931. Under the British North America Act, if the Canadian government wanted to amend its constitution, it needed a law passed by the British Parliament.

In 1949 the act was amended to give the Canadian Parliament authority to amend the constitution in some areas. But the power to amend the constitution on matters such as the use of the English and French languages and provincial affairs still required approval of the British Parliament.

In order to obtain from Great Britain the power to amend her constitution, Canada was required to create a law ratified by all the provinces and passed by the British government. And the federal government had a hard time getting all of the provincial governments to agree on a document.

In 1982, Pierre Trudeau's government passed the Constitution Act of 1982, which added a Charter of Rights to the constitution, setting up a procedure for amendment. Queen Elizabeth II of England signed the document. But Quebec's separatist premier, René Lévesque, refused to sign Trudeau's proposal on the grounds that the charter could inhibit Quebec's legislative powers over her language and culture.

In the most recent battle, the federal government again tried to secure Quebec's approval of the Constitution Act of 1982. In April 1987, Prime Minister Brian Mulroney met with the 10 premiers at a government retreat on Meech Lake. At that time, all 10 provincial ministers agreed to the draft legislation, known as the Meech Lake accord, which included five conditions added by Quebec's premier, Robert Bourassa.

Quebec's main condition was the formalization of her right to "preserve and promote" her "distinct society." The other conditions were, as reported by *Insight* magazine, "a provincial role in appointments to the Supreme Court, an increased provincial role in immigration, limits on federal spending power as it affects federal-provincial shared-cost programs and a veto for Quebec on constitutional amendments."[2]

The premiers added two proposals to the accord during the meeting, as *Insight* reported, "one securing the right of provincial governments to make Senate nominations (senators are appointed by the prime minister at present); the other setting up a yearly meeting of the premiers and the prime minister to address constitutional issues."[3]

In June 1988, the accord passed the House of Commons and the Senate and was ratified by the

Parliament of Canada. In order for the accord to go into effect, the 10 provincial governments needed to approve it by June 23, 1990.

Controversy over approval of the Meech Lake accord swept the nation. As *Insight* reported, "Canadians in outlying provinces charge that Quebec is holding national unity hostage by demanding that its five conditions be accepted—or else. Quebecers, in turn, say a no to the accord would be a rejection of their majority francophone province, an action that would fan the flames of Quebec's growing independence movement and shatter the federation."[4]

In the interim before the deadline, three new provincial premiers took office and expressed doubts about approving the accord that their predecessors had signed. Premier Frank McKenna of New Brunswick wanted to take the accord further and extend more rights to other provinces. Gary Filmon of Manitoba did not want Quebec to acquire constitutional veto power over Senate reform. Clyde Wells of Newfoundland found the proposal for Quebec's veto and the distinct society clause unacceptable.

In the end, eight premiers approved the accord. In Manitoba, Elijah Harper, a member of the legislative assembly, forced the legislature to recess indefinitely, preventing it from ratifying the Meech Lake accord. In Newfoundland, Clyde Wells complained that Ottawa was trying to manipulate him into ratification and announced that the assembly would not vote on the accord.

Despite last-minute attempts by Mulroney and

his aides to save the accord before the evening of June 23, nothing worked. The Meech Lake accord had been defeated.

On June 24, Bourassa said that Quebec would not return to the constitutional negotiating table with the nine other premiers and would boycott a federal provincial conference planned for Winnipeg in August. From now on, he said, Quebec would discuss constitutional issues only in talks with the federal government.

News of the accord's demise sparked rejoicing among several hundred thousand Quebecers, who used the June 25 celebration of St. Jean-Baptiste Day, the traditional holiday of Quebec, as a chance to show the world the power of nationalism.

Bourassa is planning to appoint a nonpartisan commission to begin a public debate on the province's future. The committee will be composed of members of the National Assembly as well as labor, business and community leaders.

Meanwhile, the process of repatriation will probably continue, according to the Canadian consul for public affairs in Los Angeles, Eric Pelletier.[5] Canadians must wait and see what will be Quebec's next move, as well as Ottawa's. It is possible that Quebec could secede from Canada, Pelletier says, but at this time it is too early to tell.

Where Does Canada Go From Here?

Although Canada's future is not yet written, the nation appears to be headed for a breakup. On both sides, English and French, leaders are unwilling to compromise for the sake of unity. It is almost incomprehensible. The issues involved are petty—nothing for a country to tear itself apart over. That's because the real issues are beneath the surface.

Canadian columnist Peter C. Newman wrote an editorial in *Maclean's* magazine entitled "Examining Canada's self-destructive psyche." In it he quotes one of Canada's leading psychiatrists, Dr. Vivian Morris Rakoff. He writes:

> When I called on Rakoff recently, I found him profoundly concerned with the Canadian psyche, while disclaiming any expertise in how to fix it. "I'm frightened about Canada shooting itself in the foot," he said. "It's quite bewildering. Here we are, one of the world's happy countries—not perfect, but essentially benign, welcoming and decent—even if we do need a kick in the ass once in a while, because we're so inert in some ways, so suspicious of excellence. At the same time, we've absorbed millions of immigrants and haven't cracked apart, and while there have been some terrible racial incidents we have had no race riots. We are at peace and perpetuate no major international quarrels. We are the seventh most prosperous country in the world and share our wealth higgeldy-piggeldy across the country.

> "And yet," he continued, "we seem to

be tearing ourselves apart as though we were a Lithuania that was annexed without legality, as though we were oppressed by some offensive, powerful, outside regime. It's madness. What are we doing it for? One reason may be that our politicians are not talking about anything that really affects us. They're not talking about the price of sausages going crazy, or hyperinflation, or death squads and secret police, or the army about to take over: they're talking about this funny, mixed-up, blessed, pluralist and decent mess of a society that most of the world envies and is desperate to get into, and that's about to tear itself apart because of constitutional lawyers' problems." . . .

Vivian Rakoff surely is right when he laments: 'Why are there people who want to break this country apart? It's like being given one of God's great gifts, deciding it may not be totally perfect, and breaking it to see what's inside.'"[6]

Canada will find the solution to her identity crisis only if she gets to the root of the karmic problems outlined in her birth chart. And she will make it through this cycle only with enlightened spiritual and political leadership.

I have confidence that the people of Canada can, if they will, provide the leadership they deserve and can, if they will, pray for the divine intervention that is indispensable to their survival as a nation.

But will they surrender their nit-picking provincialism for the larger vision of Canada's destiny? Only the people and their leaders can give answer.

The violet flame is the universal solvent that dissolves the fears and follies of men and states and statesmen. But even it cannot penetrate a psyche that will not let go of partisan politics and pride.

Yes, free will is king for a day, but tomorrow its misuse will find it a pauper without portfolio. No, the violet flame will not act against free will. It is the gift untouchable that allows us to become gods or self-destruct.

I know that every negative portent in Canada's astrology can be defeated. But what's more important is that you, the people of Canada, know it and that you seize the torch of the Goddess of Liberty and run with it as keepers of the flame and runners in the race for God's victory and your own!

I, for one, pray that you soon see that all your strength is in your union and your future in your self-dominion.

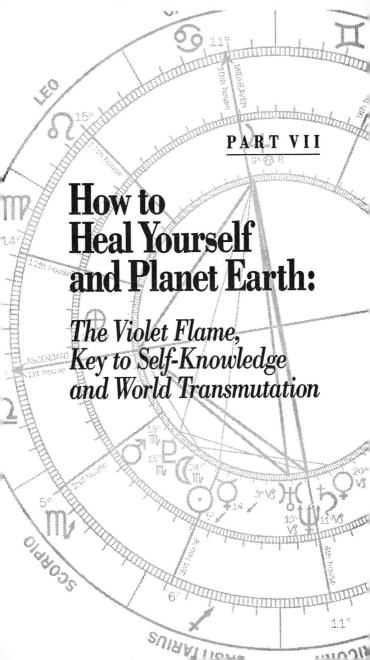

PART VII

How to Heal Yourself and Planet Earth:

*The Violet Flame,
Key to Self-Knowledge
and World Transmutation*

The Chart of Your Divine Self

CHAPTER 37

Your Divine Inheritance

Before I begin to discuss the most effective means you can use to change the prophecies I have set forth, I would like to give you a unique perspective on your spiritual destiny in the Piscean and Aquarian ages based on your relationship to the Persons of the Trinity and the Divine Mother.

The Chart of Your Divine Self reveals how these four are individualized within you as the Father-Mother God, in the I AM Presence (upper figure); as the Son, in the Holy Christ Self (middle figure); and as the Holy Spirit, who, when you have prepared yourself, may take up his abode in the body temple God provided for your soul's sojourn on planet earth (lower figure). The Chart shows the fulfillment of the Psalmist's trust:

> He that dwelleth [in consciousness] in the secret place of the Most High shall abide under the shadow of the Almighty [the Mighty I AM Presence].
> I will say of the LORD, He is my refuge and my fortress: my God; in him will I trust. [1]

"By This Name I Shall Be Invoked"

God told Moses to tell the children of Israel that his name was I AM THAT I AM and that "I AM hath sent me unto you." Moreover, he said, "Thus shalt thou say unto the children of Israel: The LORD God of your fathers, the God of Abraham, the God of Isaac, and the God of Jacob, hath sent me unto you. This is my name for ever, and this is my memorial unto all generations."[2]

The Jerusalem Bible translates the last sentence: "This is my name for all time; by this name I shall be invoked for all generations to come."

When we call upon the name of the LORD, as the prophets tell us to do,[3] we use the name I AM THAT I AM or simply I AM. Addressing "our God with us" in prayer we say, "Beloved Mighty I AM Presence..."

The Almighty, the Maker of heaven and earth, has manifest himself to each one of us as the I AM THAT I AM, who goes before us as the LORD went before the children of Israel, "by day in a pillar of a cloud and by night in a pillar of fire."[4]

The I AM Presence and the seven spheres of Light that surround it (the color bands) make up the body of First Cause, or the Causal Body. These spheres are the many mansions of our Father's house where we lay up for ourselves "treasures in heaven."[5]

Our treasures are our words and works worthy of our Creator, positive thoughts and feelings, our victories for the right, and the virtues we have embodied to the glory of God. And, as Jesus said, where our treasure is, there will our heart be also[6]— in this our heaven-world.

When we judiciously exercise our free will, the energies of God that we harmoniously qualify automatically ascend to our Causal Body. These energies are deposited in the spheres of light that correspond to the seven chakras and the seven color rays we use in our creative activities. They accrue to our lifestream as "talents," which we may increase as we put them to good use lifetime after lifetime.

John the Beloved saw and described the I AM Presence, calling it a mighty angel: "And I saw another mighty angel come down from heaven, clothed with a cloud: and a rainbow was upon his head, and his face was as it were the sun, and his feet as pillars of fire."[7]

"This Is My Body . . ."

The Holy Christ Self is the Mediator between God and man. This Universal Christ is the only begotten Son of the Father—the Light-emanation of First Cause. It is the Christ of Jesus and the Christ of you and me. Yet there is but one LORD and one Saviour.

Let us consider for a moment this mystery of the Lord's Body and the Law of the One. The ritual of the breaking of the Bread of Life is the initiation of the individualization of the God flame. Though there be one LORD and one God, yet that LORD and that God has personified himself in the I AM

Presence. As depicted in the Chart, the I AM Presence, near and dear, stands just above in direct relation to each of us.

This I AM Presence is the Divine Image of the one LORD and the one God. A thousand or 10 billion images of the One still add up to only one LORD and one God in whose Light Body we all share. One times One times One still equals *the* One.

In like manner, the only begotten Son of the Father is one Christ and one Saviour. Yet this Son is personified for each child of God in the person of the Holy Christ Self.

Our Father, out of the unfathomable depths of his love for us, has placed the Christ Image of his Son in each of our hearts. A thousand or 10 billion images of that One still add up to only one Son of God, one Christ and one Saviour.

Just think of an actual photograph of Jesus being published in *Life* magazine. Ten million copies do not add up to 10 million Jesuses, but just one.

In giving you and me a Mighty I AM Presence and a Holy Christ Self, our Father gave us the Divine Image and the Christ Image—exact replicas of the originals. These Images contain and *are* the Allness of the one LORD and the one God, and the Allness of the only begotten Son, the one Christ and the one Saviour.

Because Jesus Christ is, was and forever shall be the incarnation of the I AM THAT I AM and of the Son of God, he is always one with your Mighty I AM Presence and Holy Christ Self. It is this special relationship that you have to the Father and the Son through Jesus Christ that is the foundation of your spiritual destiny in this age.

At the Last Supper, Jesus shared with his disciples this mystery of the One, the individed Whole. He took bread and blessed it and brake it and gave it to the disciples saying, "Take, eat: this is my body, which is broken for you...."[8]

Each piece of bread Jesus gave to his disciples from the whole loaf was the gift of himself. It was the gift of his Christhood. Each piece was a portion of his Universal Light Body. Yet each piece *was* the Whole.

This is the meaning of the Law of the One and it explains the mystery of the breaking of the Lord's Body (symbolically and actually). The Lord's Body has many manifestations, but these do not detract from its essential oneness.

The disciples understood this, for Jesus had taught: "I am the Bread of Life which came down from heaven. If any man eat of this bread he shall live for ever: and the bread that I will give is my flesh, which I will give for the life of the world."[9]

The Eucharist both represents and is become by transubstantiation the Light-essence of our Lord's Body. When we partake of it, we eat "the flesh" of the Son of God and thereby assimilate a portion of the Word that he incarnated.

Jesus also took the cup of wine and gave thanks, and gave it to them saying, "Drink ye all of it. This cup is the new covenant in my blood, which is shed for many for the remission of sins."[10]

The Blood of Christ is the Light-essence of the I AM Presence. This Light is for the remission, or forgiveness, of sin that we might have the opportunity to balance our karma and pay our debts under the "new covenant" of Jesus' intercessory grace.

We have this opportunity because Jesus paid the price for our sin beforehand. He is the avatar of the Piscean age, who has borne our karma that we might live and live again to balance it.

By partaking of the sacrament of Holy Communion, we share in the I AM Presence and the Christ Presence of Jesus, who was the full embodiment of the Father and the Son. Wherefore Jesus taught: "Except ye eat the flesh of the Son of man and drink his blood, ye have no life [of God, or his Christ,] in you."[11]

In the ritual of Holy Communion Jesus opened the way for his disciples to reconnect with their Holy Christ Self. Only Jesus, the Christ, the only begotten Son of the Father, the veritable incarnation of the I AM THAT I AM, could reestablish the tie of the sons and daughters of God to that Christ, to that Son and to that God Presence.

In full comprehension of this mystery of the Lord's Body, John wrote the pivotal verses of the New Testament:

> For God so loved the world, that he gave his only begotten Son, that whosoever believeth in him should not perish, but have everlasting life.

For God sent not his Son into the world to condemn the world; but that the world through him might be saved.[12]

John also penetrated the mystery of the one LORD individualized in the I AM Presence and the one Son and Saviour personified in the Holy Christ Self for every child of God. Thus he wrote of the Life that was the Light of men and of John the Baptist, who came to bear witness of that Light.

Of this Light of the I AM THAT I AM and of the Son of God, which are one Light, John proclaimed: "That was the true Light, which lighteth every man that cometh into the world."[13]

If we do not accept the option "to become the sons of God" through Jesus (see page 494), our Lord's mission is in vain and so is ours. The mystery of the one Christ individualized and indwelling as seed potential in every child of God is the key of self-knowledge that has been taken away. It is the stone that the builders of orthodox systems have rejected.

They want to make the flesh-and-blood Jesus "very God of very God"[14] and the only begotten Son of the Father. In truth, Jesus was the Holy Grail in whom the one God and the only begotten Son of the Father dwelt bodily.[15]

Where orthodoxy misses the boat is in its claim of an exclusive Divinity and an exclusive Sonship for Jesus that denies the God-potential and the Christ-potential to all other souls. It fails to see what John the Beloved saw, that every man (every manifestation of God) that cometh into the world is ignited by the Light of the same God and the same Christ who took up their abode in the temple of Jesus.

The difference between Jesus and the rest of us is that he had the full attainment of that Godhead and that Only Begotten dwelling in him bodily. Inasmuch as we have not yet perfected our Christhood in our souls or in our bodies of flesh, the I AM Presence and the Holy Christ Self dwell above us (not in us) and go before us to light our way.

Jesus' mission was to demonstrate the path of the soul's union with the I AM Presence and the Holy Christ Self. He was the example of that which each of us must one day become. He is our Lord and Saviour because we have strayed far and wide from the house of the Father and the Son, and therefore without his mediatorship we of ourselves cannot enter into our true relationship with the Father and the Son, as illustrated on the Chart. Nor can we receive our divine inheritance without his grace.

That is why God purposed to send us THE LORD OUR RIGHTEOUSNESS,[16] prophesied by Jeremiah, who would divide the way of Good and Evil within us, teaching us right from wrong. This LORD is indeed the only begotten Son of the Father come to us in the person of our beloved Holy Christ Self. As joint-heirs, with Jesus, of the Christ,[17] we are also intended to embody that Christ; for only thus can we sup with him in glory and receive the Communion cup of eternal life.

Your Holy Christ Self overshadows you wherever you are and wherever you go. He endows you with the capacity to be "Christ conscious" at all times or, to put it another way, to have the "Christ consciousness" all ways. This beloved Friend and Teacher and Comforter is actually your Real Self, whom you will one day become if you follow in the footsteps of your Saviour.

The Lower Self Becomes the Higher Self

The lower figure is shown enveloped in the violet flame within the tube of light, which descends from the I AM Presence in answer to your call. This cylinder of steely white light sustains a forcefield of protection 24 hours a day—so long as you guard your harmony.

Your lower self consists of your soul and your spirit dressed in the garments of the four lower bodies. Your soul is the nonpermanent aspect of being that is evolving through the four planes of Matter. It is made permanent through the ritual of the ascension.

Your spirit is the distilled essence of your self. It is the pervading and predominating presence by which you are known. It is the animating, or vital, principle of your life that you take with you throughout your soul's incarnations, molding it after the likeness of the Spirit of the living God.

The ascension is the culmination of lifetimes of the soul's service to life. The prerequisites for this graduation from earth's schoolroom are (1) the soul must become one with her Holy Christ Self, (2) she must balance at least 51 percent of her karma and

(3) she must fulfill her mission on earth according to her divine plan. It is possible for the soul, walking with God, to truly embody the God flame and the God consciousness long before she is called Home in the ritual of the ascension; but not until the hour of her ascension is she fused to the I AM Presence, one forevermore.

Through the ascension the soul is become the Incorruptible One. Henceforth to be known as an Ascended Master, the soul receives the crown of everlasting life. This is the consummate goal of life, greatly to be desired. The ascension is freedom from the cycles of karma and the rounds of rebirth; it is the entering in to the joy of the LORD.

The Chart is thus a diagram—past, present and future—of your soul's pilgrimage to the Great Central Sun as year upon year up the spiral staircase of initiation you go, drawing nigh to God as he draws nigh to you.[18]

The Gift from Your Divine Parents

The threefold flame of life is your divine spark, the gift of life, liberty and consciousness from your Divine Parents. Also called the Holy Christ Flame, it is the essence of your Reality, your potential for Christhood. It is sealed in the secret chamber of your heart.

The three plumes of the threefold flame are the blue (on your left), the yellow (in the center) and the pink (on your right), corresponding to the primary attributes of Power, Wisdom and Love, respectively.

Through the Power (of the Father), the Wisdom (of the Son) and the Love (of the Holy Spirit) anchored in the threefold flame, your soul exercises her God-given free will to fulfill her reason for being in the physical plane and throughout all time and eternity.

The crystal (or silver) cord[19] is the stream of life that flows from the heart of the I AM Presence to the Holy Christ Self to nourish and sustain the soul and her vehicles of expression in time and space. John saw the crystal cord and described it as "a pure river of water of life, clear as crystal, proceeding out of the throne of God and of the Lamb."[20]

You can think of the crystal cord as an 'umbilical' cord through which the light/energy/consciousness of God flows all the way from the Great Central Sun to child-man embodied on the far-flung planets. It enters the being of man at the crown, giving impetus for the pulsation of the threefold flame as well as the physical heartbeat and all bodily functions.

Shown just above the head of the Holy Christ Self on the Chart is the dove of the Holy Spirit descending from the Father. This signifies that the Comforter attends each lifestream until the soul is spiritually ready to receive the cloven tongues of fire and the baptism of the Holy Spirit.

To that end the son of man, embracing the will of God, matures in Christ self-awareness as a Christ-filled being day by day. As he gains greater love and greater wisdom as the foundation of his self-mastery, he enters into true communion with his Holy Christ Self.

In due course, when the alchemical marriage of the soul to the Holy Christ Self is fully accomplished, the Holy Spirit will come to him and he may hear the approbation of the Father: "This is my beloved Son in whom I AM well pleased,"[21] testifying that the son of man has become the sacred vessel of the Son of God. He is now ready to begin his mission in Christ as the servant of his Lord.

The Divine Mother, the Sacred Fire and the Chakras

The Divine Mother is focused and adored in the temple of man through the sacred fire that rises as a veritable fountain of light from the base-of-the-spine chakra to the crown chakra. The seven chakras are the spiritual centers in the body that distribute the light of the Mother ascending from the base of the spine, and the light of the Father descending from the I AM Presence.

The coming together of these two radiant streams of life-energy, pulsating from above and below, establishes the union and the balance of the plus-minus (yang-yin) forces in the chakras. Thus each chakra becomes a center for the release of the light of the Father-Mother God. Each focuses one of the seven color rays and one of the seven planes of being.

In the spiritually developed, the Mother's sacred fire (known in the East as the Kundalini) rises up the spinal stalk for the quickening of the soul and the awakening of the Inner Christ and the Inner Buddha. Our Divine Mother, ever present with us,

The Seven Chakras in the Body of Man

guards and guides our footsteps, teaching us how to attain our self-mastery by taking command of our soul and our spirit, our four lower bodies, and the sacred fire that we release through our chakras.

The Four Lower Bodies

The four lower bodies are four energy fields. They are interpenetrating sheaths of consciousness, each vibrating in its own dimension. And so you have a flesh-and-blood body that is your physical body. You have a mind that cogitates, which is your mental body. You have emotions and feelings, which express through your astral, or desire, body (also called the emotional body). And you have a memory that is housed in your etheric, or memory, body, the highest vibrating of the four, which also serves as "the envelope of the soul."

These four lower bodies surround the soul and are her vehicles of expression in the material world of form. The planets also have four lower "bodies" demarcating the etheric, mental, astral and physical planes in which their evolutions live and evolve. These four quadrants of being correspond to the fire, air, water and earth of the ancient alchemists.

Our four lower bodies are intended to function as an integrated unit like "wheels within wheels." Or you might think of them as interpenetrating colanders. When the "holes" are lined up, your four lower bodies are in sync. This means they are aligned with the blueprint of your lifestream that is sustained by your Holy Christ Self, enabling you to direct the light through your chakras without obstruction to bless and heal all life.

But most of us don't have our "holes" lined up. We're out of alignment with our Real Self and so we don't experience the full benefit of our just portion of the light that descends over the crystal cord from our Mighty I AM Presence.

The problem we have to deal with if we are to emerge from earth's schoolroom as an integrated personality in God is this: During our stay on this planet we have gotten our spiritual pores clogged up with a lot of human karma and astral effluvia (i.e., the dust and debris of the misqualified energy of the centuries). In addition, each of us is carrying a percentage of the total planetary karma in our four lower bodies.

As we have misqualified God's pure life-stream perpetually flowing from our I AM Presence for our use here below, it has accumulated in the subconscious as rings on our tree of life and in the collective unconscious of the race. Like it or not, we *are* bearing one another's karmic burden, simply because we are a part of this evolution. And that, too, is our karma!

Apropos this, we saw a graphic representation of how negative energy can accumulate in the 1989 comedy *Ghostbusters II*. At the beginning of the film, the "ghostbusters" discover a river of pink-orange slime flowing in an abandoned Manhattan subway tunnel. They determine that the slime is the materialization of negative human emotions—hate, violence and anger. The slime begins to grow and multiply, gathering momentum in response to the population's continued output of negative energy; it starts pushing up through sidewalks, threatening to envelop the city and inaugurate a "season of evil." It can be counteracted only by positive energy— peace, love and good feelings.

In order to galvanize the positive energy of New Yorkers, the ghostbusters positively charge the Statue of Liberty, which comes to life and wades into Manhattan. People come out in the streets and cheer. The slime is finally overcome when the crowd sings "Auld Lang Syne."

Although we don't take it too seriously, this movie illustrates what those who are sensitive have always known: the negative energy we put out attracts more of its kind and by and by returns to overtake us unless we seek and find resolution. And sooner or later the astral slime spills over into the physical plane—and the mist becomes the crystal.

The Accumulation of Our Karma

As we near the end of the age of Pisces, we are reaping the karma of that 2,000-year cycle as well as previous cycles. In the days of Noah, God through Nature cleared the planetary computer, though not entirely, in the sinking of Atlantis, otherwise known as the Flood. Our karma has been accumulating not only since the Flood but also since the end of the last age of Pisces, 25,800 years ago.

Karma is not intended as punishment, although

those on the receiving end of it may experience it as such. Karma is intended to teach us life's lessons we have refused to learn in any other way. Karma is the effect of whatever thoughts, feelings, words and deeds we have set in motion through our freewill qualification of God's energy.

By returning to us exactly what we put out, the Great Law, as Proverbs says, forces the fool to return to his folly as the dog returns to his vomit.[22] This return of the soul to her karmic condition may recur "seventy times seven" or until the lesson is learned and we go and "make karma no more."

Most of us have set in motion good causes that have produced a harvest of good effects (very good karma!), which, as I said, are stored in our Causal Body. But we have also been putting out negative energy, and we have reencountered it as it has come full circle after gathering more of its kind, multiplying and being multiplied by negative world momentums. And we've been putting it out for a long time. Too long.

Often we have sown error unwittingly, witlessly, in ignorance of cosmic law; and we must admit that sometimes we have wittingly, witfully directed harm toward other parts of life. And now the Great Law requires us to pay the price for our unknowing wrongs as well as for our willful wrongdoings.

The message of the 1990s, the decade of transition between two ages, Pisces and Aquarius, is: We must pay our karmic debts.

Nevertheless, by the grace of our Lord we may pray, "Father, forgive us our trespasses against the law of thy bountiful love, even as we do wholeheartedly, unreservedly forgive those who have trespassed against us"[23]—and thereby truly know salvation through the mercy of God.

The Power to Become Sons of God

The reason Jesus came to demonstrate the path of personal Christhood was so that the children of the light could follow in his footsteps throughout the Piscean age and beyond. And therefore he saw to it that it was a path that they could walk and work.

But the knowledge of this path was not preserved for them by Church or State. Having had no teachers to teach them the Christian mysteries that Jesus imparted to his disciples, the children of the light have missed the point of their soul's true calling from God to walk and work this path that our Lord taught by example.

It was God's grand design that his children fulfill this calling to a personal Christhood in the Piscean dispensation. Therefore he sent his Son Jesus Christ to empower them "to become the sons of God." John the Beloved inscribed this the greatest promise of the greatest grace of all time and space:

> He came unto his own, and his own received him not. But as many as received him, to them gave he power to become the sons of God, even to them that believe on his

name: which were born not of blood, nor of
the will of the flesh, nor of the will of man,
but of God.[24]

God gave us this promise because many, by
sins against the Holy Trinity and the Divine
Mother, had allowed the divine spark, the gift of
God-identity in the beginning, to be extinguished
and thereby had also lost their connection to the
Holy Christ Self.

Therefore, for all who would work out their
own salvation "with fear and trembling,"[25] as Paul
admonished the followers of Christ at Philippi to do,
God sent his Son Jesus Christ to rekindle their
threefold flame and to reestablish the tie to their
Holy Christ Self.

What this promise recorded by John means is
that if those who are without the divine spark will
receive Jesus Christ as their Lord and Saviour, believing "on his name" and accepting him as the
Great Exemplar of the course that they themselves
must now run, the Son of God will reignite their
threefold flame, thereby giving them a second chance
"to become the sons of God"—a second chance to
bless the tie who will now bind them to their Holy
Christ Self.

The restoration of this eternal flame is the
salvation that the Son of God offers to a world that
comprehends not the Light because it abides in its
own Darkness.[26] Wherefore "the Word was made
flesh and dwelt among us (and we beheld his glory,

the glory as of the only begotten of the Father), full of grace and truth."[27]

Our partaking of Holy Communion (in any Christian church) is our acceptance of God's gift of Sonship and our commitment to go out no more from the house of the Father and the Son. Each time we celebrate the Lord's Body and his Blood, we must go forth from the altar witnessing to his Spirit by our words and our works. Each time we accept the bread and the wine, believing it is the Body and Blood of Christ, we imbibe the flame of our Christhood increment by increment, piece by piece, drop by drop.

The threefold flame and the Holy Christ Self are the means whereby every living soul who came forth from God may return to him by the path of personal Christhood—the path of words and works multiplied by the grace of Jesus Christ. This is our calling from God, beloved. It is his call to our souls to return to the altar of the Temple Beautiful in heaven. And this is the altar call that we can and must answer at this crossroads of the centuries.

The path of personal Christhood is not the beaten path, though it should be. For the wolves in sheep's clothing,[28] the embodied fallen angels who have positioned themselves in Church and State, have taken away the body of our Lord's teachings and the blood of his sacred mysteries.

Why? Because they fear that the children of the light, lawfully exercising the threefold flame of the Father, the Son and the Holy Spirit, will rise to the stature of full joint-heirship with the eternal Christ. And then these children of the light just might, in the name JESUS CHRIST and in the name of their own Holy Christ Self, rise up and overcome these reincarnated money changers and cast them out of the temples of God and man!

And so the children of the light are as shorn lambs—scattered sheep whose Shepherd the Evil One did smite.[29] They are ill-equipped for their mission in this new age of Aquarius because they do not have either the awareness of the enemy or the fullness of the self-knowledge (what the early Christians called *gnosis*) of the Universal Christ indwelling.

It is time to revisit the temples of ancient Atlantis where we find inscribed upon the walls: "Man, know thyself!" and "Man, know thy self as God!" Nor should we forget the words of Moses quoted by Jesus: "I have said, ye are gods; and all of you are sons of the Most High."[30] Therefore, O man, know the enemy within and the enemy without, who would take from thee the great truth of thy divinity.

Lightbearers of the world, you who dare to accept the option and the conditions whereby you can "become the sons of God," let us join forces with the Power-Wisdom-Love of the Trinity in the Great Central Sun. For together we can reverse the oncoming tide of karmic retribution calculated on the blackboard of the sky.

I believe, because the Ascended Master Saint Germain has told me so, that if millions of us call upon the LORD, the I AM THAT I AM, in the name

JESUS CHRIST to invoke the intercession of the heavenly hosts, we can be instrumental in turning the tide.

Lightbearers of the world, our prayers, our decrees—with the signs of our words and works following—*can make all the difference!*

CHAPTER 38

The Science of the Spoken Word

John wrote, "In the beginning was the Word, and the Word was with God, and the Word was God."[1] In the ancient Hindu Vedas we read, "In the beginning was Brahman with whom was the Word, and the Word is Brahman."[2] The essence of religion East and West is the Word.

Jesus demonstrated his great mastery of the science of the spoken Word. He commanded the sick to be whole, the elements to be still, foul spirits to come out, and even the dead to rise. He transmuted the water into wine, multiplied the loaves and fishes to feed the five thousand, and walked on the water—all by the power of the Word.

Spoken prayer is at the heart of all true religion. Christians, Jews, Moslems, Hindus, Buddhists and others offer devotions in the form of daily prayers, recitations of scripture and mantras to the Deity. These include the Our Father, the Hail Mary, the Shema and Amidah, the Shahadah, the Gayatri and the Heart Sutra. Yet today, while these traditions survive, their practice is inadequate to counteract the increasing disorder and disintegration of our civilization.

The science of the spoken Word is *the* answer. Truly, this science is the gift of the Divine Mother that we can use to heal ourselves and our planet. When applied in the recitation of dynamic decrees it infuses all religions with the sacred fire of the 2,000-year age of Aquarius.

Dynamic decrees are a step-up of all prayer forms East and West. They are the key that every pilgrim on the path of reunion with God needs to meet the coming challenges of personal and planetary karma—challenges we all must face before we can enter the high road of Aquarius.

What Is a Decree?

First of all, let us define our term. *The Oxford English Dictionary* defines *decree* as follows:

Decree, noun: An ordinance or edict set forth by the civil or other authority; an authoritative decision having the force of law. Theology, one of the eternal purposes of God whereby events are foreordained.

Decree, verb: To command (something) by decree; to order, appoint, or assign authoritatively, ordain; to ordain as by Divine appointment, or by fate. To decide or determine authoritatively; to pronounce by decree. To determine, resolve, decide (*to do* something), *obsolete* or *archaic*. To decide, determine, ordain.

The decree, as we use it, is the most powerful of all applications to the Godhead. It is the command of the son or daughter of God, spoken in the name of the Mighty I AM Presence and Holy Christ Self, for the light to descend from the unformed to the formed—from the world of Spirit to the world of Matter. The decree is the means whereby the kingdom of God becomes a reality here and now through the power of the spoken Word.

Meditations and visualizations are an important part of daily devotions, but dynamic decrees are the most powerful method of directing God's light into manifestation for individual and world action. Decrees are often accompanied by prayers, invocations, mantras, chants, fiats, affirmations, and calls to the one God, the saints (whom we refer to as the Ascended Masters) and the heavenly hosts.

Our decrees have been dictated out of the geometrization of the Ascended Masters' own Causal Bodies to the Messenger Mark L. Prophet and myself. In their affirmation of truth and their denial of error, they are the highest expression of Divine Science and all branches of metaphysics that issue therefrom.

The Divine Mother's decrees crystallize her sacred fire for the transmutation and perfectionment of our worlds. They are the tools by which the children of God might once again "pull up" the Mother Flame (the sacred fire from the base-of-the-spine chakra) and "pull down" the Father Light (from the I AM Presence).

When their practice is accompanied by a loving service to all life, a study of the scriptures and an obedience to the laws of God, the practitioner can achieve soul purification, the balancing of karma and union with God through the living Word.

Thus, let the Divine Mother's gift of the science of the spoken Word be received by those who know her vibration and desire to drink at her fount. And let her voice be heard as our own, as we deliver her decrees into her earth body that reaches out to us in pain and travail.

Jesus Christ Taught Us to Decree

It was none other than Jesus Christ himself who taught us to decree. When Jesus gave us the Lord's Prayer he said, "After this manner therefore pray ye."[3] Jesus taught us not only what to pray but also how to pray. And the manner in which he taught us to pray has been entirely overlooked, although it is as important as the prayer itself.

First Jesus taught us to address the Father, "Our Father which art in heaven," thereby establishing the contact of loving adoration from our heart to the heart of God. He then taught us to recite seven commands. Each one is spoken to our Father not as a request but as a decree in the imperative mode:

1. Hallowed be thy name!
2. Thy kingdom come!
3. Thy will be done on earth
   as it is in heaven!
4. Give us this day our daily bread!
5. And forgive us our debts
   as we forgive our debtors!

6. And lead us not into temptation!
7. But deliver us from evil![4]

When we give commands such as those Jesus taught us in the Lord's Prayer, we are actually commanding the moving stream of the river of life that flows to us over the crystal cord from our Mighty I AM Presence to crystallize into form in fulfillment of our spoken word.

These are not the pleas of miserable, guilt-ridden sinners groveling before a wrathful god. They are the commands of children of the light and loving sons and daughters whom God has entrusted with the wise and judicious use of his Word, who know they are joint-heirs with Jesus of the Christ Light.

What we learn from our Lord's prayer is that as sons and daughters of God, we need not beg our Father for our daily needs. We need only ask—in the form of the command—and he will release his light, energy and consciousness to us in the form we specify.

"By What Authority Doest Thou These Things?"

The question arises, "Who has the authority (or the audacity) to command God?" And the answer is, "Nobody I know."

While delivering the teachings of the Ascended Masters and the sacred mysteries Jesus gave my waiting heart to understand, I have had sincere religious people stand up and challenge me, saying,

"By what authority do you speak?" to which I would respond, "I speak by the authority of my Lord and Saviour Jesus Christ."

It is well, then, that we ponder by what authority any one of us may utter "commands" to the Almighty telling him what is or is not to be done on earth and in our lives.

Once when Jesus was teaching in the temple, the chief priests and elders asked him, "By what authority doest thou these things? and who gave thee this authority?"[5] Jesus did not answer them on that occasion.

But the Lord did give the secret of his authority after he healed the man at the pool of Bethesda. Using the science of the spoken Word to transfer God's light from his body to the one who sought wholeness, Jesus gave the command, "Rise, take up thy bed, and walk!"[6] When the Jews found out that Jesus had cured the man, they persecuted him for breaking the Sabbath and for saying that God was his Father. Jesus told them:

My Father worketh hitherto, and I work....

Verily, verily I say unto you, The Son can do nothing of himself, but what he seeth the Father do: for what things soever he doeth, these also doeth the Son likewise....

For as the Father raiseth up the dead and quickeneth them, even so the Son quickeneth whom he will....

All men should honour the Son, even as they honour the Father. He that honoureth not the Son honoureth not the Father which hath sent him. . . .

For as the Father hath life in himself, so hath he given to the Son to have life in himself. . . .

I can of mine own self do nothing: as I hear I judge: and my judgment is just; because I seek not mine own will, but the will of the Father which hath sent me.[7]

Jesus' claim to his divinity was based on the understanding that he, being created in the image and likeness of God, as were we all,[8] possessed all of the attributes of God himself, even as a single drop of the ocean contains the essence of the whole. Moreover, he was uniquely God incarnate, the avatar, or God-man-ifestation, of the age of Pisces.

As the Word incarnate, Jesus has the authority to utter the fiats of creation, truly fiats of the creative Word, unto the LORD. That is why he taught us to call upon the Father *in his name.* The Master transferred his authority to his disciples and he continues to transfer it to his disciples today on the condition that they give loving obedience to the Father and the Son and "love one another as I have loved you."[9]

As a Master who called his disciples, a Guru who chose his chelas, he said:

Ye have not chosen me, but I have chosen you, and ordained you, that ye should go and bring forth fruit, and that your fruit should remain: that whatsoever ye shall ask of the Father in my name, he may give it you.[10]

At the Last Supper Jesus established not only his authority in and through the Father to transfer to those who believe on him the power to do "the works that I do. . .and greater works" but also his authority to do anything his disciples should ask in his name.[11]

This is truly the authority by which we say, "In the name JESUS CHRIST, I call unto the Father and I ask (I command) that Good shall triumph over Evil upon earth this day! According to the will of God, let it be done!"

The Christ as the only begotten Son of the Father is the only true heir of God. This Son of God is your Real Self, potentially your true identity, whom God made after his own likeness. This likeness never fell into sin and disrepute but remains inviolate as the Christ—the beloved Holy Christ Self—of every man and woman and child.

To decree or to command the energies of Life is the prerogative of the Christ-identity, or Higher Self, of every son and daughter of God. The lower self, being imperfect and incomplete, does not have the authority to utter fiats of creative direction; and thus one must decree in this wise: "*In the name of* the beloved Mighty Victorious Presence of God, I AM, in me and my very own beloved Holy Christ Self. . ."

"What, then, O God, *is* man that thou art mindful of him, and the son of man that thou visitest him?"[12] Man in his I AM Presence and Holy Christ Self is truly one with God and therefore a co-creator with him. Until his lower self is fully clothed in the garment of his Christ Self and an integrated personality in God, he has no authority of his own to speak the decrees of the Word.

But God has said to man, "I will not leave you comfortless."[13] Our God has told us through his Son Jesus and through his prophets and avatars that "whosoever shall call on the name of the LORD shall be delivered."[14] Thus when we give prayers or decrees, we do so in God's name and/or in the name of his Son and solely by the authority God has given us, which authority we do not possess on our own.

The decree, the decreer and the answer to the decree make up a threefold manifestation of God himself. Recognizing this, the decreer must affirm, "God in me is giving this decree. It is God's energy flowing through me now that is obeying his command that I am voicing. And God is fulfilling his law by the power of the spoken Word that I am demonstrating."

Man (the lower self) is thus God's instrument on earth. Through him the light comes forth from the heart of God to coalesce in material form. Man is not the source of the light, neither is he a dictator over the creator or the creation; nor does he of himself have the power to cause that light to obey his command.

The Lord's Prayer—
Formula for Commanding the Father

When we command the Father, we use the scientific principle of bringing forth, or precipitating, from Spirit to Matter that which is the intent of our free will harnessed to God's will. We are confirming the commission spoken to the issue of God: "Be fruitful and multiply and replenish the earth and subdue it: and have dominion. . . ."[15]

God would not have given us this commission without the means to fulfill it. Therefore he gave us the Word in a twofold way, as: (1) the personal Christ—*the Word incarnate* in Jesus Christ and in our Holy Christ Self, who serves as Mediator of our soul's communion with God and by whose authority we command God's light, energy and consciousness; and (2) the impersonal Christ—*the spoken Word* whereby we ratify in the Matter cosmos what God has already ordained in the Spirit cosmos.

But our power to command by the Word is not without circumscription. Jesus included in the Lord's Prayer certain qualifying commands that he intended us to insert in all our prayers, or decrees. Again, this is why he said, "After this manner pray ye."

In telling us to follow our address to the Father with the command "Hallowed be thy name!" Jesus is teaching us that the name of God (I AM THAT I AM or any other name ascribed to the Godhead) must be hallowed, that is, "made holy" and adored with all our heart and soul and mind. Supreme respect for and veneration of our Father-Mother God and the Great Law that girds the cosmos is the foundation of our faith and our dynamic decrees.

In this first command of the Lord's Prayer, Jesus is affirming the first of the Ten Commandments: "Thou shalt have no other gods before me."[16] Those who pray, "Hallowed be thy name!" affirm their allegiance to the one God and are thereby signifying that God is LORD of their temple and ruler of their household—"Hear, O Israel, the LORD our God is one LORD."[17]

Therefore, in effect, they do petition that any prayer or command that is inordinate or unlawful in his sight be answered not according to the human will but the divine. This is the safety valve that protects every devotee of God from the misuse of the science of the spoken Word and the consequent misqualification of God's light.

The second command is "Thy kingdom come!" and the third is "Thy will be done on earth as it is in heaven!" In affirming these, the supplicant agrees that God's kingdom and only his kingdom shall come into manifestation as a result of his decrees and that God's will and only his will shall be done in his life. In other words, he agrees that he shall exercise his free will and the authority God has given him to command spiritual and material resources in His name in order that the earthly patterns may be established after the heavenly patterns according to God's will.[18]

When a son of God gives a command, the "plus spirals" of the Spirit creation are transferred through the nexus of the Christ to the "minus spirals" of the Matter creation. And that which is Above is manifest here below: God's kingdom is come "on earth as it is in heaven." God's will is done and that which is below is become the mirror image of that which is Above.

The fourth, fifth, sixth and seventh commands are predicated on the prior affirmation of and consent by the supplicant to the first three. These four commands are examples of our most basic physical, psychological and soul needs. They are: (4) to "Give us this day our daily bread," (5) to "Forgive us our debts as we forgive our debtors" and (6) to "Lead us not into temptation," (7) "But deliver us from evil."

God is ready to hear other commands that pour forth from our hearts and to fulfill them—as long as we subordinate them to the first three. For unless we submit our commands to God's will, even when we think we know what is best for ourselves, our loved ones, our country and our planet, we run the risk of misusing (or "misdirecting," "misapplying" or "misqualifying," as we say) the crystal-clear stream of the river of life that flows to us unceasingly from the Source.

If we use God's power to create other than as God would have us create, we defile this sacred science of the Word and therefore God himself. The consequence is injury to life and negative karma that we must one day painfully and painstakingly undo, thread by thread, as we serve to set life free.

When we create negative karma, we get out of alignment with the will of God, and drift farther and farther into the delusions of thinking man, who thinks he alone is true. But unless he is one with Christ, his mind one with the Christ mind, how can he be sure? For the plumb line of Christ Truth is the measure of our "trueness." And Paul said, "Let God be true but every [mortal] man a liar."[19]

Now, when we understand the Word as the incarnate Christ, who is our true inheritance when we walk in the footsteps of the Master, and when we understand the power of the Word when spoken in the manner Jesus taught us to pray, we can follow Jesus' example in any situation we find ourselves in.

For instance, when Jesus came upon the barren fig tree he cursed it with the command: "Let no fruit grow on thee henceforward for ever!" And when the disciples marvelled, "How soon is the fig tree withered away!" Jesus said:

> Verily I say unto you, If ye have faith, and doubt not, ye shall not only do this which is done to the fig tree, but also if ye shall say unto this mountain, Be thou removed, and be thou cast into the sea; it shall be done.
>
> And all things, whatsoever ye shall ask in prayer, believing, ye shall receive.[20]

Whether it be the fig tree or the mountain or any other offense or obstacle, we understand from this vignette that when Jesus says "whatsoever ye shall *ask* in prayer...," he often means "whatsoever ye shall *command*, believing, ye shall receive."

The final statement of the Lord's Prayer—it is actually the eighth command—is for the sealing of our prayer: "For thine is the kingdom, and the power, and the glory for ever! Amen."[21]

The sealing is our affirmation that everything we have called forth from the heart of the I AM Presence belongs to God. It is his omniscience, his kingdom (i.e., his consciousness); his omnipotence, his power; and his omnipresence, his glory, that *forever* sustain his decrees and ours, when they are in consonance with his.

The "Amen" serves a function similar to that of the Sanskrit "Aum." It is the sealing of the prayer in the heart of God for his disposition. Man has proposed, God will now dispose. Man has propounded, God will now compound.

In our sealing we are acknowledging God as the original Decreer, as the Decree and as the Answer to our Decree. We must acknowledge that the entire Creation that came forth from him, ourselves included, belongs to him—that we are his, that the kingdom is his, that the power is his and that the glory is his, forever. This final command is for our protection—lest we take God's kingdom, power and glory for the adornment of the lesser self.

Within this Allness that is God, he has made his sons and daughters to be co-creators with him. So long as we create to his kingdom, to his power, to his glory and for the very love of him, our commands for the qualification of the waters of the river of life that flow through us will be accomplished.

Why We Use the Spoken Word

The ritual of spiritual invocation requires the exercise of the spoken Word. When we raise up our voices to praise the Lord and to offer prayers in the name of Jesus Christ, we are exercising the power center, called the throat chakra (p. 489).

Through this chakra we receive from our Mighty I AM Presence the gift of speech, which is the empowerment to create. Without it we would be powerless to invoke divine intercession. By its masterful use we may bless all life as instruments of the Word of our Father-Mother God.

Saint Germain said in a dictation on May 28, 1986, "We must have the physical sounding of the Word. This is the purpose of the dynamic decree as the most efficient and accelerated means of forestalling those things coming upon the earth or upon the individual as the outplaying of karma."[22]

When Jesus raised Lazarus from the dead, he employed the power of the spoken Word to release the energy from the plane of Spirit to the plane of Matter for the restoration of the life-force. It is recorded that *"he cried with a loud voice"* when he gave the command: "Lazarus, come forth!"[23] The Gospels also record that he taught "as one that had authority, and not as the scribes."[24]

The first decree ever recorded was spoken by God: "Let there be Light!" and instantaneously there *was* Light.[25] The response to the decree of the Word sent forth by God was the Creation. And so the light of the Logos beamed forth to manifest as God Self-consciousness clothed in material form, expanding out of the infinite sea of God's being.

Thus decrees are *spoken* by man because it is the power of the Word, and none other, that is able to create, to preserve, to uncreate (or transmute), and to perfect the Divine Image in the sons and daughters of God. Therefore, decrees should always be given aloud; only if it is impossible to do so should they be offered silently.

Saint Germain has given us the following teaching on why it is necessary to use the spoken Word:

> Too frequently individuals who stress their desire for quiet meditation fail to take into account that there is a time and a place for quiet meditation, a time and a place for prayer, and a time and a place for decrees.[26] All three can be used in religious service. All three can be used in the home, individually or in groups, as one desires. But one form of worship is not a substitute for the other. . . .
>
> Decrees are synthesized manifestations of the heart flame of each one who decrees. Decrees draw together and focalize the power of the spoken Word, the visualization of the Christ mind, and the rhythm of the divine pulse. When you decree, you are releasing divinely qualified energy charged by your invocation and multiplied by the power of

the Ascended Masters. It goes forth to do its perfect work for the amplification of the power of Light upon the entire planet.

I can say little more than that which was spoken of old: "Prove me now herewith, saith the LORD of hosts, if I will not open you the windows of heaven and pour you out a blessing, that there shall not be room enough to receive it."[27]

The Anatomy of a Decree

Saint Germain has also given us a clear definition of the parts of a decree and the purpose of each part:

Decrees are generally composed of three parts, and they should be thought of as letters to God:

(1) The salutation of the decree is invocative. It is addressed to the individualized God Presence of every son and daughter of God and to those servants of God who make up the spiritual hierarchy. This salutation (the preamble to the decree), when reverently given, is a call that compels the answer from God and the ascended ones.

We could no more refuse to answer this summons in our octave than could your firemen refuse to answer a call for help in yours. The purpose of the salutation, then, is to engage immediately the energies of the Ascended Masters in answering the body of your letter to God, which you so lovingly vocalize individually or in unison.[28]

In the preamble to decrees, we call to the Ascended Masters for assistance. Commands made in the name of any and all who are one with God in heaven are an acceptable offering unto the living God. Because the Ascended Masters are one with God, hence God in manifestation and God in action, we can offer decrees in their names as well as in the name of Jesus Christ.

Contrary to what some Christians have thought, this practice in no way detracts from Jesus' central position, holding as he does the office of the only begotten Son of the Father and of World Saviour. It is no different from the Catholic practice of praying to the saints. And no Catholic would even suggest that the saints are equal to Christ, nor would the students of the Ascended Masters!

Thus it is acceptable to the Most High God that we call to any and all of the saints and heavenly hosts with our mandates imploring them to step into action in the world of material form in the service of the Lord. In fact, by cosmic law, because God has guaranteed free will to his offspring, these servants of God and his Christ are not permitted to intercede for and on behalf of mankind *unless* we invoke them in the name of the Mighty I AM Presence and Holy Christ Self.

And this form of intercessory prayer is indeed the communion of the saints on earth with the saints in heaven that is ordained by God as long as it is done through the Holy Spirit—and not psychically.

The next part of the decree is the body. Saint Germain describes it as the body of our letter to God:

> (2) It is composed of statements phrasing your desires, the qualifications you would invoke for self or others, and the supplications that would be involved even in ordinary prayer.
>
> Having released the power of the spoken Word through your outer consciousness, your subconscious mind and your superconscious, or Higher Self, you can rest assured that the supreme consciousness of the Ascended Masters whom you have invoked is also concerned with the manifestation of that which you have called forth. [29]

The final part of the decree is the closing:

> (3) Now you come to the close of your decree, the acceptance, the sealing of the letter in the heart of God, released with a sense of commitment into the realm of the Spirit whence manifestation must return to the world of material form according to the unerring laws of alchemy (the all-chemistry of God) and precipitation. [30]

How to Decree

Before actually speaking the words of a decree, sit in a comfortable, straight-backed chair in a well-lighted room where you will be undisturbed, taking care that the room has been tidied, cleaned and well aired. (Dust, untidiness, stale air and poor lighting reduce the effectiveness of the decrees because they impede the flow of light and repel the angelic hosts, who always assist the supplicant in amplifying the release of God's holy energies.)

Visualize the Presence of God above you, your lower self enveloped in the violet flame administered by your Holy Christ Self, and visualize the threefold flame pulsing and expanding from your heart—the blue plume to your left, the pink plume to your right and the yellow plume in the center.

Hold your spine and head erect; keep your legs and hands uncrossed and your feet flat on the floor. Poor posture opens the consciousness to negative forces because the solar plexus is not in control. (The solar-plexus chakra, located at the navel, is the doorway of the emotions.) Crossing the legs and hands causes a "short circuiting" of the energies that are intended to flow through the decreer to bless all mankind.

Remember Paul's words, "Know ye not that ye are the temple of God and that the Spirit of God dwelleth in you?"[31] and let the energies of God flow through your seven chakras and body temple.

Hold your book or the individual decrees at eye level so that you do not lean down while decreeing. You may prefer to sit at a desk or table where you can prop up your book in front of you, thus leaving your hands free to receive the blessings of God through the Masters. When your hands are free, they should be cupped, palms up, separated and resting in your lap. The index finger of each hand can be touching the thumb.

Speak the decree slowly and clearly without strain until you can fully comprehend the meaning of its content. Then concentrate upon the rhythm and gradually step up the tempo. You will observe the quickening of your mind as you recite with greater and greater facility.

It is important to breathe deeply and regularly, using the power of the fire breath of God to project the light through your sacred centers to bless all life with the magnetization of God's energy focused through your heart flame.

Concentration is of utmost importance while decreeing, for it is upon the flow of man's attention that the energies of the Presence travel through the superconscious to the conscious to the subconscious to the unconscious to fulfill the fiats of his spoken Word. Although you can learn to concentrate through the third eye and the crown chakra, you should stay centered in your heart; for as you now know, in the secret chamber of your heart God has placed his threefold flame for your own God self-realization.

Centering in the heart allows you to amplify God's love while balancing and expanding the threefold flame. It will develop the heart as the seat of your Christ consciousness and prevent mental strain and undue pressure on those chakras that are less developed in Western man.

Once you have mastered this, you can use the third eye and the crown chakra with the heart chakra to direct the energy flowing through you into specific situations of need.

Saint Germain has given us the following teaching on the use of rhythm and increased speed in decreeing:

> Rhythm is also important in decrees. Proper rhythm creates a most penetrating projection of spiritual vibrations that will magnetize all over the planet the qualities of God that are being invoked through the decrees. The momentum of these waves that form undulating circles over the planetary body creates an intensification of light wherever devotees come together to participate in a like endeavor.
>
> The laws governing the manifestation and distribution of physical light also apply to the flow of the currents of spiritual light. Spiritual qualities are distributed around the planetary body from every radiating focus of Ascended Master love. . . .
>
> The proper use of decrees takes practice. Individuals should not expect that the first time they make a call, the very perfection of the universe will sweep away all of the accumulated debris of their lives.
>
> Proper decreeing is an art, and as one gains greater proficiency, he will find it

possible to speed up his decrees—that is, he will be able to speed up the rate at which they are given. He will also be able to understand what is taking place as he speeds them up; for this acceleration, by raising the rate of his own electronic pattern, throws off and transmutes negative thoughts and feelings in his world. [32]

If you are interested in practicing the science of the Word and in accelerating the power and efficacy of your decrees, you may want to send for any of the decree and song cassettes I have produced with our congregation at the Royal Teton Ranch. They are listed in the back of this book.

May God bless you as you make a joyful noise unto the LORD in gratitude for the science of the spoken Word!

CHAPTER 39

What Is the Violet Flame?

Moses bore witness to the I AM THAT I AM when he exclaimed, "Our God is a consuming fire!"[1] And I bear witness to the Holy Spirit when I say the violet flame is the seventh-ray aspect of that fire.

John, the messenger of Jesus, declared the Lord's message: "God is Light, and in him is no darkness at all.... If we walk in the Light, as he is in the Light, we have fellowship one with another, and the blood of Jesus Christ his Son cleanseth us from all sin."[2]

John saw the violet light, he declared the violet light, and he walked in the violet light. He knew the violet light to be the essence of the Body and Blood of Christ. And he knew the violet flame as that all-consuming fire that transmutes the cause and core of sin and the karma that is the record of and the penalty for that sin.

(And if you ask me how I know, I will tell you that I have seen in the akashic record Jesus using the violet flame in his healings and miracles and initiating his closest disciple, John, in its use.)

The saints robed in white who gather before the Lamb and the throne of God also testify that they have washed their robes[3] in the violet flame. And every lifestream who has returned to the Source has engaged in the seventh-ray ablution—the ritual of bathing body and soul, mind and heart in the violet flame. They have washed and scrubbed, washed and scrubbed their four lower bodies, singing with the violet singing flame all the way Home!

The violet flame is the gift of the Holy Spirit that comes to us under the sponsorship of Saint Germain. As Lord of the Seventh Ray and Hierarch of the Age of Aquarius, Saint Germain reintroduced the violet flame in the twentieth century.

Not since the early days of Atlantis when its golden-age civilization was at its height have mankind had access to the alchemy of the violet flame. It was withdrawn when the priesthood and the public alike began the misuse and the disuse of the Unfed Flame on the Temple altar, compromising its seventh-ray aspect, the violet flame, as well.

With the sinking of Atlantis, the mystery schools and retreats of the adepts were removed to the Himalayas or transferred to the etheric octave. Thereafter the knowledge of the violet flame—how to invoke it, how to apply it in the alchemy of the seventh ray—was handed down from master to disciple until Saint Germain released it to the world 60 years ago.

And today the Master's students on every continent give gratitude to God for the *joie de vivre* and the positive spin they get each time they give a violet flame decree.

The violet flame is *the* key to individual and world transmutation. It works in microcosmic and macrocosmic worlds, from the smallest particle of matter to molecule to mind to materialization in man and mundane circles.

In his book *The Chela and the Path*, El Morya explains the origin and nature of the violet flame:

> The violet flame comes forth from the violet ray, that aspect of the white light that is called the seventh ray. It is indeed the seventh-ray aspect of the Holy Spirit. Just as the sunlight passing through a prism is refracted into the rainbow of the seven color rays, so through the consciousness of the Holy Spirit the light of the Christ is refracted for mankind's use in the planes of Matter.

> Each of the seven rays is a concentrated, activating force of the light of God having a specific color and frequency. Each ray can also manifest as a flame of the same color and vibration. The application of the flame results in a specific action of the Christ in body and soul, mind and heart.[4]

How does a ray become a flame, and specifically how does the violet ray become the violet flame? When you invoke the violet flame, it comes forth from the heart of your I AM Presence as a ray of light that is violet in color. That ray descends like a powerful sunbeam from its source in the Great Central Sun to what is called the plane of invocation.

Wherever you may be in the universe, in whatever socket of consciousness you find yourself, the level from which you invoke the light of God is defined as the plane of invocation.

An invocation is a call to light that is transmitted from your heart to the heart of God instantaneously. The response comes forth on the return current. When the violet ray descends from your I AM Presence to the plane of invocation, a violet flame springs up. Simply put, the flame is an intensification of a light ray that has been stepped up by the fervor of your heart's call and the zeal of the LORD's response. The phenomenon brings to mind the physical counterpart: a ray of light from the sun passed through a magnifying glass causing an object to burst into flame.

When you invoke the violet flame for the healing of a specific problem, this is how it works. It envelops each atom of your being individually. Instantaneously a polarity is set up between the nucleus of the atom (which, being Matter, assumes the negative pole) and the white-fire core of the flame (which, being Spirit, assumes the positive pole).

The dual action of the light in the nucleus of the atom and the light in the enveloping violet flame establishes an oscillation that causes the untransmuted densities to be dislodged from between the electrons. As this substance is loosened, at nonphysical, or "meta-physical," dimensions of matter the electrons begin to vibrate with an increased amount of energy, throwing the misqualified substance into the violet flame.

On contact with this fiery essence of freedom's flame, the misqualified energy is transmuted and God's energy is restored to its native purity. Relieved of the patterns of imperfection and restored to the plus-minus balance of Alpha and Omega, this energy of the Holy Spirit is returned to the individual's Causal Body, where it is stored until he elects to use it once again to bring forth the noble work of the Christ "on earth as it is in heaven."

This alchemy takes place on the material plane though not necessarily in the objective "physical" plane; for every atom of substance has its counterpart in the astral, mental and etheric compartments of the matter universe as well as in the spiritual octaves of light.

El Morya has elaborated on how the violet flame works to heal "recalcitrant conditions of the human consciousness":

> When, as an act of your free will, you make the call to the violet flame and you surrender these unwanted, untoward conditions into the flame, the fire instantaneously begins the work of breaking down particles of substance that are part of the mass accumulation of hundreds and even thousands of incarnations when in ignorance you allowed to register—through your consciousness, through your attention, thoughts and feelings, words

and actions—all of the degrading conditions to which the human race is heir.

I trust that I need not enumerate the seemingly endless but altogether finite qualities of limitation thrust upon the ethers— projectiles of the carnal mind—that have filled the wide-open spaces between the electrons and the nuclei of the atoms with the densities of mankind's carnality.

Believe it or not, this energy can be as hard as concrete or as sticky as molasses as it registers in all of the four lower bodies, causing mental recalcitrance, hardness of heart, and a lack of sensitivity to the needs of others and creating a dense mass that prevents the soul from receiving the delicate impartations of the Holy Spirit. . . .

Day by day you are ascending higher and higher in the planes of consciousness of your Christ Self as you use the scrubbing action of the violet flame and feel how the very walls of your mental body are scoured. You can think of this action in your desire body as the dunking of your emotions in a chemical solution of purple liquid that dissolves the dirt that has accumulated for decades about the latticework of your feeling world.

Every day in every way the violet flame flushes out and renews your body cells, the cells of your mind and the 'globule' of your soul. [5]

The violet flame can alter, mitigate or entirely turn back prophecy. When you invoke the violet flame in the name of your Mighty I AM Presence and Holy Christ Self through the heart of Jesus Christ and Saint Germain, angels of the seventh ray direct it into the density and discord that characterizes the out-of-alignment state of our people and our planet.

Indeed, old age, disease and death are the result of mankind's misapplication of the universal laws of God's harmony. Through giving daily decrees to the violet flame, these conditions can be forestalled and the quality of life can be greatly enhanced. Give the elderly a good diet and a daily dose of the violet flame and they will walk, skip and jog right up out of their convalescent homes (tombs for the living dead where everybody hopes they won't wind up but most everybody does)!

In a dictation Saint Germain gave on the violet flame for world transmutation and for America's fulfillment of her destiny, the Master said that the violet flame is a "physical flame" and thus the antidote for physical problems:

The violet flame is a physical flame! And what do I mean when I say this? I say the violet flame is closest in vibratory action of all of the rays to this earth substance, to these chemical elements and compounds, to all that you see in matter. And therefore, the violet flame can combine with any molecule or molecular structure, any particle of matter known or unknown, and any wave of light, electrons or electricity.

Thus, the violet flame is the supreme antidote for food poisoning, chemical waste, toxins, or drug pollution in the body. The violet flame is an elixir that you drink and imbibe like water, like the purest juice of the fruit of the harvest of the elementals' consciousness.

The violet flame is the supreme antidote for physical problems. Wherever chelas [students] gather to give the violet flame decrees, there you notice immediately an improvement in *physical* conditions!...

Whether we are dealing with organic or inorganic matter, there is a disintegration spiral that works in the buildings, in the land, in the sea and in the physical bodies of mankind that can best be counteracted by the violet flame.

The violet flame turns around the spin of electron and atom. It turns around the downward spiral of the chakras and the energy. It is forever the power of conversion—and conversion means "to turn around"! The violet flame is the buoyant joy of the Holy Ghost that turns around spirits and minds and souls and emotions![6]

If you're really ready to heal yourself and planet earth, now is the time to get to know the Ascended Master Saint Germain. He is ready, willing and able to be your private tutor in the effective and speedy balancing of your karma. He has given us many teachings on the use of the violet flame. In 1988 he told us about the personal course of instruction he prepares for each soul:

> I have prepared in my lessons and [in] all of my dictations, a course of instruction whereby the individual may make the most progress and thereby be ready for any change, major or minor, conditioned by his own karma written in his own astrology.
>
> Blessed ones, I define progress as the balancing of karma. Karma, then, is the weight that prevents the soul from flying. Therefore, emptying the ship of its cargo or a balloon of its ballast, this is my goal—thus my gift of the violet flame....
>
> The less karma you have, the greater [your] opportunity day by day. This affects all choices. It affects contracts—business, marriage and otherwise—those who are drawn to your life and those who cannot be, the children you may give birth to. Every day as percentages of karma pass through the sacred fire and that transmutation is ratified by good deeds, words and works of love and service, you are lightening the load and therefore rising and therefore, beloved, coming into new planes of realization, new associations.[7]

Saint Germain has spoken of the benefits his students have received through their increased use of the violet flame:

I bring you a report on the results of the use of my violet flame cassette by the one and the many. First and foremost the greatest good has come to the individual supplicant himself. Therefore, to those who have so loved this ritual of the seventh ray there has been an increase of the transmutation of the negative momentums of negative karma. And I have seen to it, as you count me your Master and Friend, that that violet flame that you have invoked has been directed into the most resistant and recalcitrant pockets of your subconscious, especially into those conditions which you have been the most desirous to have removed.

Therefore, in some of you a hearty amount of karma has been balanced, in others hardness of heart has truly melted around the heart chakra. There has come a new love and a new softening, a new compassion, a new sensitivity to life, a new freedom and a new joy in pursuing that freedom. There has come about a holiness as you have contacted through my flame the priesthood of the Order of Melchizedek. There has come a melting and dissolving of certain momentums of ignorance and mental density and a turning toward a dietary path more conducive to your own God-mastery.

The violet flame has assisted in relationships within families. It has served to liberate some to balance old karmas and old hurts and to set individuals on their courses according to their vibration. . . .

It is impossible to enumerate exhaustively all of the benefits of the violet flame but there is indeed an alchemy that does take place within the personality. The violet flame goes after the schisms that cause psychological problems that go back to early childhood and previous incarnations and that have established such deep grooves within the consciousness that in fact they have been difficult to shake lifetime after lifetime.[8]

Decree to the Elohim Arcturus

The best way for you to understand what the violet flame *is* is to see for yourself what it *does!* Therefore I would like to invite you to give a violet flame decree.

This dynamic decree is our invocation to God and to Arcturus and Victoria, who are God's manifestation as Elohim on the seventh ray. It is a "worded formula" that unlocks the light, energy and consciousness of the violet flame from our Father-Mother God personified in the twin flames of Arcturus and Victoria. For theirs is the consciousness of God that ensouls the age of Aquarius at the Elohimic level, the same level from which the creation was brought forth as recorded in the Book of Genesis.

Elohim, the Biblical uni-plural noun for the

"Divine Us" who created male and female in their image and likeness, is a Hebrew name for God used 2,500 times in the Old Testament. The seven Elohim embody the light of the Father-Mother God, whom they personify on each of the seven rays. These seven sets of twin God-flames are the "seven Spirits of God" referred to in Revelation.[9]

The names by which we call the Elohim are words that are keyed to their vibration and presence; these names are given to earth's evolutions to facilitate their attunement with God as Elohim and to allow them to access the power of Elohim but they are by no means the complete key to their identity.

I can assure you that if you knew just how powerful and accessible the Elohim are and how you can experience the consciousness of God as Elohim on the seventh ray when you call forth Arcturus and Victoria and their tremendous momentum of the violet flame, you would not miss a day of calling to them!

You can give this decree to Arcturus to saturate the Nature kingdom and Mother Earth with the violet transmuting flame. It is beneficial to give it on behalf of elemental life—the fiery salamanders, sylphs, undines and gnomes, who are Nature's keepers in the domains of fire, air, water and earth.

These elementals are charged by God with keeping the balance of forces in the earth, but they are bowed down with the weight of mankind's pollution of the elements as well as by the karma of man's inhumanity to man. To lighten their load and brighten your aura, won't you give this invocation to the Elohim Arcturus and Victoria and their decree that follows.

Arcturus, Blessed Being Bright

Beloved Mighty Victorious Presence of God, I AM in me, thou immortal unfed flame of Christ-Love burning within my heart, Holy Christ Selves of all mankind, beloved mighty Elohim Arcturus and Victoria, all great beings, powers and activities of Light serving the Violet Flame, the entire Spirit of the Great White Brotherhood and the World Mother, elemental life—fire, air, water and earth!

In the name JESUS CHRIST, in the name and by the magnetic power of the Presence of God which I AM and by the magnetic power of the sacred fire vested in me, I invoke the mighty presence and power of your full-gathered momentum of service to the Light of God that never fails, and I command that it be directed throughout all mankind, elemental life and the angelic hosts serving earth's evolutions to bless and heal our planet earth:

Blaze thy dazzling light of a thousand suns throughout the earth and transmute all that is not of the Light into the God-victorious, light all-glorious, flaming Jesus Christ perfection.

In thy name, O God, I decree:

1. O Arcturus, blessed being bright,
   Flood, flood, flood our world with Light;
   Bring forth perfection everywhere,
   Hear, O hear our earnest prayer.

Refrain:*
>   Charge us with thy Violet Flame,
>   Charge, O charge us in God's name;
>   Anchor in us all secure,
>   Cosmic radiance, make us pure.

2. O Arcturus, blessed Elohim,
   Let thy Light all through us stream;
   Complement our souls with Love
   From thy stronghold up above.

3. O Arcturus, Violet Flame's great Master,
   Keep us safe from all disaster;
   Secure us in the cosmic stream,
   Help expand God's loving dream.

4. O Arcturus, dearest Lord of might,
   By thy star radiance beaming bright,
   Fill us with thy cosmic Light,
   Raise, O raise us to thy height.

And in full Faith I consciously accept this manifest, manifest, manifest! (3x) right here and now with full Power, eternally sustained, all-powerfully active, ever expanding and world enfolding until all are wholly ascended in the Light and free!
Beloved I AM! Beloved I AM! Beloved I AM!

I leave it to you to experiment with the violet flame decrees in the following section along with the thoughtforms for meditation and visualization. And I urge you to prove what great good you can accomplish for yourself and the world through the ever-widening circle of your aura.

---

*Give the refrain once after each verse and repeat the body of the decree nine times.

It doesn't matter what your religion or philosophy of life is, because the violet flame belongs to all people. It is up to the spiritually quickened in every group and assembly of the religious, and especially their leaders, to take the dynamic decrees of the Ascended Masters and use them to heal themselves and planet earth.

For it is prophesied by Jeremiah, "Then shall ye call upon me, and ye shall go and pray unto me, and I will hearken unto you."[10] And it is written in the Book of Job, "Thou shalt decree a thing and it shall be established unto thee: and the light shall shine upon thy ways."[11]

CHAPTER 40

Visualizations for Violet Flame Decrees

Before you begin your session of meditation, decrees and visualizations, you should offer an invocation to God and the heavenly hosts. Following is an example of an invocation you may wish to offer to the Most High:

In the name of the Light of God that never fails, I invoke the Seven Elohim of God. O Great Central Sun, let the light rays of the Cosmic Christ pour forth in this hour through the Sacred Heart of our Lord and Saviour Jesus Christ to reignite the threefold flame and reconnect each child of God to his Holy Christ Self.

I call to the corona of the Sun. Let thy light descend, O God, upon this thy people for the healing of their souls and the healing of the nations. Come forth, O thou Master of Invocation. Come forth, O thou Master of Meditation. Come forth, O thou Master of Visualization. For in the name I AM THAT I AM we call for thy light, thy blessedness,

thy being to be directed through our chakras
for the healing of ourselves and planet earth.

As we prepare to increase and intensify the light
within our body temples, within our chakras, let us
invoke the protection of Archangel Michael and his
legions of light. We begin every decree session to the
violet flame with a decree to Archangel Michael
because the Great Law states that God will not give to
us more light than we can guard and keep in harmony. Therefore we call to Archangel Michael to
shield the light of God that we are about to invoke as
well as ourselves as servants of the light.

Archangel Michael is the Captain of the LORD's
Hosts and the protector of the servants of God. He
has unlimited legions in his command. When we
invoke his protection he is at our side. In this decree
we visualize him in his flaming presence—before,
behind, to the right and to the left of us, above,
below, wherever we go. And we affirm that the I AM
Presence is "his Love protecting here."

As you give this decree aloud, see Archangel
Michael in your mind's eye standing before you,
mighty in the LORD. See him arrayed in shining
armour with brilliant sapphire blue cape and aura.
See him wielding his sword of blue flame to deliver
you from all negative conditions that work against
your soul's progress on the Path.

See his "diamond" heart chakra blazing in the
center of his chest. (Turn to page 489 to refer to the
placement of the chakras in the body.) Through this

point of contact, meditate on the heart of God as
you say:

In the name I AM THAT I AM JESUS CHRIST,
I decree:

Lord Michael before, Lord Michael behind,
Lord Michael to the right, Lord Michael to the left,
Lord Michael above, Lord Michael below,
Lord Michael, Lord Michael wherever I go!

I AM his Love protecting here!
I AM his Love protecting here!
I AM his Love protecting here!
(Give three or nine times with joy and gusto!)

"I AM the Light of the Heart" by Saint Germain

Inasmuch as Saint Germain is the Lord of the
Seventh Ray and Hierarch of the Aquarian Age, we
give his decree "I AM the Light of the Heart" to
make contact with his heart as he sponsors us in our
violet flame decrees. Before you give this decree,
read the instructions for visualization that follow.

I AM the Light of the Heart
Shining in the darkness of being
And changing all into the golden treasury
Of the Mind of Christ.

I AM projecting my Love out into the world
To erase all errors
And to break down all barriers.

I AM the power of Infinite Love,
Amplifying itself
Until it is victorious, world without end!*

Instructions:

First, turn to page 476 and visualize the Chart of the I AM Presence and the Holy Christ Self superimposed over you. See yourself as the lower figure in the Chart surrounded by the violet flame and the tube of light. See your crystal cord as "a pure river of water of life clear as crystal proceeding out of the throne of God and of the Lamb."

See the light descending from your Mighty I AM Presence and Holy Christ Self, entering your body at the crown, flowing to your heart chakra, there to be released according to the worded matrix of your decree.

Breathe deeply and sit up tall in your seat so you have room in your diaphragm to contain the sacred fire breath of God. By the sacred fire breath, you intensify and fan the threefold flame in your heart. Let the flame, the focus of the Trinity, increase even as it is balanced through Father, Son and Holy Spirit.

In this decree you affirm that the "I AM in me is the light of the heart." Therefore center your attention in your heart. Visualize it as a dazzling sphere of white light. Picture the brilliance of the sun at noonday and transfer that picture to the center of your chest. See thousands of sunbeams going forth from your heart as light rays contacting every child of God on earth.

---

*You can give the decrees in this section three times, nine times or as many times as you want.

Remember, your God is the Limitless One, who is just waiting for your call to send you his Limitless Light! Your God is individualized for you right where you are in your Mighty I AM Presence and Holy Christ Self.

In this moment lovingly accept the heart of your Father-Mother God and the living Christ as one with your heart. Then thank God for your heart of light and know that the "sun" presence in your heart knows no limitation and that the capacity of your heart to contain it cannot be limited—except by the limitations of your own thought and feeling world!

Affirm that the light of God's heart now shining through your heart is "shining in the darkness of being"—your being and all beings on planet earth. Know that by cosmic law your call compels God's answer. Therefore, according to the fervor of your love for God and all his children, this light will be intensified in the hearts of all citizens of earth simultaneously as you give this decree and accept it done this hour in the full power of the Holy Spirit.

Affirm the power of the light of God's heart "changing all into the golden treasury of the Mind of Christ." *And decree it.* Your "golden treasury," a gift from your Father-Mother God, is the abundant life, the riches of God's wisdom, the fulfillment of your reason for being—your health, your happiness, your longevity and your opportunity to serve to set life free.

Let all that is less than this, all that is darkness, depression and despair in your life, be changed *right now* by the sun-light of God's heart into the "golden treasury of the Mind of Christ."

Project your love (which is God's love) through your heart (which is God's heart) out into the world for a specific purpose: Let love as an intense fiery pink ray like a laser beam consume all opposition to Love's victory in you, your family and the whole wide world. Then affirm that the I AM, God in you, is "the power of Infinite Love, amplifying itself until it is victorious, world without end!" See it happen in your mind's eye and accept it done right now in the full authority of the Godhead.

It's a good idea to have a lighted globe on your personal altar or in the room where you say your decrees. Use it to concentrate on the exact spot or the general area to which you are directing your decrees.

Whether standing or seated, you can raise your hands, palms outward, and visualize the light rays going forth not only through your heart but also through your hands. For example, you can direct a powerful action of Love's all-consuming violet flame to transmute the cause and core of all pollution of the environment—body, soul and mind, air and land and sea.

You can also close your eyes and visualize yourself suspended in space, directing God's light rays through your seven chakras into the planet and its people as you pray:

O God, send forth thy light! O Cosmic
Beings and evolutions of God on all systems

of worlds, radiate thy love through all light-bearers in this hour. Reach out and touch every lifestream upon earth, every part of life that is God, every elemental.

O God, let the alchemy of our oneness produce a mighty miracle in our planet this day—healing for ourselves that we may serve thee and healing for our beloved planet that all lightbearers might come into a divine oneness in the service of God for the uplift-ment of humanity.

Now turn to page 539 and give "I AM the Light of the Heart" three or nine times with deep devotion.

"I AM Light" by Kuthumi

I AM Light, glowing Light,
Radiating Light, intensified Light.
God consumes my darkness,
Transmuting it into Light.

This day I AM a focus of the Central Sun,
Flowing through me is a crystal river,
A living fountain of Light
That can never be qualified
By human thought and feeling.
I AM an outpost of the Divine.
Such darkness as has used me is swallowed up
By the mighty river of Light which I AM.

I AM, I AM, I AM Light;
I live, I live, I live in Light.

I AM Light's fullest dimension;
I AM Light's purest intention.
I AM Light, Light, Light
Flooding the world everywhere I move,
Blessing, strengthening, and conveying
The purpose of the kingdom of heaven.

This decree establishes the light of God in you for a more efficacious use of the violet flame. It also begins with God's name, I AM, in the affirmation "I AM Light, glowing Light."

Taking the verb *to be* as the name of God, as God proclaimed it to Moses, we know that that verb *to be* as the name of God has the power to release at our command infinite resources and energy from that limitless energy source of the cosmos, the Great Central Sun.

The name of God, I AM THAT I AM, is also translated "I AM WHO I AM," implying that God makes himself known in the outplaying of events: "You cannot circumscribe me by a name or a notion of what or who you think I am. You cannot predict my comings and my goings. I AM WHO I AM. I will be what I will be. Tell the children of Israel that I AM hath sent you unto them."

But one thing we do know is that God used the verb *to be* to identify his Be-ness. God is Being. When you see the words *I AM* capitalized, you know that you are saying the name of God and you are affirming that where you are as his beloved child, his son or daughter, there *God is*. For we know that the threefold flame in our hearts is the divine spark that establishes that "Be-ness."

When you say, "I AM Light, glowing Light," you are saying, "God is Being where I AM. God in me is that Light, glowing Light."

Let the following visualizations be the focus of your daily meditation on the Be-ness of God sustaining his seven rays in your seven chakras for the healing of planet earth:

I now visualize my heart chakra, 12-petaled, a fiery rose pink, sending forth this thy light as God's love to all sentient life.

I now visualize my throat chakra, 16-petaled, a fiery blue sapphire, sending forth this thy light as God's will to all nations and peoples.

I now visualize my solar-plexus chakra, 10-petaled, purple and gold with ruby flecks, sending forth this thy light as the desiring of our Lord and Saviour to receive the souls of God's desiring back to his heart.

I now visualize my third eye, 96-petaled, a fiery emerald-green sending forth this thy light as God's All-Seeing Eye focusing vision and the sacred keynote of each lifestream and the planet earth for the harmonization of all life.

I now visualize my seat-of-the-soul chakra, six-petaled, a violet-purple-pink, sending forth this thy light as violet flame to accomplish the alchemy of freedom, justice and world transmutation.

I now visualize my crown chakra, thousand-petaled, a brilliant yellow fire, sending forth this thy light as wisdom, enlightenment and illumined action to all evolutions of this planet.

I now visualize my base-of-the-spine chakra, four-petaled, pure white, sending forth this thy light for the sealing of the sacred fire of the Divine Mother in the base chakra, the soul and four lower bodies of every child of light.

Now add to your visualizations the following decrees for the purification of your chakras. Give the violet flame mantra before each chakra mantra and after the last.

In the name I AM THAT I AM, in the name Jesus Christ, Saint Germain, I decree:

I AM a being of Violet Fire!
I AM the purity God desires! (3x)

My heart is a chakra of Violet Fire,
My heart is the purity God desires! (3x)

My throat chakra is a wheel of Violet Fire,
My throat chakra is the purity God desires! (3x)

My solar plexus is a sun of Violet Fire,
My solar plexus is the purity God desires! (3x)

My third eye is a center of Violet Fire,
My third eye is the purity God desires! (3x)

My soul chakra is a sphere of Violet Fire,
My soul is the purity God desires! (3x)

My crown chakra is a lotus of Violet Fire,
My crown chakra is the purity God desires! (3x)

My base chakra is a fount of Violet Fire,
My base chakra is the purity God desires! (3x)

In the name I AM THAT I AM, in the name JESUS CHRIST, beloved Holy Christ Self, place your Electronic Presence over me, align my chakras with your chakras, let each petal be balanced and brought into attunement with the Seven Elohim, that they might send forth the vibration of the seven tones of the seven rays and the seven planes of God's Being.

Please close your eyes and visualize your seven chakras lined up. See the center of each one turning clockwise as white light spinning, each one its own fiery sun. Visualize the T'ai Chi. Experience the balance of the yang, the yin, the Alpha, the Omega within each chakra.

See the corona of each chakra and its petals in the above-named colors surrounding the center as vibrant, electric, intense. Give the "I AM Light" decree as you sustain the thoughtform of seven powerful rays of white Light going forth from the center of each chakra. Once you have established your visualization of these rays, you can see them clothed in the color ray of the chakra so that the white is no longer visible; nevertheless you continue to see it inside the outer color ray.

In the name of the Father, the Son, the Holy Spirit and the Divine Mother, in great God gratitude for this opportunity to exercise the science of the spoken Word and its power, I decree: (Turn to page 543 and give "I AM Light.")

"Heart, Head and Hand Decrees" by El Morya

Violet Fire

Heart

> Violet Fire, thou Love divine,
> Blaze within this heart of mine!
> Thou art Mercy forever true,
> Keep me always in tune with you.

Head

> I AM Light, thou Christ in me,
> Set my mind forever free;
> Violet Fire, forever shine
> Deep within this mind of mine.

> God who gives my daily bread,
> With Violet Fire fill my head
> Till thy radiance heavenlike
> Makes my mind a mind of Light.

Hand

I AM the hand of God in action,
Gaining Victory every day;
My pure soul's great satisfaction
Is to walk the Middle Way.

Tube of Light

Beloved I AM Presence bright,
Round me seal your Tube of Light
From Ascended Master flame
Called forth now in God's own name.
Let it keep my temple free
From all discord sent to me.

I AM calling forth Violet Fire
To blaze and transmute all desire,
Keeping on in Freedom's name
Till I AM one with the Violet Flame.

Forgiveness

I AM Forgiveness acting here,
Casting out all doubt and fear,
Setting men forever free
With wings of cosmic Victory.

I AM calling in full power
For Forgiveness every hour;
To all life in every place
I flood forth forgiving grace.

As you recite these "Heart, Head and Hand Decrees," visualize taking place exactly what they say. Each word or phrase carries a thoughtform that you fill in with the fiat of your mind and heart as much as you do with your spoken word.

Pour yourself into your decrees. For they give back to you *your* light, energy and consciousness multiplied many times over by the Word.

Visualize yourself surrounded by the violet flame as you see it depicted in the lower figure of the Chart of Your Divine Self. See the painting come alive as though you were looking at an animated Disney film. See the violet flame rising, pulsating in endless shades and gradations of purple-pink with violet hue and electric blue.

By and by as we decree, the violet flame, rising up from beneath our feet in answer to our call, begins to rotate. As the decree momentum builds, the pulsation intensifies and the flame begins to spin.

See yourself enveloped in the violet flame. See the violet flame passing up through your physical body, caressing the body internally and externally, healing the organs, transmuting the causes of disease within those organs, reversing negative spirals of degeneration and restoring positive spirals of regeneration.

It is good to keep an anatomy book handy so you can visualize the violet flame surrounding and penetrating each organ in your body. This is especially helpful when you are praying for yourself or others in the case of accidents, surgery and terminal illnesses. Make a specific call to God to focus the violet flame in the area of need and then hold a strong visualization of the violet flame penetrating there.

The violet flame heals the four lower bodies.

Therefore see it manifesting in the brain and also in the faculties of memory, cogitation and intelligence. See it saturating the emotions, the feelings, the desire body. See it flushing out the etheric memory, healing scars of old hurts and painful records that replay through the mind and emotions until they are transmuted.

The violet flame is indeed the missing ingredient in healing. It will work for you but you have to work with it! You cannot ignore the physical causes of physical conditions in your body. You need to be sensible about following the basic laws of health, diet and wholesome living.

Consult your doctor and take the remedies that are specific for your problem. Medical science has much to offer and the Ascended Masters expect you to avail yourself of its benefits. Of course, preventive medicine is the best medicine; but if surgery is necessary, then have it. The violet flame is an adjunct to sound scientific measures. It is not a substitute for them but should be applied as a spiritual unguent along with them.

The karma behind disease may be no more than many years of ignoring the rules of body chemistry. The law is just and impartial in all levels of being—so solve chemistry problems with chemistry and make your body the very best servant it can be for the Lord.

Then there is the karma of negative vibrations and negative habits. Your body is sensitive. It will pick up your negative vibrations and habits from your conscious and subconscious minds and outpicture them.

When you send positive messages to your four lower bodies (and your body elemental, who tends to the needs of your physical body), you clear the way for the body's reception of the violet flame. Then the physical atoms and cells will receive the violet flame, which has the ability to bond with them, giving those atoms and cells and you a positive spin and putting you back on the road to victory, victory, victory!

So, if you want to be well and you're not, but you're giving the violet flame, you'd better examine yourself to see if you are allowing negative momentums to dominate the household of your consciousness. Because they do block the efficacy of the violet flame. Besides, they make you sick.

Fear, worry, depression, low self-esteem, anger and irritability can be tied to deep-seated psychological problems that defy resolution until you get a handle on them. Getting therapy can help and so can reading books on personal psychology.

But to be healthy, happy and whole, the first requirement is to want to be. Secondly, true wholeness is oneness with God and so you have to want to be one with God. Surrender to him and to Jesus Christ is the first step. And with each succeeding step along the way, you need to invoke divine intercession and give your violet flame decrees for the transmutation of all elements in your psyche that are preventing you from getting what you really want out of life.

Replace negative vibrations with positive vibrations, bad habits with good habits. Retrain your thinking and feeling worlds. This takes determination and practice and will. The violet flame will work with you but it can't do everything. Because your free will is the deciding factor in whether God or man or angel or Master can help you.

In the final analysis, it is up to you to remake yourself in the image and likeness of God. When you decide you're going to do it and you're going to turn your life around, you will. Then you will see how the violet flame and a legion of violet flame angels and troops of elementals will work with you and see you through to the finish. And one day you'll look in the mirror and see the handiwork of God—and yourself.

When you take all the proper physical measures for the healing of a certain problem and you still do not heal, it is because the karma that caused the condition is not yet balanced, and therefore you need to: (1) Be relentless in giving your violet flame decrees until that karma itself relents and passes into the flame for transmutation. (2) Make your peace with God and man. Seek forgiveness and accept it as you forgive all who have wronged you. Then perpetually give of yourself to others. (3) Study the teachings of the Ascended Masters, which are a course on abundant, fruitful living encompassing the parallel paths of the world's religions with Jesus Christ as the chief cornerstone.

"Decree for Freedom's Holy Light"
by Saint Germain

Now visualize the globe of the world with the violet flame surrounding it just as you have visualized the violet flame pulsating up through your four lower bodies.

Fix your attention on the continents, the nations, the capitals, the cities, the great mountain ranges, the seas. See the violet flame pulsating from beneath, starting at the South Pole then sweeping up, enveloping the earth and reaching the North Pole. Now see it penetrate deeper and deeper into the strata of the earth.

Visualize a blazing violet flame sun in the center of the earth, its flames leaping out in all directions to saturate the inner planes of earth. Then see the outer flame meeting the inner sun, making the entire planet a violet flame sphere before your very eyes.

As you invoke the violet flame and sustain it where you are, where God is the I AM THAT I AM, you make yourself a counterpoint to the violet flame action you have called forth for planet earth.

Visualize a figure eight, yourself at one end and the earth at the other. See the violet flame tracing this figure eight, transmuting as it travels in, through and around yourself and the planet with the speed of light.

Visualize the Lord Jesus Christ as the World Saviour, standing at the nexus of the figure eight, with world transmutation taking place through his Sacred Heart. Sustain this visualization as you give the "Decree for Freedom's Holy Light" for the freedom of yourself and planet earth and for the healing of yourself and planet earth.

Now address your beloved Holy Christ Self:

O blessed one, let your Electronic Presence, even the Electronic Presence of the Universal Christ that is the Holy Christ Self individualized for each one, descend upon every man, woman and child evolving on this planet—in the physical octave, the astral plane, the mental plane and the etheric plane.

I ask now for the violet flame that I invoke where I am to be duplicated 10 billion times over until all evolutions assigned to this planet receive that same sustenance of light that I have called forth and that I do receive from the heart of God in the Great Central Sun by my crystal cord.

Let this light descend and let it be qualified in all hearts this day by my decree. I offer this decree for the healing of every individual soul on planet earth and for the healing of the planetary body itself. And by the Law of the One and the great mystery of the Lord's Body with us, I know that it is done in Jesus' name and I accept it done this hour in full power, O God. Amen.

Mighty Cosmic Light!
My own I AM Presence bright,
    Proclaim Freedom everywhere—
In order and by God control
I AM making all things whole!

Mighty Cosmic Light!
Stop the lawless hordes of night,
    Proclaim Freedom everywhere—
In justice and in service true
I AM coming, God, to you!

Mighty Cosmic Light!
I AM Law's prevailing might,
    Proclaim Freedom everywhere—
In magnifying all goodwill
I AM Freedom living still!

Mighty Cosmic Light!
Now make all things right,
    Proclaim Freedom everywhere—
In Love's victory all shall go,
I AM the wisdom all shall know!

I AM Freedom's holy Light
    Nevermore despairing!
I AM Freedom's holy Light
    Evermore I'm sharing!
Freedom, Freedom, Freedom!
    Expand, expand, expand!
    I AM, I AM, I AM
Forevermore I AM Freedom!

In this decree, you are calling forth the Mighty Cosmic Light. The cosmic light comes from central sun systems throughout the Spirit-Matter Cosmos, originating in the Great Central Sun and intensifying as it is anchored in the earth through your call.

When the cosmic light and Cosmic Beings descend to planet earth in answer to your call to "proclaim freedom everywhere," they proclaim the freedom of the soul, the spirit, the heart, the mind, freedom of the nations, freedom of religion, freedom of the press, freedom of assembly, freedom of speech, truly the freedom to speak what one must speak from the heart.

This is a decree for the enshrining of the four sacred freedoms in every nation and for the violet flame, the flame of cosmic freedom and cosmic light, to consume by God's law of transmutation all totalitarian regimes and all tyranny of the human ego within and without. You are decreeing for true God freedom to be made manifest in the nations and the continents and for all forces of anti-freedom as forces of the night to be bound by the hosts of the Lord.

You are calling for the cosmic light and Cosmic Beings to "stop the lawless hordes of night," all discarnate entities, all forces out of Death and Hell that move against the true light of all mankind.

As you give the "Decree for Freedom's Holy Light," allow the Great White Brotherhood and your Mighty I AM Presence to place before your third eye perpetual visions of the images that are recorded in your memory body. These would include all the pictures and films and photographs you have ever seen and scenes of all the places you have ever been. Visualize yourself standing in those places with your hands extended, releasing the cosmic light and the violet flame through your hands and your chakras.

"More Violet Fire"
by the Ascended Master Hilarion, the Apostle Paul

Lovely God Presence, I AM in me,
Hear me now I do decree:
Bring to pass each blessing for which I call
Upon the Holy Christ Self of each and all!

Let Violet Fire of Freedom roll
Round the world to make all whole
Saturate the earth and its people, too,
With increasing Christ-radiance shining through!

I AM this action from God above
Sustained by the hand of heaven's Love,
Transmuting the causes of discord here,
Removing the cores so that none do fear.

I AM, I AM, I AM
The full power of Freedom's Love
Raising all earth to heaven above
Violet Fire now blazing bright
In living beauty is God's own Light

Which right now and forever
Sets the world, myself, and all life
Eternally free in Ascended Master perfection!
Almighty I AM! Almighty I AM! Almighty I AM!

This decree is known for its rhythm and for the spiraling action of the violet flame that follows the rhythm. You need to hear it to get the rhythm and so you'll need my violet flame cassette number 1 to precipitate its full power.

You can use this decree to develop a facility for visualization by simply looking at the words and seeing those words that you are saying taking on the thoughtforms you image forth. See those mental pictures as cups being filled with violet flame by angels, Masters and Cosmic Beings.

When you recite the line "Bring to pass each blessing for which I call upon the Holy Christ Self of each and all," see in your mind's eye a huge crowd of people. First, see the figure of Jesus Christ and the Holy Christ Self descending over one person. Hold that picture strong. Focus the lens of your inner eye on it; when you've got it good and clear, multiply it and see it happening a million times!

Visualize the bleachers in Yankee Stadium filled for the World Series. See the presence of Jesus Christ and the Holy Christ Self dropping over everyone in the stadium like a mantle of light.

You can add to your mental picture as many thoughtforms as you can hold steady. You can visualize the tube of light with the violet flame in the center around yourself and every single person in the stadium. You can visualize the I AM Presence above the entire crowd. You can see the blessings flowing from your seven chakras, from your hands.

As you master the words of the decree and then

memorize them, you can close your eyes and see, with the full power of seeing that God gave you in the third eye, any blessing you want to see your violet flame decrees accomplish.

Your mind should never be idle while you decree. The idle mind is the devil's workshop. So, when you know a decree by heart, close your eyes and begin doing your work for the planet. This is what the saints have called the mighty work of the ages. What you see, what you can conceive of because you know it is the law of God, what you call forth, directing light rays through your chakras, you *will* precipitate and it *will* come into manifestation on this planet.

I have seen stupendous results on a planetary scale as the result of my private as well as public prayers and affirmations. It is astounding to me how God does take our fiats and our commands and bring them about in his good time. Sometimes it takes years, but the hour of fulfillment does come, when it is the will of God.

When you give this decree, bring to those words your very special imagination, your special images that you want to see outpictured on the screen of life. God has given you a unique ability to image forth and to imprint your image on material substance.

No two people reading this book will come up with the identical visualization or thoughtform. This is what enriches the kingdom of heaven— each individual sending forth the power of his mind, the power of his love, the power of his wisdom through the third eye to bring into manifestation the desirings of God and man, according to the will of God.

You can orchestrate a tremendous flow of light to the planet if you will just use this receiving-and-sending station, which is truly what your body temple is. Therefore, do not allow any of the components of this receiving-and-sending station to be idle, to be not in gear, to be not focused, not aligned, not tethered, not concentrated. You must master your chakras and your four lower bodies if you would master yourself and your planet.

I AM the Violet Flame

> I AM the Violet Flame
> In action in me now
> I AM the Violet Flame
> To Light alone I bow
> I AM the Violet Flame
> In mighty cosmic power
> I AM the Light of God
> Shining every hour
> I AM the Violet Flame
> Blazing like a sun
> I AM God's sacred power
> Freeing every one

My visualization with this decree is to see a violet flame sea of light enveloping the entire planet. I like to sing this decree to the melody of "Santa Lucia" because it evokes the action of the sea.

This is a powerful mantra. We call it a mantra because it is short and can be repeated many times, gathering momentum as it goes. It is also an I AM affirmation. Each time we say, "I AM the violet flame," all of the God that is in us descends to manifest as that violet flame.

The science of the spoken Word is impersonal. Whoever calls forth the violet flame with goodwill will receive it to the blessing of himself and all life.

The science of the spoken Word is based on the geometry of God and the mathematics of God, and it does not fail us when we do not fail it. The more we pour the fire of our being into our decrees, the more God pours his violet flame into us.

This is why the results are individual. It is the very fervor of our desire to heal our planet, to heal loved ones, to heal the suffering of mankind that evokes the mightiest response from God. The fervor of your desiring to heal yourself and planet earth is the fire that kindles a cosmos to your cause.

Because you are in earnest about your decrees and visualizations, you should have direct, accurate and up-to-the-minute information. Therefore, it is important to watch the news before your evening decree session so you will have an immediate eye picture.

Frame by frame it goes into the mind and into the subconscious. You don't necessarily remember all the details but you have the freshest reading of the aura of the planet in the place where the camera is focusing. And that is exactly what you need to decree effectively for the healing of conditions that make the headlines.

What most people don't know is that the camera and the audio capture the akashic records of a locale. So even if the reporting is incomplete or inaccurate, the violet flame passing through your mind and chakras can make deep incisions into the problem and go to work at sublevels that do not meet the eye but reach the soul.

So each time you say, "I AM the violet flame," you should practice developing the speed of the mind in visualization. See the ray of light shooting down the cosmic corridor that is your crystal cord all the way from the Great Central Sun, flashing through your body, through the seven chakras, focused now, for instance, on all of the world's children.

You can visualize them before you, starting with the children of your own neighborhood and moving out to the children that are deprived all over America and the world. Using your globe as a reference point, you can focus on each nation and continent, systematically directing the light into the specific needs of those children.

Of course, you can use this decree for any situation. And visualizing the violet flame sea is a very good beginning. You can see it as a peaceful sea as though on the etheric plane, saturating the mental, the astral and the physical bodies of the people and the planet.

You know the immense power of water, so

meditate on the power of the seven seas and then translate it to the violet flame sea. Imagine the weight of it, the light of it, the power of it, the energy of it! The violet flame has the capacity to totally transform the planetary body.

More Violet Flame Decrees

Radiant Spiral Violet Flame

Radiant spiral Violet Flame,
    Descend, now blaze through me!
Radiant spiral Violet Flame,
    Set free, set free, set free!

Radiant Violet Flame, O come,
    Expand and blaze thy Light through me!
Radiant Violet Flame, O come,
    Reveal God's Power for all to see!
Radiant Violet Flame, O come,
    Awake the earth and set it free!

Radiance of the Violet Flame,
    Expand and blaze through me!
Radiance of the Violet Flame,
    Expand for all to see!
Radiance of the Violet Flame,
    Establish Mercy's outpost here!
Radiance of the Violet Flame,
    Come, transmute now all fear!

O Violet Flame, Come, Violet Flame!

In the name of the beloved Mighty Victorious Presence of God, I AM in me, my very own beloved Holy Christ Self, in the name Jesus Christ, Saint Germain and Portia, Archangel Zadkiel and Holy Amethyst, Arcturus and Victoria, all great beings, powers and activities of Light serving the Violet Flame, the entire Spirit of the Great White Brotherhood and the World Mother, elemental life—fire, air, water, and earth! I decree:

O Violet Flame, come, Violet Flame,
   Now blaze and blaze and blaze!
O Violet Flame, come, Violet Flame,
   To raise and raise and raise!

(Repeat verse between the following endings:)
1. The earth and all thereon! (3x)
2. The children and their teachers! (3x)
3. The plants and elemental creatures! (3x)
4. The air, the sea, the land! (3x)
5. Make all to understand! (3x)
6. Bless all by Omri-Tas' hand! (3x)
7. I AM, I AM, I AM the fullness of God's plan fulfilled right now and forever! (3x)

And in full Faith I consciously accept this manifest, manifest, manifest! (3x) right here and now with full Power, eternally sustained, all-powerfully active, ever expanding, and world enfolding until all are wholly ascended in the Light and free! Beloved I AM! Beloved I AM! Beloved I AM!

This is what the violet flame is all about. That's why I have put together a 90-minute violet flame song-and-decree cassette, *Save the World with Violet Flame! by Saint Germain 1,* with a booklet containing all the words. How about joining me and 800 students of the Ascended Masters who did the recording and musical accompaniment? You can use this violet flame cassette daily for your soul's joyous advancement on the path and for the healing of our diseased planet.

The best way for you to become proficient in giving the violet flame is to practice along with others who have gained a proficiency. I want you to have this song-and-decree tape so you can play it in your home, office and car, and on your headsets while exercising and traveling—so you can use your chakras as sending stations to save the world with violet flame!

Glossary of Astrological Terms

Affliction. A hard or stressful aspect, such as a semi-square, square or opposition, particularly from Mars, Saturn, Uranus or Pluto.

Arc. The orbital difference between two bodies, measured in degrees along the zodiac.

Ascendant. The first-house cusp. The degree of the zodiac on the eastern horizon at the moment a horoscope is cast. It is often loosely referred to as the "rising sign." In natal astrology it gives some indication of the person's personality and temperament.

Aspect. The angular separation between any two points in the horoscope such as the position of the Sun, Moon and planets, the Ascendant and the Midheaven. Aspects are an indication of how the planets interact. "Hard" aspects (squares, oppositions, etc.) are dynamic, stressful and tend to present challenges. "Soft" aspects (sextiles, trines) usually indicate the harmonious or creative expression of the planets involved.

Aspects, Major

Conjunction. 0 degrees apart. Powerful union of energies of the planets associated. Easy or stressful depending on which planets are conjoined and the aspects they make to other planets.

Sextile. 60 degrees apart. Tends to foster cooperation in the area described by the planet, house and sign and can lead to opportunities.

Square. 90 degrees apart. Creative tension. Potentially the most discordant and destructive aspect. Can indicate conflicts, obstacles, stress and the energy needed to overcome the same.

Trine. 120 degrees apart. Indicates where there is a harmonious avenue of expression and where success may come with little effort. Natural talents.

Opposition. 180 degrees apart. If the person can integrate the planets in opposition harmoniously, the aspect acts like a conjunction. If not, the person experiences conflicts and the negative characteristics of the planets and the houses and signs they occupy.

Aspects, Minor

Semi-sextile. 30 degrees apart. Harmonious.

Semi-square. 45 degrees apart. Stressful; creative tension or frustration.

Quincunx. 150 degrees apart. Mixed influence; combination of harmony and stress. Shows duties and obligations.

Birth chart. See Natal chart.

Configuration. A planetary pattern. The association of three or more bodies (Sun, Moon, planets) and/or points (Ascendant, Midheaven) by aspect, e.g., a grand trine and T-square.

Conjunction. See Aspect.

Cusp. Lines dividing signs or houses in a horoscope.

Degree. One of 360 parts of a circle. In astrology, the circle of the zodiac has 360 degrees divided into 12 signs of 30 degrees each.

Eclipse. The partial or total obscuration of the Sun or Moon. An eclipse of the Sun (solar eclipse) occurs on the New Moon, when the Moon passes between the Sun and the Earth, cutting off the light of the Sun. The Sun and Moon are always conjoined during a solar eclipse. An eclipse of the Moon (lunar eclipse) occurs on a Full Moon, when the Earth, passing between the Sun and Moon, casts its shadow on the Moon. The Sun and Moon are always opposed during a lunar eclipse.

Ecliptic. The apparent path of the Sun around the Earth. The same as the plane of the Earth's orbit around the Sun.

Equinox. Either of two points in the year (the vernal and autumnal equinoxes) when the Sun crosses the celestial equator and day and night are equal in length everywhere on earth. The vernal equinox takes place annually around March 21 and the autumnal equinox occurs annually around

September 21. In astrology, the Sun enters the sign of Aries on the vernal equinox and the sign of Libra on the autumnal equinox.

Exalted. The sign of the zodiac in which a planet is able to easily express its best characteristics. This occurs when the nature of the planet and the sign are harmonious. A planet is exalted in one sign: Sun in Aries; Moon in Taurus; Mercury in Aquarius; Venus in Pisces; Mars in Capricorn; Jupiter in Cancer; Saturn in Libra; Uranus in Scorpio; Neptune in Cancer; Pluto in Leo.

Finger of God. A configuration that occurs when two planets sextile to one another are both quincunx to a third planet, forming an acute isosceles triangle.

Galactic Center. The center of gravity of our galaxy, around which our Sun orbits about every 250 million earth years in the same way the Earth orbits our Sun every 365 or so days.

Grand square. A configuration that occurs when four or more planets are at 90-degree angles, forming a squarelike pattern.

Grand trine. A configuration that occurs when three bodies or points are at 120-degree angles, forming an equilateral triangle.

Heliocentric nodes. The two points in a planet's orbit, 180 degrees apart, which intersect the plane of the Earth's orbit around the Sun.

Horoscope. A diagram of the heavens showing the relative positions of the Sun, Moon and planets and the signs of the zodiac with reference to a specific time and place on Earth. An astrological chart.

Houses. 12 divisions of the horoscope, distinct from the signs of the zodiac, which govern certain areas or departments of life.

Houses, rulership. (in charts of individuals)

    First house. Self, personality, appearance.

    Second house. Money, possessions, values, sense of self-worth.

    Third house. The concrete mind, communication, travel, siblings, neighbors.

    Fourth house. Home, mother, environment.

    Fifth house. Romantic affairs, creative affairs, children, social life.

    Sixth house. Health, work, service.

    Seventh house. Business and marriage partners, legal affairs, open enemies.

    Eighth house. Joint finances, taxes, legacies, death and regeneration.

    Ninth house. The higher mind, higher education, religion, foreigners, long-distance travel.

    Tenth house. Father, career, status, reputation.

    Eleventh house. Friends, hopes, wishes, community affairs.

    Twelfth house. Hidden friends and enemies, covert activities, institutions, transcendence, self-undoing.

Houses, rulership. (in mundane astrology)

First house. A nation, its self-image, the people and their psychology, interior affairs.

Second house. A nation's economy, treasury, wealth, Gross National Product, banks, financial and material resources.

Third house. A nation's newspapers, television, telephones, cinema, radio, postal system, schools, public opinion, rumors.

Fourth house. A nation's land, real estate, housing, mines, agriculture, patriotism, traditions, ideologies, the common people, opposition to the government.

Fifth house. A nation's children, birth rate, entertainment, sporting and social events, stock exchanges, high society, ambassadors.

Sixth house. A nation's work force, trade unions, the civil service, the armed forces, food reserves, public health, social security programs.

Seventh house. A nation's foreign policy, foreign relations, allies, treaties, war, declared enemies, public places, organized crime.

Eighth house. A nation's public income, taxes, the national debt, trust and insurance companies, international finance, domestic and multinational corporations, the mortality rate.

Ninth house. A nation's supreme court and court system, a nation's churches, universities, publishing industry, foreign affairs and foreign trade, international law, international bodies such as the United Nations.

Tenth house. A nation's chief executive (king, president, chancellor, dictator, etc.), the government, constitution, ruling class, the party in power, eminent people, a nation's reputation and prestige.

Eleventh house. A nation's legislature, goals, industrial development, urban renewal, fraternal organizations and social groups.

Twelfth house. A nation's hospitals, charitable institutions and prisons, hidden enemies, foreign spies, subversion, labor disturbances, plagues and epidemics, secret societies.

Meridian. The circle of longitude that passes through the North and South Poles and the Zenith and Nadir of the observer.

Midheaven. The tenth-house cusp. The point, directly overhead the place for which a horoscope is cast, where the meridian intersects the ecliptic. In natal astrology, it gives some indication of the person's career and public standing.

Moon's nodes. The two points, 180 degrees apart, where the Moon's orbit intersects the ecliptic. The north, or ascending, node occurs where the Moon's orbit crosses the ecliptic from south to north. The south, or descending, node occurs where the Moon's orbit crosses the ecliptic from north to south.

Mundane astrology. Literally, the "astrology of the world." The branch of astrology that studies nations, world leaders, and national and international economic and social developments. Described by Nicholas deVore as "an interpretation of Astrology in terms of world trends, the destinies of nations and of large groups of individuals, based on an analysis of the effects of Equinoxes, Solstices, New Moons, Eclipses, planetary conjunctions and similar phenomena; as distinguished from Natal Astrology, specifically applicable to an individual birth horoscope" (*Encyclopedia of Astrology* [New York: Philosophical Library, 1947], p. 263).

Natal astrology. The branch of astrology, also known as Genethliacal astrology, which analyzes the position at birth (and hence the influences) of the Sun, Moon, planets, other celestial bodies and astronomical phenomena (e.g., eclipses) on the life and character of an individual.

Natal chart. A horoscope, or diagram, showing the position of the Sun, Moon and planets relative to an individual on Earth at the time and place of birth.

Opposition. See Aspect.

Orb of influence. The arc of space, expressed in degrees, in which an aspect is operative; also called the "orb." There is a good deal of controversy over how many degrees astrologers should allow for an orb. A number of astrologers agree that a major aspect is effective up to 8 degrees from the point at which it is exact, and in mundane charts perhaps as much as 10 degrees.

Part of Fortune. A mildly favorable point defined as the point in a horoscope as far from the Ascendant as the Moon is from the Sun in longitude.

Planet. Literally, a "wanderer." In astrology, it generally refers to the Sun, Moon, Mercury, Venus, Mars, Jupiter, Saturn, Uranus, Neptune and Pluto. Astrologers understand that the Sun (the star at the center of our solar system) and the Moon (Earth's satellite) are not planets, but they sometimes refer to them as such as a matter of convenience.

Planets, rulership. (in natal astrology)

Sun. Individuality, will power, vitality, leadership, creativity, authority, masculine principle, father.

Moon. Emotions, habit, memory, subconscious, nurturing impulse, feminine principle, mother.

Mercury. Concrete mental faculties, thought, speech, communication, perception, intelligence, reasoning ability, mobility, adaptability.

Venus. Harmony, love, pleasure, beauty, art, social affairs and graces, financial matters.

Mars. Action based on desire, construction and destruction, assertiveness, aggression, executive authority.

Jupiter. Abstract and creative faculties, expansiveness, higher mind, wisdom, optimism, benevolence, generosity, hypocrisy.

Saturn. Concentration, crystallization, organization, caution, pessimism, responsibility, perseverance, stability, discipline, limitation, tradition, obstacles.

Uranus. Impulse for freedom and individuality, originality, ingenuity, intuition, independence, inventiveness, eccentricity, disruption.

Neptune. Inspiration, illumination, refinement, mystical tendencies, idealism, compassion, escapism, illusion, confusion, delusion.

Pluto. Regeneration, transformation, renewal, destruction, manipulation, denial, coercion, annihilation.

Planets, rulership. (in mundane astrology)

Sun. The head of state, president, king, general secretary, strongman, etc.; sometimes represents the nation or the national identity.

Moon. The people, popular opinion, crowds, women, family life, agriculture, food supplies, aquatic and maritime resources and industries.

Mercury. The communications and transportation industries, postal system, trade and commerce, young people, education, educators, the literary world, intellectual trends.

Venus. Peace (or when afflicted, war), treaties, allies, banks, currency, markets, wealth, luxuries, fashion, style, the feminine ideal, sex scandals, culture and the arts, lower courts of law.

Mars. Military, intelligence and police forces, war, crime, espionage, the masculine ideal, taxes, surgeons, sports, physical fitness, the steel industry, flammable chemicals, explosives, epidemics.

Jupiter. The highest (supreme) court and court system, churches and religious institutions, universities and higher education, judges, lawyers, clergy, wealthy people, capitalists, big business, philanthropists, advisers to the head of state, foreign relations and foreign countries, prosperity, overexpansion, waste.

Saturn. The executive branch of government, the state and its institutions, state-run businesses, corporate executives, heavy industry, leaders of powerful political parties, order and stability, authority, tradition, the status quo, repressive or controlling forces, the legal system, repressive regimes, mines and mineral resources, the elderly.

Uranus. Legislatures, civic organizations, social cohesion, the air force, civil aviation, space programs, invention, advanced technology, change, reform, revolution, rebellion, strikes, upheaval, uranium, nuclear energy.

Neptune. A nation's spiritual tradition, visions and dreams of an ideal society, the little people, mass movements, social unrest, socialism, charities, glamour, illusion, intrigue, scandals, subversion, oil, hospitals, prisons, welfare agencies, corruption, drugs, poisons, chemical warfare, the navy, counterespionage, propaganda, movies.

Pluto. The abuse of power in all forms, all things hidden and secret, widespread death and destruction especially from war, nuclear energy, toxic substances; power struggles, terrorism, totalitarian states, spy organizations, tyrants, secret police, organized crime, self-destructive activities, destructive forces outside of one's control such as war, natural catastrophes, depressions, nuclear accidents.

Planetary rulership of signs and houses. Mars rules Aries and Scorpio and the first and eighth houses; Venus rules Taurus and Libra and the second and seventh houses; Mercury rules Gemini and Virgo and the third and sixth houses; the Moon rules Cancer and the fourth house; the Sun rules Leo and the fifth house; Jupiter rules Sagittarius and the ninth house; Saturn rules Capricorn and the tenth house; Uranus rules Aquarius and the eleventh house; Neptune rules Pisces and the twelfth house.

Progressed chart. Calculated by advancing (or "progressing") the positions of the planets, Ascendant and the Midheaven at the rate of a day's movement for each year from birth. It is, as noted by Marcia Moore and Mark Douglas, "a horoscope erected for a date that is as many days after a given birthdate as the native's age in years" (*Astrology, The Divine Science* [York Harbor, Maine: Arcane

Publications, 1971], p. 758). Progressed charts are used to assess influences any time after the birth of a person, corporation, nation, etc.

Quincunx. See Aspect.

Rectification. The attempt to find the unknown moment of birth of a person or nation. The usual procedure is to compare the dates of known events in the life of that person or nation with transits and progressions to the natal chart and then to adjust the birth time so that the key transits and progressions coincide with the events.

Retrogradation. The apparent backward motion of planets as seen from Earth due to the relative speed of the planets.

Sextile. See Aspect.

Solar return. The moment when the Sun returns to the exact position it occupies in a natal chart. A chart drawn for the solar return indicates the challenges and opportunities for that year, especially when analyzed in conjunction with the natal chart.

Solstice. Literally, "standing still." One of two points on the ecliptic where the Sun's apparent position reaches its maximum distance (about 23.5 degrees) above or below the celestial equator. The Sun appears to stand still at the solstice. The summer solstice, which occurs annually when the Sun enters Cancer (around June 22), is the first day of summer and the longest day of the year in the Northern Hemisphere. The winter solstice, which occurs annually when the Sun enters Capricorn (around December 22), is the first day of winter and the shortest day of the year in the Northern Hemisphere.

Square. See Aspect.

Sunspot cycle. Refers to the cyclic increase and decrease in the number of sunspots on the surface of the sun. A cycle peaks (i.e., reaches maximum) about every 11 years.

Symbols.

Astrological Signs

♈ Aries	♎ Libra
♉ Taurus	♏ Scorpio
♊ Gemini	♐ Sagittarius
♋ Cancer	♑ Capricorn
♌ Leo	♒ Aquarius
♍ Virgo	♓ Pisces

Planets

☉ Sun	♃ Jupiter
☽ Moon	♄ Saturn
☿ Mercury	♅ Uranus
♀ Venus	♆ Neptune
♂ Mars	♇ Pluto

Transit. The passage of a celestial body such that it forms an aspect with the Sun, Moon, planets, the Ascendant, Midheaven or other important points in the natal chart. As Moore and Douglas note, "Transits are believed to indicate the nature of changing influences which impinge upon an entity from external sources" (*Astrology, the Divine Science*, p. 761).

Trine. See Aspect.

T-square. A configuration formed by three or more planets that form a right triangle. T-squares are dynamic and the most tension-producing configuration. (The tension may be creative or destructive.)

Zodiac. An imaginary belt in the heavens about 8 degrees on either side of the ecliptic. The apparent path of the Sun, Moon and planets pass through this belt. The zodiac is divided into 12 equal segments of 30 degrees each. These are known as the signs of the zodiac: Aries, Taurus, Gemini, Cancer, Leo, Virgo, Libra, Scorpio, Sagittarius, Capricorn, Aquarius, Pisces.

FOR MORE INFORMATION

Write or call for information about the dictations of the Ascended Masters published weekly as *Pearls of Wisdom*, the Keepers of the Flame Fraternity with monthly lessons, and Summit University three-month retreats, weekend seminars and quarterly conferences that convene at the Royal Teton Ranch.

At this 30,000-acre self-sufficient spiritual community-in-the-making adjacent to Yellowstone National Park in Montana, Elizabeth Clare Prophet gives teachings on the Divine Mother, the parallel paths of Christ and Buddha, Saint Germain's prophecies for our time and the exercise of the science of the spoken Word as well as dictations from the Ascended Masters and initiations of the Great White Brotherhood. These teachings are published in books and on audio- and videocassette.

Mrs. Prophet's cable TV shows air weekly with series on the Lost Teachings of Jesus, the Coming Revolution in Higher Consciousness, and a talk show entitled "Summit University Forum," where Mrs. Prophet interviews revolutionaries in every field on the critical issues of our time—from education, health and alternative healing methods to the economy and the defense of freedom.

We'll be happy to send you a free catalog of publications and audio- and videocassettes when you contact:

Summit University Press
Box A, Livingston, Montana 59047-1390
Telephone: (406) 222-8300

Be sure to ask about the Ascended Masters' library and study center nearest you.

All in our community send you our hearts' love and a joyful welcome to the Royal Teton Ranch!

Reach out for the **LIFELINE TO THE PRESENCE.**
Let us pray with you!
To all who are beset by depression, suicide,
difficulties or insurmountable problems, we say
MAKE THE CALL! (406) 848-7441

Notes

CHAPTER 1
Astrology and Karma

1. *The Encyclopedia of Eastern Philosophy and Religion* (Boston: Shamballa Publications, 1989), s.v. "karma."
2. Ibid., s.vv. "karma," "samskaras."
3. André Bareau, *Die Religionen Indiens*, vol. 3, Stuttgart, quoted in *The Encyclopedia of Eastern Philosophy and Religion*, p. 175.
4. Gal. 6:5, 7–10. For a further discussion of karma and reincarnation see Mark L. Prophet and Elizabeth Clare Prophet, *The Lost Teachings of Jesus I* (Livingston, Mont.: Summit University Press, 1986), pp. 36–41, 129–33, 178–81, 211–15, 282–83; *The Lost Teachings of Jesus II*, pp. 42–50, 52–57, 63–64, 112–21, 125–28, 226–34, 267–74, 357–59, 369–70, 373–74, 376–89, 519–21, 566 n. 56.
5. James R. Cash, Group Chairman's Factual Report of Investigation, Cockpit Voice Recorder, National Transportation Safety Board, 21 March 1990.
6. Matt. 5:18.*
7. Matt. 21:42, 44; Luke 20:17, 18.
8. I Cor. 6:20; 7:23.
9. Rom. 8:14–17; Gal. 3:26–29; 4:4–7.
10. John 13:34; 15:12.
11. Matt. 22:37, 39, 40.
12. Matt. 25:40.
13. Matt. 25:41–43, 45, 46.
14. Rom. 2:6–11 (Jerusalem Bible, hereafter cited as JB). All

*Bible references are to the King James Version unless otherwise noted.

references to the Jerusalem Bible are from *The Jerusalem Bible*, ed. Alexander Jones (Garden City, N.Y.: Doubleday and Co., 1966).

15. Deut. 10:17; II Sam. 14:14; Acts 10:34; Rom. 2:11; Eph. 6:9; Col. 3:25; I Pet. 1:17.
16. Matt. 7:2.
17. I Cor. 3:8, 13–15.
18. Heb. 11:6.
19. Eph. 2:8, 9.
20. James 1:22.
21. James 2:20, 26.
22. Heb. 12:2.
23. Matt. 5:17.
24. I Thess. 5:3.
25. *The Rubáiyát of Omar Khayyám*, trans. Edward Fitzgerald, stanza 71.

CHAPTER 2
Does God Condemn Astrology?

1. Texe Marrs, *Dark Secrets of the New Age* (Westchester, Ill.: Crossway Books, 1987), pp. 168–69.
2. Hal Lindsey, *The Late Great Planet Earth* (New York: Bantam Books, 1973), p. 110.
3. Joel C. Dobin, *The Astrological Secrets of the Hebrew Sages: To Rule Both Day and Night* (New York: Inner Traditions International, 1983), p. 193.
4. Ibid.
5. Dan. 2:2.
6. II Kings 17:17.
7. II Kings 23:5.
8. Isa. 47:6, 7. (JB)
9. Matt. 2:1, 2.
10. Matt. 2:9.
11. *The Expositor's Bible Commentary*, 12 vols. (Grand Rapids, Mich.: Zondervan Publishing House, Regency Reference Library, 1976–), 8:84, 85.
12. *The Interpreter's Bible*, 12 vols. (Nashville, Tenn.: Abingdon Press, 1951–57), 7:257.

13. *Expositor's Bible Commentary* 8:85.
14. In my book *Sanat Kumara On the Path of the Ruby Ray: The Opening of the Seventh Seal*, I associate the four beasts of Revelation 4 and 6 with the lion, Lord Maitreya; the calf, Lord Gautama; the man, Lord Jesus Christ; and the flying eagle, Lord Sanat Kumara. See *Sanat Kumara On the Path of the Ruby Ray: The Opening of the Seventh Seal*, Book I (1979 *Pearls of Wisdom*, vol. 22) (Livingston, Mont.: Summit University Press, 1989).
15. *Interpreter's Bible* 12:403, 404.
16. Ibid., p. 453.
17. Rev. 21:10.
18. *Interpreter's Bible* 12:537.
19. Job 9:2, 4. (JB)
20. Job 9:4, 6–12.
21. Joel C. Dobin, "The Legacy of Judaism," *NCGR Journal*, Winter 1987–1988, p. 8.
22. Ibid., pp. 8, 11.
23. Dobin, *Astrological Secrets of the Hebrew Sages*, p. 225.
24. Ibid.
25. *The Works of Josephus*, trans. William Whiston (Peabody, Mass.: Hendrickson Publishers, 1987), p. 32.
26. Ibid., p. 34.
27. *The Opus Majus of Roger Bacon*, trans. Robert Belle Burke, vol. 1 (Philadelphia: University of Pennsylvania Press, 1928), p. 268.
28. Ibid.
29. Ibid., pp. 267–68.
30. Ibid., p. 267.
31. Ibid.
32. Ibid.
33. Ibid., p. 401.

CHAPTER 3
What Is Prophecy?

1. Jon. 1:2. (JB)
2. Jon. 4:2. (JB)
3. Jon. 3:4. (JB)

4. Jon. 3:5. (JB)
5. Ibid.
6. Jon. 3:6. (JB)
7. Jon. 3:8. (JB)
8. Jon. 3:10. (JB)
9. Jon. 4:3. (JB)
10. Jon. 4:10, 11. (JB)
11. D. Guthrie and J. A. Moryer, eds., *The New Bible Commentary: Revised* (Grand Rapids, Mich.: Wm. B. Eerdmans Publishing, 1970), p. 721.
12. I Cor. 14:3.
13. *The Compact Edition of the Oxford English Dictionary*, s.v. "edify."
14. *Webster's Third New International Dictionary*, s.v. "edify."
15. *Compact Oxford English Dictionary*, s.v. "exhort."
16. *Webster's Third*, s.vv. "exhort," "preach."
17. Isa. 40:1, 3–5.
18. I Thess. 5:3.
19. Mark 10:27; Matt. 19:26; Luke 18:27.

CHAPTER 4
A Messenger and a Prophet

1. John 13:16; 15:20.
2. John 1:9.
3. John 3:14, 15.
4. John 3:16, 17.
5. Num. 21:4–9.
6. Rom. 8:16, 17.
7. John 14:12–15.
8. Exod. 3:13–15.
9. *Gospel of Philip* 67:26–27, in James M. Robinson, ed., *The Nag Hammadi Library in English*, 3d ed., rev. (San Francisco: Harper and Row, 1988), p. 150.
10. *Gospel of Thomas*, logia 13, 108, quoted in Elaine Pagels, *The Gnostic Gospels* (New York: Random House, Vintage Books, 1981), p. xx.
11. Arya Maitreya and Asanga, *The Changeless Nature (The Mahayana Uttara Tantra Shastra)*, trans. Katia Holmes

and Ken Tsultim Gyamtso (Eskdalemuir, Scotland: Karma
Drubgyud Darjay Ling, n.d.), p. 21.
12. Rev. 7:9, 10, 13–17.
13. Rev. 14:6.
14. Isa. 61:1.
15. John 12:44, 45.
16. Matt. 25:21, 23.

CHAPTER 5
What You Can Do about Your Karma

1. Matt. 2:7–12.
2. *Encyclopedia of Eastern Philosophy and Religion*, s.v.
   "karma."
3. Deut. 4:24; 9:3; Heb. 12:29.
4. Abraham Lincoln, speech to the Republican State Con-
   vention, Springfield Illinois, 16 June 1858.

CHAPTER 6
An Eventful Two Years

1. Telephone interview with financial analyst Robert Kwasny,
   30 June 1990.
2. *Webster's New World Dictionary*, 2d college ed., s.vv. "conservative," "reactionary," "reaction."
3. "Uzbekistan Jumps on Bandwagon," *Washington Times*,
   21 June 1990, p. A7.
4. Adrian Karatnycky, "Now It's the Ukraine's Turn," *Wall
   Street Journal*, 18 July 1990, p. A8.
5. *Webster's New World Dictionary*, s.v. "liquidate."
6. "Bonfires of the S&Ls," *Newsweek*, 21 May 1990, p. 23.
7. Robert E. Litan, R. Dan Brumbaugh and Andrew S.
   Carron, "Cleaning Up the Depository Institutions Mess,"
   Brookings Papers on Economic Activity, 1989:1. In a telephone interview on December 11, 1989, Litan said that
   losses in the banking industry may well be greater than
   those in the thrift industry "if we have a significant recession and if the FDIC is not given the funds to do the job so
   that we delay cleaning up the mess."
8. "It'll Be a Hard Sell," *Business Week*, 29 January 1990, p. 30.

9. "Wall Street Era Ends As Drexel Burnham Decides to Liquidate," *Wall Street Journal*, 14 February 1990, p. A1.

10. "The Great Liquidation," *Kwasny Economics*, 19 June 1990, p. 1.

11. "Going for the Broke," *Newsweek*, 2 April 1990, p. 40.

12. Telephone interview with Trisha Morris, National Association of Realtors, 3 August 1990.

13. "Is It the Banks' Turn?" *U.S. News & World Report*, 2 July 1990, p. 38.

14. Eric Schmitt, "Collapse in Region's Housing Market Is Taking a Toll on Owners' Emotions," *New York Times*, 13 April 1990, p. A13.

15. Barbara Rudolph, "Pop! Goes the Bubble," *Time*, 2 April 1990, p. 50.

16. Elizabeth Clare Prophet, "Prophecy for the 1990s II," in *Saint Germain: Prophecy to the Nations*, Book II (1988 *Pearls of Wisdom*, vol. 31) (Livingston, Mont.: Summit University Press, 1990), p. 116.

17. Craig Torres, "A Curious Bull Market: Bloodletting Doesn't Stop," *Wall Street Journal*, 20 July 1990, p. C1.

18. *Kwasny Economics*, 18 December 1989, p. 2.

19. Ibid.

20. *Kwasny Economics*, 30 April 1990, p. 4.

21. Stock Market Data Bank, *Wall Street Journal*, 1 August 1990, p. C2.

22. Douglas R. Sease and Craig Torres, "Growth Stocks Take a Pounding, Showing Market's Vulnerability," *Wall Street Journal*, 24 July 1990, p. A1.

23. *For Your Eyes Only*, 14 May 1990, p. 1.

24. Walter S. Mossberg and Gerald F. Seib, "White House Mulls U.S. Participation in Effort to Shore Up Soviet Economy," *Wall Street Journal*, 20 June 1990, p. A3.

CHAPTER 7
The Astrology of World Karma

1. Abraham Lincoln, "Perpetuation of Our Political Institutions," address to the Young Men's Lyceum of Springfield, Illinois, 27 January 1838.

2. Hos. 8:7.
3. Uranus will enter Aquarius on April 1, 1995, and remain there until June 8, 1995, when it retrogrades back into Capricorn to complete its transit of that sign.
4. See Rev. 6:1–8.
5. Rev. 4:4, 10; 5:8, 14; 11:16; 19:4.

CHAPTER 8
The Portents of Saturn-Uranus Conjunctions

1. Richard Nolle, "Saturn-Uranus Triple Whammy of '88," *Star Tech*, Pisces 1988, p. 4.
2. Ibid. As with many historical questions, there are differences of opinion about when the classical period of Greece came to an end. Some historians argue it ended at the start of the Greco-Macedonian empire in 338 B.C., others say it ended with the incorporation of Greece into the Roman Empire, and still others at various points of time during the reign of Alexander the Great. In any case, Alexander—who was the primary disseminator of classical Greek culture—died four years after his invasion of India. After his death the Greco-Macedonian empire was fragmented into three competing units that declined in power.
3. "Greece enjoyed a period of prosperity that lasted until about 280 B.C. Thereafter the same conditions that had led to the crisis of the 4th century came to the fore again, aggravated now by perpetual and increasingly devastating wars. Wealth was concentrated in fewer hands; the market for Greek exports contracted as the new Greco-Oriental communities in the East began to compete with Greece. The wages of free laborers were sharply depressed; the middle class, owners of moderate-sized farms or factories, likewise became impoverished. Infanticide and abortion became common among both rich and poor. Class war became acute and open in many Greek cities apart from those, like Rhodes and Athens, still rich enough to subsidize the proletariat. The chief points in the program of the social revolutionists were still, as in the 4th century B.C., cancellation of debts and redistribution of land" (*Encyclopedia Americana*, s.v. "Greece").

4. For more information about the Galactic Center see Michael Baigent, Nicholas Campion, and Charles Harvey, *Mundane Astrology: An Introduction to the Astrology of Nations and Groups* (Wellingborough, Northamptonshire, England: Aquarian Press, 1984), pp. 336–38; Philip Sedgwick, *The Astrology of Deep Space* (Birmingham, Mich.: Seek-It Publications, 1984), pp. 93–99; Michael Erlewine and Margaret Erlewine, *Astrophysical Directions* (Ann Arbor, Mich.: Heart Center School of Astrology, 1977).

5. Other astrologers investigating the effects of the Galactic Center include Michael Erlewine, Richard Nolle and Philip Sedgwick.

6. George Santayana, *Reason in Common Sense*, vol. 1 of *The Life of Reason* (1905; reprint, New York: Dover Publications, 1980), p. 284.

CHAPTER 9
The Portents of Saturn-Uranus-Neptune Conjunctions

1. See Dylan Warren-Davis, "The Black Death," *Astrological Journal*, November/December 1988, pp. 302–9.

2. See Diana Rosenberg, "A Preliminary Investigation of Black Hole Effects in Personal and Mundane Horoscopes," *Heliogram*, May Day 1988, p. 19.

3. Barbara W. Tuchman, *A Distant Mirror: The Calamitous 14th Century* (New York: Alfred A. Knopf, 1978), p. xii.

4. Telephone interview with Richard Nolle, astrologer, 12 February 1988.

5. The thesis that the AIDS virus was created in the laboratory by genetic manipulation of deadly animal viruses, enabling them to cross the species barrier and attack the human immune system, is examined by Elizabeth Clare Prophet and her guests on the Summit University Forum "The AIDS Conspiracy: Establishment Cover-up, Pharmaceutical Scam or Biological Warfare?" on 4 audiocassettes, 4³/4 hr., $23.80 (add $.95 for postage), A88113; 3 videocassettes, 4¹/2 hr., $59.95 (add $1.90 for postage), GP88078. See also Appendix A, "A Startling Thesis on the Origin of AIDS,"

in *Saint Germain: Prophecy to the Nations*, Book II (1988 *Pearls of Wisdom*), pp. 124–28.

6. John Townley, *Astrological Cycles & the Life Crisis Periods* (New York: Samuel Weiser, 1977), p. 46.

CHAPTER 10
The Spirit of the Prophets Then and Now

1. Ezek. 18:30–32.
2. Isa. 1:16–20.
3. In the Jerusalem Bible, the Hebrew *YHVH* (rendered in other English translations of the Bible as "the LORD") is translated as "Yahweh"—the name for the I AM THAT I AM, referred to by the Ascended Masters as the Mighty I AM Presence.
4. Jer. 18:7–11. (JB)
5. Jer. 20:4.
6. Eph. 6:12.
7. *Yang* and *yin* are the two opposing but complementary energies, forces or principles in Chinese philosophy whose interactions cause the universe to come into being. The interplay of yang and yin forces govern all formation, movement and change. The yang force in the universe has characteristics that are masculine, active, bright, positive, hot and contracting. The yin force in the universe has characteristics that are feminine, passive, dark, negative, cold and expansive. Traditional Chinese medicine teaches that perfect harmony between the yang and yin elements in the body brings health. Conversely, the undue preponderance of one or the other results in disease and death.
8. Rev. 16:7; 19:2.
9. Phil. 2:7.
10. Jer. 1:14; 4:6; 6:1.
11. Jer. 32:35. (JB)
12. Rom. 8:16, 17.
13. See *The Life of Saint Issa* 12:10, in Elizabeth Clare Prophet, *The Lost Years of Jesus* (Livingston, Mont.: Summit University Press, 1984), pp. 215, 274.

14. Biblical references to child sacrifice: Lev. 18:21; 20:2–5; Deut. 12:31; 18:10; II Kings 16:3; 17:17; 21:6; 23:10; II Chron. 28:3; 33:6; Ps. 106:37, 38; Isa. 57:5; Jer. 7:31, 32; 19:1–6; 32:35; Ezek. 16:20, 21, 36; 20:26, 31; 23:37–39; Mic. 6:7.

15. Saint Germain, January 6, 1982, in *Kuan Yin Opens the Door to the Golden Age*, Book I (1982 *Pearls of Wisdom*, vol. 25) (Livingston, Mont.: Summit University Press, 1983), p. 179.

16. Saint Germain and Portia, July 4, 1990, 1990 *Pearls of Wisdom*, vol. 33, p. 360.

17. Ibid., p. 363. In an article in Spring 1983 issue of *Heart: For the Coming Revolution in Higher Consciousness*, I said, "I will concede that because there is not free will or consent involved in rape, a woman can make the choice within 36 hours not to accept the condition of pregnancy." Until Saint Germain gave his July 4, 1990 dictation, I sincerely believed that abortion was permissible if conception occured in cases of rape or incest. After the dictation, the Master explained to me that the only reason abortion should be allowed is in the case of jeopardy to the life of the mother. If conception occurs as a result of rape or incest, then it is the will of God and should be accepted as a karma between father and mother and the incoming soul. I stand corrected.

18. Jer. 19:3–9. (JB)
19. Jer. 19:15. (JB)
20. Jer. 20:3, 4. (JB)
21. Jer. 11:21. (JB)
22. Jer. 22:13, 15, 17. (JB)
23. Jer. 23:14. (JB)
24. Jer. 7:3, 4, 8–11. (JB)
25. Jer. 14:13. (JB)
26. Jer. 6:13, 14. (JB)
27. Jer. 4:16–19. (JB)
28. Jer. 25:8, 9, 11. (JB)
29. Jer. 28:13, 14. (JB)
30. Jer. 28:15. (JB)
31. Jer. 52:6. (JB)

CHAPTER 11
El Morya Unlocks the Mystery

1. There is some confusion as to when Congress signed the Declaration of Independence. Popular belief holds that the Declaration was signed on July 4, 1776, by the 56 men whose signatures are appended to the document. But scholars have demonstrated that this is unlikely. The *Secret Journal* of Congress records that on July 19, 1776, Congress resolved to have the Declaration engrossed (written on parchment) and signed when it was ready and that it was signed on August 22, 1776. In addition, one quarter of the men who signed the Declaration were not in Congress on July 4—either they were not in Philadelphia on that day or they had not yet been elected to Congress. Nevertheless, the document was signed on July 4 "by Order and in Behalf of the Congress" by at least John Hancock, president of Congress, and Charles Thompson, secretary of Congress. The *Journals of the Continental Congress* say that Congress "agreed to a Declaration" on the fourth and ordered that it be "authenticated and printed." In order to be "authenticated" a document had to be signed by Hancock and his signature had to be attested to by Thompson. The nation was conceived on July 4 since Hancock and Thompson were acting as instruments of the entire Congress.

2. Garry Wills, *Inventing America: Jefferson's Declaration of Independence* (Garden City, N.Y.: Doubleday and Co., 1978), p. 331.

3. Ibid., pp. 331–32.

4. Warren E. Burger, "The Right to Bear Arms," *Parade*, 14 January 1990, p. 5.

5. Worthington Chauncey Ford, ed., *Journals of the Continental Congress 1774–1789*, 34 vols. (Washington, D.C.: Government Printing Office, 1904–37), 2:155.

6. See Michael Baigent, "Ebenezer Sibly and the Declaration of Independence 1776: An Investigation," *NCGR Journal*, Spring 1985, p. 46.

7. N. N. Sukhanov, *The Russian Revolution 1917*, ed., abr. and trans. Joel Carmichael (Princeton, N.J.: Princeton University Press, 1984), p. 629.

CHAPTER 12
The Portents of the United States Conceptional Chart

1. Sirius, now at 13° 56′ Cancer was at 11° 0′ Cancer in 1776, still conjoined the U.S. conceptional Sun. Like all fixed stars, Sirius moves about 1° every 72 years.
2. Richard Hinckley Allen, *Star Names: Their Lore and Meaning* (New York: Dover Publications, 1963), p. 121.
3. Nicholas Davidson, "Life Without Father: America's Greatest Social Catastrophe," *Policy Review*, Winter 1990, p. 40.
4. Dane Rudhyar, *The Astrology of America's Destiny* (New York: Random House, 1974), pp. 71–72.
5. John Adams to Thomas Jefferson, 1815, quoted in Bernard Bailyn, *The Ideological Origins of the American Revolution* (Cambridge: Harvard University Press, Belknap Press, 1967), p. 1.
6. Dane Rudhyar, *Astrological Timing: The Transition to the New Age* (New York: Harper and Row, Harper Colophon Books, 1969), p. 58.
7. James M. Perry, "As Panama Outcome Is Praised, Details Emerge of Bungling during the 1983 Grenada Invasion," *Wall Street Journal*, 15 January 1990.
8. Ibid.
9. Thomas Paine, quoted in Rudhyar, *The Astrology of America's Destiny*, p. 109.

CHAPTER 14
The Portents of the Birth Chart of the Soviet Union

1. See Elizabeth Clare Prophet, "Nostradamus: The Four Horsemen," in *Saint Germain On Prophecy*, Book Two (Livingston, Mont.: Summit University Press, 1986), pp. 27–47.

CHAPTER 15
A Capricorn Conjunction Triggers the Great Depression

1. Arch Crawford, "Harmonic Convergence," *Crawford Perspectives*, 8 August 1987, p. 2.
2. Mark Twain, *Pudd'nhead Wilson and Those Extraordinary Twins* (New York: P. F. Collier and Son, 1922), p. 108.

3. See "Author Believes August Heralds New Age of Peace for World," *Salt Lake City Tribune*, 1 August 1987; José Argüelles, *The Mayan Factor: Path Beyond Technology* (Santa Fe, N.Mex.: Bear and Co., 1987), pp. 146, 159, 165, 169–70, 193–94.

4. I Thess. 5:3.

CHAPTER 16
My Vision of the Four Horsemen

1. Rev. 1:1.
2. Rom. 8:6, 7.
3. Rev. 12:17.
4. Rev. 20:12, 13; II Cor. 5:10; 11:15.
5. Dan. 7:9, 13, 22; Rev. 4; 5; 6:16; 7:9–12; 14:3; 19:1–6; 20:11–15; 22:1, 3.
6. The Revised Standard Version and the Jerusalem Bible omit the words *and see* which appear in the King James Version after the word *Come* in Rev. 6:1, 3, 5, 7. *The Interpreter's Bible* says that the additional words *and see* are "not well attested." "Come!" is a command upon which the horses appear in turn. The words *and see* are extraneous and change the meaning of the verses. Consequently, they are omitted in this citation of the King James Version.
7. Rev. 5:1–4; 6:1–8, King James Version. Compare with the Jerusalem Bible translation of Rev. 6:1–8: "Then I saw the Lamb break one of the seven seals, and I heard one of the four animals shout in a voice like thunder, 'Come.' Immediately a white horse appeared, and the rider on it was holding a bow; he was given the victor's crown and he went away, to go from victory to victory. When he broke the second seal, I heard the second animal shout, 'Come.' And out came another horse, bright red, and its rider was given this duty: to take away peace from the earth and set people killing each other. He was given a huge sword. When he broke the third seal, I heard the third animal shout, 'Come.' Immediately a black horse appeared, and its rider was holding a pair of scales; and I seemed to hear a voice shout from among the four animals and say, 'A ration of corn for a day's wages, and three rations of barley for a day's

wages, but do not tamper with the oil or the wine.' When he broke the fourth seal, I heard the voice of the fourth animal shout, 'Come.' Immediately another horse appeared, deathly pale, and its rider was called Plague, and Hades followed at his heels. They were given authority over a quarter of the earth, to kill by the sword, by famine, by plague and wild beasts."

8. Matt. 24:22; Mark 13:20.
9. *Interpreter's Bible* 12:412.
10. Saint Germain, November 27, 1986, in *The Handwriting on the Wall*, Book II (1986 *Pearls of Wisdom*, vol. 29) (Livingston, Mont.: Summit University Press, 1988), pp. 647–48, 650; also published in *Saint Germain On Prophecy*, Book Four, pp. 207, 208, 212.
11. Saint Germain, October 3, 1987, in *A Year of Prophecy*, Book I (1987 *Pearls of Wisdom*, vol. 30) (Livingston, Mont.: Summit University Press, 1989), pp. 484–85.
12. Ibid., pp. 487–88.
13. Vesta, October 19, 1987, in *A Year of Prophecy*, Book I (1987 *Pearls of Wisdom*), pp. 544–45.

CHAPTER 17
How the February 1988 Conjunction Affects the United States

1. Dan Brumbaugh, "Nightline," ABC News, 31 July 1990.
2. Frank Anunzio, "Nightline," ABC News, 31 July 1990.

CHAPTER 18
Capricorn Conjunctions in 1989, 1990, 1991, and 1994

1. See Ravi Batra, *The Great Depression of 1990: Why It's Got to Happen—How to Protect Yourself* (New York: Simon and Schuster, 1985).
2. Telephone interview with Marsha Adams, biologist and specialist on the correlation of earthquakes and sunspot cycles, 10 February 1988.
3. Baigent, Campion, and Harvey, *Mundane Astrology*, p. 169.
4. Ibid., pp. 169–74.

CHAPTER 20
Uranus—the Great Awakener

1. I Thess. 5:2.
2. II Pet. 3:10–14.
3. William Shakespeare, *Julius Caesar*, act 4, sc. 3, line 217.
4. Matt. 10:28.

CHAPTER 21
The Power Elite and Their Hidden Agenda

1. Telephone interview with Joe Cobb, Republican staff director of the Joint Economic Committee, 6 September 1990.
2. C. Wright Mills, *The Power Elite* (New York: Oxford University Press, 1956), p. 270.
3. Ibid., p. 271.
4. President Franklin Delano Roosevelt to Col. Edward Mandell House, November 21, 1933, *F.D.R.: His Personal Letters* (New York: Duell, Sloan and Pearce, 1950), p. 373.
5. Mills, *Power Elite*, p. 271.
6. Ibid., p. 95.
7. Frederick C. Howe, *Confessions of a Monopolist* (Chicago: Public Publishing, 1906), pp. 157, 145.
8. Antony C. Sutton, *Wall Street and FDR* (New Rochelle, N.Y.: Arlington House Publishers, 1975), p. 72.
9. Howe, *Confessions*, pp. v–vi.
10. Sutton, *Wall Street and FDR*, p. 75.
11. Antony C. Sutton, *The War on Gold* (Seal Beach, Calif.: '76 Press, 1977), p. 84.
12. Ibid.
13. Matt. 7:16–20; 12:33; Luke 6:43–45.

CHAPTER 22
"How Are the Mighty Fallen!"

1. II Sam. 1:19, 25.
2. Barbara H. Watters, *Horary Astrology and the Judgment of Events* (Washington, D.C.: Valhalla Paperbacks, 1973), p. 61.

3. Hilary Stout, "U.S. Foreign Debt Widened Last Year; Nation Remains World's Largest Debtor," *Wall Street Journal*, 3 July 1990, p. A2.
4. Ibid.

CHAPTER 23
Opportunity Knocks

1. Archeia Hope, January 2, 1987, in *A Year of Prophecy*, Book I (1987 *Pearls of Wisdom*), p. 79.
2. Gautama Buddha, April 4, 1983, 1983 *Pearls of Wisdom*, vol. 26, pp. 464, 465.
3. Gen. 18:23–33.
4. Saint Germain, May 28, 1986, in *The Handwriting on the Wall*, Book II (1986 *Pearls of Wisdom*), p. 523; also published in *Saint Germain On Prophecy*, Book Four, pp. 170–71.
5. Dan. 12:1.
6. *Saint Germain On Alchemy* (Livingston, Mont.: Summit University Press, 1985), pp. 350–52.

CHAPTER 24
The Astrology of War between the Superpowers

1. For an excellent discussion of this phenomenon see Baigent, Campion, and Harvey, *Mundane Astrology*, pp. 183, 201–2.
2. Nostradamus, Century III, quatrain 95, quoted in Edgar Leoni, *Nostradamus and His Prophecies* (New York: Bell Publishing Co., 1961), p. 217.
3. Telephone interview with Joseph Douglass, Jr., author, 27 June 1990.

CHAPTER 25
Haven't You Heard the Cold War Is Over?

1. Meg Greenfield, "It Wasn't War, It Isn't Over," *Newsweek*, 16 April 1990, p. 96.
2. *Encyclopaedia Britannica*, 15th ed., s.v. "International Relations."
3. Judy Shelton, *The Coming Soviet Crash: Gorbachev's*

Desperate Pursuit of Credit in Western Financial Markets (New York: Macmillan, Free Press, 1989), p. 201.

4. John M. Collins and Dianne E. Rennack, *U.S./Soviet Military Balance: Statistical Trends, 1980–1989*, Congressional Research Service, Library of Congress, 6 August 1990, pp. 16, 19, 24, 29, 39, 58.

5. Ibid, p. 29.

6. "Soviets Seen Doubling Stock of Mobile ICBMs," *FPI International Report*, 27 July 1990, p. 1.

7. Douglass, telephone interview.

8. *FPI International Report*, 15 June 1990, p. 3.

9. Joseph K. Woodard, "Perestroika and Grand Strategy," *Global Affairs*, Winter 1990, p. 30.

10. Ibid., p. 31.

11. Telephone interview with Maj. Gen. George J. Keegan, Jr. USAF (Ret.), 9 August 1990.

12. "The Changing U.S.-Soviet Strategic Balance," *Global Affairs*, Spring 1990, pp. 12–13.

13. Keegan, telephone interview.

14. Telephone interview with Dr. Steven S. Rosefielde, professor of economics at the University of North Carolina at Chapel Hill, 20 August 1990.

15. *FPI International Report*, 27 July 1990, p. 3.

16. Rosefielde, telephone interview.

17. Ibid.

18. *FPI International Report*, 15 June 1990, p. 7.

19. Ibid.

20. *For Your Eyes Only*, 2 April 1990, p. 3.

21. Telephone interview with John M. Collins, senior specialist in national defense at the Library of Congress, 20 August 1990.

22. Telephone interview with intelligence analyst Stephen Cole, 11 September 1990.

23. Collins and Rennack, *U.S./Soviet Military Balance*, pp. 143, 155.

24. Department of Defense, *Soviet Military Power 1989* (Washington, D.C.: Government Printing Office, 1989), p. 111; *For Your Eyes Only*, 14 May 1990, p. 6.

25. "Bring on the B-Team," *New York Times*, 18 July 1990, p. A15.

CHAPTER 26
Have the Soviets Lost Eastern Europe?

1. John Lenczowski, "A Dash of Skepticism Wouldn't Hurt," *Los Angeles Times*, 11 January 1990.
2. Anatoliy Golitsyn, *New Lies for Old* (New York: Dodd, Mead and Co., 1984), pp. 327–28.
3. Ibid., pp. 327, 89.
4. Ibid., p. 340.
5. Telephone interview with Dr. Harold Rood, professor at the Center for Defense and Strategic Studies, Southwest Missouri State University, 9 August 1990.
6. Barrie Dunsmore, "Nightline," ABC News, 14 June 1990.
7. David B. Funderburk, "How the U.S. State Department Supported Ceausescu," *Conservative Review*, February 1990, p. 3.
8. Ibid., p. 2.
9. Ibid., p. 3.
10. *FPI International Report*, 24 August 1990, p. 7.
11. Ted Koppel, "Nightline," ABC News, 14 June 1990.
12. Telephone interview with James Sherr, specialist on Soviet defense and security policy at Oxford University, England, 28 August 1990.
13. "Poland's Feud in the Family," *U.S. News & World Report*, 10 September 1990, p. 52.
14. "Reform Hits the Skids," *Newsweek*, 10 September 1990, p. 36.
15. Sherr, telephone interview.
16. Paul Gray, "She Just Can't Get Any Respect," Grapevine, *Time*, 20 August 1990, p. 17.

CHAPTER 27
The KGB Handle on Eastern Europe

1. Jim Holmes, "Behind the Scenes, Communists Cling to Power," *West Watch*, 19 May 1990, pp. 3–4; telephone interview with defense consultant Dr. Avigdor Haselkorn, 30 August 1990.
2. Holmes, "Behind the Scenes," p. 4.
3. Haselkorn, telephone interview.

4. Telephone interview with Charles Via, chairman of the Center for Intelligence Studies, 9 August 1990.

5. Steven Emerson, "Where Have All His Spies Gone?" *New York Times Magazine*, 12 August 1990, p. 28.

6. Ibid., p. 18.

7. Holmes, "Behind the Scenes," p. 5.

8. Ibid.

9. Telephone interview with Jan Sejna, former secretary of the Czech Defense Council, 22 August 1990; telephone interview with Jim Holmes, an associate with the Council for InterAmerican Security, 14 August 1990.

10. Avigdor Haselkorn, "The KGB, a Key Part of Perestroika, Still Has Its Sights Set on the West," *New York City Tribune*, 3 August 1990, p. 1.

CHAPTER 28
Is the Warsaw Pact Finished?

1. ADN International Service, East Berlin, 12 June 1990.

2. Holmes, telephone interview, 14 August 1990.

3. *FPI International Report*, 27 July 1990, p. 3; Collins and Rennack, *U.S./Soviet Military Balance*, pp. 7, 8.

4. Holmes, telephone interview, 14 August 1990.

5. *FPI International Report*, 10 August 1990, p. 7.

6. *FPI International Report*, 27 June 1990, p. 3.

7. Sejna, telephone interview.

8. Sherr, telephone interview.

9. Ibid.

10. Ibid.

CHAPTER 29
The Astrology of Iraq's Invasion of Kuwait

1. Richard Murphy, "A Line in the Sand," ABC News, 12 September 1990.

2. Nicholas Campion, *The Book of World Horoscopes* (Wellingborough, Northamptonshire, England: Aquarian Press, 1988), p. 163.

3. Malcolm W. Browne, "Hussein's Achilles' Heel," *New York Times*, 14 August 1990, p. 8.

4. "The Making of a Monster," *Newsweek*, 20 August 1990, p. 29.
5. Robert S. Greenberger, "Iraqi Documents Show U.S. Lawmakers, in Baghdad Visit, Didn't Signal Concerns," *Wall Street Journal*, 20 September 1990, p. A6.
6. Otto Friedrich, "Master of His Universe," *Time*, 13 August 1990, p. 23.
7. Watters, *Horary Astrology*, p. 47.

CHAPTER 30
Dangerous Liaisons

1. Margaret Garrard Warner, "The Moscow Connection: The Inside Story of Secret Diplomacy between the Superpowers," *Newsweek*, 17 September 1990, p. 24.
2. Morton Kondracke, "Interested Parties," *New Republic*, 24 September 1990, p. 16.
3. Warner, "Moscow Connection," p. 24.
4. Kondracke, "Interested Parties," pp. 16, 18.
5. Warner, "Moscow Connection," p. 24.
6. Bill Keller, "Moscow Joins U.S. in Criticizing Iraq," *New York Times*, 4 August 1990, p. 6.
7. Kondracke, "Interested Parties," p. 18.
8. Ibid.
9. "Text of Joint Statement: Aggression 'Will Not Pay,'" *New York Times*, 10 September 1990, p. 5.
10. Edward Jay Epstein, "Virtual Ally," *New Republic*, 3 September 1990, p. 19.
11. Peter Schweizer, "Is Moscow Playing Cute on Kuwait?" *New York Times*, 22 August 1990, p. 23.
12. Ibid.
13. Telephone interview with Charles Via, 13 August 1990.
14. Telephone interview with Harriet Scott, editor of *Soviet Military Strategy*, 10 August 1990.
15. *For Your Eyes Only*, 17 September 1990, p. 2.
16. "A Line in the Sand," ABC News, 11 September 1990.
17. Schweizer, "Is Moscow Playing Cute?" p. 23.
18. Ibid.
19. "Soviet Went to Baghdad before the Invasion," Intelligence

Briefing, *Insight*, 27 August 1990, p. 38.

20. Schweizer, "Is Moscow Playing Cute?" p. 23; Bill Gertz, "Soviets Oppose Iraqi Move, State Department Insists," *Washington Times*, 16 August 1990, p. A9.

21. Telephone interview with Peter Schweizer, research analyst with the American Foreign Policy Council, 28 August 1990.

22. Bill Gertz and Martin Sieff, "Soviet Military Aiding Saddam: Officers May Have Gone 'Rogue,'" *Washington Times*, 23 August 1990, p. A1.

23. Paul Bedard, "White House Discounts Soviet Presence in Iraq," *Washington Times*, 6 September 1990, p. A1.

24. Schweizer, "Is Moscow Playing Cute?" p. 23.

25. Bedard, "White House Discounts Soviet Presence," p. A10.

26. Martin Sieff, "U.S. Nudges Soviets to Pull Advisers," *Washington Times*, 24 August 1990, p. A1.

27. Bedard, "White House Discounts Soviet Presence," p. A10.

28. Ibid.

29. Ibid.

30. Ibid.

31. Ibid.

32. "Transcript of Bush-Gorbachev News Conference at Summit," *New York Times*, 10 September 1990, p. A6.

33. Ibid.

34. Ibid., p. A7.

35. Peter Samuel, "Moscow Still Providing Iraq with Military Aid, CIA Says," *New York City Tribune*, 21 September 1990, p. 1.

36. Ibid.

37. Epstein, "Virtual Ally," pp. 19, 20.

38. Ibid., p. 19.

39. "George Bush, Diplomat," *U.S. News & World Report*, 10 September 1990, p. 26; *The World Almanac and Book of Facts 1989*, p. 756.

CHAPTER 31

What Are We Going to Do About All Those Nuclear Weapons?

1. James T. Hackett, "The Ballistic Missile Epidemic," *Global Affairs*, Winter 1990, p. 40.

2. Via, telephone interview, 9 August 1990.

3. Hackett, "Ballistic Missile Epidemic," pp. 53, 52.

4. "A Line in the Sand," ABC News, 11 September 1990.

5. *For Your Eyes Only*, 17 September 1990, p. 2.

6. Marc S. Palevitz, "Beyond Deterrence: What the U.S. Should Do About Ballistic Missiles in the Third World," *Strategic Review*, Summer 1990, p. 50; *Collier's Encyclopedia*, s.v. "Warfare."

7. "Israel Successfully Launches First Antiballistic Missile," *Aviation Week & Space Technology*, 13 August 1990, p. 23.

8. Angelo M. Codevilla, *While Others Build: The Commonsense Approach to the Strategic Defense Initiative* (New York: Free Press, 1988), p. 48.

9. Weekly Compilation of Presidential Documents, Congressional Research Service, Library of Congress, 23 March 1983, p. 448.

10. Angelo M. Codevilla, "A Shield in Space?" *Strategic Review*, Summer 1990, p. 64.

11. Collins and Rennack, *U.S./Soviet Military Balance*, p. 32; *Soviet Military Power 1989*, pp. 50–51.

12. Hackett, "Ballistic Missile Epidemic," p. 56.

13. John Gardner et al., *Missile Defense in the 1990s* (Washington, D.C.: George C. Marshall Institute, 1987), pp. 39–40.

CHAPTER 32
Why I Believe We Can and Should Survive a Nuclear War

1. Richard Pipes, "How to Cope With the Soviet Threat: A Long-Term Strategy for the West," *Commentary*, August 1984, p. 16.

2. Ibid., pp. 16–17.

3. Ibid., p. 17.

4. Nevil Shute, *On the Beach* (New York: William Morrow and Co., 1957), p. 97.

5. Collins and Rennack, *U.S./Soviet Military Balance*, pp. 16, 17, 18, 21, 23, 26, 27, 28.

6. Edward Zuckerman, *The Day After World War III: The*

U.S. Government's Plans for Surviving a Nuclear War (New York: Viking Press, 1984), p. 128.

7. William C. Martel and Paul L. Savage, *Strategic Nuclear War: What the Superpowers Target and Why* (Westport, Conn.: Greenwood Press, 1986), pp. 85, 87, 88, 92, 100, 101; *Soviet Military Power 1989*, p. 45.

8. Carl Sagan, "Nuclear War and Climatic Catastrophe: Some Policy Implications," *Foreign Affairs*, Winter 1983/84, pp. 259, 267, 292.

9. Starley L. Thompson and Stephen H. Schneider, "Nuclear Winter Reappraised," *Foreign Affairs*, Summer 1986, pp. 984–85.

10. "Milder Nuclear Winter," *Newsweek*, 31 March 1986, p. 65.

11. Thompson and Schneider, "Nuclear Winter Reappraised," p. 994.

12. Ibid., p. 991.

13. Office of Technology Assessment, *The Effects of Nuclear War* (Washington, D.C.: Government Printing Office, 1979), p. 7.

14. Ibid., p. 85.

15. Zuckerman, *Day After World War III*, pp. 125–26.

16. Leon Gouré, *Shelters in Soviet War Survival Strategy* (Coral Gables, Fla.: University of Miami, Advanced International Studies Institute, 1978), p. vii.

17. Thomas F. Nieman, *Better Read Than Dead: The Complete Book of Nuclear Survival* (Boulder, Co.: Paladin Press, 1981), p. 47.

18. Zuckerman, *Day After World War III*, p. 134.

19. Ibid, p. 135.

20. Ibid.

21. Ibid., p. 137.

22. Cresson H. Kearny, *Nuclear War Survival Skills* (Cave Junction, Ore.: Oregon Institute of Science and Medicine, 1987), p. 13.

23. Nieman, *Better Read Than Dead*, p. 114.

24. For information on how to build and stock an expedient fallout shelter see Cresson H. Kearny, *Nuclear War Survival Skills*, available through Summit University Press,

$10.50, paperback (add $2.00 for postage); Bruce D. Clayton, *Life After Doomsday: A Survivalist Guide to Nuclear War and Other Major Disasters* (Boulder, Colo.: Paladin Press, 1980), available through Summit University Press, $21.95, hardbound (add $2.00 for postage).
25. Deut. 30:19, 20.

CHAPTER 33
Why I Believe the Soviet Union Intends to Launch a Nuclear First Strike

1. Department of Defense, *Posture Statement: Fiscal Year 1966*, pp. 49–50, cited in Codevilla, *While Others Build*, p. 27.
2. Codevilla, *While Others Build*, p. 27.
3. Ibid., p. 236.
4. "The Changing U.S.-Soviet Strategic Balance," p. 13.
5. Department of Defense, *Soviet Military Power 1988* (Washington, D.C.: Government Printing Office, 1988), p. 56.
6. Codevilla, *While Others Build*, p. 122.
7. Ibid.
8. Ibid., p. 12.
9. Bill Gertz, "Soviets' Radar Boost Might Violate Treaty," *Washington Times*, 2 December 1989, p. A6.
10. Codevilla, *While Others Build*, p. 122.
11. "Gorbachev Interview: The Arms Agreement, Nicaragua and Human Rights," *New York Times*, 1 December 1987, p. 6.
12. Department of Defense, *Soviet Military Power 1987* (Washington, D.C.: Government Printing Office, 1987), p. 45.
13. Ibid., p. 53. See Elizabeth Clare Prophet, January 3, 1988, "The Race for Space," in *Saint Germain: Prophecy to the Nations*, Book I (1988 *Pearls of Wisdom*), pp. 63–88.
14. Gouré, *Shelters in Soviet War Survival Strategy*, p. vii; *Soviet Military Power 1987*, p. 52.
15. Joseph D. Douglass, Jr., *Red Cocaine: The Drugging of America* (Atlanta, Ga.: Clarion House, 1990), p. 224.
16. Ibid., p. 8.

17. Jan Sejna, November 28, 1987, Summit University Forum "Gen. Jan Sejna and Dr. Joseph Douglass, Jr.: Inside Soviet Military Strategy." Full-length interview, 4-3/4 hr., available on three audiocassettes, $19.50 (add $.95 for postage), A88016, or three videocassettes, $59.95 (add $1.90 for postage), GP88001; also available on five 1-hr. cable TV shows, parts 1-5, $19.95 each (add $1.10 each for postage), HL89001–HL89005.
18. William R. Van Cleave, "Surprise Nuclear Attack," in Brian D. Dailey and Patrick J. Parker, eds., *Soviet Strategic Deception* (Lexington, Mass.: Lexington Books, 1987), pp. 459–61.
19. Ibid., p. 455.
20. Department of Defense, *Strategic Modernization Issues,* July 1990, p. 17.
21. Saint Germain, November 27, 1986, in *The Handwriting on the Wall,* Book II (1986 *Pearls of Wisdom*), p. 648; also published in *Saint Germain On Prophecy,* Book Four, p. 208.
22. Saint Germain, February 13, 1988, in *Saint Germain: Prophecy to the Nations,* Book I (1988 *Pearls of Wisdom*), pp. 163–64.
23. Saint Germain, October 8, 1989, 1989 *Pearls of Wisdom,* p. 710.
24. Ibid., p. 709.
25. Gautama Buddha, May 20, 1989, 1989 *Pearls of Wisdom,* p. 414.

CHAPTER 36
Canada's Future

1. "In Search of a Nation's Heart," *Maclean's,* 11 June 1990, p. 20.
2. Deanna Hodgin, "Separate Dreams Divide a Country," *Insight,* 18 June 1990, p. 11.
3. Ibid.
4. Ibid., pp. 11–12.
5. Telephone interview with Eric Pelletier, Canadian consul for Public Affairs in Los Angeles, August 1990.

6. Peter C. Newman, "Examining Canada's Self-Destructive Psyche," *Maclean's*, 2 July 1990, p. 53.

CHAPTER 37
Your Divine Inheritance

1. Ps. 91:1, 2.
2. Exod. 3:13–15.
3. Gen. 4:26; 12:8; 26:25; Ps. 99:6; Joel 2:32; Acts 2:21; Rom. 10:12, 13.
4. Exod. 13:21, 22; Num. 14:14; Neh. 9:12, 19; Ps. 78:14.
5. Matt. 6:19, 20; John 14:2.
6. Matt. 6:21; Luke 12:34.
7. Rev. 10:1.
8. Cor. 11:24; Matt. 26:26; Mark 14:22; Luke 22:19.
9. John 6:35, 51.
10. Matt. 26:27, 28; I Cor. 11:25. (JB)
11. John 6:53.
12. John 3:16, 17.
13. John 1:3–9.
14. The Nicene Creed.
15. Col. 2:9.
16. Jer. 23:5, 6; 33:15, 16.
17. Rom. 8:14–17; Gal. 3:26–29; 4:4–7.
18. James 4:8.
19. Eccles. 12:6.
20. Rev. 22:1.
21. Matt. 3:16, 17; 17:5; Mark 1:10, 11; Luke 3:21, 22; II Pet. 1:17, 18; Matt. 12:18; Isa. 42:1.
22. Prov. 26:11.
23. See the Lord's Prayer. Matt. 6:9–15; Mark 11:25, 26; Luke 11:1–4.
24. John 1:11–13.
25. Phil. 2:12.
26. John 1:5.
27. John 1:14.
28. Matt. 7:15.
29. Zech. 13:7; Matt. 26:31; Mark 14:27.
30. Ps. 82:6 (see Jerusalem Bible); John 10:34.

CHAPTER 38
The Science of the Spoken Word

1. John 1:1, 2.
2. John Woodroffe, *The Garland of Letters* (Pondicherry, India: Ganesh and Co., n.d.) pp. 4–5.
3. Matt. 6:9.
4. Matt. 6:9–13; Luke 11:1–4.
5. Matt. 21:23; Mark 11:27, 28; Luke 20:1, 2.
6. John 5:1–9.
7. John 5:17, 19, 21, 23, 26, 30.
8. Gen. 1:26, 27; 5:1; 9:6.
9. John 13:34; 15:12.
10. John 15:16.
11. John 14:10–14.
12. Ps. 8:4; Heb. 2:6.
13. John 14:18.
14. Joel 2:32.
15. Gen. 1:28; 9: 1–3, 7.
16. Exod. 20:3; Deut. 5:7.
17. Deut. 6:4; Mark 12:29.
18. Heb. 9:23.
19. Rom. 3:4.
20. Matt. 21:21, 22.
21. Matt. 6:13.
22. Saint Germain, May 28, 1986, in *The Handwriting on the Wall*, Book II (1986 *Pearls of Wisdom*), p. 521; also published in *Saint Germain On Prophecy*, Book Four, p. 166.
23. John 11:43.
24. Matt. 7:29; Mark 1:22.
25. Gen. 1:3.
26. See Jesus and Kuthumi, *Prayer and Meditation* (Livingston, Mont.: Summit University Press, 1978).
27. Mal. 3:10; Saint Germain, "The Power of the Spoken Word," in Mark L. Prophet and Elizabeth Clare Prophet, *The Science of the Spoken Word* (Livingston, Mont.: Summit University Press, 1983), pp. 42–43, 44.
28. Saint Germain, "The Power of the Spoken Word," p. 40.
29. Ibid.

30. Ibid.
31. I Cor. 3:16, 17; 6:19, 20; II Cor. 6:16.
32. Saint Germain, "The Power of the Spoken Word," pp. 41–42, 44–45.

CHAPTER 39
What Is the Violet Flame?

1. Exod. 3:2; Deut. 4:24; 9:3; Heb. 12:29.
2. I John 1:5, 7.
3. Rev. 7:9, 10, 13–15.
4. El Morya, *The Chela and the Path* (Livingston, Mont.: Summit University Press, 1976), p. 47.
5. Ibid., pp. 47–48, 49.
6. Saint Germain, December 2, 1984, in *Maitreya On the Image of God*, Book II (1984 *Pearls of Wisdom*, vol. 27) (Livingston, Mont.: Summit University Press, 1990), p. 553; also published in Mark L. Prophet and Elizabeth Clare Prophet, *The Lost Teachings of Jesus II*, pp. 479–80.
7. Saint Germain, April 16, 1988, in *Saint Germain: Prophecy to the Nations*, Book II (1988 *Pearls of Wisdom*), p. 405.
8. Saint Germain, July 4, 1988, in *Saint Germain: Prophecy to the Nations*, Book II (1988 *Pearls of Wisdom*), pp. 546–47.
9. Rev. 1:4; 3:1; 4:5; 5:6.
10. Jer. 29:12.
11. Job 22:28.

A Note About the Media
by Erin Prophet Reed

There has been so much national and international media coverage of Elizabeth Clare Prophet in the past year that you are likely to have seen it. Since the coverage has been for the most part inaccurate, shallow and sensationalistic, I thought it necessary to write this note to provide some balance and perspective.

Beneath the headline "Loser of the Week, Elizabeth Prophet," *Time* magazine wrote in its April 30, 1990 issue, "The charismatic Guru Ma drew thousands of believers to a Montana valley to prepare shelters for apocalyptic nuclear dangers, particularly on April 23. If you've read this far, she was wrong."

It sounds like an open-and-shut case. "She was wrong." The only problem is, *Time* was wrong. *Time* never interviewed Mrs. Prophet or a spokesman before publishing this item. And Mrs. Prophet never said that she expected nuclear war on April 23 or any other date; she has simply urged civil defense preparedness. She did say that April 23 was a date of the acceleration of returning negative karma but that she did not expect any catastrophe on that date. *Time* refused to print a retraction or correction, despite numerous requests.

The moral of this story is: if you have unpopular or controversial beliefs, don't expect accurate media coverage.

A month earlier, *Time* had printed another inaccurate piece that claimed, "In 1987 [Mrs. Prophet] predicted that California would fall into the sea." She did no such thing.

It appears that *Time* set out to misrepresent the church. When church spokesman Murray Steinman asked a lawyer for *Time* why Mrs. Prophet had received such shoddy treatment, he replied, "I think there's a lot of skepticism concerning the church and its so-called teachings. From what I've read, I am very dubious about the premises of Mrs. Prophet."

Steinman asked, "So are you saying that if our religious philosophy was considered to be more legitimate by *Time*, we might get a different kind of coverage?"

The lawyer responded, "Yeah, that's fair."

Time's coverage is typical of the way the media has treated Mrs. Prophet and her prophecies. Since it's almost impossible today for a public figure to win a libel suit, I have decided to at least set the record straight on a few issues.

Another area of confusion is Mrs. Prophet's purported self-aggrandizement. As head of a religious community, she is called "Mother" by her students. But in 1985, *People* magazine erroneously reported that she calls herself "Mother of the Universe."

When Forrest Sawyer came to Montana in May 1990 to report the opening segment for a planned "Nightline," I informed him of *People's* error and requested that he not make the same mistake. He assured me that he did all his own reporting and that he *never* copied another reporter's stories. In fact, he said that he had often been the victim of errors resurrected from clip files by sloppy reporters. Therefore, he said, he knew how I felt.

You can imagine my surprise when I heard Sawyer say during his opening segment, "To her church members she is the Mother of the Universe."

I was even more surprised when I saw *People's* June 4, 1990 issue. The reporter had been duly warned about the past "Mother of the Universe" error. But his New York editors had come up with a new twist. They inserted the words "she refers to herself as Mistress of the Universe" into the story. *People* denied all requests to print a correction or even an explanatory letter to the editor.

In addition, by omitting an important detail of an incident that occurred when he interviewed Mrs. Prophet, the reporter implied that she is "worshiped" by her followers. He reported that "a female worshipper dropped to her bare knees in the gravel" before Mrs. Prophet outside a restaurant. He failed to report that Mrs. Prophet immediately asked the woman to stand up, helped her to her feet, and explained to her that we worship one God and not a human being.

This incident was a fluke. Futhermore, the woman was from India, where kneeling before religious teachers is a sign of respect rather than worship.

People also reported that Mrs. Prophet "has prepared for the apocalypse at least six times." This is categorically untrue. Perhaps this statement was based in part on a clipping from the Knight-Ridder news service and *The Philadelphia Inquirer*, which in November 1989 reported that Mrs. Prophet had predicted nuclear war would begin December 31, 1989. In fact, she had merely advised people to try to have fallout shelters completed by December 31. Knight-Ridder and the *Inquirer* ran a retraction.

Reporters who say she predicted the apocalypse (or Armageddon, or a holocaust, or the end of the world) never use a direct quote. That is because she has simply never "predicted" any of the above.

The facts that *Time* and *People* had such a hard time grasping were quite easy for a college student from the University of Washington newspaper, *The Daily*, to report.

Karl Braun, the assistant editor of the newspaper, wrote, "The major factual error that . . . [most] national publications ran is that the Church said the world was going to end on Monday, April 23. Church members never made this proclamation. (If anyone can find a statement from Church leaders or any documentation, other than newspapers, proclaiming the 'END OF THE WORLD,' I would be very surprised.) This statement was originally printed in one publication and was repeated many times over."

Let's take a look at what really happened in Montana:

Mrs. Prophet is the leader of Church Universal and Triumphant, a worldwide organization whose international headquarters is a spiritual community, the 30,000-acre Royal Teton Ranch in Montana.

People from all over the world visit the ranch for conferences, seminars and 12-week courses at Summit University, where they study the teachings of the Ascended Masters. Some church members who want to live close to the ranch so they can participate in religious services have built homes on private land nearby.

Mrs. Prophet has been promoting civil defense in lectures across the United States for nearly two decades. In May of 1989, staff at the Royal Teton Ranch broke ground on a 13-acre fallout shelter project for the 750 men, women and children who are a part of the church's staff. Other church members all over the world as well as in Montana had already begun building shelters on their own private land.

In 1989, Mrs. Prophet said that over the next 12 years there would be dangerous periods in which the potential for nuclear war would be greater than usual.

In February 1990, she told her members that March and April would be dangerous months during which there would be an increased likelihood of nuclear war. She advised them to have a fallout shelter in or near their home and to have a supply of food and water. Some church members who already had shelters in Montana came to the area to join in a prayer vigil for world peace that was held during those two months.

Holger Jensen of *Maclean's* magazine reported that "believers...[paid] up to $12,000 each for space in the church's bomb shelters." The church does not sell shelter spaces. Some church members who built their own shelters on private land have sold spaces to other members. Prices have reportedly ranged from several hundred dollars to ten thousand dollars. In some cases, the price of a shelter space may have included a supply of food, medical supplies, a generator and decontamination facilities. The shelters are not a money-making scam, as Jensen implied.

The shelter for staff at the Royal Teton Ranch was nearly complete when three of the underground storage tanks that held fuel for the shelter generators began leaking. They leaked a total of 21,000 gallons of diesel fuel and 11,500 gallons of gasoline.

As of this writing, 9,900 gallons (86 percent) of the gasoline and 6,600 gallons (31 percent) of the diesel have been recovered and removed from the site. Government officials, including representatives of the State of Montana, the Environmental Protection Agency, and Montana's Environmental Quality Council, have praised the church's swift response and clean-up effort. The State of Montana's on-site inspector called it "exemplary." The fuel spill was an unfortunate tragedy that the church believes was caused by faulty tank manufacture, since each of the tanks split at the welded seams.

So that's what happened in Montana.

In this brief catalog of media errors, I don't want to give the impression that every reporter who visited the ranch in the past year was lazy or sloppy.

Some reporters *have* written accurate and balanced stories. And some of these were published. But on several occasions, editors have refused to print them. For example, one reporter for a major newspaper wanted to write a story on how well the fuel spill cleanup was going. "That's not the story," his editor said. "The story is how they're ruining the environment."

Because "that's the story," Forrest Sawyer chose to do a mediocre reporting job on the environmental impact of the Royal Teton Ranch.

The 12,500-acre Royal Teton Ranch-South borders Yellowstone National Park. Inside the Park, 40 miles from the ranch, the Old Faithful geyser attracts tourists from all over the world. Sawyer said that according to park officials, "the most extraordinary hot springs in the world could be harmed if the church follows through on plans to tap its own springs."

Sawyer neglected to report that the church's geothermal well has been capped since the day it was drilled, that a U.S. Geological Survey team is currently studying the relationship between the church's well and Yellowstone geothermal features, and that the church has agreed to abide by the results of the study. The church has no intention of using the well if there is danger that it will harm any park features. Sawyer did not interview Mike Sorey, head of the USGS team, who recently said, "There is no chance that development at the church could affect the hot springs and geysers at Old Faithful."

Sawyer also reported that "the main bomb shelter. . . is being built in what was once prime habitat for grizzly bears, elk and pronghorn antelope." What Sawyer neglected to mention is that the shelter site is about 13 acres of our 12,500-acre ranch, 98 percent of which is pristine habitat for all kinds of wildlife.

With under 2 percent of its acreage developed, the Royal Teton Ranch is *less* developed than Yellowstone National Park, which has 5 percent of its acreage developed, including six towns with a residential capacity of 17,000. The fallout shelter site is smaller than the parking lots at Old Faithful!

Sawyer based his report on the claims of park officials. But can these claims be taken seriously when the park plans extensive new building on 30 acres of its Canyon Village complex in a high-density grizzly bear area? Furthermore, Sawyer didn't mention that the grizzly bear population is recovering in the Yellowstone area and there is even talk of taking it off of the threatened species list.

People reported, "Yellowstone Park officials complain that the ranch sits astride prime range for elk, bison and the threatened pronghorn antelope; where once the animals could forage through the valley, they are now thwarted by fences, buildings and roads."

While there is no doubt that park officials made these claims, they are not true. And *People* did not print a balancing comment. I had personally shown the reporter the wooden jackleg fence on our border with the park (the only significant fence we have built) and told him that it replaced a 100-year-old barbed wire fence that was harmful to wildlife. He observed pronghorn antelope grazing peacefully on the ranch side of the fence near one of the 21 open gates.

In our experience, the fence does not hinder wildlife migration out of the park. Every winter, the Royal Teton Ranch is covered with elk, antelope and deer—even bison when it is cold enough. If they manage to get onto the ranch land to graze, how can the fence be "thwarting" them?

There isn't time or space here to discuss all of the other inaccurate reporting. I invite you to visit and tour the beautiful Royal Teton Ranch and see exactly what it is that the press didn't tell you.

You won't see a perfect community. You will see a group of people who are doing their best to live a spiritual life according to the traditions of the world's monastic communities, raise their children in peace (away from urban crime and pollution), offer intercessory prayer for world problems, pursue organic farming and live in harmony with nature.

For a guided tour of the Royal Teton Ranch and church community, call (406) 848-7381.

Discover the most powerful means of invoking God's intercession in your life— the science of the spoken Word

These professionally recorded tapes are designed to help you build a momentum of invoking positive change into your life. Decree and sing along with Elizabeth Clare Prophet and the congregation at the Royal Teton Ranch. Full musical accompaniment.

SAVE THE WORLD WITH VIOLET FLAME! BY SAINT GERMAIN 1

This cassette contains violet flame decrees and songs for personal and planetary transmutation. This spiritual fire can dissolve inharmonious thought and feeling—stress, anger, depression—into God's light, peace and love. The violet flame

can cleanse your system of emotional and physical poisons and transmute karma. Included with each 90-minute cassette are 2 booklets containing all the words. **#B88019 $5.95**

EL MORYA, LORD OF THE FIRST RAY 1

This cassette contains prayers and ballads composed by and for the Darjeeling Master as well as dynamic decrees to the Masters of the First Ray. This ray of God's will—of his divine plan made manifest through his perfection, power and protection—is the key to unlock your creative potential and make your dreams a reality.

A celebration of the soul's reunion with God through devotion to his Law, his Will and his Divine Plan. Included with each 90-minute cassette are 2 booklets. **#B88125 $5.95**

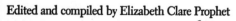